Parody in the Age of Remix

Mashup Creativity vs. the Takedown

Ragnhild Brøvig

The MIT Press
Cambridge, Massachusetts
London, England

© 2023 Massachusetts Institute of Technology

This work is subject to a Creative Commons CC-BY-NC-ND license.

Subject to such license, all rights are reserved.

CC BY-NC-ND

The MIT Press would like to thank the anonymous peer reviewers who provided comments on drafts of this book. The generous work of academic experts is essential for establishing the authority and quality of our publications. We acknowledge with gratitude the contributions of these otherwise uncredited readers.

This book was set in ITC Stone Serif Std and ITC Stone Sans Std by New Best-set Typesetters Ltd. Printed and bound in the United States of America.

Library of Congress Cataloging-in-Publication Data

Names: Brøvig, Ragnhild, author.
Title: Parody in the age of remix : mashup creativity vs. the takedown / Ragnhild Brøvig.
Description: Cambridge, Massachusetts : The MIT Press, 2023. | Includes bibliographical references and index.
Identifiers: LCCN 2022021534 (print) | LCCN 2022021535 (ebook) | ISBN 9780262545396 (paperback) | ISBN 9780262374118 (epub) | ISBN 9780262374125 (pdf)
Subjects: LCSH: Mashups (Music)—Philosophy and aesthetics. | Mashups (Music)—History and criticism. | Parody in music.
Classification: LCC ML3877 .B7707 2023 (print) | LCC ML3877 (ebook) | DDC 781.1/7—dc23/eng/20220809
LC record available at https://lccn.loc.gov/2022021534
LC ebook record available at https://lccn.loc.gov/2022021535

10 9 8 7 6 5 4 3 2 1

To my beautiful daughters, Hedvig and Agnes

Contents

Acknowledgments   ix

1   Introduction: Mashups and Takedowns   1
2   Mashup Music as Parody: Its Roots and Specificity   27
3   Producing Mashups and the Pleasure of Play   53
4   The HAHA, AHA, and AH Impacts of Mashups   93
5   Sampling Ethics and Mashups' Legality   137
6   How Platform Moderation Affects Mashup Producers   175
7   Authorship and Ownership in the Age of Remix
    and Takedowns   209

Appendix: Notes on MASHED Interview and Survey Methods   231
Notes   237
References   269
Index   299

Acknowledgments

I am deeply thankful to Noah Springer and the rest of the MIT Press crew for believing in this book's proposal and for the smooth and positive journey it has been to publishing it. I also thank the Press's anonymous reviewers of the manuscript for providing valuable feedback that enabled me to improve the content considerably. My profound gratitude goes to Nils Nadeau for his consistently excellent and thorough copyediting, including of this manuscript, and for a very good collaboration over the years.

I owe profound gratitude to the Research Council of Norway, which provided me with financial support over three years (2018–2021) to embark on the research project MASHED: Mashup Music, Copyright, and Platform Regulation and enabled me to put together an interdisciplinary research team. This solid team consisted of then-postdocs Alan Hui and Ellis Jones; researchers Irina Eidsvold-Tøien, Miloš Novović, and Elisabeth Staksrud; and research assistants Eirik Jacobsen and Øyvind Skjerdal. Research assistants Vemund Hegstad Alm, Ole Kristian Bekkevold, Oskar Holldorff, and Solveig Wang also worked for the project for short periods to perform specific tasks. My greatest thanks go to all of them for their wonderful contributions and collaboration—and, not least, for making these three years fun! Thanks also to the mashup producers who took the survey and were willing to be interviewed. Without your generous accounts, this book would have been a completely different one.

I also thank the project's scientific advisory board—Nancy Baym, Lionel Bentley, Serge Lacasse, and Aram Sinnreich—for contributing to the research in different ways. My thanks also go to Owen Gallagher, who visited the research group midway along and provided invaluable feedback on the research, and to Patricia Aufderheide, Georgina Born, Nicola Dibben,

Paul Harkins, and my colleagues in my faculty's Career Development Programme (especially Ellen Reese), as well as several researchers within the Art of Record Production community, for their fruitful discussions about my initial ideas for this project.

A big thanks to everyone at the Department of Musicology and the Center of Excellence RITMO at the University of Oslo, with which I am affiliated. I am especially grateful to my colleagues Anne Danielsen, Kyle Devine, Stan Hawkins, Yngvar Kjus, and Áine Mangaoang, as well as the MASHED researchers and research assistants, for reading and commenting on drafts of this book. Thanks also to the students and PhD candidates whom I have had the pleasure of teaching or supervising for your thoughts, questions, and research, all of which have been a great source of inspiration to me. I further thank the many scholars worldwide who have inspired me through their work, their presentations, and through stimulating conversations.

I am deeply thankful to my family and friends for always supporting, encouraging, and inspiring me and for filling my life with the most precious and meaningful moments.

RB
Oslo, March 2022

1 Introduction: Mashups and Takedowns

Why write another book on remix when so many rich contributions have already been provided by other scholars?[1] To some, remix may seem like a niche, but it is in fact one of the most widespread expressions of contemporary culture of the past two decades or more.[2] There is still much to be said about it; it remains a worthy object of attention in itself and the major challenges that mashup and remix artists currently face are symptomatic of bigger societal challenges as well.

Together with the expansion of remixes, online platforms have increasingly implemented substantial content-moderation measures designed to mitigate copyright infringement. These measures rely on algorithms and automatic decision making, and given that mashups are primarily constructed by merging uncleared samples from other recordings, these works have represented a ready target for blocking and takedown. As a result, mashup producers experience such blocking and takedown solutions by platforms as a huge challenge. Many of these artists find themselves less motivated to do their work, and some have even stopped producing or distributing mashups altogether because of the hurdles they face. What is troubling is not the content moderation as such but the fact that the major hosting platforms are ill equipped to handle copyright exceptions, which has important consequences for content residing in the contested area of copyright law, including mashups.

In this book, I argue that mashups should be understood as a form of parody and that this status should protect them from removal from hosting platforms. That is, several national laws and international treaties recognize parody, via copyright exceptions, as noninfringing. Some may find the association of mashup music and other remixes with parody to be a bit of a stretch; others may assume that by making this connection, I will then ignore the many mashups and remixes that are not either experienced as parody by the listener or intended as such by the producer. Note, however, that parody as a concept has been considerably diminished in many contexts (including dictionaries!) until it has become simply a label for content with a satirical impulse or the ability to evoke laughter.[3] This is not how I define parody in this book. In line with parody scholars and the historical use of the concept, I apply the term to *acknowledged appropriations that instigate an ironic critical distance from the parodied works*.[4] Put differently, the concept of parody applies to any works that expose the fact that they appropriate other works, and that in turn instigate a playful contrast with them. Likewise, mashup music is an acknowledged appropriation of other musical sources, and, like parody, it displays an ironic critical distance toward its sources (more on this below).

In the historical context of art, parody is understood quite broadly and does not necessarily involve either satire or humor understood in terms of the laughable. As we will see in chapters 5, 6, and 7, the legal concept of parody is sometimes narrower but not incompatibly so. Long-simmering debates regarding the scope of legal exceptions seem, however, to matter less now, in the sense that the content-moderation systems of online platforms often make them redundant. That is, what is carefully assessed in court on a case-by-case basis is often summarily judged by algorithms and automated decision making on the platforms. Given that platforms such as YouTube have become global media dominators, this is a dramatic turn of events, since it effectively erases the exceptions of copyright, which have been carefully carved out in the law to maintain a balance between property rights and freedom of expression.

When blockings and takedowns become entirely automatic as well as systematic—and then, regrettably, symptomatic of an entire music genre and a culture of remix-based parodies—we have indeed reached a crossroads. The availability of one's content on the major online platforms of the day determines one's creative place (and fate) in the cultural sphere at large. As such, the concerns addressed in this book are not only about mashups and these platforms' imperfect content-moderation measures but also about the current architecture of (and structures of hegemony in) a cultural sphere within which deeply rooted and socially valuable art forms persist or perish not according to the law or the fading interests of artists and consumers but according to a deceptively simple moderation rule.

What's more, this rule is enforced via an extrajuridical procedure performed by privately owned entities more concerned with the market than with plurality and democracy.

The motivations behind this book are, on the one hand, the pleasure and enrichment that I personally find in mashups and other remixes and my recognition of their larger social value, and, on the other hand, my conviction that these works are treated unjustly and that we as a society are risking valuable cultural expressions in the name of overly brittle principles of copyright protection. The latter does not only concern copyright law or platform regulation but also bigger societal issues, including positional power, the privatization of the law, and the unjust (as opposed to just) regulation of culture.

The tension between sample-based music and copyright holders has not been lost on scholars. Yet compared to the fuss raised around this music and copyright regulation in the 1990s and the early 2000s (especially within the hip-hop and electronic dance music scenes), they have paid much less attention to the new threat that sample-based music faces with respect to content moderation, despite that it is an existential one.[5] Thus, there is an urgent need to spotlight this situation, which affects millions of producers and content creators every day. The focus of this book is mashup music in a European and North American context. I hope, however, that the impact of presenting a solid case for these works as parody will be far-reaching in terms of its relevance to other sample-based content and geographical (and thus legal) contexts as well.

What Is Mashup Music?

Before delving further into the content of this book, including my methodological approach, I must explain what I mean by mashup music and situate it in a sociohistorical context. The term *mashup* can be applied to the artistic mashing of two or more images, image and subtext, or image and sound, or to the nonartistic fusion of disparate elements, such as a web page's combination of data from different sources.[6] Here, I use it more narrowly to refer to a particular musical style that mashes musical sources. Mashup music is, in this context and as defined above, *an acknowledged appropriation of other musical sources that displays an ironic critical distance toward these sources.*

This definition, though, warrants elaboration. Michael D. Ayers, among others, accepts the standard definition of a musical mashup as a production "in which the creator takes two or more tracks and blends them together" (2006, 128), which points to the important notion that mashups are montages, consisting of more than one source. However, such an inclusive understanding appears to encompass much hip-hop music, medleys, and other sample-based productions as well. A more pragmatic use of the term, then, would point to a particular form of juxtaposition, one that consists of nothing but samples from prior music recordings that are aligned vertically as well as horizontally (in contrast to medleys, where songs follow one another sequentially). Moreover, these samples are, for the most part, strategically selected from recordings that are familiar to a broad group of listeners, whether they are contemporary tracks or old-time classics. The samples' origins are also exposed by means of the samples' significant duration and subtle (as opposed to drastic) manipulation, including pitch and tempo alteration or structural rearrangement, or both. Mashups are often audiovisual, and, in these instances, the video footage usually consists of mashed-up clips from the original tracks' official music videos or live performances. This formalistic definition of mashup music can be further supplemented with the aesthetic principles that prevail within the mashup scene. First, mashup producers make a conscious effort to *credit* their sources (which is why I include *acknowledged* appropriation in the definition above). Second, they strive to *match* the sources sonically so that the resulting montage sounds coherent—like an "original," as they put it. Third, the producers make sure to *distance* their own work from their sources through irony (an aspect also included in the main definition above). And fourth, their ultimate goal is to *repurpose* the sources, creating something new out of the old. These principles are discussed in chapter 3, where I also identify play as an important motivation for making mashups in the first place.

When mashups started to coalesce into a scene at the turn of the millennium, they usually consisted of a full-length a cappella version of a given track placed atop an instrumental version of another track (sometimes three or even four tracks were combined in this way). Two examples of such mashups from this initial phase are Freelance Hellraiser's "A Stroke of Genius" (2001), which blends the vocals of Christina Aguilera's "Genie in a Bottle" (1999) with the instrumental version of the Strokes's "Hard to Explain" (2001), and Go Home Productions' "Ray of Gob (Madonna vs Sex

Pistols mashup)" (2003), which combines Madonna's vocal from "Ray of Light" (1998) with the music of the Sex Pistols' "God Save the Queen" and "Pretty Vacant" (both 1977). These particular works gained much attention in the early media coverage of mashups and thus contributed to mashup music's mainstream success. This type of mashup is often referred to as the "basic" or A+B mashup. Another type of mashup is the so-called megamix, where several or many tracks are restructured in succession and with overlaps (but with much shorter intervals between them, and much more integration, than a DJ set or mixtape, for example). Although producers like DJ Earworm, Girl Talk, and Osymyso created bootlegs consisting of several tracks during the scene's early phase, it was only during its second decade of existence that megamixes started to proliferate. Prime examples of megamix mashups include DJ Earworm's annual "United States of Pop" works (such as "United State of Pop 2014 [Do What You Wanna Do]" [2014]) or AnDyWuMusicland's "year-end megamixes" (such as "Mashup 2016 'We Were Young' [Best 90 Songs of 2016]" [2016]).

The producers interviewed for this study generally referred to the megamix and A+B formats as different subcategories of mashup, though a few producers from the "old school" reserved *mashup* for the latter alone. Some of the informants, including Danny Neyman, also referred to a third category, called the "minimix": "I usually say a mashup is anywhere from two to three songs, a minimix is anywhere from four to twenty songs, and a megamix is anything above that. . . . [The number of mashed songs in a minimix] is more of a subjective question, but it's basically the intermediate step between a mashup and a megamix." In this book, I subdivide mashups only into the A+B and megamix categories, since these seem to be the categories most commonly used by the producers themselves. Although the megamix mashup is much more prevalent now than it was during the initial phase of the mashup scene, most of the interviewed and surveyed producers said that they either stuck to the A+B format or worked on a combination of A+B and megamix mashups.[7] It is therefore not the case that megamixes have overtaken A+B mashups in the last decade, or that the younger generation makes megamixes whereas the old-school producers stick to the basic mashup format; instead, the basic mashup has simply come to be complemented by the megamix over the years.

In addition to these different forms, mashup producers also adhere to different concepts. They may, for example, mash clashing genres; shape end-of-year/month/decade mashups out of whatever the hits actually were; mash tracks that, when taken together, comment on a specific theme (such as Christmas or Halloween); patch together lyrics that say something new or share a topic; or make tribute mashups to various artists. I elaborate on these different concepts in chapter 3.

Given that it consists of prior sources, mashup music is also a particular type of remix. The term *remix* has its roots in the Jamaican dub music of the late 1960s and the US and European dance floor scene of the 1970s and 1980s, where it initially referred to the musical alteration of a single preexisting track. Since the turn of the century, its meaning has shifted from implying only a new mix of a given source to implying in addition a mixture of found content. Lawrence Lessig, who is often credited as the coiner of the phrase "remix culture," explains: "They remix, or quote, a wide range of 'texts' to produce something new . . . remixed media may quote sounds over images, or video over text, or text over sounds. The quotes thus get mixed together. The mix produces the new creative work—the 'remix'" (Lessig 2008, 69). In the context to which Lessig refers, *remix* serves as an umbrella term for art that recycles, alters, and recombines preexisting sources into a new version.[8] As such, it functions as what David Gunkel calls a "quasi synonym"—an exchangeable term with small but significant differences in its iterations—for terms such as *collage*, *bricolage*, or *culture jamming* (2016, 22). As Owen Gallagher points out, scholars have been inconsistent about whether the term remix encompasses non-sampled content, and he proposes that "the presence of sampled source material is the defining aesthetic characteristic of remix that distinguishes it from other forms of media" (2018, 3). I agree with this definition and, as I explain below, therefore view remix as a concept enmeshed in the digital context of the new millennium, and mashup music as one of remix's numerous manifestations.

The Changing Context of Mashups

Mashup is associated with not only a particular music form or style but also a scene. In what follows, I provide some background on how the mashup scene emerged and has since developed. I base this narrative on a combination of interview data and prior scholarly and journalistic encounters.

Mashups' Early Phase: Bastard, GYBO, and Bootie

As Roberta Cruger (2003) points out, "Mash-ups might be better understood as part of a continuum rather than a new trend." While the mashup format and underlying aesthetic principles have a history predating the digital era (see chapter 2), it was at the turn of the twenty-first century that mashups began to mushroom into a distinct milieu and that the term became associated with a particular musical style and scene. The mashup scene primarily manifests online via dedicated mashup forums and networks on social media platforms such as YouTube, Facebook, Twitter, and Soundcloud. Yet initially, the scene centered around a tiny London club with a monthly club night called "Bastard."[9] McSlzy (aka Mc Sleazy) recalled:

> I think legally it would have held about a hundred [people], but there were always about two hundred in there. . . . And they invited me down to play. I must have played there about half a dozen times. There was no bouncer at the door, nobody charged to get in, but the only people that were there, it was people that were just there for the bootlegs, and they would just go crazy for them. . . . It was really honest, and it was, it was quite punk, actually. . . . It wasn't like a normal club at all. It was like a house party in a movie . . . it was this dingy sweat box of a room where people would just be going ape. And that was the honest side of it . . . when we did the clubs, and when we did the music, it wasn't to earn money.

Initially, these A+B blends were in fact called "bastard pop" or "bootlegs"— "mashups" (at first spelled with a hyphen: "mash-ups") came later, when the scene went mainstream and spread to the United States as well. During this initial phase, mashup tracks were also sometimes played on the alternative radio station XFM London during its Friday night show "The Remix" (Cruger 2003; McGranahan 2010, 12).

In 2001, a couple of years after he started making mashups, McSlzy established a website called GYBO—short for "Get Your Bootlegs On." GYBO became the nexus of the mashup scene in its first decade. According to him, it involved only half a dozen people at first, mostly from the United Kingdom, but then the membership started to change in size and geography, first encompassing continental Europeans and then Americans as well; at its peak, there were about sixteen thousand members. The website was basically a message board through which the members communicated, organized or announced mashup events, and posted links to their mashups and got feedback from one another.[10] According to McSlzy, there were no MP3 files on GYBO; they were instead posted via a third-party file host:

"Everyone hosted their own files . . . there were a lot of free web posts, like Angelfire and Tripod, so people would try and find space where they could. And this was a time when, if Virgin was your internet supplier, then you got like ten megabytes, which was an awful lot . . . it would take you a long time to upload an MP3." This decision to use a third-party host for its MP3 files made GYBO immune to copyright issues as well.

During this initial phase of mashups, there were no social networking sites such as Facebook, SoundCloud, or YouTube. Myspace did exist, and some producers used it as their online site for data storage and sharing, but streaming was not possible there, so one had to download the files to listen to them. Several producers also used peer-to-peer services such as Napster or Soulseek to share their mashups and to acquire files to mash. As such, McSlzy explained, their archives of music to mash were quite limited: "The only way that you could get tunes, at that point, that you didn't have in the house, was if you went to something like Napster, or something like that, and illegally downloaded the tune. It isn't like today where you could just go into iTunes and then download it. . . . So, yeah, you tended to be using that many tunes as you got, and that was stuff you bought because you liked it."

Another blog that also emerged in 2001 but only lasted for a year or so was Boom Selection, run by Daniel Sheldon—a fifteen-year-old Manchester-based mashup producer who went by the moniker The_Dr. In contrast to GYBO, Boom Selection allowed producers to make their mashups available for download from its site (McGranahan 2010, 12). Yet it did not function as a hub like GYBO and soon faded away. It is perhaps best remembered for its *Boom Selection_Issue 01*, aka *Never Mind the Bootlegs* (2002), a three-disk MP3 compilation consisting of 432 tracks and 11 DJ mixes.[11] This compilation album caught the attention of the widely influential US online music magazine *Pitchfork*, which described it as "one of (if not the) first pseudo-historical CDR compilation," as it consisted of MP3 files and an invitation to the listener to "burn your own audio CD compilation" (quoted in Mitchum 2005).

Another (more ordinary) mashup CD that was circulating at the same time and caught the attention of the US magazine *Entertainment Weekly* (Brod 2002), as well as the worldwide readership of the *New York Times* (Strauss 2002a), was the compilation *The Best Bootlegs in the World Ever* (2001). The CD contained seventeen mashups (or "bootlegs," as they were called), including "A Stroke of Genius" by Freelance Hellraiser.[12] In 2002, the Belgian duo Soulwax, aka 2ManyDJs, released the hour-long mashup compilation *As Heard on Radio Soulwax, Pt. 2*, consisting of forty-five tracks that were either remixes or mashups. The album sleeve informs us that it took the record company six months to clear 114 out of 187 samples (Soulwax n.d.), but, according to Cruger (2003) and Liam McGranahan (2010, 27), these were only cleared for the Benelux (Belgium, the Netherlands, and Luxembourg) countries. Yet, the album had enormous success worldwide. It topped the charts in several countries and was endorsed by influential media outlets, including the *New York Times* (Strauss 2002b) and *Pitchfork* (Mitchum 2002), thus contributing to the popularity of mashups far beyond Europe. While mashup producers and fans relied heavily on peer-to-peer downloading of files during mashups' initial phase, then, the circulation of bootleg CDs (as well as twelve-inch "white labels") was also important to the scene's expansion.

Paul V. and Adriana A (aka DJ Adrian), who were among the US mashup pioneers, both referred to this latter CD and its reviews in US magazines when asked about how they discovered mashups. Adriana A recalled:

> It's funny—I read about mashups actually before I heard one. There was a national magazine here in the US called *Entertainment Weekly*, and I read just a small little review in 2002. I'm almost positive I actually still have that article, because it was so, you know, it was so life changing in a way. But it reviewed a bootleg CD coming out in the UK called *The Best Bootlegs in the World Ever*. And it described it as, like, "You'll hear Christina Aguilera singing with the Strokes, and Destiny's Child over 'Smells Like Teen Spirit' by Nirvana." And I'm just like "Oh my god! That sounds amazing! This sounds like everything that I love!" . . . So I ordered it online from Rough Trade in the UK. It arrived in my mailbox two weeks later. Put it on, and the very first mashup I ever heard was [Freelance Hellraiser's] "Smells Like Booty," which is Destiny's Child "Bootylicious" over "Smells Like Teen Spirit." And I was just, like, "Oh my god, I love this!" And I just fell in love immediately. It really summed up what I wanted to do as a DJ. And then that just kicked off me going down a rabbit hole of discovering [more mashups]—you know, because where do you find these things?

The discovery of that CD also brought both Adriana A and Paul V. to the mashup community at GYBO.

Adriana A explained that she and Mysterious D (who together went by the artist name A+D) soon started to integrate mashups into their DJ sets: "And, you know, we're talking 2002, people had no idea what this stuff was. You'd be in a club or a bar, and you'd be playing these tracks, and they hear the familiar, they hear Daft Punk, or they'd hear the familiar opening chords of whatever song it is, and then a completely different vocal comes in instead of the one they want, and they're just like '*What?* What is this?' Some people would get very angry about it. I mean other people were like, you know, fell in love with it as much as we did." They then decided to start a party dedicated to mashups, which resulted in the 2003 introduction of a monthly Wednesday mashup night at a club in San Francisco. Although *mash-up* was the more commonly used term in the United States at that time, they called their club nights *Bootie* "as an homage to the roots of the early 2000s UK scene," Adriana A recalled, adding "and [to the phrase] 'shake your booty.'" According to Adriana A, the club night built up quite quickly from a hundred people to a thousand, and soon it was held every Saturday. Bootie mashup nights soon appeared in other US cities as well, including New York, Los Angeles, Seattle, and Boston, but also in cities elsewhere, including Berlin, Paris, London, and Rio de Janeiro. DJ Schmolli from Austria recalled that those producers running the Bootie nights encouraged people around the world to have their own Bootie parties: "It was not like they were getting money to use their brand . . . they just left everything to you—they gave you all the graphics and everything, and you could run your own Bootie parties. There's like this concept that has to be followed, you know: it's just mashups all night, and they had, like, a certain style of the creation of the party, which they told you. . . . The only thing they wanted [was that] you invited them like once a year, and you made a party with them. But, on the other hand, you got invited too, so I got, like, to play Bootie parties in the United States. Also, I got to Brazil . . . and same goes for Berlin." Adriana A and colleagues also initiated a Bootie website with mashup compilations, challenges, news, and events. This website, together with the various Bootie clubs, became another anchor point for the mashup community, along with GYBO. Whereas GYBO only lasted for the first decade of the mashup scene, the Bootie website, as well as some of the Bootie clubs (including those in San Francisco and Los Angeles), is still active today.

Mashups Go Mainstream
The *New York Times*, *Entertainment Weekly*, and *Pitchfork* were but a few of the magazines and newspapers that paid attention to the mashup scene during

its emergence. Mary Huhn (2005) from the *New York Post* described mashups as "the hottest trend fans can look forward to in 2005," which indicates the hype around these works. Mashups also generated extensive radio play and a dedicated MTV show—*MTV Mash*—that launched in Europe in 2004. Huhn cites MTV executive vice president Tom Calderone's description of the show's origins: "We took it from the indie underground and are trying a mainstream approach." MTV had also planned to launch a mashup series in the United States and first contacted Jay-Z about the idea, who suggested that he make mashups with Linkin Park. The planned US MTV mashup series never came about, but the initiative did result in a Jay-Z/Linkin Park mashup concert (on July 18, 2004) and one of the first mashup albums cleared and signed by a label—*Collision Course* (2004)—featuring four Jay-Z/Linkin Park mashups and a documentary about the collaboration, which was also aired on MTV.[13] There was also a live festival in 2005, AmsterJam, that embraced the mashup concept courtesy of artists including Garbage, Snoop Dogg, Red Hot Chili Peppers, and Bootsy Collins (Aquilante 2005; Breihan 2005).

Other major acts picked up on the trend; for example, David Bowie held a mashup contest in 2004 where he invited people to mash his latest album.[14] Kylie Minogue also performed a mashup at the Brit Awards as early as 2002, singing her hit "Can't Get You Out of My Head" over the backing track "Blue Monday" by New Order (titled "Can't Get Blue Monday out of My Head"). In his review of the Minogue live mashup, *Guardian* journalist Dom Phillips wrote, "This dramatic new version had been created in secret by her record label for maximum impact. And it worked. Minogue was cleverly cashing in on the vogue for unofficial records that mix two or three wildly different songs into a new track. No trendy London party is complete these days if the DJ doesn't play one of these illegal 'mash-up,' 'bastard pop,' or 'bootleg' records" (Phillips 2002). Some of the producers, including Simon Iddol, recalled that during this time when mashups were starting to take off, several mashup producers were invited to work with established acts as well: "Many artists contacted us, like we are talking about [the] top twenty artists worldwide, who just gave up the a cappellas because mashups are the best viral marketing tools." For example, mashup producer Freelance Hellraiser was contacted by Christina Aguilera to remix her next single and by Paul McCartney to perform mashups as a preshow for his concerts (Serazio 2008, 88), and 2ManyDJs were contacted by record labels that offered their back catalogs to be mashed (Shiga 2007, 107). Several mashup producers, including McSlzy, were also invited to contribute to the development of Activision's *DJ Hero* 1 and 2 (released in 2009 and 2010), a musical video game spinoff of *Guitar Hero* that allowed users to blend tracks using a controller made into a turntable.[15] Some of the producers accepted these invitations from the "official" music industry—for example, Freelance Hellraiser remixed Aguilera's "Fighter" (2003) and accepted McCartney's touring invitation, which in turn led to *Twin Freaks* (2005), a collaborative album with McCartney. Other producers, including 2ManyDJs, refused them (Shiga 2007, 107), presumably because they regarded such gestures as selling out. Today, there are fewer connections between the mainstream industry and mashup producers, who tend not to seek material gain in and of itself.

Mashup music was symptomatic of a much larger remix trend during the early 2000s, and as it achieved mainstream status, it came to serve, as Ellis Jones (2021b) points out, as a kind of poster child for the democratic promise of Web 2.0. The initial decade of the mashup scene saw much excitement about the music, in fact, not only because it was novel but also because it was part of a perfect storm of optimistic developments. First, the 1990s saw huge developments in the market's ability to offer powerful computers at an affordable price, as well as high-quality, user-friendly, and low-cost music-editing software. By the late 1990s and early 2000s, that is, music production had become accessible to the many, and the capacities of music software programs—so-called DAWs (digital audio workstations)—also advanced swiftly. For example, Acid, a popular DAW among mashup producers at this time, made it relatively easy to align individual tracks, including the matching of their tempos and keys. In contrast to analog speed alteration, digital software allowed for the manipulation of tempo and pitch independent of one another and without otherwise affecting the sonic result (that is, the pitch-altered sounds maintained their original tempo and the speed-altered sounds retained their original pitch levels, all while also retaining their particular formative qualities as well).

Second, the combination of the rapid improvement and increasing availability of high-speed internet connections, the introduction of the MP3 format, and the development of peer-to-peer file-sharing services made it easier than ever before to discover and acquire a diverse range of music to be mashed as well as distribute mashups to a broad group of listeners.

Introduction

While mashup music did not emerge exclusively as an internet phenomenon, internet forums such as GYBO did contribute to the mashup community's growth and geographic expansion. The bottom-up model of Web 2.0, in which content is shared among the masses instead of supplied to them by a broadcasting agency, enabled users to circulate content outside the traditional industry model of distribution, which contributed tremendously to the proliferation, visibility, and impact of mashup music, especially given that this music resides in a legal gray area due to its excessive use of uncleared samples.

This larger trend, then, was characterized by the cultural participation of the masses (Jenkins 2006), its medium configurability (Sinnreich 2010), and its new networking opportunities, as well as the increasingly apparent tendency of the binaries of production/consumption and professional/amateur to dissolve.[16] While Lessig and his peers[17] have singled out the act of remixing sampled content into a new work as a defining feature of our recorded, digital, malleable, and networked society, Margie Borschke (2017) emphasizes that rather than being an inevitable consequence of technological change, remixing is a testament to consumers' deeply rooted agency and innovation. She is particularly skeptical of Lessig's argument that with the introduction of digital and networked technologies, we have moved from a read/only (RO) culture centered on consumption to a read/write (RW) culture centered on the idea of talking back (Lessig 2008, 28–31). Still, while I agree with Borschke that it is important to acknowledge consumers' enduring participation and agency, the digital era has clearly lowered the barriers for citizens to produce, circulate, and engage with cultural content, and thus I find *remix culture* to be a fitting name.

Jones (2021b) describes early scholarly encounters with mashups as opportunities to justify the hope that Web 2.0 would significantly challenge market economies and copyright practices. Such a hope was also associated with mashups in the open-source documentaries *Good Copy Bad Copy* (Johnsen, Christensen, and Moltke 2007) and *RiP!: A Remix Manifesto* (Gaylor 2008), thanks to the appearances of the producers Girl Talk and Danger Mouse (here fronted as mashup artists).[18] Notions of the internet's capacity as an advanced democratizing media sphere have since been challenged by the reality of Web 2.0; it neither turned out to be an egalitarian, noncommercial space nor remained free of market constraints, copyright control, and other traditional gatekeepers.[19] Still, these early scholarly encounters capture some of the enthusiasm that many of the producers, including McSlzy, felt at that time:

> At the beginning it was, like, a "we don't know what we are doing here but we're onto something" kind of a vibe. . . . It seemed to be a fresh cycle of interest in it and that was a combination of having the internet, to make that stuff known, but also people having the technology to be able to do that in their rooms. So, it was a perfect storm of things at that time, and I think it was really the first time that music distribution could happen on a global scale without record companies being involved. And you couldn't hear music from the other side of the world prior to that, unless there was some late-night show on the radio, that was it. All of a sudden you could. So, it was pretty raw and no one was governing this.

Producing and consuming mashups in this early phase appear to have given producers a sense of being part of the future in terms of both creating something novel and being part of an important movement toward cultural democracy.

Between about 2005 and 2010, as new platforms such as Facebook, SoundCloud, and YouTube went mainstream, most of the producers started to post their mashups there as well as on GYBO and other mashup websites such as mashuptown.com.[20] While GYBO was basically a message board, these major social media hubs allowed for the hosting of music files and images as well, and YouTube also allowed for videos. They further facilitated new forms of dissemination and communication: producers could share links to other mashups and also comment on and communicate about particular audio or audiovisual mashup files in the comment sections beneath their work. The "like" function that several such platforms featured also presented a kind of voting system that helped to boost the popularity of certain producers and their mashups. Colatron, who joined Facebook in 2007, pointed to it as "a massive thing" and "the biggest thing that happened for us guys." Others considered SoundCloud to represent mashups' next go-to space after Facebook (adding ruefully that this was before they were "kicked out" due to SoundCloud's harsh moderation of assumed copyright-infringing content). The emergence of these major hosting opportunities eventually led to GYBO's fadeout, and although certain other dedicated mashup sites would emerge, they tended to function only as complements to the major platforms. Despite GYBO's decline, several of the interviewed producers said that mashup activity clearly picked up around 2010 as a consequence of the emergence of Facebook, SoundCloud, and YouTube, along with the relative ubiquity and user-friendliness of music-production software during this time.²¹ They also lamented the way in which the scene became more fractured after GYBO.

Although the old-school producers recalled the mainstreaming of mashups with pride and gusto—especially the major magazine reviews, radio and MTV play time, and approaches by established acts—several of them, including Colatron, regretted what was already being lost as well: "It was an exciting time to be alive, you know. You would just discover all these new and wonderful sorts of creators out there, before the days of YouTube, when everyone became a blogger—it was just crazy. You had these people on the other side of the world constantly entertaining you for free via whatever platform it was. . . . But, again, I just don't think you're ever gonna [experience] those days again, you know? What the kids are doing now is great, but it's missing that spark. I can't quite put my finger on it, but it's just not how it was." Colatron's lament recalls Michael Serazio's observation that "ubiquity dulls the edge of any innovative cultural blade" (2008, 88). Writing about how the commercial music culture appropriated the initially underground mashup concept, both Serazio (2008, 88) and John Shiga (2007, 95) see mashups as the perfect example of what Dick Hebdige identifies as the common trajectory of subcultures: while they are often formed through an act of resistance, they eventually become commodified by "entrepreneurs" who appropriate, incorporate, and market them to mainstream ends (Hebdige 1979). Hebdige further observes that this trajectory often leads to the given subculture's demise, yet mashups nevertheless remain viable, if somewhat changed.

While acknowledging these developments in the context and enthusiasm surrounding mashups, Adriana A simply saw a new phase for the art form: "There's an entire generation of people now that have grown up with the concept of a mashup, that it's not like this weird subversive thing anymore. This is just simply music. . . . And I remember when, in the early days of Bootie, the early days of mashup culture, people would say to us, 'Do you think it's a fad?' . . . But they never went away. Remixes are just part of the musical landscape now, and, in exactly the same way, [mashup music] is simply part of the musical landscape. It's simply a way that people create and consume music." In the two decades since the mashup scene was acknowledged as such, it has become an integral part of internet culture. The most-viewed mashups on YouTube have accumulated more than fifty million views, and other mashups go into the millions of views as well. There is still an active producer and consumer group dedicated to mashups, as became overwhelmingly clear to us when we identified mashup producers to interview and survey. In this book (especially in chapters 2, 3, and 4), I will try to identify some of the factors that attract so many people to making or consuming mashups, including their double-codedness, play, humor, enlightenment, and beauty aspects. Despite all the change, both within the scene and in the world, the mashup format and its producers and fans have stood the test of time. Yet, while the first phase of the mashup scene both welcomed and promptly exploited technological developments such as readily available and inexpensive computers, software, and internet connections, the second phase has been faced with a technological development that is rather less constructive to mashups: the algorithmic and automatic blocking and takedown measures of major hosting platforms.

Mashups Face Takedowns
Despite the enormous and abiding popularity of mashups and other user-generated remixes on online distribution platforms, they continue to occupy a contested area of copyright law, thanks to their substantial use of samples from prior musical recordings. The use of copyrighted material without permission represents infringement unless the use falls under copyright's limitations and exceptions. Copyright, that is, is softened by exceptions intended to balance property rights with user rights to ensure that the former do not override the fundamental right to freedom of expression. The law considers a careful balance between copyright and its exceptions to be critical to fostering cultural production and diversity. Such exceptions vary according to respective copyright laws, but most encompass the right to parody or appropriate existing content in some form. The scope of the legal concept of parody, or any other exception, also varies across nations and is generally unpredictably applied as well because it relies on a careful case-by-case evaluation that considers the specific context and details of the case and its interrelation with certain other legal factors. Mashup music has never been tested in court as such, so its legal status remains unclear (see chapter 5).

In the early 2000s, mashup producers and radio shows playing mashups soon started to receive cease-and-desist orders from record labels or rights enforcement organizations.[22] Several of these producers found this confusing, given the positive attention they had received from established artists or their labels. The most famous such order is perhaps that which Danger Mouse (aka Brian Burton) received from Capitol Records after having mashed the Beatles' *The White Album* (1969) with Jay-Z's *The Black Album* (2003) in a full-length album blend he called *The Grey Album* (2004). Because Burton had not sought permission for the Beatles samples,[23] the copyright holders of the band's sound recordings in the United States, Capitol Records, required that Burton withdraw his music from the internet, as well as what remained of the three thousand pressed CDs, which he did. But the case was taken up by the nonprofit copyright activist organization Downhill Battle as part of their campaign promoting a "participatory culture" (Downhill Battle 2004). On February 24, 2004, Downhill Battle arranged the now legendary Grey Tuesday, which they described as a "day of digital civil disobedience against a copyright regime that routinely suppresses musical innovation" (Downhill Battle n.d.). As part of this campaign, approximately 170 blogs and other websites made the album available as a free download.[24] But whereas Downhill Battle's intention was to front free file sharing and protest copyright law, Burton simply continued to insist in interviews that it was not his intention to break the law but rather to make an art project (Rimmer 2005, 40). This statement correlates with the perspectives of the interviewed and surveyed producers, who respected copyright in principle and did not see mashups as necessarily counter to that principle (see chapter 5).

When interactive social media platforms first emerged, they relied on manual moderation, including community-led surveillance. With the explosive growth in users and their uploaded content, however, several platforms that had started as small enterprises entered into agreements with or were purchased by major corporations and became hugely successful businesses through the generation of revenue from advertisements attached to their content. Whereas the popularity of social media platforms initially derived from the concept of hosting user-generated content with which other users could interact through comments and likes, they soon started to host (and ultimately rely on) corporate media content as well. Their alliances with big media corporations, together with various associated legal threats and lawsuits, spurred changes in how they moderated content, including copyrighted material. Through the subsequent US Digital Millennium Copyright Act (1998)[25] and the European Union's e-Commerce Directive (2000),[26] the platforms were not to be held liable for hosting copyright-infringing content but only for notifying copyright holders upon becoming aware of possible infringement. Still, mounting legal and economic pressures compelled the platforms to incorporate more substantial content-moderation systems relying on algorithmic detection technology. This shift would completely change both the profiles and the user experiences of the major platforms. Their copyright-related content moderation systems now typically scan content for infringement by comparing it to a database of copyrighted content provided to the platform by copyright holders (see chapter 6). When automatically notified of a match, the copyright holder may choose to ignore or monitor the use, place an advertisement on it and collect the revenue, or block or remove the content altogether. The sheer amount of content on these platforms means that the matching and disposition processes are generally automated and definitely not the product of deliberate case-by-case legal analysis. As such, content residing in the contested area of copyright law, including that which can be defended under copyright law's exceptions, is often blocked along with the black-and-white situations (see chapter 6). This is mashup music's sometime fate as well.

The empirical interview and survey data suggest that platforms' content-moderation systems have had significant and detrimental impacts on the mashup scene. It is not only that the mashups themselves are blocked or removed but also that valuable archives of comments and likes are lost upon a producer's account termination, and the followers of that account may not accompany the producer to their new account either. Several of the interviewed and surveyed producers had been forced off their preferred platforms and banished to less visited sites, and some had stopped making mashups altogether. Others had changed how they made mashups, including what samples they used and how they treated them. Hosting platforms, once understood as the saviors of sample-based music producers, have now become in some ways their greatest threat as well, since content moderation and its chilling effects have hurt the creation of new mashups and shortened the public life of existing ones. If mashups are banned from these platforms, that is, they have few other places through which to be disseminated.

It is this new crossroads between extensive remix activity, on the one hand, and substantial algorithmic and automatic copyright-related moderation, on the other, that this book takes as its point of departure. As we trend toward stricter regulation policy concerning internet content, we need to understand what we risk losing along the way and, most important, why it matters.

Outset and Outline

Between about 2005 and 2009, McGranahan and Aram Sinnreich conducted interviews with mashup producers for their respective research efforts (McGranahan 2010; Sinnreich 2010). Much has happened since then. In the interests of finding out more about the mashup scene writ large and its producers' current situation, I started an interdisciplinary three-year research project in 2018, "MASHED: Mashup Music, Copyright, and Platform Regulation," which received funding from the Research Council of Norway, allowing me to establish a research team. In 2019, my project colleagues and I carried out thirty hour-long semistructured interviews with mashup producers and conducted a survey via an online form (with open and closed scaled questions) involving ninety-two mashup-producer respondents.[27] This material has been the principal source for the analysis presented in this book, along with other sources, including mashup music, academic texts, media output, legal documents, and many fruitful discussions with fellow researchers, students, practitioners, and other stakeholders. Whereas the survey responses were anonymous, the interviewed producers were given the choice (via an informed consent form) of remaining anonymous or being referred to by their artist pseudonym; the majority chose the latter option.

The producers were identified via mashup forums, social media platforms, and word of mouth. To limit our focus relative to the field of law, we mainly reached out to producers residing in European countries and the United States. The producers interviewed were spread across fifteen countries, whereas the surveyed producers were spread across twenty-two countries, and some had residences outside Europe and the United States as well (including elsewhere in North America, South America, Asia, and Oceania). Other than that, we specifically attempted to capture the diversity of the scene in terms of various subcommunities, a producer's location, background, age, and gender, as well as their choice of distribution platforms, their mashup style, their level of popularity, and the extent of their current involvement in mashups. The mapping of the scene attests to the scene's current fragmentation. Frequently mentioned subcommunities included the Bootie website and clubs discussed previously; an internet forum focused on the engineering aspect of mashups; a Discord-based forum; a small group of producers known as the Crumplbangers; a community based around a SoundCloud clone platform; the subset of relatively meme-based mashup producers; and individuals who were not part of any community.[28] All of these various groupings encompass both first- and second-generation producers whose birth years range from 1962 to 2001 (with a lull between 1984 and 1993; hence, I sometimes refer to the producers as "old-school" and "new-school"). With respect to the dissemination of these producers' mashups, the scene's primary manifestation is presently on social media platforms including YouTube, Facebook, SoundCloud, Twitter, and dedicated mashup sites. Despite the scene's expansion and subsequent fracturing, it remains quite male dominated, though several interviewees identified themselves as nonbinary and LGBT. The demography of the producers was otherwise quite varied even beyond age and geography. For example, their educations and current occupations ranged from designers, music producers, and club managers to economists, biomedical scientists, and artificial intelligence engineers. Their music backgrounds varied too. A couple of the old-school producers lamented that whereas most of the producers who were active in mashups' early phase had music backgrounds, this seemed not to be the case any longer. Such assumptions, however, did not correlate with the findings of the interviews and survey; that is, the scene seems to be quite varied with regard to music background, but it does not appear to be a split between old-school and new-school producers as such.[29] (For more on the interview and survey methods, including the sample selection, see the appendix.)

When I started this project, I wanted to approach mashups via integrated insights from three vantage points: (1) the field of art, and specifically popular music and remix studies, as well as studies on parody, montage, and appropriation; (2) the field of new media, with a particular focus on the content-moderation measures of internet platforms; and (3) the field of copyright law, principally in terms of the ways in which sample-based music is positioned in relation to European Union and US copyright law. I made this interdisciplinary commitment because I believe that important insights arise in the border areas where these specific scopes and vantage points meet. To fully understand the ramifications of the current situation that today's mashup producers face requires grasping what it is that motivates them, as well as the abiding social value of this art form. Conversely, to fully understand mashup music, one must pay attention to these producers' technological, political, and legal circumstances, since they have a profound impact on the music itself, as well as the ways and places in which this music circulates. To delve into these interdisciplinary border areas with more confidence than that supplied by book learning alone, I put together a team of scholars with expertise in law and new media since I am already situated within the interdisciplinary fields of popular music and remix studies.[30] Although this book is not a collaborative project as such (the project members have all been working on individual projects, save for some coauthored articles), the team's collaboration has significantly enhanced my expertise in the relevant areas of law and new media. Of course, any oversights are mine alone.

I start, in chapter 2, by situating mashups in the larger context of intertextual music practices and parody. I emphasize that sampling, as well as musical appropriation more generally, is not a single thing but a whole field of endeavor. While this may seem perfectly obvious, sample-based music is all too often treated quite reductively in a legal context. I first discuss some of the many variables of appropriation relevant to mashup music. These variables are here divided into three categories involving different aspects of appropriation: (1) the nature of the appropriation (deliberate versus unconscious; based on specific works versus stylistic features; sample-based versus recreated; acknowledged versus hidden); (2) the arrangement of the sources (appearing successively or in parallel; several sources versus one source; purely recycled material versus partly recycled; bisociative versus associative sources); and (3) the perspective or stance regarding the sources (evaluatively open versus evaluatively determined; repetition with ironic critical distance or imitative repetition). I then elaborate why I believe that much mashup music, as well as other forms of remix, represents a uniquely contemporary take on parody, and I also point to precursors other than those typically mentioned in scholarly accounts on mashups. These kinds of associations with historical precursors and the long-established art form of parody legitimize mashups as an artistic practice and provide for a better understanding of their sociocultural value. Moreover, the identification of sampling as a whole field, and of mashups as parodies, also has important legal ramifications that should be acknowledged in the context of copyright regulation.

Another important dimension of mashups' social value is their meaning to their producers, and in chapter 3 I let the producers explain the aesthetic principles behind their work. While accommodating and unpacking the variety in these narratives, I also discern certain shared underlying principles, including that mashup music is intended to be an acknowledged form of appropriation (*crediting*); that the sources it brings together are made to match in various ways, making the resultant track sound musically coherent in and of itself (*matching*); that the producers tend to instigate an ironic critical distance toward their mashed sources, including a conceptual clash, incongruity, or surprise of some sort (*ironic distancing*); and that the producers share the goal that a mashup should repurpose its sources, bringing something new to the originals by means of contextual and synergetic transformation (*repurposing*). I then point to the striking similarities between mashup music's underlying principles and the principles commonly associated with parody. Returning to the interview data, I next speculate that part of the pleasure of making mashups recalls participation in various forms of play, specifically in terms of overcoming given constraints. That is, mashup producers seem to derive pleasure from the act of mastering, and in turn plumbing the potential of, the mashups' explicitly and implicitly articulated limitations. This impression is strengthened by the fact that producers often layer further challenges atop mashup's basic "rules," such as the conceit of the concept mashup, for example. But alongside the challenges offered by the making of a mashup, it is also the aesthetic result of that work that motivates mashup producers.

As we know, the listener's particular engagement with a mashup will not necessarily correspond to its producer's particular engagement or intentions. Since listening experiences are most often intuitive and subconscious in nature, any analytical grasp of them depends more on empirically informed theoretical perspectives (derived systematically from numerous encounters) than on a few individual encounters. In chapter 4, I therefore elaborate on the centrality of certain aspects of mashups via a synthesis of theories that complement my encounters with the mashup experience as parody and play (as mentioned in chapters 2 and 3). These perspectives are empirically grounded, in that they are informed by the mashup producers' accounts. While I am wary of presenting them as definitive viewpoints or objective, all-encompassing understandings (which simply do not exist), I believe that these constructions may contribute to a better understanding of the sociocultural value and profound meaning of this music.

First, I situate mashups within the discourse of intertextuality, arguing that it is what is beyond their sounds, images, and words that explains people's continuing fascination with these works. The core of mashups, as well as parody and several other types of acknowledged appropriation is, in short, how the various recycled features function anew thanks to their relocation and reactivation and why they do so. A copy in this context is never only a copy because the text is at once transformed *and* reproduced; a sample may be "the same" as its source, but its implications have clearly changed through the recontextualization performed by the appropriation. As such, this work can (to make a Barthian distinction) represent a very thick text (with respect to its meaning) despite its apparent manifestation as a thin text (with respect to its concrete content). Inspired by Arthur Koestler, I next frame the perspectives presented in this chapter as mashups' "HAHA," "AHA," and "AH" impacts, respectively. That is, I first situate humor as a central component of mashups deriving from listeners' impression that the mashed tracks do not make sense even as they experience them as making a lot of sense at the same time (mashups' HAHA). This recognition of their inherent incongruity derives in turn from the mashups' sociopolitically pregnant breach of expectations, conventions, and stereotypical notions (mashups' AHA). In addition, the humor and edification of mashups are significantly shaped by the mashups' aesthetic and affective dimensions (their AH)—that is, mashups' artistic or pleasurable attraction contributes to their humor and illumination while also being shaped by them. The discussions in this chapter not only provide insights into the larger sociocultural value of parody and mashup but also serve as a foundation for my argument in chapter 5 that the heart of parody and mashup cannot be found in the representation alone. It must also encompass the associations and connotations that mashup's representational features trigger, and this reality must inform the reception of mashups in the courts.

In chapter 5, I explain that mashup sampling is, according to the producers, governed by its own set of internal ethical guidelines that emphasize that (1) producers must not profit from their mashups and (2) they must always credit the artists whom they sample. I argue that the mashup community's ethical guidelines and general approach to copyright and sampling clash with the popular narrative linked to sampling artists—one suggesting that unauthorized sampling is a matter of "theft" or "piracy," that it is eroding the revenue and recognition of otherwise hard-working musicians, or that it is an act of civil disobedience or resistance to copyright or an anti–music industry approach. Instead, it would appear that the reasons mashup producers do not license their samples have more to do with the fact that licensing is replete with both practical and economic hurdles and that some producers do not think they even need to license because they believe that permission is already granted to them by copyright law's exceptions. I discuss the intricacies of those exceptions with a focus on sample-based music and copyright law in both US and EU contexts. Instead of providing a yes/no answer regarding the legality of mashups, I argue that much mashup music may have a good case for being identified and defended as parody in court while also acknowledging that copyright is highly complex and overlaps with other legal issues; after all, any legal conclusion regarding assumed copyright infringement will be case specific and inherently unpredictable. I thus position mashups in the legal gray area while arguing for the defense of mashups as parody. Moreover, I emphasize that licensing samples is currently not regarded as a viable alternative by mashup producers.

In chapter 6, I unpack the reasons that content moderation presents a major threat to sample-based music by pointing out that its handling of content does not guarantee the adequate accommodation of copyright exceptions. I also discuss mashup producers' experience with platform moderation. Here, I refer to their descriptions of the ways in which content moderation has restricted their creative choices, directed where and how they distribute their mashups, and otherwise had a significant impact on their overall motivation to produce this music. I argue that sampling currently faces a crossroads regarding its ultimate fate, in that platforms' content-moderation regimes at once represent a major threat and bring with them some cause for hope—that is, they encompass the prospect of getting samples more efficiently licensed through the option of monetizing this content. Still, of course, the latter alternative only gets us halfway and may be considered simply a means of bypassing the current threat rather than remedying the situation. This chapter contributes to my argument in this book by questioning the presumed neutrality of the major platforms, arguing that they exercise considerable power and influence in shaping the contemporary and future cultural sphere because they are pivotal forums for expression in today's society. As such, their lack of transparency and ineptitude in accommodating copyright exceptions has important ramifications not only for mashups but also for culture and society at large.

Pulling together my main findings and arguments in chapter 7, I highlight the broader relevance of this book by engaging its findings and arguments in three wide-ranging discussions. The first concerns various, and sometimes conflicting, ideologies underpinning musical discourses. I argue that popular music has deep roots in a rock ideology that sees true musicianship as the fruit of not only talent but also diligence and labor. Mashups are seen to push at the boundaries of the concepts of music authenticity, musicianship, and authorship through their reliance on nothing but samples and their shameless embrace of the manipulated, ironic, and fabricated. But even in this context, a rock ideology lurks beneath the surface of not only the outside reception of this music but also the very mashup scene that appears to dismiss it. Still, there are also other important artistic ideologies that are in circulation and that inform the scene. I argue that to maintain cultural diversity, we need to acknowledge that what people find meaningful in relation to creative expressions is diverse as well.

The second discussion in this final chapter addresses the significant gap between legal reasoning and artistic practice, including these respective fields' corresponding terms but conflicting concepts. The concept of parody as understood in the field of art is sometimes insufficiently reflected in the legal concept of parody in, for example, EU law. I argue that while the legal context remains separate from the context of the arts and thus operates with its own definitions, one should not underestimate the power that laws and legal enforcement have when it comes to incentivizing or discouraging art. The law should function as both a cultural incentive and a cultural regulator, but in either case it must be adequately informed by artistic practice.

The third discussion concerns the positional power of corporations with regard to copyright enforcement. I begin by interrogating the power that platforms currently possess, including the fact that they have the final word in classifying what art forms should and should not be part of the cultural sphere. I extend this discussion by pointing to recent legal developments that may encourage platforms to include parody detection as part of their content moderation in order to meet the legislative requirement of accommodating copyright exceptions. I argue that machine-learning technology is ill suited to identifying parody and that it risks reducing parody to its representational and paratextual features alone. An algorithm, though programmed by humans, is not capable of considering contextual information in the same way that a human interpreter can, and, in the case of parody, context is key. The combined power and opacity of these platforms threaten not only the culture itself but also the relevance of copyright law's exceptions, which in turn undermines the position of the law in relation to the platforms.

I encourage the interested reader to peruse the whole book because each chapter contributes to the others and to the overall argument. If one were primarily concerned with the producers' perspectives, however, one could prioritize chapters 3, 4 (from HAHA), 5 (the first half), and 6 (the last half). If one wanted to learn more about this music's aesthetic and social value, one could concentrate on chapters 2, 3, and 4. If one's main interest were the legal aspects, one could prioritize chapters 5 and 6 (although chapters 2, 3 and 4 provide important background); if it were platform regulation, one could prioritize chapter 6 (and ideally the last half of chapter 5).

Whereas much research on copyright regulation and platform moderation has downplayed individual and broader artistic experiences in the interests of seeing a bigger critical picture, I believe that these aspects represent a crucial part of that picture. That is, why should we care about the threat to a particular art form if we know nothing about this art form or its sociocultural significance? Insight into the value of a particular art form is furthermore worthwhile in itself. After all, artistic engagement (via either production or consumption) is a crucial aspect of human life: it is part of what makes people flourish. Of course, art may also function as a window to understanding the broader social, historical, and economic context, which is in turn decisive for art's position, or even existence, in society. As such, mashup producers' experiences with the platforms' content moderation point to the interdependent relations among art, law, and media, and thus also to society's critical responsibility to carefully balance the act of regulating art with the act of preserving it. In other words, I hope that this book will remind us that we, as a society, must rise to the occasion in terms of how we shape—as we always do, for better or worse—our contemporary and future cultural spheres.[31]

2 Mashup Music as Parody: Its Roots and Specificity

> Knowledge of the ways existing music has been reworked in other times and by other composers can clarify the historical place of those we focus on, helping us recognize what is unusual or innovative in their approach to the uses of existing music and, just as important, what has long-established precedent.
>
> —Peter Burkholder (1994, 851)

Scholars and journalists have traced the origins of mashup music to earlier sample-based genres in the field of popular music, including hip-hop, dub, and club DJ-ing, as well as avant-garde music, including musique concrète (a compositional technique, developed by Pierre Schaeffer, centered around the manipulation of recorded sounds).[1] They have also pointed to non-sample-based music, such as jazz and folk, as predecessors in the practice of versioning familiar music, and to medieval organum (a type of polyphonic composition), fourteenth-century motets (a polyphonic composition with iterations), baroque quodlibets (compositions combining well-known tunes), Western art music, and African American music as other historical and contemporary examples of new music that relies on and combines existing music.[2] Quite specific examples from the 1950s onward have been delineated as mashups' direct predecessors or as early examples of a mashup aesthetics, including Buchanan and Goodman's 1956 hit "The Flying Saucer," in which a spoof news report is combined with clips from eighteen contemporary music hits; Alan Copeland's 1968 arrangement of the lyrics and melody of the Beatles' "Norwegian Wood" with the "Mission: Impossible" theme; the Beatles' 1968 sound montage "Revolution 9," which includes several tape excerpts from well-known classical music works by, among others, Beethoven, Sibelius, and Schumann; and John Oswald's 1989 album

Plunderphonics, in which each track presents a thoroughly manipulated version of a familiar recording.[3] These associations with historical precursors are valuable not only as a way to legitimize mashups as an artistic practice but also as a way to gain a better understanding of the aesthetics behind them. Still, such comparisons often lead to conflations and sweeping generalizations; for example, they can reduce mashup music to the enduring practice of musical "borrowing" or equate it with prior forms of sampling. As Peter Burkholder (1994, 851) stresses, musical "borrowing," as he calls it, is not any one thing but a whole field. This urge to refer to prior musical practices should be considered only a point of departure for exploring the many ways in which recycling is enacted and the wide range of functions or effects it is able to produce.

There have been several attempts to provide a typology for the different forms of appropriation or intertextual practice, in which the types are constructed according to a combination of factors or qualities that are regarded as particularly relevant. One of the most detailed is provided by Burkholder (1994) in relation to his analysis of Charles Ives's music, in which he identifies fourteen different types (including "modelling," "cantus firmus," "medley," "collage," and "patchwork") that are based on combinations of features that distinguish them.[4] When trying to identify mashup music's roots and specificity in relation to other intertextual practices, in this chapter I first discuss the variables of appropriation in and of themselves rather than resorting to these various typologies.[5] It here becomes clear that although mashup music shares some qualities with other forms of musical appropriation, it also differs in important ways. After having considered the many variables of appropriations, I turn to a typology that is less fine-grained than those of Burkholder and other scholars but is nevertheless firmly established within both the field of art and the legal context—one that distinguishes among parody, satire, homage, pastiche, and plagiarism. I ultimately conclude that the characteristics of mashup music correspond to those of parody. Important studies within the field of popular musicology have already established that parody, as well as irony and intertextuality, is a fundamental aspect of popular music.[6] Here, however, I argue that mashup music goes beyond simply embracing parody as an attribute (in the sense of its enactment of parodic gestures); its very construction and underlying principles qualify it as parody, understood as an artistic category in the field of art. When one is evaluating the legality of specific musical cases, it is crucial to possess a clear sense of the variety of ways in which music can be recycled and of the effects this work can generate. Understanding mashups (and other forms of remixes) as parody thus may also have legal implications, since parody is accepted as a legitimate form of appropriation in several national laws and international treaties. I start, however, by clarifying my use of the concept of appropriation.

The Concept of Appropriation

Lori Burns and Serge Lacasse remind us that "popular music is undoubtedly a multilayered palimpsest: we find not only innumerable versions of preexisting songs reborn in different styles but also entire genres based on borrowing or hybridization (e.g., hip-hop, mash-ups)" (Burns and Lacasse 2018, 1). The palimpsestic nature of music is often theorized in terms of intertextuality, but this concept tends to be used in two different (yet related) ways. The first is the notion that all texts draw on other texts implicitly or explicitly. The study of intertextuality in this sense often involves the structural analysis of different types of specific intertextual relations or the source study of specific appropriations. The second is the notion that intertextuality triggers a specific kind of meaning via the transposition of a text from one context to another. The study of intertextuality in this sense is less concerned with the tracing of a text's sources than with the transformation that those sources undergo when moved from one context to another.[7] This chapter is interested in the former—intertextuality as appropriation strategy—whereas chapter 4 deals with the latter—the meaning making of appropriations.

Burkholder (1994) is one of several scholars who refer to the act of using prior music as musical "borrowing."[8] However, as Justin Williams (2014, 7) points out (even as he uses the term as well), "borrowing" indicates a use of something that belongs to someone else and is in one's possession only for a certain amount of time before one is supposed to return it.[9] This metaphor thus does not align with the described practice, and it may, moreover, imply a proprietary view of music that ignores copyright exceptions. I therefore regard *recycling* as a better metaphorical term than borrowing, though, like *borrowing*, this alludes only to the activity (to recycle), not to the work itself. The use of prior work in music is sometimes referred to as a musical "quotation"—especially uses that are acknowledged[10]—yet this term does not refer to the type of work as a whole either, but instead points specifically to an extracted fragment. A more established concept, and one that alludes to the art form (as opposed to the activity) that relies on the recycling of prior works, is appropriation, which has been used within a variety of art forms to refer to the act of "seizing something that belongs to others and making it one's own" (Boon 2007, 3).[11] While acknowledging that *appropriation* can be used as an umbrella term for a range of intertextual practices, Eduardo Navas, Owen Gallagher, and xtine burrough and colleagues (2018, 20) lament that to them, it implies that "(1) culture may be a form of 'property,' and (2) the owner of the cultural property suffers a loss when it's 'appropriated' by someone else." Yet as Lacasse and Andy Bennett point out, appropriation can also refer to taking something else and making it part of a personal identity (2018, 326)—that is, to putting one's personal stamp on what someone else has created. Paul Ricoeur similarly describes appropriation as the counterpart of "distanciation"; while the latter is linked to "any objective and objectifying study of a text," the former refers to "the 'playful' transposition of the text, and play itself will appear as the modality appropriate to the reader *potentialis*, that is, to anyone who can read" (1991, 87). In other words, appropriation can also imply interpretation, or the idea that instead of merely repeating a passage of a work, one engages with it more thoroughly and analytically, hence making it one's own.

According to Marcus Boon, the term has two divergent implications for ownership:

> First of all, the sense in which it is used above, that of taking something and making or claiming it as one's own, or using it as if it was one's own. Secondly, that which is proper to a situation or a person—that which is "appropriate." Appropriation, according to the first definition, often involves taking something that arguably belongs to someone else. There is the sense of seizing, of making a claim on something that has already been claimed by someone else. According to the second definition, it is that which one has a right to claim as one's own, which is "properly" one's own (we will set aside for now the question of where this right and claim come from). (Boon 2007, 2–3)

In contrast to "borrowing," which clearly indicates that the relevant content belongs to someone, "appropriation"—if we endorse Boon's second meaning—confirms that it is a reuse but one that is "appropriate." This implication is also somewhat problematic, of course, since appropriated material often resides in the gray area of copyright law, meaning that its legal status is unclear (I return to this issue in chapter 5), and the ethical perspective regarding whether it is appropriate will vary depending on both the use and the evaluator. This ambiguity, however, allows for a more "neutral" (to the extent that such a thing is even possible) position with regard to ownership than that suggested by the related concept of borrowing, and I therefore use it throughout the book.[12]

Appropriation Variables: Its Nature, Arrangement, and Perspective

In scrutinizing various typologies of appropriation, I have teased out the common variables on which they are based and grouped them into three categories: (1) the nature of the appropriation (whether the use is deliberate or unconscious, sample based or recreated, acknowledged or hidden, for example); (2) the arrangement of the sources (whether they appear successively or in parallel, for example); or (3) the appropriation's apparent perspective or stand toward its sources (whether it is benign or satiric, for example). In what follows, I discuss the variables within each of these categories in turn.

The Nature of the Appropriation

Cultural appropriation can take many forms and be understood in different ways. An important distinction, which tells much about the nature of the appropriation, involves whether it is the result of unconscious and inevitable forms of referentiality or of a more deliberate act.[13] The former concerns influence and is related to intertextuality, here broadly understood as the condition through which any utterance is "a link in a very complex organized chain of other utterances" (Bakhtin 1986, 69).[14] When appropriation is used in relation to a specific artwork, it is, of course, a signal of a deliberate act of referentiality. Mashups clearly represent the latter.

Deliberate forms of appropriation can also vary in character depending on whether they recycle specific works or rather reference stylistic features. Does the appropriation, for example, quote a specific Motown recording or simply adopt the signature stylistic features of the Motown sound?[15] Stylistic evocation thus asserts a common stylistic language or shared competency with the characteristics of a particular style, whereas the appropriation of a specific work asserts a familiarity with that work, which is then made to serve as the new work's referent. Mashups are clearly situated within the latter practice of appropriation rather than the former.

So far, then, mashups could be traced back to practices related to medieval organum and motets, Western art music, African slave songs, oral folk traditions, jazz and blues music, and the long tradition of cover songs, to mention but a few, that are also deliberate appropriations of specific works. Yet another variable of musical appropriation with respect to its nature involves whether it is an act of re-creation (or performance) or a sample (understood here as a technologically extracted sequence from a recorded musical work).[16] A cover song, for example, or the way in which Mozart borrowed from Bach or Rachmaninoff borrowed from Beethoven represents the former, because they appropriate by means of re-creating a musical sequence in a performance (or in a transcription that will later be performed). Mashups or hip-hop tracks represent the latter because they rely on samples from preexisting recordings. The difference between re-creational and sample-based forms of appropriation is much more than a technicality; it has a major impact on the sonic result as well as the meaning making of the music. When an audio file is extracted, the prior music's melody, rhythm, harmony, and instrumentation, as well as the performances of the instrumentalists and singers, will not simply be similar but actually duplicated, meaning that all the nuances in terms of microrhythm and intonation, for example, will be exactly the same. Moreover, the exact "sound,"[17] or sonic timbre, of the music is likewise extracted, the uniqueness of which often leads to immediate recognition. Thus, the sampled quotation arguably evokes its source more profoundly than the re-created or performed quotation and brings with it a sense of experiencing exact sameness even though the quoted music is now presented in a different context and takes on a new meaning. Functioning as indexical signs from the past,[18] samples furthermore often evoke strong cultural memories associated with their source, including the source's contextual connotations. This rather profound distinction between sampled and re-created or performed forms of appropriation carries over to copyright issues as well, as I discuss in chapter 5.[19]

In terms of its sample-based appropriation, mashup music can be linked to Western avant-garde music and sample-based practices within the field of popular music, including dub, DJ culture, remixes, hip-hop, and EDM. These are important roots that should not be neglected, but they should not be conflated either. For example, these other forms of sample-based appropriation do not always manifest themselves in an acknowledged manner. Hip-hop sampling, for example, sometimes exposes its sources but other times disguises or obscures them to the point of unrecognizability. This brings us to yet another variable with respect to the appropriation's nature: whether its references are more or less hidden or acknowledged, the latter implying that they are signaled explicitly.[20]

Harold Bloom (1973) points out that authors often hide, via transformation, their "borrowing" due to their anxiety about being revealed as unoriginal (that is, their "anxiety of influence"). This possibility also underpins the many copyright cases that have centered around the question of whether a musical sequence is an act of deliberate plagiarism (using another's music but pretending that it is one's own) or an instance of coincidental similarity. Appropriations that are acknowledged, however, are meant to be perceived as appropriations. The use of prior material is baldly signaled, either textually or paratextually—that is, via contextual cues or "secondary signals" that are closely linked to the text (Genette 1997, 3–4).[21] As I demonstrate in the following chapter, mashups are firmly situated within this latter category of acknowledged appropriation. A high priority for mashup producers, for example, is to announce that their mashups are mashups. In terms of textual signaling, they often mine widely known sources or expose their sources through the use of relatively lengthy passages that are treated only subtly or not at all. In terms of paratextual cues, they often include the sources' song titles and artists, and/or the term *mashup* or *megamix* in the mashups' titles or in the descriptions beneath the audio or video files.

The roots of mashups with respect to their nature, then, can be traced to various types of deliberate appropriation of specific works, and more specifically to those that are *sample based* as well as acknowledged (see figure 2.1). But even if these features connect them, these types may differ in terms of their arrangement of the sources, as well as the perspective they take toward their reused sources. For example, hip-hop music may be a deliberate, acknowledged, and sample-based form of appropriation, but it differs from mashup in that it often loops short samples instead of using full-length samples or shorter samples that are not looped, and it also usually combines its samples with nonsampled musical elements, including vocals.

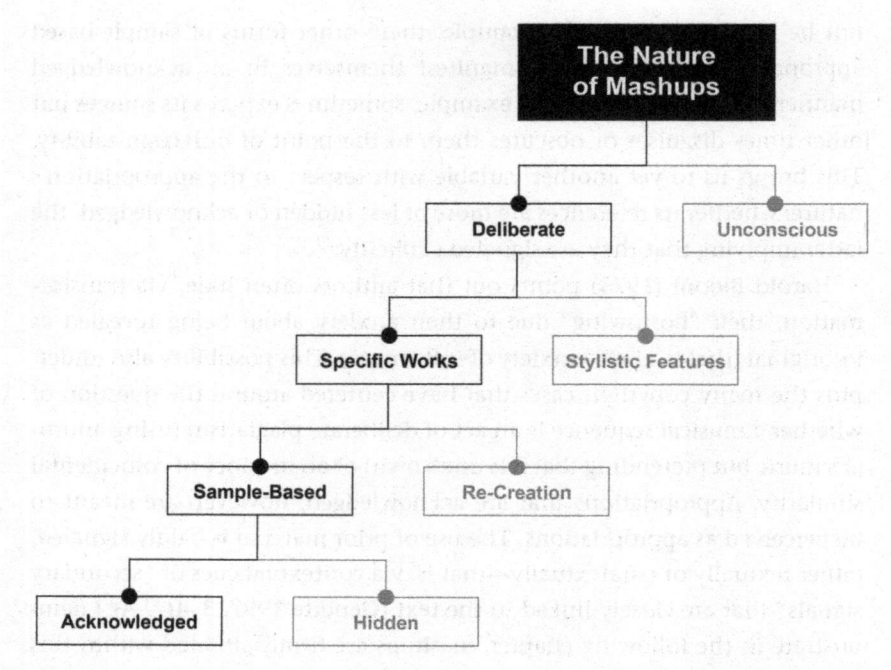

Figure 2.1
The specificity of the nature of mashup music in relation to other appropriations.

The Arrangement of the Sources

Acknowledged appropriations (including parody) can involve one or several prior works.[22] Examples of the former include covers and many EDM remixes, whereas much hip-hop and mashup music exemplifies the latter. Yet, there is another variable as well with respect to the arrangement of sources—that is, whether they are purely recycled or partly recycled. If the acknowledged appropriation is based on several prior works, it can consist of nothing but passages from these works, or it can combine those passages with "new" or nonappropriated material. Hip-hop music generally exemplifies the latter case, whereas mashup music (and often other internet remixes) generally exemplifies the former case. Appropriations consisting of nothing but prior material (as in mashups) are commonly referred to as montage or collage works, though sometimes they are also given more genre- or area-specific names such as *assemblage, cento, medley, pasticcio,* and *quodlibet*.[23]

The principle of montage (or collage) predates the advent of film and the various avant-garde movements with which it is commonly associated. Across all of its historical manifestations as well, the extent varies to which it draws attention to itself as such and insists on its construction as integral to its meaning. This brings us to a third variable with respect to the arrangement of sources: whether the sources are associative or bisociative. Inspired by the early Russian film theorist Vsevolod Pudovkin, who emphasized editing, as opposed to space-time continuity, as the foundation of film (Harrah 1954, 167), Sergej Eisenstein theorizes montage by arguing that "the juxtaposition of two separate shots . . . resembles not so much a simple sum as it does a creation" (Eisenstein 1986, 7). Something new occurs at the meeting point between sources. He further describes the juxtaposition of shots as a collision rather than a linkage (1986, 37) and notes that some forms of montage feature a smoother collision or are more "neutral" in their juxtaposition of shots than others (Eisenstein 1977, 4).[24] The perceptually profound collision of sources (that, according to him, leads to a "sensation of duality" [1986, 15]) might also be characterized as bisociative—a term introduced by Arthur Koestler as an antonym to that which is associative: "Bisociation means combining two hitherto unrelated cognitive matrices in such a way that a new level is added to the hierarchy, which contains the previously separate structures as its members" (Koestler 1967, 183). In contrast to associative processes through which one idea leads to another, bisociation refers to the integration of independent matrices otherwise thought to be incompatible (Koestler 1964, 657–660). Acknowledged appropriations (including mashups) are, in a sense, bisociative by definition since they emphasize the contrast or incongruity between the source's new and original contexts. But the term *bisociative* can also describe the montage, in which two or more combined sources are experienced as conceptually contrasting due to their difference in original forms or their diverse styles or connotations. Whereas mashup music is inherently bisociative, in the sense that it juxtaposes previously unrelated sources, some mashups emphasize this bisociative nature by appropriating material that does not blend conceptually (although it might blend musically) due to a perceived clash of styles or connotations. Along the lines of Eisenstein's distinction between more or less neutral juxtapositions in montage, then, we can perhaps distinguish between more or less bisociative and associative

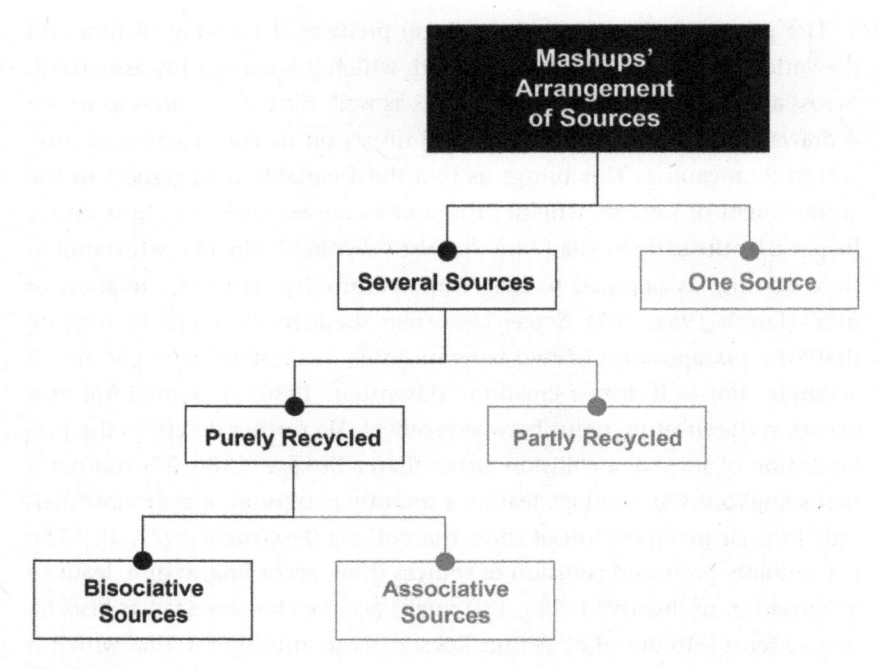

Figure 2.2
The specificity of the arrangement of mashup music in relation to other appropriations.

forms of montage, wherein mashups—and particularly the A+B mashup—tend to exemplify the former.

Whereas EDM remixes, hip-hop, and mashup music have much in common in terms of their nature—they are all deliberate, acknowledged, and sample-based appropriations of specific works—they often differ with respect to their arrangement of sources. That is, EDM remixes often rely on only one source, whereas mashups, and potentially hip-hop music as well, rely on several. And whereas EDM remixes and hip-hop music usually combine their source(s) with non-appropriated material, mashups use nothing but prior works and furthermore often combine their sources in a bisociative montage (see figure 2.2). Mashups cannot, however, be reduced to a montage in the sense that the concept of montage encompasses several variables with respect to its nature, as discussed above. Nor does the identification of the mashup as a montage imply a particular perspective toward its sources, to which I turn next.

The Appropriation's Perspective toward Its Sources

An alternative to seeking mashups' roots and specificity in the nature of their appropriation and the ways in which the appropriated material is used in terms of its arrangement involves looking for similarities and differences based on the stand they take toward their sources. Richard Dyer (2007, 35) points out that all forms of appropriation (or "imitations," as he prefers) imply an evaluative attitude in terms of expressing a valuation or position regarding the recycled material. He then introduces the useful distinction between appropriations that are evaluatively open and those that are evaluatively predetermined. The former implies that the appropriation's perspective toward its source(s) is either ambiguous or varied, whereas the latter implies an explicit intention, whether friendly or mocking in nature. Because of its multiple and often ambiguous functions, mashup music in its entirety belongs to the category that Dyer describes as "evaluatively open," although particular instances of it could be interpreted as "evaluatively predetermined." The same applies to dub, hip-hop, and EDM sampling, as well as internet remixes and memes. Although several types of hip-hop music could be interpreted as homage and several forms of internet remixes as satirical, they are, viewed as a whole, evaluatively open because of these genres' broad variety and ambiguity when it comes to their perceived intent.[25]

Another related yet quite distinct pair of concepts revolves around whether an appropriation is an act of imitative repetition or repetition with ironic critical distance. "Critical distance" here does not necessarily imply an explicit critique as such but rather an act of distancing oneself from the material by dramatizing the contrast between how it appears in its original context and how it appears in its new, appropriated context. If the appropriation involves ironic critical distance, it self-reflexively acknowledges that it is not an imitation but rather a new take—one that playfully transforms the original content by means of recontextualization or alteration. It comments on what it recycles by presenting it from a different point of view. Such repetition with ironic critical distance can be either evaluatively open or predetermined, and if it is the latter, it can be either an act of homage or a satire. Mashup music presents itself as an interpretation and a reworking of its sources, which differentiates it from the mixtape or several other forms of medley that do not emphasize the contrast between their new and original contexts to the same extent.[26] That is, along with being

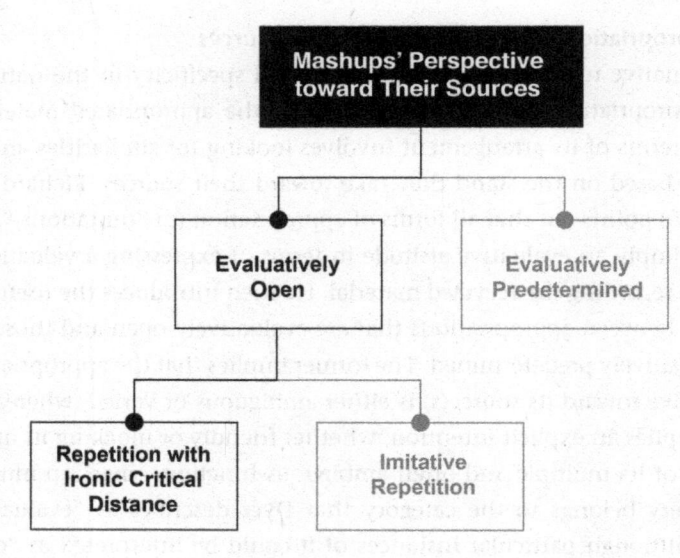

```
                    ┌─────────────────────┐
                    │ Mashups' Perspective│
                    │  toward Their Sources│
                    └──────────┬──────────┘
                   ┌───────────┴───────────┐
           ┌───────┴───────┐       ┌───────┴───────┐
           │  Evaluatively │       │  Evaluatively │
           │     Open      │       │ Predetermined │
           └───────┬───────┘       └───────────────┘
        ┌─────────┴─────────┐
┌───────┴────────┐  ┌───────┴────────┐
│ Repetition with│  │   Imitative    │
│ Ironic Critical│  │   Repetition   │
│    Distance    │  │                │
└────────────────┘  └────────────────┘
```

Figure 2.3
The specificity of mashup music's perspective toward its sources in relation to other appropriations.

evaluative open, mashup music displays an ironic critical distance toward its sources (see figure 2.3).

To summarize, mashups can be distinguished from as well as compared to other appropriations by means of the following criteria: they are deliberate as opposed to unconscious; they sample specific works as opposed to stylistic features; they are sample based as opposed to re-creational; and they acknowledge their sources as opposed to hiding them. Furthermore, they rely on several sources as opposed to one alone, they consist purely of recycled material as opposed to mingling that material with other elements, and their montages of sources usually result in bisociative collisions rather than associative amalgamations. Finally, their perspective on their sources is evaluatively open as opposed to predetermined, and they display an ironic critical distance toward those sources as opposed to presenting them as imitative repetitions. All of these variables testify to the gross simplification inherent in regarding various forms of musical appropriation, or sample-based music more specifically, as one and the same. Moreover, once one has identified these characteristics of mashup music, it becomes clear that this music actually exhibits the characteristic features of parody.

Mashups as Parody

Typologies rely on a combination of selected variables, including those mentioned above. A typology of appropriation that is firmly established within both the fields of art and law is the one that distinguishes among plagiarism, homage, satire, pastiche, and parody (sometimes a more fine-grained typology also includes terms such as *cento*, *burlesque*, *travesty*, *irony*, *nostalgia*, and *allusion*, among others). In what follows, I delineate the differences among these types with a special attention to parody. Furthermore, I point to the corresponding qualities of mashup music and parody and trace the roots of mashup music to concrete examples of bisociative, montage-based parodies.

Plagiarism, Homage, Satire, Pastiche, and Parody

Dyer (2007, 24) helpfully identifies the three criteria, each consisting of a binary alternative, that most often inform the distinctions between plagiarism, homage, satire, pastiche, and parody: (1) whether the recycled material is concealed or unconcealed, (2) whether it is textually signaled or unsignaled, and (3) whether it is evaluatively open or predetermined. (As demonstrated, there are several more variables among appropriations but each typology emphasizes a specific selection.) The first two criteria that Dyer mentions involve whether the appropriation is acknowledged; if it is (meaning it is unconcealed), it can be signaled as such either textually or merely contextually (23). Among the types mentioned above, plagiarism is the only one that is (textually and paratextually) concealed and unsignaled (see figure 2.4); it is, in contrast to the other types, "an author's false claim of another's work" (Demers 2006, 29).[27] I thus focus primarily on the third category that Dyer introduces—whether it is evaluatively open or predetermined—while also adding a fourth closely related criterion that is often mentioned when one is defining these types: whether the appropriation is an instance of imitative repetition or of repetition with ironic critical distance, as discussed above.[28]

When suggesting the categories "evaluatively open" and "evaluatively predetermined," Dyer points out that satire and homage are obvious examples of types that are evaluatively predetermined. Satire displays a scornful and disdainful attitude or a denigrating attitude of mockery or ridicule—one whose target is either the appropriated text itself or something external to it that it somehow represents. As Linda Hutcheon points out (2000, 56), satire can be understood as "encoded anger" and is thus destructive due to its contempt and disdain, but it can also be didactic in its earnest attempt to bring about change. Travesty and burlesque can be seen as subcategories of satire, as they also involve a degree of mockery and ridicule. Like satire, homage is evaluatively predetermined but resides at the other end of the spectrum, paying tribute to what it recycles. Homage is a reverence or respectful attestation of the quality and greatness, and perhaps also influence, of an artist or their works or a musical style of the past, and it can thus also involve an element of nostalgia.

Whereas satire and homage are sometimes referred to as appropriation types,[29] they are also used as adverbs to describe the perceived evaluative intent of other appropriation types. For example, parodies are sometimes seen as being a form of homage and other times as having a satirical sting. The primary feature that distinguishes homage and satire from parody as well as pastiche is exactly this category of evaluative attitude—that is, in contrast to homage and satire, pastiche and parody are evaluatively open. While this is the most common understanding among parody scholars (see below), not everyone agrees with it. Dyer (2007, 23–24) argues that parody, unlike pastiche, is evaluatively predetermined, based on his understanding of parody as fundamentally satirical. Genette (1997, 12, 25) suggests that the debate regarding whether parody is a form of mockery or a form of ridicule can be traced to the etymology of the word,[30] in which "para" can imply either (1) the diversion of an existing text into something new that is invested with new meaning (a playful distortion) or (2) mockery (the satirical imitation of a style). Still, Hutcheon (2000, 32) points out that there is nothing in the concept per se that necessitates the involvement of ridicule, so she finds it problematic that several dictionaries define *parody* as such. Margaret Rose agrees. In her thorough historical review of the term, she finds that the occasional linking of parody to mockery can be partly explained by the way in which ancient descriptions of parody as comic have sometimes wrongly been interpreted as implying ridicule and mockery. Moreover, where the term *ridicule* is used, subsequent interpretations and translations have often failed to account for its shifting meaning: whereas ridicule is now understood as mockery—a "laughing *at*"—it was previously understood as something funny and amusing—a "laughing *with*" (*rideo* means to laugh) (Rose 1993, 9). She contends that it is the latter sense of ridicule that ancient descriptions are applying to parody (25) and cites the similar conclusions of scholarly parody authorities Fred W. Householder (1944) and F. J. Lelièvre (1954) (22). Another explanation for the confusion of satire with parody is that they are often used in combination; as both Rose (1993, 83) and Hutcheon (2000, 43) point out, parody has been a common vehicle for satire since ancient times, but this does not make the two concepts synonymous. Whereas satire can take many forms, it always sends an unambiguous message. Parody is a more specific form but sends multiple messages, including those that are ambiguous and even relatively neutral. Moreover, whereas parody always comments on an artwork or what it represents from within or through that specific work, satire does not necessarily do so; it can comment on its target by using means other than the "voice" of any particular work as such (Hutcheon 2000, 43).

Whereas Genette (1997, 27) argues that parody is never satirical (if it is, it should be defined instead as travesty, he insists), there is now, with certain exceptions including Dyer (2007), a consensus among parody scholars that parody has always boasted a range of possible functions.[31] Sabine Jacques sums up: "[History] reveals that parody is *multi-functional*: provoking laughter, conveying criticism, providing (positive or negative) social or political commentary, paying homage, and developing or testing artistic or musical rules and techniques" (2019, 5). Or, as Genette writes, parody is "a form in search of a function" (1997, 71). In addition to having different functions—some humorous, some ambiguous, others satirical—parody in itself can also be ambivalent or invite more than one interpretation, several scholars observe.[32] Simon Dentith (2000, 11 fn.12) accordingly describes parody as a playful rather than satirical transformation. For all these reasons, I remain convinced that parody falls within the category of being evaluatively open.

The other related yet quite distinct pair of concepts—that is, whether an appropriation is an act of imitative repetition or repetition with ironic critical distance—is not part of the table Dyer uses to distinguish pastiche from parody and other related types, but it is exactly this trait that several other scholars identify as the main difference between parody and pastiche. What unites parody and pastiche is that both are evaluatively open. What several scholars see as distinguishing them, however, is that pastiche, like plagiarism and often homage as well, is a more or less imitative repetition that emphasizes similarity, whereas parody, like satire, is a repetition with critical difference. For example, Rose points out that pastiche is "a more neutral practice of compilation which is neither necessarily critical of its sources, nor necessarily comic" (1993, 72), and Genette also observes that pastiche imitates more than it transforms (1997, 34 fn.60). Hutcheon similarly argues that whereas pastiche operates according to similarity and correspondence (2000, 38), parody is "a form of repetition with ironic critical distance, marking difference rather than similarity" between the parody and the parodied text (Hutcheon 2000, xii). Dyer refers to Mirella Billi, who similarly suggests that "parody may be distinguished from pastiche chiefly because it brings out the difference between the two texts . . . rather than the similarity. . . . Whereas parody is transformative, pastiche is imitative" (Billi [1993, 36] as quoted in Dyer 2007, 47). Dyer himself has a broader understanding of pastiche:

> One of the connotations of the word "pastiche," perhaps always, certainly since Jameson's discussion of it in the context of postmodernism (1984), is that it cannot be critical, indeed that its very closeness to what it imitates prevents it from having the distance necessary to critique. Certainly pastiche is not, like parody, by definition critical (or, come to that, like homage, by definition evaluative in a positive sense). None the less, that does not mean that it cannot be used critically. Ludovica Koch (1983, 11) maintains that pastiche is always subversive: beneath its apparent elegance, pastiche is always "bringing to light the arbitrariness, generic basis and indifference" of the forms it imitates, qualities that otherwise give the illusion of life and originality to art. I would not want to go as far as always, but I do want to show that pastiche can be used critically. (Dyer 2007, 157)

This broader definition, whereby pastiche may be seen to sometimes encompass a critical distance toward its sources, makes the terms *parody* and *pastiche* overlap, and Dyer also admits that several of the works that Hutcheon calls parody, he calls pastiche (2007, 51 fn.54). According to this broader definition, mashups could also be labeled pastiche; parody and pastiche both represent a broad range of manifestations, many of which overlap with one another. Whether one chooses parody or pastiche to label content falling within this overlapping range may not be that important in an everyday context (especially given that these concepts often seem to be misguided in terms of their historical use). But in a legal context, it well might matter, which is why I stick to parody: it has a strong legal defense.

With the "ironic critical distance" of parody, Hutcheon refers to the ways in which parody self-consciously acknowledges, and even exposes, not only its status as an appropriation (that is, a new take on something old) but also its specific textual or contextual transformation of the parodied work of art. "Ironic" in this context points to the way in which the parodied work of art is inverted by its new context: the parody instigates a playful contrast with that which is expected in terms of transforming while repeating. This transformation goes beyond the inevitable one—that is, that repetition always involves a degree of difference[33]—in that parody transforms explicitly in terms of emphasizing and dramatizing the difference between the parodied text's original and new contexts, thus resulting in a recoding that in turn introduces new meaning to the familiar (which leads to a rereading of it). "Ironic" also points to the act of communicating two messages at once, in which one is communicated directly (the "said") and the other indirectly ("the unsaid"); in parody (as well as mashups), the direct message is what is heard and seen, whereas the indirect message encompasses the many associations that the sources trigger. Parody's ironic critical distance does not communicate one version in place of the other but instead presents both through the technique of irony. According to Hutcheon, "it is the superimposition or rubbing together of these meanings (the said and plural unsaid) with a critical edge created by a difference of context that makes irony happen" (Hutcheon 1994, 19).

Although *parody* is an old term that has had many definitions throughout history, most of them seem to agree on the centrality of this critical and distancing aspect. More than merely imitating or slightly varying an existing work, parody transforms it in a way that makes the result incongruent with its source. For example, Lelievre defines parody as "singing after the style of an original but with a difference" (1954, 66, 72); Mikhail Bakhtin, as "an intentional dialogized hybrid" (1981, 76); Rose, as "the comic refunctioning of preformed linguistic or artistic material" (1993, 52); Hutcheon, as "a form of repetition with ironic critical distance, marking difference rather than similarity" (2000, xii); Genette, as a "playful transformation of a particular text" (1997, 202); and Dentith, as "a relatively polemic allusive imitation of another cultural production or practice" (2000, 9). What these descriptions have in common is that terms such as *difference*, *dialogized hybrid*, *comic refunctioning*, *ironic critical distance*, *playful transformation*, and *polemic imitation* all point to the characteristic critical distance that parody introduces in relation to its acknowledged recycled work.

This critical distance is also related to the notion of humor. Pastiche is generally not seen as evocative of a humorous response, precisely because it lacks parody's ironic critical distance. Parody, on the other hand, triggers a feeling of incongruity—and, moreover, the combination of incongruity and sense making that humor scholars have identified as a key trigger of humor (see chapter 4). That is, parody is inherently incongruent—it is an acknowledged reworking of a prior work—yet it makes sense as a work in itself as well and thus depends on a structure that readily triggers humor. Nevertheless, parody scholars disagree as to whether humor is a defining characteristic of parody. Rose, for example, insists that humor is essential to parody and thus includes it in her definition of the term: "[Parody is] the comic refunctioning of preformed linguistic or artistic material" (1993, 52). She expands on this comic refunctioning by referring to how parody often evokes a feeling of incongruity: "The creation of comic incongruity or discrepancy will be taken as a significant distinguishing factor in parody in the definitions given of it in this book and may also be said to explain both the production of the comic effect in the parody and how the parody may continue to be defined as comic" (31). Rose further argues that because of the inherent incongruity between the parodied text and the parody, "the parody may still be said to be 'comic' even when its comic aspects are not noticed or understood by a recipient" (32). Hutcheon takes issue with this definition, preferring the less-loaded alternative of "repetition with critical difference" since this "would allow for the range of intent and effect possible in modern parodic works" (2000, 20).[34] She does not include humor in her definition of parody because parody does not always trigger a humorous response, at least according to her understanding of the concept of humor. However, as several humor scholars maintain, humor should be seen to encompass experiences, responses, and emotions ranging broadly from laughter (scornful or otherwise) to a knowing smile when one is in on the joke to an inward, unexpressed amusement over something playfully and unexpectedly subversive, disruptive, or puzzling (see, for example, Kitts and Baxter-Moore 2019, and Raskin 2008). And it is in this context that the humor of parody should be understood. The characteristic structure of what triggers humor is the nearest we can come to an objective classification of something as humorous or nonhumorous, which may be why Rose (1993) and other parody scholars include the comic in their definitions of parody while embracing a generous understanding of humor. Stating that

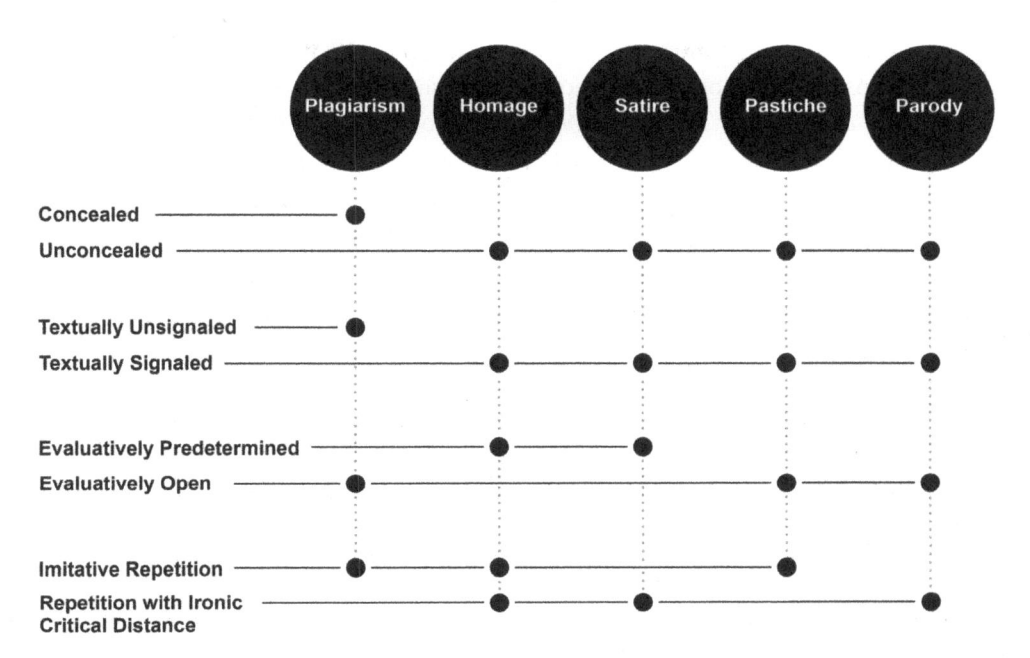

Figure 2.4
Differences and similarities among plagiarism, homage, satire, pastiche, and parody.

parody depends on ironic critical distance is, from this perspective, almost synonymous with saying that it contains the key triggers of humor, if one accepts the dominant theories of humor.

To sum up, then, and as illustrated in figure 2.4, plagiarism is a concealed and textually unsignaled form of appropriation, whereas homage, satire, pastiche, and parody are unconcealed and textually signaled forms. Furthermore, homage and satire are evaluatively predetermined forms of appropriation, whereas plagiarism, pastiche, and parody are evaluatively open. Finally, plagiarism and pastiche represent an imitative repetition of sources, whereas parody and satire represent repetition with ironic critical distance, and homage can do both.

Parody, then, is an acknowledged and multifunctional (evaluatively open) appropriation that displays an ironic critical distance toward its sources:

- *Acknowledged appropriation* here points to an act of referentiality that is deliberate, as opposed to unconscious, and to the parody being signaled as a parody. In contrast to plagiarism, which hides its sources, parody exposes them in order to be recognized as such. Its effectiveness requires that it is understood to be a reworking of something existing.

- In contrast to satire and homage, which are evaluatively predetermined, parody is also *multifunctional*, ranging, for example, from a satirical mockery to an entertaining social critique or a benign source of amusement.
- And more than merely imitating an artwork (the act that often defines pastiche), parody presents its appropriated material from an *ironic critical distance*—that is, in a way that is incongruent with how it was presented before. It transforms while it repeats, and it does so by communicating two texts at once—one directly (the parody itself) and one indirectly (the parodied text). In fact, the parody functions as a parody exactly because its appropriated material is recognized as belonging to two contexts at once.

It should further be obvious by now that mashups have much in common with parody: mashup music is also an acknowledged appropriation of specific artworks, and, like parody, it displays an ironic critical distance toward its sources. It does so by embracing the contrast between the sources' new and old contexts, and sometimes also between the combined sources and their connotations—and this in turn emphasizes the contrast between the familiar and the novel, and thus also its ironic critical distance. By introducing this critical distance with regard to their sources, mashups function as comments, but as I discuss in chapter 4, their received and intended messages are multifunctional—sometimes playfully benign, other times explicitly political, and still other times ambiguous or relatively neutral. Based on the striking similarities between the abiding definitions of parody and my understanding of mashup music (on which I elaborate in the following chapters), I conclude that mashup music is not only like parody but also in fact a contemporary manifestation of parody.

Mashup's Roots in Bisociative, Montage-Based Parody

In the courtroom, sampling is often reduced to a single thing, but as this chapter demonstrates, sampling, as well as appropriation more generally, is a whole field of practices and activities. Sampling is also not opposed to parody but can even manifest itself as parody. In this chapter, I have argued that although mashup music has many common traits with various other forms of appropriation, including hip-hop music, its particular specificity must be sourced not only in its sample-based nature but also in parody. Moreover, the roots of mashups can be traced to the bisociative montage, which merges sources not commonly thought of in combination. It thus becomes apparent that it also has predecessors beyond those usually referred to, as the following historical examples demonstrate.

Catherine A. Bradley's (2018) detailed account of thirteenth-century music points out that within certain forms of sacred music such as motets, it was common to appropriate secular melodies, including those otherwise associated with vernacular love songs—two musical categories often thought of as polar opposites. She explains: "This spirit of compositional play, and a profound interest in quotation, are consonant with the beginnings of the motet as a vernacular genre that delights in the combination of apparently contradictory materials. . . . This aesthetic arguably reached its summation in the proliferation of three- and four-voice polytextual motets, which present unparalleled opportunities to explore multi-layered semantic, allegorical, and/or parodic interactions between texts, as well as intricate and overlapping relationships between melodic lines" (249–250). As such, the motet of the thirteenth century actually shares some common features with mashups in terms of their playful mix of divergent songs.[35]

If we look to Western art music in general, there are several other examples to pick from. For example, in "Golliwog's Cakewalk" from the piano suite *Children's Corner* (1908), Claude Debussy both juxtaposes and instigates a dialogue between a danceable and cheerful ragtime cakewalk named Golliwog (after a popular minstrel caricature doll) and excerpts from Wagner's "Prelude" to *Tristan und Isolde*. In her thorough analysis of this movement, Elizabeth de Martelly points to the stylistic incongruity between Wagner's music and the cakewalk:

> The musical volley between the Tristan quotations and the syncopated gestures of the cakewalk presents a tension between two apparently disparate musical styles: where Wagner's opera is harmonically complex and "refined," the syncopated cakewalk represents a lowbrow, "wild," and "animalistic" musical idiom. Here, Debussy frames Wagner and the cakewalk as "humorously" incompatible, from disparate worlds incapable of communicating with one another. (Martelly 2010, 26)

By emphasizing their contrast, Debussy introduces a critical distance regarding both forms of music. Martelly goes on to observe that this stylistic incongruity also evokes a confrontational clash between the two social contexts represented by these divergent styles: "Golliwog as Africanized 'primitive' and Wagner as the epitomized figure of high Western culture" (2010, 26).[36] Debussy's bisociative montage thus serves as an example of how the parodic dramatization of music-stylistic and social differences that characterizes many mashups has also long been explored in Western art music.

Sinfonia (1969) by the Italian composer Luciano Berio is another bisociative montage juxtaposing passages from Mahler and Beethoven, as well as Schoenberg, Debussy, Hindemith, Ravel, Berlioz, Stravinsky, Strauss, Bach, Berg, Webern, and Stockhausen. Its parodic critical distance toward these passages is clearly evident, as Marion Hestholm explains: "Instead of 'killing' the precursors by writing something else, as Bloom's theory proclaims, Berio plays them up against each other and gives them new life" (2010, 94). Noting that montage "feeds on the dynamic of this confrontation of authorial voices" (94), she refers to the sleeve notes of the Erato recording, in which Berio writes: "The combination and unification of musical characters that are foreign to each other is probably the main driving force behind this third part of Sinfonia, a meditation on a Mahlerian 'objet trouvé'" (Berio 1986, 2).

Avant-garde composer Karlheinz Stockhausen's "Hymnen" (1969), which juxtaposes national anthems from around the word, is conceptually similar to mashup music, though it manipulates its sources much more excessively. Likewise, Glenn Gould's 1955 piano superimposition of the national anthems of the United States and the United Kingdom—"Star-Spangled Banner" and "God Save the King [or Queen]"—is even more resonant with mashup music, in that its sources are made perfectly explicit in their very subtle manipulation and also used as the primary foundation of the work. According to Benjamin Givan, Gould gave the following explanation of his alignment of these anthems to his recording engineer:

> By the way, I have a quodlibet of my own which came to me in the bath tub the other night. One of these times I'm going to be invited to give a concert on the fourth of July, I am sure, and when I do, I've figured out that, by leaving out the repeats in "The Star-Spangled Banner," and starting your entry at the thirteenth bar of "God Save the King," and then playing "God Save the King" over again, and altering the harmony in the second half of "The King" to modulate to the supertonic region, it has the most marvelous effect. (Givan 2015)

With only a few minor alterations, the anthems can be made harmonically compatible, even as they continue to carry with them the weight of their respective nation's political history.

There are also several obvious examples of parodic, bisociative montage in the field of popular music. For example, Nina Simone's "Little Girl Blue" (1958) combines the song with the same title from 1935 (with music by Richard Rodgers and lyrics by Lorenz Hart) with the melody of the widely known Christmas carol "Good King Wenceslas." Whereas the songs are incongruent in terms of their context, they sound stylistically congruent in Simone's version, and the Christmas carol may also function to underline the lyrics of "Little Girl Blue" for some listeners, as both songs are about struggle and disappointment. A more humorous example of a bisociative parodic montage is the aforementioned release "Mission: Impossible Theme/Norwegian Wood" (1968) by Copeland. Lalo Shifrin's familiar "Mission: Impossible" theme from the popular TV series of the same name (1966–1973) is used as the instrumental accompaniment to the lyrics and melody of the Beatles single "Norwegian Wood" (1965) as performed by Alan Copeland Singers. The latter song remains in G major, but in Copeland's arrangement, its original 6/8 time signature is changed to 5/4. The instrumental accompaniment from the "Mission: Impossible" theme remains in 5/4 and its original key of G minor, but, interestingly, the minor and major tonalities do not clash, although the associations and connotations of this soundtrack and the music of the Beatles certainly do.[37]

Whereas all these examples reperform their excerpts of existing music (save for Stockhausen's "Hymnen"), one of the earliest examples of bisociative montage-based parody that relies on samples is the Evolution Control Committee's "The Whipped Cream Mixes" from 1996 (first released on cassette in 1994). In the two tracks constituting "The Whipped Cream Mixes," the music by Herb Alpert's Tijuana Brass from their album *Whipped Cream and Other Delights* (1965) is overlaid with the rap vocals of Public Enemy's Chuck D from 1988 and 1991 releases in a manner sonically similar to an A+B mashup. In my analysis with Paul Harkins (2012) of one of these mixes, "By the Time I Get to Arizona," we point out that by combining the rap vocals of Public Enemy's "By the Time I Get to Arizona" with the music of Herb Alpert's "Whipped Cream," the Evolution Control Committee juxtaposes two tracks that work together musically in this new context while continuing to clash profoundly in terms of both style and connotations.

Whereas the lyrics of Public Enemy are "expressing a Malcom-X-inspired militancy about racism and other socio-political problems in America," Herb Alpert's Tijuana Brass "had no agenda other than entertaining their vast and diverse 1960s audience" (Brøvig-Hanssen and Harkins 2012, 94). When replacing the dense and sample-heavy montage of Public Enemy's music—which functions to underline the political message—with the light and cheerful music of Herb Albert, the contrast becomes humorous, as described by *Salon* journalist Charles Taylor: "Every time Chuck D lights into some new target of his righteous rage you hear those horns saying, 'Lighten the fuck up!'" (Taylor 2003). The bisociative nature of the two tracks is thus obvious, and so is the Evolution Control Committee's parodic critical distance from both tracks, making the work more evocative of mashup music than most examples of hip-hop or dub music, among others.[38]

These examples represent but a brief historical introduction to bisociative montage-based parodies.[39] Still, they serve to demonstrate that there are paths to tracing mashup music's roots in history other than either those limiting it to, or even equating it with, the sampling practices of hip-hop and dub music or those making the sweeping claim that the act of appropriating others' music belongs to all times. While it is fruitful to understand these practices as important roots of mashups, conflating notions or generalizations dismiss the fact that appropriation represents a diverse but dedicated artistic practice, as does sampling. Thus, while mashup music shares certain structural and technological similarities with hip-hop music, dub, and remixes in terms of being sample based, it is not, as Michael D. Ayers claims, "a logical derivation of hip-hop" (2006, 129). Such a positioning denies the fact that the formation of any practice is always quite complex in character and that the practice itself is likely traceable to multiple sources depending on what one's focus happens to be. This idea that sample-based music is not a single thing but several and that mashup music is simply a recent manifestation of the long-standing practice of parody is critical when it comes to defining the legal status of mashups and other forms of sample-based music. Moreover, as several poststructuralists have reminded us, texts are not isolated entities placed in a random social and historical context; they are saturated by their context, which informs both the production and the experience of those texts. As such, a contemporary hip-hop track from Turku differs from a 1990s hip-hop track from the Bronx, not only because the tracks themselves differ but also because the time and place in which they were produced and consumed provide them with very different meanings. It is uninformed to regard contemporary types of appropriation as something completely new, but it is also uninformed to regard them as nothing more than the latest incarnations of earlier forms. They are likely to be unique not only in their combinations of the many variables mentioned in this chapter but also in the sense that they have been produced and consumed within a unique social and historical context that contributes to their meaning.

3 Producing Mashups and the Pleasure of Play

[Mashups] appealed to me because it was incredible to hear a lot of these original songs being reimagined in different ways.
—Anonymous mashup producer (personal interview)

If you're able to take a piece of that composition [that resonates with people], if it still retains that original resonance—whether it's the vocals or the instrumental or a sample or whatever—but maintaining that resonance and then creating something I would argue to be brand new out of it, then it's new and old at the same time. And that's very unique, I think, because people instantly can connect to it through what they knew already, but you're also making something new out of that.
—CFLO (personal interview)

The previous chapter identified the specificity of mashups among the myriad appropriations from a descriptive perspective and further highlighted mashup music's correspondence to the parody concept. This chapter describes what the mashup producers who were interviewed and surveyed for this study regarded as significant to mashup aesthetics and how they realize these aspects in the creative processes of producing mashups. Several of them acknowledged that mashups are frequently dismissed out of hand, for two reasons: people engage with the music at a surface level without ever activating or even realizing its full potential, or they only know poor mashups, which are ubiquitous now given the ready availability of the specialized technological tools with which to make them and the social networks through which to distribute them. Raheem D noted, "The thing is: anyone can really pick up and do a mashup if they wanted to. And especially with social media—now you can post it to anyone that will listen. A lot of people tend to not know about keys and stuff being offbeat. So, then, someone will be, like, 'Oh, this sounds so messy and out of key and stuff. I don't like this. I prefer the original songs.' And then they just say they don't like mashups, when they've probably not listened to a good one." The insights into what mashup producers emphasize when making mashups is important to gain a better understanding of the mashup aesthetics.

While there are several variants of mashup music, there seem to be certain abiding and fundamental aesthetic guidelines or criteria of the genre among the producers—guidelines that constantly recurred in the interviews and survey responses and are also symptomatic of the mashups themselves.[1] I have here grouped these empirical findings into four "principles" that I have labeled as follows: *crediting, matching, ironic distancing*, and *repurposing*. *Crediting* here implies that the producers want their mashups to be recognized as acknowledged appropriations; that is, they expose the fact that their music relies heavily on the sampling of existing music recordings. The samples should be from well-known sources, so the listener will recognize them; if not, it must be made obvious in some other way that the mashup's music is not "new" as such. *Matching* refers to the producers' emphasis on making the sources they bring together match in various ways, so that the new track is musically (and potentially visually) coherent in and of itself. To many producers, it is not enough to align the key and the tempo; sound, harmony, rhythm, lyrics, and video represent equally high priorities. With *ironic distancing*, I point to the mashup producers' urge to instigate a conceptual clash, incongruity, or surprise of some sort. This may result from the simple fact that prior tracks from different sources have been juxtaposed, but it may also result from a difference in respective source era, lyrical theme, mood, or genre and associated stereotypes. I here question the assumption (proposed by several scholars and journalists) that the heart of mashup music is the genre clash that it often embraces and argue instead that what is actually crucial is the ironic critical distance that mashup music displays toward its sampled sources (thus my choice of the words *ironic distancing*). Finally, *repurposing* refers to the producers' aspiration to present their sources in a new light, primarily by means of letting the new context transform the listener's impression of them.[2]

These four aesthetic principles have much in common with parody. As noted in the previous chapter, parody is an acknowledged appropriation that repurposes its sources while retaining an ironic critical distance, and if several sources are combined, they are made to come together in a coherent whole as well. As such, the producers' underlying aesthetic principles support the notion that much mashup music corresponds to the concept of parody.

In the second part of this chapter, I interpret the producers' perspectives on the aesthetics behind mashups, and their motivations for making them, as a fascination with play, understood both as a particular form of activity and as a mind-set. That is, mashup activity has much in common with play, I observe, in the sense that it is motivated by, as well as premised on, one's mastery of the particular constraints that define it. Mashup producers seem to thrive on making the most out of the possibilities inherent in the frame of constraints set up by the mashup's underlying principles. Play, I believe, functions well as a rubric for the study of mashups as it contributes to illuminating the sociocultural significance of mashups and mashup activity. Moreover, I argue that another reason that mashups are easily dismissed is because their play frame, and its internal rules and logic, is not always recognized as such, or at least not understood properly, so that the activity deriving from it may thus be experienced as trivial.

Principle 1: Crediting

The first aesthetic principle emphasized by the producers is crediting, not only in terms of accreditation but also in terms of exposing the fact that their mashup is a mashup—that is, they seek to tap into the listener's ready understanding of mashup music as a calculated collision of prior musical sources. This principle is reflected in my notion that, contrary to plagiarism, mashup music constitutes an acknowledged form of appropriation, as discussed in the previous chapter. Several mashup producers emphasized the importance of the careful accreditation of their sources in the video or audio file descriptions and said that they even add a more general disclaimer announcing that the purpose of the mashup is purely recreational. Likewise, mashup titles often incorporate the terms *mashup* or *megamix* or the names of the artists or bands responsible for the original tracks (such as "Highasakite vs. Coldplay" or "Highasakite But It's Coldplay"). Alternatively, producers might use the titles of the original tracks to form a referential wordplay, such as titling a mashup of George Michael's "Careless Whisper" and Billy Idol's "Rebel Yell" as "Careless Rebel (George Michael +

Billy Idol Mashup)" (Wax Audio, 2012), or titling a mashup of Chic's "Good Times" and Iron Maiden's "Iron Chic—Rime of the Ancient Mariner" as "Rime of the Good Times" (Bill McClintock, 2020).[3]

The principle of crediting also transcends such annotations and paratextual information to encompass other means of forging a more immediate recognition of the sources in question. For example, the producers generally select samples from sources with which a broad group of listeners is already well acquainted, including popular contemporary tracks and historical or traditional classics.[4] In contrast to many hip-hop producers, then, mashup producers generally avoid esotericism. This timeliness can, of course, limit a mashup's longevity, but it seemed to be more important to the producers to enhance listeners' accessibility to the material and in turn broaden and expand the audience. Because the listener's acknowledgment of mashup music as a deliberate juxtaposition of existing music tracks is fundamental to the producers, they favor music samples (and video clips) of a duration that is adequate to enable easy recognition.[5] Furthermore, they tend to edit these sources only subtly or transparently.[6] As I expand on later, tempo and key changes are as slight as possible, and editing and mixing of tracks are done solely to make their juxtaposition successful while still keeping them as close to the originals as possible.

To some of the mashup producers, it was vital that listeners instantly recognize the mashed sources. Kap Slap said, "You can't mash up things that people don't know, 'cause what's the point?" and PhilRetroSpector concurred: "That's why mashups work. There is that familiarity with them." To others, it was more important that their listeners categorize what they hear as a mixture of existing music. Adriana A emphasized this point: "Well, I think the recognizability is what makes a mashup interesting and fun. . . . If it's manipulated too much . . . what's the point? I call those 'what's-the-point-mashups.' . . . Ideally you want to be able to recognize it. Or, if you don't necessarily recognize one of the songs, you'll at least recognize that it's mashed up, because it's so radically different from the original." If the tracks are very different in style or sound already, this will help listeners acknowledge and appreciate the mashup *as mashup*, even when they do not know the sources, said Adriana A: "Say you take a hip-hop song, but then you mash it up with some heavy metal band—I don't necessarily need to know what that heavy metal band is, but it sounds crazy with this hip-hop artist over loud guitars." Adriana A's point here echoes hip-hop scholar Justin Williams's (2014) notion that a musical quotation can draw attention to itself as a quotation even if the listener is not familiar with the source; the quotation's sonic or stylistic contrast with the rest of the music can be just as revealing and valuable as its referential function (or even more so).[7] As Adriana A pointed out, the stylistic differences between hip-hop and metal are often ingrained in the listener as divergent, so that even if one does not know a mashup's sources as such, one understands it to be a juxtaposition of incongruent styles.

As Jeanette Bicknell points out, so long as unfamiliar quotations are comprehended as quotations, they need not be permanently exclusionary: "It can also be an invitation to noncomprehending listeners to discover the original context of the quoted phrase and join the group of those who do recognize it without further clues" (2001, 188). Once listeners acknowledge the mashup as appropriation, they can explore its original sources as they see fit, regardless of their familiarity beforehand. Listeners may even find this comparison between the mashup and its origins—which are readily available in our age of "ubiquitous music" (Kassabian 2013)—to be particularly diverting. Some of the interviewed producers described themselves as a type of curator who introduces legendary but neglected music to younger generations or reintroduces familiar music with a twist, so that those who once found it stale might experience it anew. DJ Paul V. explained: "To me, the greatest gift of a good mashup is that it's hopefully going to take a fan of only one part of that song and turn them into a fan of the second or third or fourth part that's also used." Adriana A agreed: "I hated hip-hop. Hated it! Didn't understand it . . . until mashups. And then I would hear songs that I liked, but there's a rap on top of it. And, all of a sudden, I'm hearing the rap and I'm noticing the artistry of the rap. And it's because it offers an entry point for me. . . . I was basically tricked into listening with a more open mind and not being immediately prejudiced toward [it]. And now I totally have an appreciation for hip-hop that I never would have had before, if it wasn't for hearing hip-hop mashups fifteen years ago." She added that she sometimes tries to broaden musical horizons by introducing listeners at pop parties to indie, alternative, and goth music by "wrapping pop vocals on top," combining, for example, an instrumental track by My Chemical Romance with the vocals of Katy Perry's "Fireworks." As I discuss in chapter 4, mashup music thus represents a means of bridging the gap between divergent fan bases, opening ears to various genres, or animating those genres' differences. Yet most of the producers preferred to use recognizable sources, since the crux of the mashup aesthetic is the making of something new out of something "old." While the mashup can function as such even when the sources are not so obvious, thanks to the many ways in which producers expose its nature, instantly recognizable samples can trigger the listener's *immediate* response.

Obstacles Related to Crediting

Given that the principle of crediting involves mashup producers' prioritization of recognizable samples from existing and preferably well-known recordings, a sample library such as Splice or a sample database that provides authorized short musical sequences will not work for them because the samples are too short. Nor will a creative-commons sample database or a sample database such as Tracklib help. While such databases feature entire songs, including songs that may be familiar to some listeners, they do not have the really famous music that mashup producers seek. And whereas the re-creation of a whole track is an option in some forms of music appropriation, mashup producers shun this alternative because part of the joy of both making and experiencing mashups is that the mashed music sounds exactly the same yet completely different (see chapter 2 for a discussion of the importance of medium specificity).

As I discuss in depth in chapter 5, mashup producers find the process of seeking permission to use samples from famous songs to be confusing, and they also assume it to be time-consuming and unfeasibly expensive. The samples they use, then, are typically unauthorized and retrieved in alternative ways. Raheem D pointed out that it was easier to acquire official instrumental and a cappella tracks—so-called stems—some years ago, when promotional CDs that often included these versions were still available. Yet some contemporary recordings still make such stripped audio files available, or they are leaked by the artists, record companies, or radio stations, for example. Colatron recalled that in the early phase of the mashup scene, "there was always this race to get the most obscure source files to make stuff with, so some of the a cappellas, you know, people would pay hundreds of pounds for, behind the scenes, to get their hands on, like, the most exclusive vocal that no one else had used" (here, "obscure" describes the original file source of the track, not the sort of music one might turn up while crate digging, for example). He then added that because these official versions were quite rare, producers often ended up extracting the vocal or instrumental parts themselves: "We would hand cut vocal stems, instrumentals—we would do it by hand, you know. I did a 30-channel cut-and-paste of the 'Bohemian Rhapsody' a cappella, all 27 channels of vocals of it, and it took me four to five months. And it was insane, but it was rewarding to do that." The process he describes is made easier if one has the instrumental-only version already and can then use phase cancellation to extract the vocal from a full mix.

While official instrumental versions may be rarer than they once were, the digital library of recordings from which to extract them is considerably vaster today than it was in the early 2000s, when producers had to either buy the tracks they wanted or download them illegally from peer-to-peer file-sharing sites such as Napster. There are also software programs that make such inversions or extractions more straightforward, and they have advanced considerably over the past twenty years in terms of both scope and availability.[8] Some of the interviewed mashup producers considered such techniques to generate less than pristine results, even after their attempts to clean things up with an equalizer and other processing effects (thanks to certain persistent middle frequencies, for example). They preferred to make them manually or acquire them from websites dedicated to providing stems. The sound quality of the manipulated stems (and music catalogs) varies significantly among these websites, and while certain sites offer stems for free, most require a pay-by-the-month arrangement that can be quite expensive. Some producers therefore share stems within Facebook groups or forums, but most feel obliged to pay for them, including Happy Cat Disco: "[I want to] support the people who support us." There are also community websites on which one earns credit when one posts stems; this credit can be used in turn to acquire other stems. Stems can also be found in YouTube or Google searches, but the producers noted that there are fewer stems on the internet than there used to be, mainly due to copyright regulations. Dedicated stem websites have decreased in number as well due to copyright regulations. Still, producers strive to overcome the hassle of finding sources and the legal challenges associated with using unauthorized samples because the alternative of employing nothing but unfamiliar samples would mean that the mashup would be almost dead on arrival.

Principle 2: Matching

The second aesthetic principle that the producers emphasized is the *matching* of sources. John Shiga, who wrote an article (2007) on the mashup in its early phase, quotes an anonymous contributor to the mashup website GYBO who wrote that talent in the context of a mashup is "the capacity to recognize shared properties between different songs, or the capacity to reorganize the musical and aural relations of recordings so that they sound like they are components of the same song" (Shiga's paraphrasing of the quote; Shiga 2007, 103). This statement rings true for the current mashup scene as well, wherein one of the primary aesthetic goals remains to juxtapose samples in a way that makes the disparate tracks sound musically coherent—that is, they are made to match. The producers make the mashed tracks share the same tempo and pitch, they align their rhythm and harmony, they make them fit together structurally (in terms of either vertical or horizontal alignment), and they sometimes also relate the tracks' lyrical themes in some way. If the mashup consists of a video as well, the footage is usually edited to match the new audio track and shaped into a coherent montage of clips in and of itself. In this section, I first expand on the mashup producers' alignment of source keys and tempos by also focusing on the ways in which they try to align the tracks' harmonies and rhythms. I then address the parameter of sound, a clear priority of the producers, before discussing how the producers approach lyrics and video in the mashup.

Key, Tempo, Harmony, and Rhythm

According to the producers, matching the tempos and keys is crucial to making mashed tracks sound coherent, as though they belong together. Experienced producers described this process as much more time-consuming when they had to manipulate those elements manually; today, software does it automatically, though it can be a tricky affair. Poolboy noted that mashing music whose recorded performance does not keep perfect time (which is especially true for older music) can entail stretching certain passages in a track while tempo-compressing other passages. Other producers also indicated that tempo and key manipulation should be kept to a minimum in order to preserve the original tracks' sound quality and keep the samples as true to their sources as possible. To some, this meant pitching the tracks by two semitones at most and altering the tempo by no more than ten beats per minute; to others, it meant making the tracks meet halfway in terms of both tempo and pitch rather than placing an excessive burden on one track rather than the other. Some said that they developed an idea for a mashup, then found and matched the sources (for example, they heard a song that they associated with another song and decided to try out the combination)—a method requiring a good ear in terms of anticipating what might fit together. Others said that they worked more systematically, extracting the vocals and instrumentals from popular songs, duplicating the tracks, and manipulating the keys and tempos variously on each version to produce the same a cappella track in different pitches and tempos. After executing this process on multiple songs, they organized their tracks in a mashup "database" consisting of a cappella and instrumental folders for every key and tempo. This time-consuming work allowed them to experiment more freely with different track combinations in the sequencer program.

Less present than key and tempo manipulation in academic discussions of mashups is the producers' imperative to make the tracks' harmony and rhythm compatible. Some of the interviewees were not particularly concerned about this, but many insisted that the mashup had to be harmonically perfect. Several, including Tom Boates Everybody, admitted that they were frustrated with people who posted mashups with little regard for harmony:

> I'm a production-minded person—like, a music-minded person—so I like having things in the same key or having a rhythm play off the vocals of a different song, like, all that stuff kind of matters to me. And I started to get really frustrated with some other DJ friends who would make mashups but not care about those things. . . . So, there is a level of artistry to it, because there are definitely mashup artists out there who are just, like, "Oh, this bpm and this bpm, and it says it's in the same key, so let's just put them together." Like, it's hard for me to call that art. That's luck—I don't know what it is.

According to the producers' standards, harmonic "perfection" does not require the mashed songs to share a tonality and harmonic progression (though this does happen). In fact, mashing tracks that differ in these areas will often heighten the listener's surprise at the (potential) success of their combination.

The latter can be exemplified by the Reborn Identity's "Portishead vs Blondie vs Kanye West—Sour Glass (mashup)" (2009), which mashes the music of Portishead's "Sour Times" (1994) with the vocals of Blondie's

"Heart of Glass" (1978) and, toward the end, a twenty-second vocal phrase from Kanye West's "Love Lockdown" (2008). Here, a familiar vocal line is set to a new harmonic progression. Portishead's "Sour Times" is in a minor key, staying on C♯m with a descending bassline in the verses, then repeating the descending harmonic progression F♯m–C♯m/E–D♯–in the choruses. Blondie's "Heart of Glass" is, in contrast, in a major key, using the chords E–C♯–C♯m–E–in the verses and A–E–A–E (or F♯–B, depending on the round) in the choruses. The Portishead song is therefore in the relative minor key to Blondie's song, meaning that the two tracks share the same scale and, in the mashup, retain their original keys (though the Blondie vocals are slowed from 114 to 110 beats per minute). Blondie vocalist Debbie Harry starts singing on the sixth tone relative to the E major chord, but in the mashup, it is the tonic center of C♯m. She descends in the original to the fifth tone of the C♯ major chord (which then turns into C♯m), then to the third, second, and first tones of the major chord E, which in the mashup becomes the fifth tone of the *minor* chord C♯m, then remains in that chord for the fifth, fourth, and third tones. Here, then, Harry's original major melody becomes a minor melody with an emphasized minor third that strengthens the impression of a minor tonality. An originally "optimistic" melodic line (despite its lyrical content) now sounds rather dejected (although also somewhat detached), given the way in which minor chords are often experienced as sadder, more emotionally freighted, and less energetic than major chords (Moore 2016, 69–76). Even more striking is that when the characteristic second chord of Blondie's original version, the C♯, goes away, so does much of the melody's characteristic expressiveness, which contributes to its general deflation in the mashup. This shift is sharpened by Portishead's lo-fi, jazz-inflected film noir sound, drawing on a sample from Lalo Schifrin's "The Danube Incident" from 1969 (from the TV show *Mission: Impossible*) that is characterized by the sound of a jangly cimbalom and features a prominent descending bassline. Even the mashup's footage contributes to turning Harry's nonchalance into misery, combining close-ups of Harry's face with clips from the "Sour Times" video (which is based on Portishead's 1994 short film *To Kill a Dead Man*), all converted to black and white for consistency. With this example, we see clearly how the alteration of harmony, together with other elements (such as the video content), can produce a harmonically coherent mashup while reinventing an existing vocal track in the context of a mashup.[9]

DJ Prince has doubled down on the idea that if you do not get the harmony right, you will not achieve legitimacy within the mashup community, by developing a tool called "harmonic mixing" to assist those with limited musical competence or music-listening skills. This tool, which is available at a tutorial website, presents the circle of fifths as the "Camelot Wheel," in which the names of the twelve tones' key signatures and associated major and minor keys are switched out with letters and numbers for ease of navigation (A is minor and B is major, and 1A and 1B are parallel keys, so that "Heart of Glass," discussed above, would be 12B, whereas "Sour Times" would be 12A).[10] This tool is used in the software program Mixed in Key to analyze songs' tonality and harmonies and then translate the chords into the codes of the Camelot Wheel.[11] Though such tools did not come up in the other interviews, I suspect that some of the producers would have welcomed such help, while others would have rejected it as ruining the spirit, challenge, and fun of making mashups.

Some producers also transposed individual tones in a given vocal melody in order to make it fit with a new harmonic progression. For example, DJ Cummerbund recalled a mashup in which he made every major third into a minor one in order to better suit the harmony. Many of the other producers, including DJ Schmolli, were purists:

> [If an instrumental] has a certain chord structure, four bars, and the last chord in the fourth bar is not going well with the vocals, I would usually just kick this idea and not re-pitch just the certain notes or certain phrases from the last chord where it doesn't fit. I don't do re-pitching at all. I have done it a couple of times, but I usually don't re-pitch. If I hear a mashup, I wanna sing along with the original vocal melody, and I get distracted if there's like only the last word that is pitched up or pitched down a semi-tone. . . . I mean, it's not that bad, but I wanna keep the vocals as original as possible, so everybody instantly knows these are the vocals, and they're not being altered or pitched or things like that.

He does alter tracks in other ways—for example, pitching up the whole track by a semitone or slowing or speeding it up by a couple of beats per minute—but people usually miss such subtle changes. "The thing is," he explained, "if it sounds forced, then I would not do it. Simple as that."

The various means of mixing the tracks' harmony often challenge the producers in terms of musical skills and creativity. Accordingly, producers including PhilRetroSpector regarded the mashing of a rap a cappella with an instrumental track as a lazy solution: "If somebody had a rap—say if your a cappella was a rap track—there was always the snobbery there, that that was easier to cut. . . . Because, you know, I mean, you're not harmonically mixing anything." Happy Cat Disco disagreed, insisting that a rap vocal can be just as challenging because of its rhythmic complexity: "There's something about the polyrhythm stuff—they need to work. And specifically with hip-hop, because a lot of people say hip-hop isn't a mashup art because it's too easy, because there's no harmonic content. And I'm like, no, but there's rhythmic, there's polyrhythmic content, and a lot of people who say that can't make rap mashups, because they think it's easy. It's not. You gotta get that. It's why Eminem is good, because he knows how to play off the rhythms of the backbeat."

Happy Cat Disco here touches on another alignment priority for several of the producers—the tracks' rhythmic profiles—in the interests of forming a coherent groove.[12] DJ Schmolli noted that this rhythmic alignment is important to the mashing of pop vocals as well: "There's a flow in vocal tracks that fits to the original music, but if you take the vocal track, which has a certain flow on it, and put it on another instrumental that has a different flow on it, even if it's in time . . . you don't feel the flow of the lyrics and the vocals. It's not good." His purist approach prohibits him from "groove-correcting" tracks (using specialized software) to force the vocals to fit the instrumental track(s); he would rather find a different track instead.

Sometimes, however, the mashing of tracks that have completely different types of flow can generate an interesting and reinvigorating result, which is the case, for example, with oneboredjeu's "Flo Good Inc.—Gorillaz feat. De La Soul vs. Flo Rida feat. T-Pain (mashup)" (2019), which blends the music of "Feel Good Inc." (2005) by Gorillaz featuring De La Soul with the vocals of "Low" (2007) by Flo Rida featuring T-Pain. The original version of "Low" has a tempo of 128 beats per minute; in the mashup, however, the vocals are sped up to match the faster tempo of the instrumental track at 139 beats per minute, which alters the perceived vocal performance significantly. This altered impression of the vocals is made even more profound with the replacement of their instrumental accompaniment. In the original version of "Low," the vocals of Flo Rida and T-Pain sound a bit pushed forward relative to the beat in their performance style, whereas the instrumental accompaniment is more laidback; the groove is quite minimalistic and leans toward the house end of the hip-hop spectrum, with prominent synthesizers and house claps and a less prominent syncopated kick drum. In the original version of "Feel Good Inc.," it is the vocals that are laidback, whereas the instrumental accompaniment is more pushed forward. The instrumental of "Feel Good Inc." can be described as a vigorous, rock-inspired groove involving a straight but intense lo-fi drum beat with punchy snare and bass drum sounds and an insistent, regular hi-hat. Moreover, an energetic and melodic syncopated bassline supplies the song's centerpiece. Via the mashup, this music groove by Gorillaz reenergizes T-Pain and Flo Rida's vocals even more than their changed tempo, making them funkier and more energetic, while these replaced vocals also highlight the effectiveness of Gorillaz's groovy bassline.

As demonstrated, several mashup producers are concerned not only with key and tempo alignment but also with harmony and rhythm, including the potential that lies in combining tracks in which the harmonic progression and rhythmic flow diverge. The replacement of these parameters can transform the familiar elements significantly, with a surprising effect on the listener—one sometimes accompanied by humor or even awe.

Sound

The interviews and survey suggest that different mashup producers devote different amounts of time and energy to the mixing process. Some are concerned mostly with making sure the volume levels across the tracks are consistent throughout the song, or they send the mashed version through a mastering plugin to create stronger uniformity and consistency between the tracks. MsMiep further explained that some producers, including herself, value imperfect stems (a vocal track, for example, in which one can hear the bleed of the instrumental accompaniment in the background), probably to introduce a DIY vibe. Danny Neyman privileged track availability over sound quality: "If there's a song that I really, really want to incorporate, and I just can't find a high quality a cappella but I can find a low quality [version] that might work, I'll do that." Purist producers including DJ Faroff even eschew processing effects altogether: "So I was kind of, in a way, proud of using some shitty software, that, you know—I didn't really have any effects or anything." Other producers, though, are obsessed with sound quality in terms of obtaining or making stems with the best quality possible and mixing their mashed tracks to achieve superior sonic coherence.

"I think what happens in the general public is that they think that all we do in mashups is that we just take an a cappella and throw it over an instrumental and call it a day," one of the anonymous interviewees explained. "But no, we don't do that, right? We do a lot more than that. We add reverb, we add delay, we do all the things that an audio engineer would do. We have to make them sound good. And that's how your general public will appreciate them at the end of the day. If they sound like originals." Indeed, "sounding like an original" was a mantra for many of the interviewed mashup producers, and Happy Cat Disco elaborated on it: "When we say it 'sounds like an original,' [we] mean it sounds like it was always intended to be like that. That means you got the rhythm right, you got the harmonics right, you got the engineering right, and the personality's there. When somebody says that to you, that's a good thing. That's a really good thing. . . . So yeah, we do need to try and make it sound like it was meant to be of a recording." Simon Iddol agreed that mashups are often underrated in terms of their engineering but lamented the reason:

> Since it's easy to do, there are so many bad mashups, and so many bad remixes and everything out there. So that's why we have kind of a bad reputation now for mashups and also for remixes. . . . To make a good mashup is not easy because of the basic fact that those songs were not made for each other. We have a saying in the mashup community that "these songs were made for each other—this is a match made in heaven," blah blah. But it's not true. I mean, those songs were made in a different period of time, different mindset, different continent, different artist—so many differences. *You* are the bridge. *You're* the connection, the artist.

This ideal of "sounding like an original" demands much more than simply matching the respective tracks' keys and tempos, the producers insisted, though they felt that too many mashups suffer from doing only those things.

Several of these producers had backgrounds as audio engineers, and Happy Cat Disco pointed out that mixing tracks from prior recordings to sound coherent is often more challenging than mixing a new track: "I do sound effects for a living, I do recordings, I do editing, I do mixing. But the best engineering skill I've gotten, by EQ [a sound engineering tool used to adjust the volume of different audio frequencies] or settling the mix—I mean everything—has come from mashups. I've learned more from doing that than I ever have from sound effects, so . . . EQing, trying to get things to sit in the mix, using multiband compressors, using sidechains—every single mashup that anybody does has a unique problem. And this is sort of

Producing Mashups and the Pleasure of Play 67

where the art comes in. So, if you're gonna ask me, 'Where is the art?' it's coming from an engineering aspect, I think. Engineering is an art form." Among the challenges in this regard, as introduced above, is improving the quality of the stems that are not already studio versions. Another is making mashed tracks that were never intended to cohere share the mix in terms of sound. Happy Cat Disco said, "Trying to get my Michael Jackson vocal, [which was] recorded back in 1984, on top of something that's recorded nowadays, it's an engineering feat trying to get that to work. It takes a great deal of, like, compression and EQing and effects and things like that to kind of get things to sit in the mix professionally."[13] A "dry" a cappella track might need more reverb or sonic aggression to succeed; the volume of a frequency area of an instrumental track might need to be modified by a few decibels (using a sound equalizer [EQ]) to make space for the vocal; an overall reverb or multiband compression might help the mashup's discrete tracks come together better, they explained. To Happy Cat Disco, the engineering was so important that if the sound was not good, he would not post it; he felt that his mashup name, and his engineering reputation, was at stake.[14]

Several of the other producers who prioritized the mixing of mashup tracks described in detail their use of reverb, delay, EQ, compression, leveling and panning, and other sound-processing effects. Given his general reluctance to alter his source tracks, DJ Schmolli described himself as "really picky" when it came to mixing them with equalizer, compressor, reverb, and so on. The sonic result of his considerable effort is still subtle in terms of its relationship to the original; he did not want to make audible changes to particular sounds but instead sought to integrate the sources as best he could.[15] As mentioned, there was a consensus among the mashup producers that while the tracks should sound as though they belong together, it should also be obvious that they are independent as well. As one of the survey respondents put it, "You must believe that it's a whole new song but one that you've already heard." This discrepancy enhances the experience of "same yet different" or "old yet new" that defines the mashup as a work of art.

At least one of the current dedicated mashup forums is centered on sound and engineering, and several of the interviewed producers were part of that forum. They likened it to a peer-reviewing system through which a producer posts a mashup "draft" on the site and others provide constructive feedback on its engineering that can be worked into the mashup ahead of its reposting to the site. This back-and-forth process—which can, they said, be quite lengthy—exemplifies a form of social authorship that has become common on the internet.[16] McSlzy described one of the earliest mashup forums, GYBO, as functioning as a quality control system as well, but also as "a self-regulating community" in the sense that producers would not post their mashups if their peers did not approve.

To most of the interviewed and surveyed mashup producers, the art of the mashup resided in the bridging of tracks in such a way that the combination sounds "like an original" even as it remains obvious that the tracks are from different (often very different) sources already. But the ways in which producers achieved this varied, with some focusing on sound and others on key and tempo, and potentially also harmony and rhythm. Still others focused on the lyrical themes in their respective sources, or on creating a coherent audiovisual experience by merging footage associated with the mashed tracks or using independent footage to which the mashup functioned as a soundtrack.

Structure, Lyrics, and Video
Although the structure of mashups adheres to the montage form in that several prior sources are merged, as discussed in the previous chapter, mashup producers structure their samples quite differently within this format. In the most basic A+B mashup, an a cappella track is aligned horizontally with an instrumental track. As producers mash the two sources, some retain the structures of both samples in their entirety (or close to it), whereas others retain the structure of one of the samples (the a cappella track, for example) while rearranging the structure of the other, often so as to make the harmonies work together. However, A+B mashups are often more complex than this, consisting of more than two tracks that are aligned along both axes. And whereas it is often either the vocals or the instrumentals of a given source track that are used, bits of the other are often used as well, to spice up the mix. When several sources have been mashed into a megamix mashup, the samples' duration and frequency of appearance vary considerably. This mosaic form of making mashups allows for more structural experimentation than a typical A+B mashup, which often aims to make the mashed tracks appear to be as close to their original versions as possible. In megamix mashups, the producers use a combination of instrumentals,

a cappella tracks, and complete (unmanipulated) samples that are aligned both vertically and horizontally.

Jeffrey S. Yunek, Benjamin K. Wadsworth, and Simon Needle (2020) point out that when producers structure their mashup samples, they often align the sections' new placements with their placements in the original tracks. For example, if two samples stemming from a chorus are used within a mashup chorus, they serve to boost the sense of the section as a chorus. That way, the listener benefits from associations not only to the sources as such but also to the formal function of the selected sequences (as a verse or a chorus, for example). These scholars further refer to DJ Earworm, who states that he bears the samples' formal functions in mind when he structures them (3). In an interview, DJ Earworm revealed his preference for the verse-chorus form in megamixes: "I decided the initial combination of hooks would be my chorus, and then I set about filling in the rest. A normal pop song will have a verse/chorus/bridge structure, with the choruses being identical, the verse being fairly similar, and the bridge standing out as different . . . the whole thing will sound like a single song. . . . My goal is to make the perfect pop song rather than a DJ mix. My mashups have a beginning, a middle and an end, they all happens [sic] in four minutes. Verse, bridge, chorus, intro, outro, enough repetition but not too much, parts that repeats, parts that mimic each other—pop, basically" (quoted in Yunek et al. 2020; for the original interview, see Morse 2011). Although megamix mashups, as well as A+B mashups, often do use the typical pop form of alternating verses and choruses (Boone 2013, 146–150), the arrangements of mashups are otherwise quite diverse. After demonstrating the complexity and sophistication of mashup arrangements in his study, Liam McGranahan concludes, "It would be impossible to create rules, or generalize, about the specific editing and rearranging strategies that mashup artists use because they vary so significantly from mashup to mashup and are so reliant on the particular sources and number of sources that are sampled" (2010, 51–52).

In his *Audio Mashup Construction Kit*, DJ Earworm (who authored the book under his proper name Jordan Roseman) points out that when structuring the samples, it is not only form or melody that is relevant but also the lyrics and an overarching narrative (Roseman 2007, 80). That is, his samples are also selected and arranged in order to create new lyrics. He writes: "The words of the songs can inspire the particular combination. If you are using vocal elements from more than one song and if the words relate to each other, it can be wonderful. Songs may share key words or simply relate to each other thematically. One song may twist the meaning of the other, altering the context. Another song may ask a question that the other song answers. A worthwhile goal is to somehow tell one continuous story from the lyrics of several songs" (Roseman 2007, 80). He then discusses what he calls the call-and-response technique, in which phrases from different sources alternate in a dialogue, and the "cut-up" technique, in which the words (or even the syllables and phonemes) of vocal tracks are spliced together into new sentences (231–232).[17] When interviewed by McGranahan, he gave an example of this procedure:

> For instance, I was listening to that Beyoncé song "If I Were a Boy," and all of a sudden it was like, "oh, that sounds just like 'Free Fallin' [by Tom Petty]." . . . And you know you find out what words do relate. I was like, "oh, it ['If I Were a Boy'] is kind of about a girl complaining about this guy who is taking her for granted. And then he [Tom Petty] is really singing about, in a way, being free." Then I was thinking, well for her his freedom is just really annoying. So I said, this could be kind of a conflict, the male version and the female version. So you just, you can take almost two random songs and you just see what in them relates to each other. (DJ Earworm as quoted in McGranahan 2010, 68)[18]

Several of the other producers interviewed for this study also emphasized the relevance of the lyrics for the structural arrangement of mashups. They explained that mashups might expose a coherent linear narrative across the songs, a repetitive emphasis on certain words, a new conversation between the artists, or a gesture of wordplay when initially opposed narratives come together in unexpected ways. CFLO provided an example of the latter approach: "I had Kanye West's 'Jesus Walks' versus Jay-Z's 'Lucifer,' right? So they're opposite, and . . . there's some sort of string between them that you connect as an artist and put them together. And if they sound good, it's even better." Raheem D favored mashups that sounded as though the mashed artists were singing together in the studio, so he generally took the a cappella version of the tracks he was mashing and cut them so that they make sense lyrically.[19] Isosine also gravitated toward exposing a common lyrical theme between the mashed tracks: "I just like it, because, I mean, what makes a song—like, a non-mashup, like, a normal song—good is that, on top of it having catchy lyrics or good song structure or whatever, I think that the theme is very important, and how well the singer or the producer can tie together the theme. And so, I kind of like to extend that concept into the mashup. And it gets interesting with mashups because now you have the opportunity to use as many samples as you want. . . . There's gonna be lots of songs falling within the same themes, and I kinda like the synergy of combining all of that, just to reinforce the idea of a certain theme."

More often than not, a mashup features a video, leading many producers to use YouTube as their preferred distribution channel (although there are other reasons as well that contribute to its alignment with mashup producers, including its large and active audience). There are even dedicated mashup-video producers—some make only videos and collaborate with another producer who makes the music; others do both. Mashup videos tend to use footage involving their source songs—either the actual music videos from the sampled songs or related concert footage or a combination of the two. The video footage of the sampled sources has the added benefit of associating the source songs with their artists, even when the songs in question are not recognized as such, which may heighten the experience of mashups as something old but also new. In megamix mashups, the footage and the audio that belong together are usually displayed simultaneously, whereas in the basic A+B mashups, the footage of the mashed tracks is often intermingled in various ways, since both tracks are present simultaneously (for examples, see chapter 4). Sometimes the intermingling of footage and its alignment with the audio is done quite artistically.[20] For example, in AnDyWuMUSICLAND's "Beyoncé—Sorry, Single Ladies (feat. Justin Bieber) [Remix]" (2015), which mashes the vocals of Beyoncé's "Single Ladies (Put a Ring on It)" (2009) with the instrumental version of Bieber's "Sorry" (2015), the screen is divided in two, with alternating clips from the two videos on each half and occasionally the same clip mirrored across both halves. Both tracks' music videos consist of women dancing against a white background. Though Beyoncé's video is black and white while Bieber's is in color, the mashup converts Bieber's video into black and white to match Beyoncé's and create a seamless "original" out of the two disparate sources—one that comments on the similarities between them. In some mashups, other footage is added as well. In chapter 4, for example, I analyze DJ Cummerbund's "Blurry in the USA" (2020), in which the combined footage of the mashed songs is complemented by audiovisual news report clips of the Black Lives Matter protests, which serve to underline the mashup's overall theme of a nation in decline.

Other mashup producers rely on footage that is independent of the mashed tracks, so that the mashup serves as the soundtrack to a new or altered third-party video. Alternative footage might include cartoons—for example, Happy Cat Disco's "Bruno Mars vs. Caravan Palace(24K Digger)—Mashup" (2016) uses segments from Fleischer Studio's "color classic" cartoon titled "Hold It" from 1938, and his "The Weeknd vs. 2Pac & Eazy-E ft. Lucien Hughes & Memeguy1997 (I Feel The 90's Coming)" (2017) uses selected segments from the animated sitcom *The Simpsons*. The latter video was made by Lucien Hughes, who was described by *Pitchfork* in 2016 as "the most visible Simpsonwave artist working right now" and as "the internet denizen who gave the [Simpsonwave] genre its name" (Lozano 2016). Simpsonwave is a subgenre, or perhaps a feature, of vaporwave that is characterized by YouTube montage videos of edited clips from "The Simpsons."[21] In the *Pitchfork* interview, Hughes explains that the Simpsonwave videos are very much about nostalgia: "'The Simpsons' is pretty unique in that it's something that almost everyone born between the late '80s and early '00s grew up watching. Vaporwave is very much about creating an atmosphere of nostalgia, so I feel 'The Simpsons' just perfectly fits the whole aesthetic" (Lozano 2016). The nostalgic 1990s tinge to the Simpsons video for the mashup certainly also fits the theme of the mashup itself, as revealed by both the selection of samples (which are mostly from the 1990s or early 2000s)[22] and in the title of the mashup ("I Feel the 90's Coming"). The collaboration between Happy Cat Disco and Simpsonwave artist Lucien Hughes also reminds us that mashups are part of a larger internet scene that relies on the visual to capture attention and inform its dominant aesthetic forms.

Danny Neyman's main reason for making mashup videos was to hold the audience's attention on the mashup: "I'm sure you've noticed [that] plenty of people are talking about how, especially in younger generations, the attention span of everyone has kinda decreased a little. So, if you're just listening to the audio and looking at one picture on the screen just consistently, it gets a little boring." MsMiep linked mashup videos to contemporary society's general orientation toward the audiovisual: "I think that that's how mashups have been consumed. That's how I feel, like, that's where I see mashups sort of being shared around different groups on social media. If it's got a video, it'll do the rounds. If it doesn't have a video along with it, then it just kind of drops off pretty quickly. People aren't necessarily interested. I think it needs to be that full audiovisual package these days." While some producers persist in accompanying their mashups with a still image, others consider the video to be an integral part of the mashup and an artwork in itself. Still, the interviewees were more interested in talking about mashup music than mashup video footage, although the questions may have led them in that direction.

As demonstrated thus far, a commonly emphasized aesthetic principle of the mashup producers was to make the mashed tracks sound like an original (the *matching*) while clearly delineating, through various acts of signaling, that the result is nevertheless a mashup—that is, a combination of disparate tracks (the *crediting*). This act of doubled utterance was part of the challenge and fun of making mashups, the producers explained, and it inspired a range of solutions. Given the ongoing development of tools that assist with the mixing process, one might think that the old-school mashup producers would dedicate more time to the mixing process than the younger generation would, but this quality was instead clearly person specific regardless of generation. A given producer's approach to mashups might also vary according to what type of mashup was being made; they might devote more time to lyrical coherence in megamixes and to "harmonic mixing" in A+B mashups, for example—but this particular distinction did not arise in the interviews, perhaps because the line between these two formats is often blurred. Despite their individual idiosyncrasies, however, all the producers adhered to the transparent mediation paradigm.[23] That is, their manipulation of the original sources was discreet and usually transparent; the tempos and keys were altered but only slightly, for example, and processing effects were used primarily to refine the sound of the sampled audio files and integrate them more completely. As one survey respondent put it, a good mashup must reflect a "lack of audible technical tricks." While the structure of the source songs might be significantly rearranged in a megamix mashup, a basic A+B mashup usually features only the structural edits that are absolutely necessary to integrating its sources. In keeping with this rather purist and minimalist production paradigm, most mashups also consist of samples alone, with no additional self-produced musical material. In general, the interviewed mashup producers wanted to give the impression that the blended tracks fit together perfectly *as they are*, since this apparent effortlessness enhances the intended audience response ("these sources shouldn't go together but they do!").

Principle 3: Ironic Distancing

After extolling the perfect blend between source tracks, DJ Surda cautioned that it only got you halfway there: "[The blend] is one thing . . . and the other thing for me is that the good mashups are a clash. . . . So, for me, the good mashups are . . . the clash ones, and the ones that, when you're listening, it totally works." In addition to establishing a musical dialogue between the mashed tracks, that is, mashup producers use these sources to instigate a conceptual clash, incongruity or surprise of some sort.[24] I have labeled this specific aspiration the aesthetic principle of *ironic distancing*. As we shall see, this quality can arise from a profound disparity in its sources' genres, stereotypes, or eras, for example, but also from the obviousness of the juxtaposition itself (that is, from the simple fact that prior tracks from different sources have been juxtaposed).

The Clashing of Genres and Disparate Tracks

A common feature of the more fundamental aesthetic principle of ironic distancing is the genre clash. Scholars and journalists concerned with mashup music have long remarked on the fact that mashups often combine sources associated with contrasting genres, such as pop and rock or hip-hop and metal.[25] So in 2003, *Salon* journalist Roberta Cruger wrote, "The more disparate the genre-blending is, the better; the best mash-ups blend punk with funk or Top 40 with heavy metal, boosting the tension between slick and raw" (Cruger 2003). This blending of disparate genres was particularly pronounced during mashup's early phase, when the A+B form dominated the scene. DJ Paul V., a cofounder of the Bootie mashup organization in Los Angeles and a prominent mashup radio host, recalled that he always sought out mashups with prominent genre clashes to play on his radio show. Those were his favorites, he said, thanks to their "surprise element" that "will really blow people away." He pointed to the early British mashup classics, such as Freelance Hellraiser's "A Stroke of Genius" (2001) (combining the Strokes' "Hard to Explain" [2001] and Christina Aguilera's "Genie in a Bottle" [1999]) and Go Home Productions' "Ray of Gob (Madonna vs Sex Pistols mashup)" (2003) (combining Madonna's "Ray of Light" [1998] and the Sex Pistols' "God Save the Queen" and "Pretty Vacant" [both 1977]):

> Taking like, again, Christina Aguilera with the Strokes. You'd never think of it. So, I sought out the people—you know, like Go Home Productions, [who] was

the king at the time. And he would do amazing stuff like Madonna with the Sex Pistols, or ABBA with Echo and the Bunnymen, or you know, you fill in the blank. He did so many great ones and he made them work. . . . If you didn't know the original sources and you just heard that track, like if you heard Madonna singing "Ray of Light" over "Pretty Vacant" and "God Save the Queen," you would be, like, "Wow, that girl has a really hot punk band that she just record[ed with]."

Today, genre-clashing mashups remain relevant, whether they involve rock versus pop or other genre combinations. For example, InanimateMashups's "We Are Extraterrestrial—Robbie Rotten vs Katy Perry (Mashup)" (2016) blends the pop vocals of Katy Perry's "E.T." (2010) with a soundtrack from a children's TV series—the music of "We Are Number One" (2014) from the Icelandic (but English-speaking) children's TV series *LazyTown*.[26] William Maranci is another mashup producer who takes the concept of blending ostensibly antithetical music styles to the limit. In his mashup "The Black Eyed Peas—My Humps (feat. Mozart)" (2020), for example, he mashes the vocals of "My Humps" (2004) by the hip-hop band Black Eyed Peas with the music of the "Turkish Rondo" by Mozart (the third movement of Piano Sonata No. 11 in A major, K. 331, late 1700s). "My Humps" sparked much controversy because of its objectification of women and the materialistic focus of the lyrics and music video, and it has been parodied by several artists, including Alanis Morrisette. The result of this particular mashup is thus not only a clash of genres and (very disparate) eras but also a clash between high and low within the firmly established Western music hierarchy. As one viewer commented ironically: "This is frankly disturbing, why would you ruin a song with as much artistic value as 'My Humps'?" In another mashup, "Eminem—Lose Yourself But It's 4'33" by John Cage" (2020), William Maranci combines the (silent) music of Cage's "4'33"" with the vocals of Eminem's "Lose Yourself," where Eminem's lyrics about giving yourself over to "this opportunity that comes once in a lifetime" become a kind of sports announcer commentary on the video performance of Cage's piece.[27] Here, the mashup's humor arises from the listener's notion that the respective works are far apart in every way yet are made to fit so perfectly together.

Still, the taste for genre clashes seems to vary among producers and sometimes depends on the type of mashup in question (that is, A+B or megamix).[28] Adriana A insisted that while nonclashing mashups do flourish on the internet, the clashing ones are more popular: "I've noticed that the mashups in, you know, this day and age—the ones that go viral are the ones that have that classic early-mashup-scene genre clash. 'Cause that's really what resonates. That's what made me fall in love with mashup culture." CFLO agreed, saying that his favorite mashups "are the ones where, if you write it down on paper and you're like 'This shouldn't go together,' but then you hear it and it does go together.... Like it doesn't make sense, but it does. That's, I think, the best." NodaMixMusic even regarded the induced collaboration of artists who would never make anything together as the whole point of the mashup. Some of those producers who leaned toward genre-clashing mashups, such as DJ Cummerbund, found nonclashing mashups to be lacking in ambition: "It was just EDM tracks mixed with EDM tracks, and that was just boring. It's like, what was the point?" DJ Faroff added that while a blend of genre-aligned contemporary music might work perfectly well at the club, in that it makes people dance, it is less interesting artistically and intellectually. The group of producers known as the Crumplbangers came about as a statement against boring mashups, as member pomDeter explained: "Basically, it's a reaction to the swath of bland mashups that were around at the time. Mostly current pop versus current pop that, if you didn't know any source, you might think it was an original track. They're technically good but they just lack some of the early bootleg spirit. So, we just made a small community to try and inject the fun back into it. Have a laugh and make silly music."[29]

Other producers saw a time and place for nonclashing mashups depending on whether the work was mainly meant to be humorous (for which a genre clash would be preferable) or aesthetically pleasing or made for the dance floor (for which a genre clash would not be necessary as such). And while the interviewees acknowledged a generational shift away from genre-clashing mashups, there were plenty of exceptions to it, including several old-school producers who embraced the complexities of megamix mashups over the clash of genres above all else, and vice versa.

As I discuss further in chapter 4, the clashing of genres is not only about musical style but also about those genres' strong cultural connotations and implications for identity. As such, genre-clashing mashups serve as sociocultural commentaries on habitual conventions and expectations, and some producers and listeners seem to value this ironic critical play. Moreover, mashup music's blending of genres often produces a humorous effect because radically antithetical musical and attitudinal norms are somehow made to match. And humor, understood in its broadest sense and as stemming from the combination of incongruity and congruity, is an important aspect of the mashup aesthetic and approach, although not all mashup producers intend their work to be humorous (see chapter 4).

Explicit Juxtaposition of Distinct Tracks

Whereas A+B genre-clash mashups dominated the early phase of this art form, megamixes have grown in popularity in recent years. The concept of megamix mashups is to blend several or many sources, regardless of whether the clashing of genres occurs. Year-end megamixes, for example, blend the greatest hits from annual charts such as *Billboard*'s Hot 100 Songs, and they are often from very similar genres. Other megamixes emphasize an existing or imposed common theme across the sampled sources. Isosine explained that sometimes what matters here is how many samples one can use, not what genre they represent: "And, you know, three years ago I thought having forty samples was a massive amount. And I think last year someone came out, and there was like 120 different songs in one year-end mix. And every year it grows." But the quantity of samples is, of course, not important to all forms of megamix. Instead, the point may be to make a musically coherent and pleasant result out of the juxtaposition of several or many distinct tracks. Although it is perhaps more obvious in the genre-clashing A+B mashups, megamixes also signal an ironic critical distance from their sampled sources in terms of exposing the concepts behind them—that is, they are meant to be understood as juxtapositions of distinct sources. This is part of the intriguing challenge and pleasure of both creating and listening to megamixes. Various forms of signaling—including the choice of sources and the sampled sequences within them, the length and treatment of the samples, the mention of the sources under the video/music files, and the mashup titles, which often include the word *megamix*—together make it obvious that these tracks are not made from scratch or from independent samples from a database. Instead, they are clearly indicated to derive from selected samples from publicly available tracks by other artists that were initially made for a different musical and sociocultural context.

This form of ironic distancing—one that is less about genre clash than about the explicit juxtaposition of disparate sources—can also be present in A+B mashups that are pushed in directions other than the genre clash. For example, Raheem D said that, rather than combining genre "opposites," he devised dream collaborations, including artists who were no longer with us:

"So that's one thing that's magical, I think, is those star collaborations that people have always wanted but never had the chance to happen." While several of the interviewed mashup producers were interested in mashing clashing sources who were unlikely to collaborate in real life, Raheem D flipped this script by mashing sources who probably *could* have collaborated or who would be great to hear together (for example, Justin Bieber and Justin Timberlake). He pointed out that he actually started making mashups to perpetuate the cultural relevance of the urban pop artist Aaliyah, who died in a plane crash in 2001 at just twenty-two years old, by making posthumous songs featuring her vocal performances. This work obviously lacks the humorous aspect of the genre-clash mashup, but its combination can generate a similar feeling of surprise, and, for some, surprise was the most important aspect of all.

As we have seen, mashup producers exploit an ironic distancing toward the sources they mash, whether the tracks in question are strange bedfellows or not, because they explicitly play on the fact that what is heard is something that initially belonged to a different context. Whether the sources represent a clash of associated conventional genre categories or not, the mashup itself represents a clash between the listener's existing understanding of its sources and their presentation in a new context. The oscillation between the sources' initial and new contexts may, in turn, serve to repurpose existing material to the edification (and pleasure) of the listener.

Principle 4: Repurposing

A mashup that satisfies only the first three principles—crediting, matching, and ironic distancing—can still be considered a bad or boring mashup by one's fellow producers. A good mashup must also say something on its own or add some synergy to its sources, and, most important, it must shed new light on the mashed tracks. To various extents, mashups bring something new out of something familiar by transforming the samples via recontextualization (or, more specifically, "transcontextualization" [Hutcheon 2000, 12]; see chapter 4). CFLO echoed the notion that while the sampled tracks are relatively unaltered, they are nevertheless extrinsically transformed by their new musical context: "For me, one of the things I think makes a really good mashup is when, all of a sudden, the context of the song has changed while still retaining the original elements." And it is this repurposing of the tracks—the way in which mashups enable people to understand them from a different perspective from what was initially intended—that engages the producers and fans of mashup music. "It's quite hard to make something new," NodaMixMusic admitted: "That's why we need to dig deeper, like make this kind of stuff. Give these old tracks, or tracks that already exist, give it a new sound, new meaning." This combination of familiarity and unpredictability, of repetition and change, was considered fundamental to the mashup aesthetics by the producers, including PhilRetroSpector: "If you're not shining a new light on it, I don't see the point of doing it. I think it gets tired very, very quick."

MsMiep appreciated how the juxtaposition of tracks can completely change the vibe of the song: "It's just about changing the scenery, really.... It's like in a green screen, you got this one piece in here, and depending on what you put in the background it can totally change the atmosphere. And I think that is fun. It's a good challenge." Such a challenge can also emerge from mashups that try to blend tracks with different moods; for example, an energetic recording can become lounge music, or a melancholic or aggressive track can become a feel-good song, or a frivolous ditty can become a serious statement. For example, the Reborn Identity's mashup of Portishead and Blondie, discussed above, reshapes the ennui and insouciance of the latter's vocals into utter misery via the music (and footage) of Portishead and Kanye West. Two disparate mashups of Miley Cyrus's "Wrecking Ball" (2013) prove this point as well. The initial version of "Wrecking Ball" is a power ballad of sorts; its gentle, almost delicate verse gives way to a powerful, weighty, soaring chorus with a tormented vocal delivery. In "Wrecking People (Village People vs Miley Cyrus)" (2014), DeeM blends Cyrus's vocal with the instrumental track of the disco classic "Y.M.C.A." (1978). By slowing the music and speeding up the vocals, the latter becomes positively punchy atop the ebullient, energetic, and upbeat 1970s disco song. Owen Gallagher's (aka ragaman7) mashup "Miley/O'Connor Mashup—Nothing Compares to a Wrecking Ball" (2013) goes in the opposite direction, mashing Cyrus's vocals with an instrumental track that is even more dejected than "Wrecking Ball": Sinéad O'Connor's 1990 hit "Nothing Compares 2 U." While the tracks are already in the same tempo, the mashup's replacement of the pulsing beat of Cyrus's music with the immersive synth strings and reverb that were typical of early 1990s pop adds another layer of sorrow and affliction to the vocal line.[30] While the mashup's combination of sources is not necessarily any better than the sources were on their own, it adds value by being something different. Its sources meld together but never completely abandon their initial forms and meanings, existing in the mashup alongside the listener's intact memory of what they were.

It is the unexpected outcomes of particular combinations of tracks that producers were most passionate about, as Deep End explained: "Just the realization that combinations of two or more pop and other genres of songs can make something potentially amazing got my attention and [has] kept it ever since." And McSlzy described a happy DJ experience when "people [at the club] turn around and nod and smile at you, and it's not just because they know the tune, it's, 'Ah, I see what you did there.'" BringMeTheMashup pointed out that their infectious sense of surprise at their discovery of something new in the already familiar may sometimes be particularly pertinent: "It's more of a shock value, I'd say, in the sense that 'I didn't know that these songs would work together.'" dicksoak agreed: "I think, for a lot of people, the reason they find it entertaining is probably because, like I said, something unexpected—the shock factor, right?" Maya Jacobson noted that this surprise aspect emerges directly from the thrill of discovery in the production process: "From the production point of view . . . it's like this chemical explosion, a tiny explosion in your mind, when you say, 'Oh, this would work with this.' That's the fun about it." dicksoak stated that the easiest way to surprise the listener was to overcome the inherent disparateness of one's sources and pull off what Adriana A calls the "OMG-WTF mashup." But sources that are not that different from one another can impart a feeling of surprise as well, in their very defamiliarization—that is, in the revelation of hearing them from a new perspective, not the familiar ones.[31]

In chapter 4, I will explore the ways in which mashups are able to repurpose their sources via the processes and priorities of humor, critical commentary, and artistic or emotional appeal. There, I frame these impacts as part of what makes mashup music attractive to both producers and listeners, in turn shaping its sociocultural significance. In chapter 5, I discuss how this repurposing of sources, which is in a legal context referred to as *transformativeness*, is relevant when one is considering copyright exceptions. For now, I simply say that to many listeners, mashups' impact transcends their shock value in their articulation of a completely different take on existing songs—people find great pleasure in recognizing *how* (not only *that*) the sampled tracks have been transformed and in the meanings that emerge from this repurposing of sources.

It bears repeating that mashups have much in common with parody, and this notion can also be gleaned from the aesthetic principles to which the mashup producers adhere. As I explained in the previous chapter, parody is an acknowledged form of appropriation that displays both autonomy, in terms of functioning as a work on its own, and dependence, in terms of fundamentally relying on one or more prior text(s). By presenting an ironic critical distance toward the parodied text(s), it transforms that text by providing it with new meaning. In his lengthy study of parody, Robert Chambers summarizes the essential work of parody: "Parodists bang, bind, and blend the material they target into multiple kinds of contrasted pairings" (2010, 5). Banging refers to the incongruent and disruptive shock that parodists produce in their transformation of the familiar by means of instigated contrasts, which creates, in turn, "an oddly surreal landscape [coexisting] alongside the world of the familiar" (2010, 75). Binding and blending refer to the parodist's means of maintaining the coherence of the parody's "seemingly inappropriate pairings" (2010, 84) by making them seem as though they belong together. This description is strikingly evocative of the producers' accounts of mashups' underlying principles, including their emphasis on the combined clashing and matching of the sources. This very combination instigates a critical, ironic distance in relation to the reused material that separates mashup music from pastiche, which is more about imitation than difference (see chapter 2).

Mashup as Play

The producers' perspectives on the underlying aesthetic principles and creative processes of making mashups suggest to me that the making of mashups has much in common with play (which is a much broader notion, in fact, than "game," with which it is most often associated). I do not mean that play is yet another aesthetic principle to which they adhere but rather that underpinning their descriptions of these principles seems to be a fascination with play (even though they do not identify it as such). More precisely, part of their attraction to making this music is the challenge of mastering the constraints set up by the framework of mashups and plumbing the potential that resides within those constraints.

Play and game scholars agree that play is premised on the mastery of the particular constraints that define a given activity. Although not all forms of play are fun, the fun of play resides in making the most out of the possibilities inherent in the framework of its accepted constraints. The Dutch historian and cultural theorist Johan Huizinga has had a major influence on play theory and game studies through his *Homo Ludens: The Study of the Play-Element in Culture* (1955). Huizinga insists that play is not only about games or fun but also about an entire mind-set that we bring to our surroundings when we deliberately manipulate them: "[Play is] a free activity standing quite consciously outside 'ordinary' life as being 'not serious,' but at the same time absorbing the player intensely and utterly. It is an activity connected with no material interest, and no profit can be gained by it. It proceeds within its own proper boundaries of time and space according to fixed rules and in an orderly manner" (1955, 13). The French sociologist Roger Caillois similarly characterizes play as inherently free, separate (in time and space), unproductive, and governed by locally defined laws. He also adds that play is typically uncertain in terms of its course and result, as it depends on the players' agency and innovation (2001, 9–10), and that it is "accompanied by a special awareness of a second reality or of a free unreality, as against real life" (10). Other scholars of play agree that it boils down to a mastery of constraints that is generally enacted freely and that it involves rules differing from those that apply outside the play situation. In what follows, I link these characteristics to the work involved in mashups.

The Pleasure of Mastering and Overcoming Constraints

The influential philosopher Bernard Suits, who bases his definition of play on a critical review of the large body of literature on the nature of game-playing, states, "To play a game is to engage in activity directed toward bringing about a specific state of affairs, using only means permitted by specific rules, where the means permitted by the rules are more limited in scope than they would be in the absence of the rules, and where the sole reason for accepting such limitation is to make possible such activity" (1967, 148). The constraints or rules are what enable the play activity in the first place; a game of soccer, for example, would be meaningless if not for the rules that define it.

If we frame the making of mashup music as play, its basic rules or constraints would be the fashioning of an aesthetically successful whole out of disparate, already existing parts. Moreover, they would correspond to the widely recognized aesthetic principles of the genre, including crediting (exposing the mashup as a mashup), matching (aligning the samples), ironic distancing (instigating a clash or surprise of some sort), and repurposing (rendering something new from something existing). While all music genres operate within certain constraints and expectations, mashup producers use them as motivation above and beyond the simple alignment with stylistic norms.[32] The art of mashup music derives not only from satisfying these identified principles but also from making the most out of the least in terms of seeking the most forceful sample-blending effect using the fewest (audible) means possible. For example, producers generally use nothing but samples (save for processing effects) while trying to stay as close to the samples' original presentations as possible. For the same reason, they usually alter the tracks only subtly or transparently, as opposed to manipulating them in a way that will attract the listener's attention. To DJ Faroff, working within these constraints involved in the mashup can be challenging but is also part of what defines the genre: "I think mashup is a form of art. . . . Mashups at their best are sometimes brilliant and can be seen as a form of songwriting; you're just writing music with other people's music. That's how I think about it. As I said, when you impose yourself some constraints, it's kinda hard, actually."

Technological development has eased some of the challenges of making mashups. For example, certain producers told us that mashups used to be cleverer than they are now, because new digital tools have made it so much easier to match tracks in terms of tempo and key, for example, or to extract stems. They lamented that those challenges were part of the fun and of the artistry. Still, while software can assist in making a perfect blend, it cannot make a perfect mashup; there is much more to it.

Another indication that mashup producers enjoy plumbing the potential within the explicitly and implicitly articulated constraints of mashup music is that they often layer further challenges atop them, such as the conceit of the concept mashup, for example. Motivating concepts include mashing clashing genres, patching together lyrics that say something new, or making end-of-year mashups out of whatever the hits were. Some producers also define a niche and then stick to it; for example, Kap Slap usually blends pop and dance music; DJ Paul V. prefers to make rock mashups; NodaMixMusic specializes in making mashups of 2Pac's music; Raheem D makes "dream collaborations"; Colatron, DJ Schmolli, and PhilRetroSpector create "emotional mashups"; and Simon Iddol usually mashes mainstream music with less familiar tracks. The way in which many producers also mash topical tracks (often with classics) and post them as close to those tracks' initial release as possible also represents a form of constraint that goes beyond the underlying principles mentioned above.

The embrace of theme-based challenges started early on in mashup culture. McSlzy, who ran one of the first internet mashup forums, GetYourBootlegOn (GYBO), recalled that he put out challenges every couple of weeks revolving around topics such as "girls and guitars" or "punk." The latter, in fact, gave rise to the mashup classic "Ray of Gob (Madonna vs Sex Pistols mashup)" (2003) by Go Home Productions. Such concept challenges have been central to the mashup scene ever since; MsMiep explained that, on the Crumplbangers forum, there are monthly challenges in which the winner gets to choose the challenge for the next month: "And Rudec this month has chosen 'make it sad.' Basically, by the end of the song, any genre, anything you want, mash it up, and by the end it's gotta be a sad song. And that's quite a good challenge, because . . . it kind of makes you start thinking about, actually, 'how can I take this piece of music and completely flip it on its head, and make it something really, really different?'" Such collective and time-specific challenges suggest that play is not only about individual creativity, including the desire to overcome "unnecessary" demands; it also has a social dimension to it, in that shared challenges can produce group solidarity and a feeling of togetherness, as well as playful and energizing competition (and perhaps less playful competition too).

The mashup collective associated with the Bootie clubs and website also develops mashup concept challenges. For example, Bootie regularly launches theme parties through which producers send in mashups based on the theme ahead of time, and they are all played at the party and later released as a compilation album. Sometimes compilation albums are also based on the curation of existing mashups (usually by Adriana A), such as the *A Very Bootie Christmas* albums, the *Halloween Bootie* albums, and *Bootie: Gay Pride!* (2013). Other concept albums are based on genres (such as *Bootie Goes Goth* [2018]) or artists (such as Fleetwood *Mashed* [2020] or

Queen—Mash Aid [2019]). Bootie has also released several tribute mashup compilations, including *Bootie Loves Prince* (2016), *Bootie Loves Bowie— Mashup Tribute to David Bowie* (2016), *Bootie Loves Whitney: Mashup Tribute to Whitney Houston* (2012), and *Bootie Mashes Michael Jackson* (2009).[33] Another category involves film—*Disney Mashed* (2020) features mashups at least partly based on music from Disney films, while *Bootie: Beyond Thunderdome* (2019) sets up a mashup soundtrack for the film *Mad Max beyond Thunderdome* (1985). Adriana A, who compiled the latter, wrote the following on the Bootie website: "The mashups chosen for this set are meant to fit the Death Guild aesthetic of dark, angry energy, while also having some of that cheeky Bootie Mashup vibe, often with pop vocals meant to troll the fighters in the dome!" For example, the album starts with the DJs From Mars mashup "Catalyst Carmina Burana (Linkin Park vs. Carl Orff)," which mixes Linkin Park's "The Catalyst" (2010) with Carl Orff's famous *Cantata Carmina Burana* (1937) and revels in the source tracks' metrical differences (Orff's uneven meter is straightened out to fit Linkin Park's music) but also their shared majestic grandeur and rhythmic pace.

A rather different form of extra mashup challenge is what the producers referred to as "72": in this time-restricted and collaborative challenge, participants have seventy-two hours to complete a three-minute mix before passing it on to the next person, who makes another three-minute mix by building on and transforming the previous version by adding new elements before passing it on again. At the end, the total time of the mashups must be seventy-two minutes, or the approximate length of a compact disc (listen to *72* [2009], *72 mix 2* [2010], *72 mix 3* [2012], and *72 rebooted 2* [2019]). MsMiep noted that this challenge was popular ten years ago and has now been taken up again due to its tenth anniversary:

> So that's what's going on at the moment. So, we've signed up and are kind of going through, and every seventy-two hours it gets passed to the next person. And you've got no idea what you're gonna be given, or what time of the morning it's gonna be when your seventy-two hours start, or if you're at work or anything. And then you gotta kinda carry it on. And there's some of the old guard that are joining . . . and it's really diverse: some of the newer people like me, and you know, all the different genres, and [it's diverse in terms of] what people like to listen to, and what they like to mash up, and what they put together. It's really cool. . . . And luckily it kinda caught me in the weekend, so I was able to spend a bit of time. But you have to try and mix into something that, you know, a producer that I really respect [would be] thinking, "Oh gosh! How do I follow

that?" . . . You know, without kind of letting the whole team down. Yeah, it was fun. It was a good challenge.

It is not only rising to such challenges but reaping the rewards, in terms of the aesthetic result, that motivates mashup producers. And, as ToToM has experienced, more restrictions sometimes make things easier: "I noticed [that] answering to this kind of challenge sometimes . . . some of my best work came from this." ToToM's notion echoes the Russian-born composer Igor Stravinsky, who once stated, "My freedom will be so much the greater and more meaningful the more narrowly I limit my field of action and the more I surround myself with obstacles. Whatever diminishes constraint diminishes strength. The more constraints one imposes, the more one frees one's self of the chains that shackle the spirit" (2003 [1947], 51).

Mashup's inherent exercise of creative agency within an intentionally limited aesthetic framework resonates with the perspective of game designer and scholar Ian Bogost, who sees play as "working a system of interacting with the bits of logic within it" (2016, 114). The pleasure of limits, Bogost points out, resides not in the limits themselves but in the exploration of the "possibility space" that those limits both enable and restrict: "Minecraft asks you to survive in a world made of inhospitable cubes you can use as resources. Candy Crush asks you to solve a puzzle given a limited supply of powers. Golf asks you to get a tiny ball into a slightly larger hole many hundreds of yards away by striking it with a stick" (2016, 93). Another example of the creative embrace of limitations is Oulipo, a French collective of writers and mathematicians who explore the potential of constrained writing techniques such as the lipogram (which avoids particular letters) and the palindrome (a phrase that reads the same in both directions). Similarly, the "Dogme 95 Manifesto" and "Vows of Chastity," both written in 1995 by the Danish filmmakers Lars von Trier and Thomas Vinterberg, are self-imposed rules that, among other things, eschew special effects, added sounds, optical work and filters, and static (nonhandheld) cameras—the goal being to purify filmmaking in order to emphasize narrative and acting above all else. In the context of music, the twelve-tone composition often associated with Josef Matthias Hauer and Arnold Schoenberg requires that all twelve tones of the chromatic scale are given equal importance throughout the composition. In all of these examples, it is not enough to follow the rules; one must make the most out of the possibilities that lie within the framework of the given constraints. This is where the true challenge lies and also where the art, and fun, is to be found. Mashups cannot be reduced to the mashing and clashing of their sources, as DJ Poulpi pointed out: "Even with the same combination or idea, there is still some decision process. And I think it's not a technical decision process—I think it's an artistic decision process."

The fascination with play, in which specific aims and rules apply, also derives from the accompanying feeling of being somewhat detached from ordinary life, play theorists point out, or of being within a separate time and space.[34] Huizinga compares this isolated, bounded space with a playground or "magic circle" (that is, a ritual space) while clarifying that it can be an ideal or conceptual space as well as a material space (1955, 10). The rules that constitute the playframe within that space differ from the rules outside it; they only apply within the playframe and to those who participate in it at a specific point in time. Since this playframe exists in its own space and time and has its own rules and logic, it can be experienced as both meaningful and nonsensical, depending on whether one is inside or outside the frame. Regarding the mashup's playframe, Kap Slap stated:

> It's art that people don't really realize the value of, the possibilities of. You know, like, it seems so easy to just throw a vocal over something else and whatnot, but you can really get.... You can make something really powerful just by using the voices of others. And that's kind of the way I look at mashups. But it's just, again, it's so hard to do.... I would feel like a sellout if I only just did the basics. And it would be good—like, obviously, I do do that. And, like, [the mashup of] "Call Me Maybe" and "Greyhound"[35] [is] literally one of the biggest releases I've done. People loved that, and I still play it to this date. People still go crazy for it, [but] I still don't really get it. [It] seemed very easy to me. It was, like, "Okay, sure." But [when making mashups beyond the basics], in my head I would say, like, I really hope that like one person listens to it and says, "Wow! I see that now the way he saw that." Like, "Holy shit!" you know. 'Cause those people are the ones that become, like, the really hardcore fans.

From an outside perspective, that is, mashups might be reduced to their underlying principles and thus seem creatively and artistically limited, but for those who have explored or experienced their playframe, the mashup format may be seen to offer countless challenges and opportunities.

Mihaly Csikszentmihalyi, the late Hungarian American psychologist best known for his theory of flow, argued that the times when people strive to overcome challenges are the most enjoyable of their lives, assuming that the challenges align with their skills or capabilities (that is, they are neither too hard nor too easy). "Enjoyment," he argued, "appears at the boundary between boredom and anxiety, when the challenges are just balanced with the person's capacity to act" (2008, 52). Whereas passive activities may feel pleasurably relaxing, Csikszentmihalyi linked the best moments in life with active involvement in terms of either mental or physical effort (such as reading or playing a sport) or the work of production or manipulation (such as creating or performing art), especially when people are pushed to their limits or accomplish something new (3, 45–46). Whereas several producers continued to make mashups twenty years later and still found new challenges, others got bored and either stopped making music altogether or started making other forms of music instead. The constricted rules of mashups thus may also limit the creative process. What I am suggesting is less that the play aspect of mashups is particularly beneficial compared to other ways of making music than that it explains some of the motivations behind people's involvement with this art form.

A Free and Intrinsically Motivated Activity

Another motivation for participating in an activity framed as play is that it can be experienced as both escapist and empowering. The restrictions inherent to the playframe can affect people differently from many other forms of restrictions. Huizinga and Caillois both point out that play is free and voluntary—one can choose to participate or not.[36] Suits agrees that play is essentially a *"voluntary* attempt to overcome *unnecessary* obstacles" (Suits 2005 [1978], 55, my emphasis). Instead of enforcing external rules or goals imposed by others, the rules of the playframe are voluntarily accepted by players as a condition of participation. This feeling of taking control over rules, in the sense that one has voluntarily entered the playframe, rather than being controlled by them can be quite empowering. Of course, in mashup music, losing a bit of the autonomy of controlling the result is part of the fun, but entering into the mashup playframe is still a way to take control over the rules that dictate the art form. Within the playframe, if one does not master the rules or decides to break them rather than follow them, the consequences are limited to the frame, and one can always leave. As such, play momentarily frees the player from the mandatory activities of the real world and thus imparts a sense of escapism, as Deep End points out: "Listening to pop music to me is a form of escapism, as is making mashups."

Huizinga's definition of play foregrounds intrinsic motivation as a key characteristic as well: "It is an activity connected with no material interest, and no profit can be gained by it" (1955, 13). The notion of intrinsically motivated activity arises in numerous and diverse scholarly contexts, including discussions of leisure, emotions, recreation, play, and gaming. It is often related to a particular mind-set that is centered on the activity rather than any potentially related external goal. Such a mind-set is often referred to as "autotelic" (Csikszentmihalyi 2008; Klinger 1971) or "paratelic" (Apter 1982), as opposed to "telic"—*telic* is Greek for end or goal, *para* is Greek for beside or alongside, and *auto* is Greek for self.[37] Of course, the notion that an activity is intrinsically motivated—that is, that its primary motivation is not the achievement of an external goal—does not imply that external goals are altogether irrelevant. Motivation, as I see it, will always be somewhat socially contingent and constructed. Although most of the mashup-interviewed producers insisted that they were making mashups for the pleasure of doing so, they also lamented that platforms other than the major ones had smaller audiences and that they experienced the blocking and takedowns of their mashups as truly demotivating, which points to their desire to achieve some recognition or at least share what they do with others. Still, the material conditions of real life do not mean that activities cannot be inherently motivated as well. For example, the clichéd argument among musicians across genres that they make music out of passion and not for the money is not entirely convincing, since the "not for money" part does not tie in with either their practice or life's requirements. Still, the commercial aspects of the work allow for the passion as well; obviously, these producers' motivation can be twofold. Sometimes, however, one aspect does dominate the other. If an external goal is accomplished in an autotelic/paratelic activity, it is seen as a bonus—conversely, with telic activities, it is the pleasurable sensation of the activity that is seen as a bonus (Apter 1982, 47). And with mashup producers, who rarely make any money from mashups and rarely aspire to a career in the activity, the intrinsic motivation of making the music usually seems to dominate the extrinsic ones. While the making of a mashup might also satisfy external goals, such as gaining recognition, popularity, and viewer clicks, this was, according to the producers, not the main point (see chapter 5 for more). Instead, most of them described mashup making as a hobby and said that they primarily did it for fun. Maya Jacobson recalled that the first thing she learned about making mashup music was that she would never get paid for it, to which she quickly added: "Not that I ever thought about that. I mean, my point was only about the fun and creation." DJ Surda agreed: "The motivation is enjoyment and not money: You do something that you love, you know. . . . There's no money that could pay that." Although intrinsically motivated activities may not serve a higher purpose, they can give life meaning and inspire great commitment in terms of dedication, time, and energy.

Building on Huizinga's playground metaphor, Bogost describes play as "a practice of manipulating the things you happen to find in a playground" (2016, 22). This deliberate reworking of things we encounter into something new and personal can produce the feeling of making the world one's own. As mentioned in chapter 1, *participatory culture* became a buzzword in the mid-2000s (popularized by media scholar Henry Jenkins, among others), but the notion is much older than that. For example, in his examination of the practices of everyday life (reading, talking, dwelling, cooking, and so on), Michel de Certeau argues that consumers are active agents who make "everyday life invent itself by poaching in countless ways on the property of others" (1984, xii). This particular mode of production, often described in terms of consumption, is characterized by its fragmentation, poaching, and quasi-invisibility, since it manifests itself only through the art of using the products imposed upon it (31). Certeau also famously distinguishes between strategies and tactics, whereby the former are used by those with institutional power and defined as "proper" (a city's streets represent a "strategic" grid), and the latter are used by ordinary people as they navigate, negotiate, and appropriate these "proper" measures (shortcuts across town represent a tactical appropriation of the grid of streets). Strategies produce, tabulate, and impose spaces, and tactics use, manipulate, and divert these spaces (30). Whereas Certeau is interested in "the multitude of 'tactics' articulated in the details of everyday life" (xiv) that are of a clandestine nature (such as reading what one wants or walking where one wants in the city), his description of them also recalls mashups and other user-generated remixes.[38] Both, for example, draw on "the vocabularies of established languages . . . in order to trace out the ruses of other interests and desires that are neither determined nor captured by the systems in which they develop" (xviii). Certeau's notion of consumption and participation also suggests that this drive to manipulate what we consume and otherwise make do with what we have is an expression of an innate capacity: "The child still scrawls and daubs on his schoolbooks; even if he is punished for this crime, he has made a space for himself and signs his existence as an author on it" (31).

The difference between the strategies and tactics that Certeau describes and those of mashups is, of course, that the mashup activity is not necessarily oppositional to the same degree as tactics, since the constraints are, unlike strategies, primarily self-imposed.[39] Yet mashups and remixes reflect this same drive to sign one's existence onto something—that is, to appropriate. Ultimately, according to Certeau, tactics inform one's identity because "being is measured by doing" and development is characterized by detachment (1984, 137). Moreover, they represent an important source of pleasure: "There is a certain art of placing one's blows, a pleasure in getting around the rules of a constraining space" (18). As a form of play, mashup creation is not only about making the most out of the agreed-on constraints but also about creating something meaningful by renewing the sources and extending their reach (the repurposing principle). Kap Slap described the mashup approach as taking a pop song with impact and saying, "Let's flip that on its head. What if it was like that?" Thanks to the mashup producer's reengagement with the source tracks, something new appears, and a mark has been made on the world.

Signing one's existence onto something further compels profound attentiveness to that something. In *Playing Along: Digital Games, YouTube, and Virtual Performances* (2012), Kiri Miller examines the experience of playing *Guitar Hero* and *Rock Band*, interactive video games in which players accompany famous songs on "instruments" by triggering the correct buttons on the controller at the exact moments demanded by the scrolling notation on the screen. Joining Csikszentmihalyi, Huizinga, and several other play theorists discussed in this chapter, Miller notes that the participants' experience of playing along and "exploring the boundaries of one's potential" implies both intense engagement and focused attention (2012, 222), particularly with the music itself, thanks to the heightened listening required to compete. This intimate attentiveness offers players a new way of hearing music with which they are otherwise very familiar (112–113). She then recalls Simon Frith's description of the musical engagement of dancers, who "have a heightened, more intense, above all more concentrated sense *of the music*. Dancing (if not watching dancing), is, in this respect, a form of enhanced listening" (Frith 1998, 223, emphasis in original; see also Miller 2012, 113). Mashup producers also perform a close auditory inspection and analysis of the music they mash, which in turn allows them to experience it very differently. This depth of engagement transfers its benefits directly to mashup listeners as well via the work of defamiliarization.

Such active involvement and participation in the activity, and the challenge of making the most out of the particular constraints of the genre, may provide feelings of accomplishment, proficiency, empowerment, liberation, escapism, and, not least, fun.[40] While some continue to see play as trivial, frivolous, or a waste of time, Bogost disagrees and paraphrases Huizinga: "Man is not primarily a knower (*Homo sapiens*) nor a creator (*Homo faber*), but a player—*Humo ludens*" (2016, 99). For producers, mashup music functions as a conceptual playframe within which they manipulate the things they find and explore the potential amid the constraints. Even when a mashup fails, it is still a meaningful activity. As such, play seems to be one of several factors that contributes to shaping the sociocultural significance of mashup music.

This chapter has focused on the production side of mashups, describing what mashup producers regard as significant to the art form and identifying play as central to their motivation. The next chapter focuses on the experience of listening to the music and watching the videos. Of course, these two perspectives are intrinsically related; it is, for example, not only the process but the product, and its reception, that motivates producers. In the following chapter, I discuss how mashups (as products) can trigger different experiential responses, including humor, critical awareness, and aesthetic pleasure. As will be clear from the following discussions, play is a relevant aspect of the listening experience too. An awareness of the constraints relevant to a given mashup is also what heightens the experience of the listener/viewer: they invite the listener into the playframe by revealing the concept behind it, and they challenge the listener's memory and musical knowledge in terms of the recognition of the sources, as well as the ways in which they have been (textually and contextually) altered. In short, the listener has to "play" to discover the hidden surprises of this particular playground—a form of participation that also includes filling in the gaps.

4   The HAHA, AHA, and AH Impacts of Mashups

[If mashups no longer existed,] we would be losing this kind of magical effect of surprise which you have when it clicks, when it works. We would lose the smile that people get when they hear a nice combination or mix.
—DJ Poulpi (personal interview)

Insane how you can take your medium of creating mashups and still send such a powerful message.
—Anonymous (YouTube commenter)

You don't know whether to laugh or cry, because it's beautiful, but it's ridiculous. And I love that.
—DJ Earworm (personal interview)

A better understanding of the sociocultural significance of mashup music is crucial as we approach a crossroads wherein platforms' detection and blocking procedures pose a threat to it that is close to existential. We need to know what it is we risk losing.[1] When trying to grasp that significance—including what it is that continues to fascinate and motivate listeners twenty years after the emergence of mashup music—it becomes clear that the producers' perspectives, as discussed in the previous chapter, can be limited despite their valuable insights. Any form of interview with a mashup audience member would be likewise limited. This is because individual experience is usually quite intuitive and operates at an unconscious level, so one has only a limited ability to articulate the full complexity of one's experience. Theoretical accounts are also limited in that they offer more of a general framework than an explanation of the particular, but they can nevertheless help us to understand the particular in all of its multiplicity—that is, they can ground subjective interpretations as well as contextualize empirical encounters within a larger discourse. This chapter, then, does not attempt to explain *the* experience of a mashup but rather to provide some insights into mashups' potential (and profound) meanings. I chose the theories and perspectives presented here based on my own analysis and interpretation of mashups and according to their resonance with the mashup producers' accounts as well. I further illustrate my points with reference to particular mashups and my personal experiences with and interpretation of them.

The main focus of this chapter is how mashup music can lead to experiences related to humor, enlightenment, and beauty. I use Arthur Koestler's concepts of the HAHA, the AHA, and the AH to frame my discussion: The first (his HAHA) is a humorous reaction in which the discord or incongruence between two mutually exclusive contexts that are made to interact is highlighted and results in a conceptual clash that registers as funny. The second (AHA, a concept he borrows from the Gestalt psychologists) is the reaction in which one experiences intellectual enlightenment—that is, when one sees something from a new perspective. The third (AH) is an affective reaction that evokes the experience of beauty (Koestler 1967, 185–188). These categories—the HAHA, the AHA, and the AH—capture the three potential outcomes of experiencing mashups that were emphasized by the interviewed producers and that resonate with my own observations while watching and listening to mashups and while witnessing my students, colleagues, and friends' reactions to this music. In the case of mashups, the HAHA, AHA, and AH impacts are intrinsically related, though they are often weighted and realized differently among individual works. For pragmatic reasons in this chapter, I discuss them one at a time while acknowledging that each will be incomplete in isolation. First, I demonstrate the way in which the fundamental design of mashup music is very much characterized by what scholars (primarily within the fields of philosophy, linguistics, and psychology) have established as a key trigger of humor: the combination of incongruity and congruity. I also emphasize the range of responses to humor, from outright laughter to a knowing smile or twinkle of amusement. Next, I discuss how the HAHA impact of mashups stems in part from their AHA impact—that is, from the enlightenment that accompanies the experience of something from a new perspective. I also demonstrate that mashup music can comprise a broad range of utterances that are framed as commentaries in more or less explicit ways. Finally, I point out that the experiential effects of the HAHA and AHA are significantly shaped by the AH dimension, which encompasses the affective experience of finding the audiovisual features of the mashup artistically pleasing and attractive.

Fundamental to all these impacts are intertextuality, double codedness, and bisociation. I therefore start with a more general discussion of the concept of intertextuality and then apply it to the abiding understanding of the aesthetics of mashup music (as well as acknowledged appropriations more generally). I also draw on the related concepts of the double coded, montage, and bisociation.

Intertextuality and the Pleasure of the Doubled and Merged

Despite their many differences, acknowledged appropriations share certain aesthetic features or implications that also inform their enduring popularity and uniqueness in relation to what is often otherwise taken to be "original" music. One of these core qualities, which propels their aesthetic effects and unique communicative abilities, involves intertextuality. Here, I am not only thinking about the notion that all texts draw on other texts, either implicitly or explicitly, or about the specifically structural analysis of different types of intertextual relations or the source study of specific appropriations (as discussed in chapter 2). Instead, I am primarily referring to intertextuality as the triggering of a specific kind of meaning via the transposition of a text from one context to another, or, as put by Julia Kristeva, who first coined the term *intertextualité*, "from one sign system to another" (Kristeva 1984, 59).

Intertextuality is closely related to semiology and semiotics—the term even sprang from Kristeva's reworking of Ferdinand de Saussure's notion of the differential sign and her reading of Mikhail Bakhtin's dialogism. Saussure's linguistic theory (or semiology/semiotics) objects to the notion that a word (the signifier) functions as a unified referent to a given object in the world (the signified). Instead, it can only refer to our concept of that object, which is, in turn, shaped in relation to associative concepts. *Tree* does not refer to a tree in the world but only to our conception of what a tree is. Moreover, he argues, a signifier's meaning further derives from the text's structure—from how it is positioned in relation to other signifiers. Drawing on Saussure's linguistic theory, Bakhtin emphasizes the social situatedness of the signifier—that a signifier's meaning stems not only from an abstract linguistic system and from the way it is linguistically structured but also from its existence among specific individuals or groups of users within specific social contexts at specific moments of utterance or reception. Relevant here is also what Bakhtin calls the "speech genre," which concerns the notion that we speak differently depending on the context and discourse, with regard to both what we say and what we mean by what we say.

These notions are also relevant to our understanding of music: specific music, or a specific musical performance, is not understood in isolation but in the context of other music as well as in relation to a specific discourse, including that of a musical genre. A scream in the context of heavy metal may, for example, signify anger and frustration, not only because of the way it is performed or its musical accompaniment but also because of our conception of the heavy metal genre, which in turn derives from previous encounters with the genre, including the ways in which it is framed and manifested. A scream in the context of a pop song may have less aggressive connotations, even if the scream itself is the same as the one in the heavy metal song. As such, Bakhtin states, utterances are always dialogic; all utterances, and the ways we understand them, are shaped by other utterances that precede them (1986, 93–94). Moreover, our recognition of utterances as belonging to a specific speech genre or discourse makes us perceive some of them as congruent within that context and others as incongruent. Graham Allen explains: "'Hello darling!' might be a perfectly acceptable way in which to greet a close friend; one would hardly employ it in a formal introduction to a local dignitary. The words we select in any specific situation have an 'otherness' about them: they belong to specific speech genres, they bear the traces of previous utterances" (Allen 2011, 20). As we will see later in this chapter, this notion also applies to musical elements that are transferred from one genre context to another. The notion that utterances are socially situated in terms of both their production and their reception and that they draw on and are understood in relation to other texts or discourses is also the core of the principle of intertextuality and intertextual transformation.[2]

Intertextual Transformation
Drawing on Saussure's notion that the textual sign is not fixed but relational, Kristeva (1969) proposes a more general conception of meaning that disrupts any notion of singularity, unity, stability, or predetermination.

Meaning (as well as subjectivity) is not fixed, she argues; it is dependent on multiple factors and always in process. She combines this conception with her reading of the works of Bakhtin and particularly his notion that a sign's meaning is specific to the exact social and historical contexts of addresser and addressees. Kristeva extends this notion by arguing that texts cannot be reduced to representations because the very context within which a text is produced and consumed is crucial to how it is experienced, and thus to its meaning. The paintings of Edvard Munch, for example, were informed by the time in which he lived, and our experiences and understandings of those paintings are informed by both our own time and our knowledge of the discourse of Munch and his paintings. This social and historical situatedness of addresser and addressees must be understood not only as part of the text's context, she argues, but also as an integral part of the text itself. A text's "inside" (the meaning in the text itself) and "outside" (its historical and social situatedness) together comprise its meaning, and thus its phenomenological existence, so that the text's outside is also its inside (Kristeva 1980). As Jacques Derrida puts it, "Il n'y a pas de hors-texte"—there is no outside text (1976 [1967], 158). The consumption of a text, Kristeva (1980) then concludes, must be a process of coproduction: the text's meaning is generated from the intersection between the representation and the readers' interpretation of it. Consequently, texts are always in a state of becoming, and they take on different meanings depending on the given reader's subject position and historical and social context. Mashups, for example, are experienced differently depending on the listener's foreknowledge about the mashed sources and their connotations (or at least about the genres or stereotypes that they represent). The text never contains meaning as such; its meaning occurs in the process of its consumption.

Roland Barthes, who was inspired by Kristeva's theories as well as Derrida's insistence that concepts derive their meanings from their opposites, similarly challenges the positioning of the text's contextual situatedness as external to the text or its meaning. He does so by distinguishing between the work and the text: "The work can be held in the hand, the text is held in language; it only exists in the movement of a discourse" (1977, 157–159). Elsewhere, he similarly distinguishes between what he calls the readerly text and the writerly text (1975a, 3–4). The readerly text (or work) is the representation, which may give the illusion of a singular and stable meaning. The writerly text (or just text) refers to the text's infinite potential for multiple meanings via its consumption from different subject positions. The latter, then, is the former but informed by past experiences, discursive knowledge, and internalized cultural codes and sociolects. It is therefore never stable or fixed but rather plural and endless as it manifests in ceaseless and various discourses. Barthes (1981, 43–44) furthermore distinguishes between the consumer and the reader: the former limits the *work* to one stable meaning, whereas the latter encounters it generatively and becomes a coproducer of a *text*. He continues, "A text's unity lies not in its origin but in its destination . . . the birth of the reader must be at the cost of the death of the Author" (Barthes 1977, 148). While many people have interpreted this line as an argument against authorial agency, others have stressed that what Barthes is actually saying is that the text is never the product of the author alone. The author is a "scriptor" who compiles elements of already existing texts and discourses, but the reader does this as well in the subsequent encounter with the text (that is, when experiencing texts, we always draw on associations with prior texts and discourses).³ As such, the author is able to limit the text's meaning to a certain extent but never to determine it.

It is within this larger theoretical framework that Kristeva coined the term *intertextualité*, which not only addresses influence, appropriation, and context but also, more pertinent, the text's passage from one context to another: "The term *inter-textuality* denotes this transposition of one (or several) sign-system(s) into another; but since this term has often been understood in the banal sense of 'study of sources,' we prefer the term *transposition* because it specifies that the passage from one signifying system to another demands a new articulation of the thetic—of enunciative and denotative positionality. If one grants that every signifying practice is a field of transpositions of various signifying systems (an intertextuality), one then understands that its 'place' of enunciation and its denoted 'object' are never single, complete, and identical to themselves" (Kristeva 1984, 59–60). Since texts consist of much more content than what they actually present, the term *intertextuality* tries to capture and describe the effect of the initial text's transposition from a prior context to a new one—the way in which it takes on new meanings, for example, and enters into a new signifying system. This transformation is at the heart of Kristeva's concept of intertextuality, and it is what makes that concept especially relevant to a discussion of the aesthetics of acknowledged appropriations, including mashups.

Arguments reminiscent of those of Kristeva and Barthes are to be found in texts and discourses by Gilles Deleuze, Derrida, Michel Foucault, Linda Hutcheon, Paul de Man, Roman Ingarden, and Søren Kierkegaard, among others, and in the numerous scholarly considerations of irony, but the salient point has already been made: the ultimate state of being, or heart, or core of the "text" is what its representation or articulation triggers above and beyond its initial (and authorial) words, images, or sounds (among other things). The notion of intertextuality is not only relevant to appropriated art but also to art in general, if one accepts the notion that art is never created from nothing (creatio ex nihilio). As Derrida states in his critique of Claude Lévi-Strauss's distinction between the *bricoleur*, who takes whatever is at hand, and the engineer, who uses raw materials, the engineer is in fact a myth, as every discourse is bound by bricolage (see Smith-Laing 2018). Still, if intertextuality is present in any text, some texts remain more explicitly intertextual, in the sense that this quality is self-consciously and self-reflexively exposed, as in avant-garde art or parody that copies prior works or "found" sounds/objects. A copy is never a copy in a strict sense because the text is transformed in the act of recontextualization implied by that copy. As Henry Louis Gates Jr. puts it, "Intertextuality represents a process of repetition and revision, by definition" (1988, 60). When one experiences something familiar as copied or imitated in a new context, an inevitable transformation happens, in the sense that one must negotiate the meaning of that which lies beyond the representation itself but is still intrinsically tied to it. This transformation lies at the heart of parody. In the case of the mashup, that is, the source tracks may be "the same" but their implications have changed. What makes mashups interesting, then, is how these various musical elements function anew thanks to their relocation and why they do so. If one accounts only for the mashup's readerly level—if one consumes rather than reads the mashup (in the Barthian sense), for example by seeing it as nothing more than the merging of two tracks—one bypasses the art, as well as the mashup's message (because the text is then reduced to a work).

The Pleasure of the Doubled
When the transposition is self-reflexively exposed, as in parody, the meaning is not only changed but doubled; a parody is a reworking of an existing artwork meant to be experienced as something familiar *and* new—as a

parallel *and* a contrast to a given model or background text. It has a heterogeneous plot through which the same text can be understood within two different contexts: the original context of the parodied text and the new context of the parody. To acknowledge this duality of context, the Russian formalist Yury Tynyanov describes parody as "double-coded" (1975 [1921]). He frames this nature in terms of a dialectical play with a "dual-planed existence" or "double life"—one that must be "perceived through a double angle of vision" (1975 [1921]). This notion of the doubled was later taken up by Bakhtin, who was inspired by the Russian formalists in his own discussions of narrative and parody. He insists that we experience parody via an inner dialogue between how we are used to experiencing the parodied text and how this text is presented in the parody (1981, 76). In parody, Bakhtin states, "The author employs the speech of another, but . . . introduces into that other speech an intention which is directly opposed to the original one . . . and forces it to serve directly opposite aims" (Bakhtin 1971 [1929], 185). To him, then, parody is based on both dialogue and contrast—that is, it is meant to be experienced as a heterogeneous dialogue. Gary Saul Morson explains, "The audience of a double-voiced world is therefore meant to hear both a version of the original utterance as the embodiment of its speaker's point of view (or 'semantic position') and the second speaker's evaluation of that utterance from a different point of view. I find it helpful to picture a double-voiced word as a special sort of palimpsest in which the upper-most inscription is a commentary on the one beneath it, which the reader (or audience) can know only by reading through the commentary that obscures in the very process of evaluating" (1981, 71). Parody is, in other words, meant to be experienced as interpretation and as commentary from within, and this doubled discourse, and double layer of meaning, is its core, as well as that of other forms of acknowledged appropriation.

The overarching notion here of a dialogical or heterogeneous experience implies that the two respective versions do not fuse into one—that is, the parody is always perceived against the backdrop of a contradictory reality. Hutcheon suggests the neologism "transcontextualizing" (2000, 12) to recognize that this form of recontextualization is something more than *re*-contextualization, because one text is experienced from the perspective of two contexts at once. She then distinguishes parody and pastiche by calling the former "bitextual" and the latter "monotextual" (33). Parody's inherent incongruity or critical distance, after all, derives from its double meaning. As opposed to many other forms of musical sampling, mashup music deliberately dramatizes its critical ironic distance from its sources. The pleasure of parodic texts (such as mashups) emerges, according to Hutcheon, from its "very paradoxical essence" (2000, 77)—the way in which it sets up a combination of recognition, or conservative repetition, and critical and revolutionary difference, instigating, in turn, a participatory hermeneutic activity for the listener (92). In her work on adaptation, another form of doubled discourse, Hutcheon writes that the intertextual engagement of the reader "creates the doubled pleasure of the palimpsests: more than one text is experienced and knowingly so" (2006, 116). Perhaps even more relevant than "doubled pleasure," I might add, is the "pleasure of the doubled"—the pleasurable tension between the familiar way of hearing texts and an unfamiliar and novel representation of those texts.

The notion of double-voiced discourse also relates to Gates's discussion of the black tradition, or the indigenously African, in which he explains that the African American concept of Signifyin(g) (with a capital "S" and a parenthetical "g") denotes "formal revision that is at all points double-voiced" (1988, 22). Signifyin(g) differs from signification in standard English; whereas the latter denotes meaning, or that something is signified, the former denotes ways of meaning, or the ways in which that something is signified (81). Signifyin(g), in other words, refers to a rhetorical play, or a conscious rhetorical strategy—one that endorses indirect communication, revision of texts, the play of signification and differences, displacement of meanings, and open-ended interpretation. It is fundamental to African American literature, Gates explains, as well as black music forms such as jazz, blues, the spirituals, and ragtime. As an example, he refers to jazz musicians and their audiences and states that if they are well trained, they are both playing and listening with expectations: "Signifyin(g) disappoints these expectations; caesuras, or breaks, achieve the same function. This form of disappointment creates a dialogue between what the listener expects and what the artist plays. Whereas younger, less mature musicians accentuate the beat, more accomplished musicians do not have to do so. They feel free to imply it" (1988, 81).[4] Gates concludes, "[Signifyin(g)] depends on the success of the signifier at invoking an absent meaning ambiguously 'present' in a carefully wrought statement" (1988, 49). Signifyin(g), that is, revels in the play that exists at the crossroads between surface and latent meanings. As such, this tradition has much in common with parody and other acknowledged forms of appropriation, in that they all emphasize indirection, intertextuality, double-voiced discourse, and repetition with revision. Gates notes that the originality of much of the black tradition lies in this particular rhetorical act—that is, in the ways of Signifyin(g) rather than the representation of novel content (79). The same applies to all forms of acknowledged appropriation. As such, the heart of mashup music cannot be reduced to the representational level but must also take into account that which lies outside the (audiovisual) representation itself; it is the sum of the divergent associations that the given mashup sets into motion that makes it an effective and valuable aesthetic and communicative resource.

An alternative way of approaching the doubled coded is to relate it to Michael Apter's (1982) notion of "synergy," which he includes in his reversal theory—a grand explanation of human motivation, emotions, and personality. Synergies occur when opposite meanings coexist conceptually—that is, when an identity is assigned oppositional characteristics so that two contexts are simultaneously present in the mind (163). For example, an actor is understood to be both the character being acted and the person who is acting. In the same way, an antique vase can be experienced as both rare and a personal belonging but also as commonplace and belonging to many people if considered from the perspective of its users in the past. In these instances, the identity in question acquires two parallel levels of meaning, and thus a "double nature" (163), in the sense that two contexts are simultaneously present in the mind. Apter explains: "There is no ambiguity here in the normal sense of the word, and the qualities are not, logically, mutually exclusive, since two different meaning levels are involved. But, phenomenologically, both contrasting sets of properties may be assigned simultaneously to the same object and feelings of synergy arise" (155). He further argues that this binary tension is part of the fascination of the experience. In a synergy, in the reversal theory sense, incompatible meanings are brought together "to produce a special phenomenological effect which could not have been produced by either alone" (141). He continues: "There is momentarily a feeling of bewilderment while the two contradictory meanings compete, and this experience of the two different meanings is synergetic" (142). Synergy can arise as one switches between the alternatives or attends to both at once (142). In the examples of the actor and the antique vase, synergy is the product of an identity or object being grasped as having contrasting attributes or qualities that coexist. Mashup music likewise resides in the collision between foreknowledge and immediate experience, which evokes a sense of the juxtaposed sources as both old and new, familiar and unfamiliar.

"Make-believe" synergy, one of the subcategories Apter mentions, arises when a phenomenon is seen to belong to both an imaginary world and the "real" world: "A given identity has one set of real characteristics and is then assigned another set of imaginary characteristics" (Apter 1982, 157). Mashup music can also be understood as a make-believe synergy, in that its explicit juxtaposition of elements belonging to divergent contexts produces a synergy that makes up an imaginary world, understood as a secondary context that emphasizes a revisionary play of references and the displacement of their meanings. Put differently, make-believe synergy describes an understanding of the sources as simultaneously part of the mashup's virtual collaboration with the original artists and part of their prior contexts. Synergy, that is, exists between what is presented in the mashup's world (a virtual or imaginary world) and this content's reference to its original contexts. The experience of make-believe synergy involves two fundamental steps, Apter explains. The first involves the acknowledgment that something is make-believe or has imaginary qualities. This step usually happens if the synergy is meta-communicating to its audience that what it presents is make believe; as mentioned, the mashup signals this to the listener by putting the listener in a position to readily recognize its sources (by both textual and paratextual means) and thus also understand it as a montage and not an actual collaboration between those sources. The second step involves the acceptance and internalization of those imaginary qualities—that is, a process of "entering actively into the spirit of the make-believe by imagining that the imaginary qualities are real" (Apter 1982, 161). In the case of mashup music, this would mean accepting it as a playful interpretation or versioning of its sources and experiencing it with an open mind, taking it for what it is, not only for what it used to be. Through each of these acts of the listener—acknowledging and accepting—the make-believe acquires a "double nature" (163), in which both the imaginary and the "real" are simultaneously present in consciousness and generate a synergetic effect. This effect, Apter says, then triggers a feeling of pleasant excitement: "Much of fantasy is exciting not in spite of it being only imaginary, but *because* it is imaginary and contrasts synergically with what is known to be the case" (169).[5] In the same way, the playframe of the mashup exposes this dialectic relationship by making it obvious that it is a play reality and making its references explicit. As such, the mashup functions, on the meta-level, as a commentary on its sources, fostering a supreme awareness of their coexistence and interaction, which in turn represents a source of our enjoyment of it. The fact that the mashup is a montage allows for synergetic experiences at several levels—that is, meaning emerges in the individual tracks' transposition from one context to another *and* in the collision of individual tracks and their associations. Mashup music can thus be characterized in the same way that Gates describes Signifyin(g): "[It] luxuriates in the inclusion of the free play of these associative rhetorical and semantic relations" (1988, 49).

The Aesthetics of Montage and Bisociation

Montage, like other acknowledged appropriations, plays with references to prior works and their connotations but also with the peculiar synergetic oscillation of signs that the juxtaposition of works puts into motion. In her extensive study of montage, Marion Hestholm (2010, 35–50) refers to Peter Bürger's discussion of that concept in his seminal *Theory of the Avant-Garde* (1984) and to Theodor W. Adorno's understanding of it in *Aesthetic Theory* (1997 [1970]), which inspired Bürger in turn. According to both, the motivation behind montage is to shock. This is certainly true for Dada, Fluxus, and surrealism—and, as mentioned in the previous chapter, mashup producers also value the surprise effect—but as Hestholm points out, this notion is a simplification of the montage aesthetic that, in addition, does not actually capture the form (or even the avant-garde) more generally (2010, 38). She also objects to Bürger's idea that the recipient's experience of the montage derives from its principles of construction (that is, that its meaning emerges from its arrangement), since this implies "a non-relation between the original meaning of the fragment and the 'posited meaning' created by the montage" (39). Instead, Hestholm insists that the fragments matter in themselves, not only in how they are structured: "The fragment is chosen by virtue of its function in its original context, and while its meaning may change dramatically—even to the opposite of what it was before—the fragment is always (and necessarily) interpreted as part of both contexts at once" (40). This notion is in line with the theories of intertextuality and the double coded presented above and finds even more support, she notes, in Barthes's notion of the montage as a constellation of "pregnant moments": "The pregnant moment is just this presence of all the absences (memories, lessons, promises) to whose rhythm History becomes both intelligible and desirable" (Barthes 1977, 73). This notion of the pregnant moment, which also evokes an intertextual transformation resulting in a double-coded reading, is perhaps the core of all acknowledged appropriations more generally, but what distinguishes montage from other forms of appropriation is that the juxtaposition of passages from prior works also allows for new meanings to arise.

In his discussion of the collage principle in music and especially how we experience juxtaposition and discontinuity, Nicholas Cook compares it to the museological principle described by Peter Vergo (1989, 54): "The same material can be made to tell quite different stories not just by means of captions or information panels or explanatory texts but by the sequence in which works are displayed" (quoted in Cook 2006, 116). Cook elaborates on this notion: "Any object by itself has an indefinite range of potentially meaningful properties, but the juxtaposition with a second object brings certain of those attributes into play and de-emphasizes others. For instance, the juxtaposition of a vase with another artifact might variously foreground its shape, its material, a manufacturing technique, an ornament motive or painted representation, its use, or its social connotations" (116). Similarly, he points out, the juxtaposition of contrasting musical passages "serves to problematize each of them, their meanings unraveling one another" (120). What "sticks in the ears" thus cannot be readily generalized, he points out, because everything in the concrete instance contributes to creating the effect (121). Cook's point echoes the notion of appropriation's double-codedness, as well as Sergej Eisenstein's (1986) notion that new meaning is produced in the collision of elements—that is, when disparate elements intersect, a concept or quality emerges that is "qualitatively distinguishable from each component element viewed separately" (14).

As suggested in chapter 2, montage can also be described as bisociation, which is the act of connecting previously unconnected frames of reference or juxtaposing or integrating independent matrices otherwise thought to be incompatible strangers. Koestler notes that when faced with bisociation, we experience a peculiar kind of synthesis that is more heterogeneous than its associative counterpart: "It compels us to perceive the situation at the same time in two self-consistent but habitually incompatible frames of reference; it makes us function on two wave-lengths simultaneously. While this unusual condition lasts, the event is not, as is normally the case, perceived in a single frame of reference, but *bisociated* with the two" (1967, 186). He continues: "The more familiar the previously unrelated structures are, the more striking the emergent synthesis" (184). Mashup music is inherently bisociative in the sense that it juxtaposes sources not previously considered in combination; some mashups also emphasize their bisociative nature by juxtaposing especially divergent sources. Moreover, as discussed previously, the mashup is bisociative in its "double codedness" (Bakhtin 1984 [1963]; Tynyanov 1975 [1921]) and "ironic, critical distance" (Hutcheon 2000)—that is, the listener experiences its sources as belonging to two contexts at once. Koestler then notes that the synergy (or synthesis, as he calls it) that emerges from bisociative combinations can lead to three different forms of reaction or response that may be overlapping or complementary: the HAHA, the AHA, and the AH. It is to these various impacts that I turn next.

The HAHA Impact of Mashups

While not all mashups are experienced as or intended to be funny, their fundamental design associates them with humor, amusement, goofiness, and fun. Before I elaborate on this point, however, I discuss what I mean by humor using influential humor theories that see it as deriving from a combination of incongruity and congruity or sense making.[6]

Koestler's notion that humor results from bisociation, or from seeing a phenomenon from two perspectives at once, is very much in line with dominant humor theories. Until the middle of the eighteenth century, humor was generally understood to be an expression of superior and hostile feelings toward a joke's target. As such, it was negatively connoted and prompted moral objections (Morreall 2008, 211). This perspective, now referred to as the superiority theory of humor, has since been challenged by theories positing that (1) humor does not necessarily involve a supercilious attitude and may not be negatively loaded; (2) jokes do not need a butt or target; and (3) even when they have one, the target need not be a victim of the joke as such but rather some value for which that "victim" is a signifier.[7] After the middle of the eighteenth century, then, other theories of humor evolved, including what is known now as the *relief theory*, which sees humor as resulting from the release of repressed nervous energy, and the *incongruity theory*, which sees humor as resulting from understanding something as out of place.[8] These theories ushered in a more positive view of humor, thanks to the fact that they did not reduce it to the realization of an unsympathetic or aggressive attitude (Morreall 2008, 211). The notion that incongruity is a necessary condition of humor, which has informed much pioneering humor theory (frequently through the work of linguists and psychologists), seems especially relevant to the experience of mashups as humorous; after all, mashups display a uniquely synergetic combination of incongruity and congruity.[9]

The connection between humor and incongruity was already recognized by Aristotle in *Rhetoric* and later by Cicero in *On the Orator*; both pointed out that laughter often results from a violation of expectations (Morreall 2008, 215–216). James Beattie, who contributed to a more comprehensive incongruity theory in the eighteenth century, expanded on this notion: "Laughter [or humor] arises from the view of two or more inconsistent, unsuitable, or incongruous parts or circumstances, considered as united in complex object or assemblage, or as acquiring a sort of mutual relation from the peculiar manner in which the mind takes notice of them" (Beattie 1971 [1776], 602). To Beattie, then, humor (or laughter, which is his focus) boils down to the experience of two or more things that are united or related as divergent from one another. Similarly, Arthur Schopenhauer argued that laughter or humor is "simply the sudden perception of the incongruity between a concept and the real object" (1957 [1819], 76), and Kierkegaard relatedly noted, "Wherever there is contradiction, the comical is present" (1987, 83). The basic idea behind the incongruity theory of humor, then, is that humor derives from a violation of our usual ways of perceiving things—that is, from a mismatch or a surprising deviation between that which we expect and that which we confront.

Two of the most influential contemporary theories of humor are Victor Raskin's (1985) script-based semantic theory of humor (SSTH) and Salvatore Attardo and Raskin's (1991) revision of that theory, in turn known as the general theory of verbal humor (GTVH). The SSTH posits that humor arises when at least two opposing scripts (or sets of information typically associated with individual objects or events) overlap while somehow being forced to make sense.[10] Similarly, GTVH identifies script opposition as one of humor's common characteristics. The two theories identify various types of script opposition, including actual/nonactual, normal/abnormal, possible/

impossible, good/bad, obscene/nonobscene, stupid/intelligent, clean/dirty, alive/dead, and so forth. And as Attardo, Hempelmann, and Di Maio point out, multiples of such incongruities can be present in a text at the same time (2002, 27).

Such recent humor theories, however, also argue that while incongruity is a necessary condition of humor, it is not enough to trigger a humorous response. In order to find something humorous, we must also perceive it to be congruent or even normal from a certain perspective—that is, the incongruity must also somehow make sense. For example, Elliott Oring (1989, 349) notes that the incongruity must be "appropriate," and Thomas C. Veatch proposes that "humor occurs when it seems that things are normal while at the same time something seems wrong" and that this simultaneity and ambiguity together produce an "affective absurdity" (1998, 164, 205).[11] Put differently, it is the imaginary play with multiple views of a situation occurring simultaneously—one that exploits an incongruity; another that guarantees a certain viability—that evokes a humorous response.[12]

Although the combination of incongruity and congruity often triggers a humorous response, it does not always do so. Central to Raskin's (1985) concept of the "script" is the observation that humor results from a combination of the text itself and the connotative and extratextual information that the audience brings to its experience of that text. It is, in other words, the supplementary information in the perceiver's mind that gives rise to the experience of the text as incongruous. Since humor depends extensively on the audience's readings and cultural and social knowledge, it is clear that what one person might find humorous, another might not. Some may not have the requisite knowledge of or relationship to the content's explicit and implicit components to understand it as warped or bent—that is, the particular expectation that is played with and violated is not necessarily present in the first place. Different listeners will also have different affective commitments to a given joke's target or target weapon. Some, then, may experience a joke or a parody's violation or twisting of expectations as offensive rather than humorous. Finally, the experience of humor depends on the joke or parody's design, to which I will return. But, as mentioned in chapter 2, the characteristic structure of what triggers humor (incongruity and sense making) is, nevertheless, the closest we can come to an objective classification of something as humorous or nonhumorous, which is why I identify humor as central to mashups with the understanding that humor encompasses a broad range of experiences, responses, and emotions.[13] We must remember that humorous amusement is a mental state that does not necessarily culminate in laughter but allows for a range of responses, including a smile of enjoyment or an inward feeling of slight amusement.[14] This broad range of potential responses leads Oring to identify humor as "an amusement-provoking stimulus that is recognized as such by someone who smiles or laughs, is disposed to smile or laugh, or even rejects the enticement to smile or laugh" (Oring 2003, 163n.1).

Humor's Role in Mashups

This potential ambiguity between structural and experiential features is also present in the mashup. As discussed, not all producers intend their mashups to be humorous, and mashups are not necessarily experienced as such. Still, most of the producers in this study saw humor as central to mashup music. DJ Earworm recalled that many in the mashup community, especially in the early days, sought to make "jokes." PhilRetroSpector similarly allowed that while he does not consider humor to be important to his own mashups, many of them are very "tongue in cheek," by which he meant that they combined two sources that no one would have expected to hear together. Humor seemed to be important to "new-school" mashup producers as well. For example, dicksoak preferred to structure a mashup like a joke and noted the profound influence of stand-up comedy; MsMiep said that when she made her mashups, making someone laugh mattered more to her than anything else; and Poolboy said his main priority was to make funny music. In fact, funny was more important than musically enjoyable, he added. He recalled his first encounter with Neil Cicierega's mashup albums *Mouth Sounds* (2014), *Mouth Silence* (2014), and *Mouth Moods* (2017): "They were so absurd that they were the funniest things I've ever heard. . . . If music was like a big circle of just a spectrum of genres, he'd go for the furthest two genres he could get to. . . . It wasn't until I heard the Neil [Cicierega] albums [that] I was like, 'I wanna make funny [music]. I wanna focus on humor.'" To several of the mashup producers, surprise was central to the mashup's humor. BringMeTheMashup explained: "They're smiling and laughing because they didn't expect a song in there that they know." The surprise that BringMeTheMashup describes is one born of incongruity, and what makes it humorous is when the idea that something does not make sense is combined with the realization that it actually does make sense.

The juxtaposition of incongruity and congruity that triggers humor is a common feature of mashups. On a basic level, the experience of mashup incongruity derives, on the one hand, from the listener's recognition that the mashup version departs significantly from the respective initial versions of the mashed sources, and, on the other hand, from the listener's preconceived notion that the sources are otherwise somehow incompatible with one another. Mashup incongruity transcends the source material as well to engage other divergent connotations. It can be recognized at different levels depending on the listener's familiarity with the particular tracks that are mashed, or with those tracks' cultural, artistic, or political connotations. If one is familiar with the mashed tracks or accepts the mashup's invitation to revisit them, one will experience it as having a double identity: it is at once a reworking of familiar tracks and a new track in its own right. The original versions function as expectancy schemes against which the listener compares the new version, and it is this effort that produces a violation of expectations and thus an experience of incongruity. On the other hand, the experience of the mashup also introduces a sense of congruity or internal logic in its combination of divergent tracks. As discussed in chapter 3, producers manipulate the tracks so that they share the same pitch material and tempo, their harmony and rhythm are aligned, and they are mixed to sound congruent or like an "original." Often lyrics or video footage are made to match as well. This work of combining them thus enables a musical dialogue between the tracks that links them despite their differences.

If we recall Barthes's distinction between the "readerly text" and the "writerly text" (1975a, 3–4), in which the former is the representational level of the text and the latter is what the text signifies, we might further note that these dimensions always work together but are nevertheless distinguishable at an analytical level. For example, in a music video, the readerly level consists of its complex matrix of sounds, visuals, and lyrics, whereas its writerly level consists of individual readings of those audiovisual and linguistic signs, including the many associations and connotations they evoke. Mashup humor, then, arises from the tension between an experience of the mashed tracks as not making sense at the writerly level—that is, the knowledge that the tracks do not belong to one another and sometimes also that the tracks have divergent connotations—alongside the fresh realization that the juxtaposition does make sense at its readerly level—that is, the musical, visual, and lyrical levels coalesce.[15]

The experience of the text as a whole is thus confronted with a conflict or friction that foregrounds the double-codedness and ironic, critical distance of mashups, which I identified in chapter 2 as central aesthetic features of parody as a whole. Mashup music's signature accommodation of incongruity and congruity suggests a central role for humor in this genre as well, even if humor is not the primary concern of every mashup producer. What one finds humorous here, again, is the tension that the mashups set up between an understanding of the tracks as (1) incongruous—the tracks diverge from their original presentation and diverge from one another (in that they should not go together)—and as (2) making perfect sense—the tracks instigate a congruent musical (and possibly also lyrical or visual) dialogue with one another. It is this abiding tension between incongruity and congruity, or between two heterogeneous halves forming a compelling whole, that suggests a humorous response. Two logics are operating at once: one is breached (the sources should not go together) and the other is fulfilled (the combination makes sense). In what follows, I explain more closely how these two logics arise and how this overall feeling of incongruity may be strengthened or diminished.

Incongruity and Congruity in Mashups

An example of this multivalence of incongruity and congruity is Bill McClintock's mashup "Slayer and Katrina & The Waves—'Chemical Warfare (Don't It Feel Good?)'" (2019), which combines the vocals of Slayer's "Chemical Warfare" (1984) with the instrumental, as well as some short vocal clips, of "Walking on Sunshine" (1985) by Katrina and the Waves. The tracks are associated with radically different genres and personas. Slayer is one of the most influential pioneers of extreme or "trash" metal, which merges heavy metal with punk. The band's music and performance styles are characterized by a massive sound, fast tempo, emphatic drumbeats, distorted power chords, guttural shouting, and overall aggression and intensity. The band's lyrics are also dark, with topics including violence, war, torture, hate, and Satanism. (In fact, the band was sued in the mid-1990s—the suit was ultimately dismissed—by the parents of a murdered child who held the group responsible for encouraging kids to kill.) "Chemical Warfare" is from Slayer's early days but has remained one of its signature tracks, and the band regularly returns to it in live shows. Slayer's mashup partner here, Katrina and the Waves, is the British American pop/rock band fronted by Katrina Leskanich. The band is particularly known for its 1997 Eurovision Song Contest winner, "Love Shine a Light," along with the hit "Walking on Sunshine." The latter, which has appeared in several TV commercials and films and boasts several cover versions, is a Motown-influenced song characterized by a live-sounding upbeat drum groove; a riff-based accompaniment of bass guitar, guitars, piano, and organ; and a punchy and cheerful horn section, as well as Leskanich's vigorous professions of love over a memorable feel-good melody.

In the mashup, the vocals of "Chemical Warfare" and the instrumentals of "Walking on Sunshine" appear in their entirety without structural edits. Yet the mashup is not a straightforward A+B form, as Bill McClintock inserts a few other clips atop his two base layers, including selected vocal clips from Leskanich's performance of "Walking on Sunshine." Moreover, at 1:17, an audiovisual clip of Slayer drummer Dave Lombardo performing a blistering sixteenth-note (repeated) drum fill supplies the transition to the prechorus of the Katrina and the Waves accompaniment in a sort of musical dialogue. In the midst of the song, Joe Satriani shows up to perform a guitar solo from his 2010 Montreal live performance of "Satch Boogie" (1988). Whereas Satriani's guitar style is entirely dissimilar to the shredding solos of Slayer guitarists Kerry King and Jeff Hanneman, it fits the upbeat music of the mashup, stylistically serving as a bridge between these antithetical musical styles.

The mashup video combines the official music video of "Walking on Sunshine" with official footage of Slayer's live performance of "Chemical Warfare" at a concert in Sweden on July 3, 2011. The mashup video starts like "Walking on Sunshine," with Leskanich dancing in a warehouse, but at the moment when the original video depicts Leskanich humming the note B♭, the mashup instead shows Slayer's Tom Araya screaming the same note in a tight metal-falsetto style. For the rest of the mashup video, clips from Slayer's concert dominate but are occasionally joined by clips of Leskanich singing and dancing on stage or walking contentedly along the River Thames.

This mashup, then, implies multiple concrete incongruities, as well as several more abstract ones. Among the former is the mashup's collision of completely divergent musical and performative moods and styles, and lyrical messages. In the original versions, the individual tracks' music, performance, and lyrics complement one another, which is not the case with the mashup. Instead, Araya's fury and pessimism seem radically othered by the positive energy of Katrina and the Waves. Moreover, the fact that Araya's performance is intermingled with selected clips of Leskanich's vocal performance adds to the generally bizarre result. For example, as Araya describes the deadly gas that brings troops to their knees, Leskanich burbles a response about feeling alive and feeling the love; when Araya grunts that the demons are not ready to die, Leskanich pipes in with "No, no, no!"; and when Araya evokes bodies that lie dormant and lifeless, she shrieks, "Ooh, yeah!" In the chorus, there is a culminating back and forth: Araya screams, "Chemical warfare!" to which she replies, with infectious enthusiasm, "And don't it feel good?" followed by Araya roaring, "Yeeaaah!" What drives this mashup's humor home, while also providing it with a political dimension, is that although these two lyrics are antithetical to one another—one lamenting war and death and the other reveling in romance and contentment—Leskanich's outbursts seem to attempt to justify the horror that Araya proclaims while dulling his tormented rage. Conversely, the Slayer singer makes for an uncomfortable duet partner in the "Walking on Sunshine" universe. The mashup's combination of audio and footage also contributes to the absurdity. The cheerful, upbeat music simply does not jibe with the performance style of Slayer dominating the mashup's video, so we find Araya's introductory roars accompanied by images of Leskanich doing a joyful "pin-up" jump in a warehouse, which, together with the Waves' punchy brass section and generally upbeat music, transforms his anguished yowls into hoorays.

Appreciating this incongruity does not necessarily require any knowledge about the tracks. John Covach (1991, 1995) and Asbjørn Eriksen (2016) observe that humor in music often arises directly from radical juxtapositions of conflicting musical styles, which rely only on the listener's ability to tell nonnormative/incongruent stylistic features from normative/congruent ones. Stylistic incongruity requires only a low-level competency in the listener, even if the fullest appreciation of the humor depends on a more advanced stylistic competency (Covach 1995, 407). A low-level competency in metal and pop would still enable the observation that growling vocals simply do not complement the stylistic features of the accompaniment by Katrina and the Waves, regardless of whether the melody itself works with the rhythm and harmony of the instrumentals. We recognize the various elements as different speech genres, as Bakhtin calls them, or, following Kristeva, as taken from one context and discourse to another. However, the feeling of absurdity is, of course, especially profound if one is familiar with the original versions of the tracks and has an existing relationship to the bands or the genres they represent. The experience of incongruity will then not only derive from the clash but also from the recognition that the mashup scenario is absolutely antithetical to the original versions of the mashed tracks. This will, in turn, allow us to attend to the transformation that happens when the various elements are transposed from one context to another. For example, when Araya's original accompaniment of frenetic double-bass drum kit and massive guitar riffs is replaced in the mashup by the cheery, upbeat music of Katrina and the Waves, his aggressive guttural vocal delivery seems completely out of place.

In addition to being a bizarre juxtaposition of divergent lyrical content, musical expressions, and performing styles, this mashup is also a pointed play with more abstract incongruities, including that between divergent connotations. In previous chapters, we saw that genre blending was a priority for several of the producers, especially in the early days, and this aspect of the mashup has also been widely remarked on by scholars and journalists. The concept of the music genre centers on certain common stylistic features, including, among other things, signature rhythmic patterns, timing profiles, song forms, harmonic formulas, instrumentation, sound, lyrical themes, performance style, and underlying aesthetic principles. Yet the music genre is also often understood as discourse, or, as Robert Walser puts it, as a "socially produced way of thinking and communicating" (2014, 29). He adds, "The analytical notion of discourse enables us to pursue an integrated investigation of musical and social aspects of popular music" (28). In his elaboration of genre as discourse, Walser draws on Bakhtin's idea of genre as a historically situated "horizon of expectations" (27). These expectations concern not only music-stylistic parameters but also shared values and norms, collective image construction, notions of authenticity, economic and organizational traits, the social and historical context, and any relevant sense of community. Music genres thus set up many normative expectations with regard to both musical and social dimensions, and these dimensions are intrinsically related in practice and thus tend to tangle up in each other's associations.[16] That is, we do not experience music in a sociocultural vacuum but instead as deeply inscribed in a specific historical and sociocultural context with a particular tradition of social rituals, values, and norms, as well as music-stylistic conventions. When mashups merge metal and pop, then, the result represents not only a clash of musical style but also a clash of social identity and genre categorization.

Despite genres' contingency, they are not arbitrary but formed through a social and historical chain and network of other utterances; they also continue to form future expressions as well as interpretations. As such, genre discourses function as a guide for both performers and listeners in terms of what is perceived as normative or nonnormative within a given one. Stan Hawkins points out, "We can exist in numerous discursive communities at the same time" (Hawkins 2002, 151), but, I will add, we are still very context sensitive in the way in which we discern the normative from the nonnormative within those different discourses, including their different notions of authenticity. When a sample is taken from one genre discourse and inserted into another, it may be perceived as clashing with that discourse even if it works well at a musical level, and this combination often produces a humorous response. With reference to Ben Urish, who identifies humor as a function of culture, Lori Burns and Alyssa Woods remind us, "For humor to be properly understood in the selected music videos [that they analyze], it is essential to understand the contexts of the musical genres to which they refer; more specifically, it is important to identify and connect with the codes and conventions of those genres and to be familiar with their realization within the larger network of popular music texts. Also fundamental to the understanding of humor is the notion of cultural critique and commentary on social values and ideals" (Burns and Woods 2019, 312). Mashups and their humor thus both function as and are symptomatic of a self-reflexive awareness of genre discourses, as well as the acknowledgment that genre constructions, stereotypes, and different notions of authenticity are founded on and strengthened by an antagonist or "other." For example, in the "Chemical Warfare (Don't It Feel Good?)" mashup, the assumptions about and stereotypes associated with both metal and pop are reinforced by their appearance in such close company.

Yet the tracks' similarities, as well as their contextual transformation, also challenge the assumption that they are binaries, as the mashup introduces the possibility that genres and identity constructions are fragile things. They are, after all, social constructs that acquire their meaning only within a limited purview—that is, what convinces in one context might not convince in another. Moreover, they depend on an entire apparatus working in synchrony to convince us of their validity. For example, in the "Chemical Warfare (Don't It Feel Good?)" mashup, the aggressive metalhead image of frontman Araya, which functions as a marker of male masculinity in the context of heavy metal, is emasculated, and his screams are transformed from markers of resistance and rebellion to camp shrieks of pure joy. This move represents a stark contrast to the conventional male masculinity with which Slayer, and metal music (or "cock rock") more generally, is usually associated, and it demonstrates that what functions in one context may be perceived as utterly staged and out of place in another.[17] By changing the context of Araya's performance, the mashup participates in what Hawkins calls "genderplay," which concerns "the switching of roles and toying with norms that are intentionally designed to entertain" (Hawkins 2016, 28 n.5).[18] When that staging is dismantled, an identity construction is laid bare, and an "authentic core" or "naturalness" is rejected. Through humor, then, mashup has the potential to evoke critical reflections regarding any notion that identity or genre possesses some "essence" or "naturalness," acknowledging instead that they are breakable constructs that rely on their discourse.

Whereas the experience of mashups as incongruent is symptomatic for mashups' AHA impact, their congruity or sense making is crucial to their AH impact, and it is the combination of these aspects that allows for their HAHA impact. Despite the cultural, ideological, and music-stylistic incongruity of the two sampled tracks, they nevertheless manage to mingle and form a coherent musical amalgam. Just as a joke is fundamentally dependent on congruity for its incongruity to be perceived as humorous, the HAHA impact of mashups is fundamentally dependent on the musical congruity between the tracks, which allows it to function on an aesthetic level. If two incongruent tracks are put together without this musical dialogue, it would not be funny. Put simply, mashup humor arises from the tension between an experience of the mashed tracks as not making sense and the creeping awareness that the juxtaposition does make sense. One of the YouTube comments on this mashup describes its combination of "Walking on Sunshine" with "Chemical Warfare" as a "well-made vegan pizza: You hear about it and you think 'ehh,' but then you eat it and it's delicious."

When mashing the growling vocals of Slayer's Araya with the music (as well as some selected vocals) of Katrina and the Waves, Bill McClintock aligns the tracks' pace by slowing down the vocals considerably—from 110 bpm to 101 bpm—to match the original tempo of "Walking on Sunshine." This unrushed version of Araya's vocal performance reveals a more defined rhythm while also surrendering some of its intensity and anger. The tonality of the two tracks is left unaltered even though they are originally in different keys; "Walking on Sunshine" is in B♭ major, whereas "Chemical Warfare" is based on the power chord E♭5.[19] The reason Bill McClintock had to do relatively little to match the tracks in terms of their tonality is that Araya performs in a monotone guttural shout throughout the song. However, in the prechorus, his vocal style becomes less distorted as he ascends to what is, in the original version, the accompanying chord's root note, which, in the new version, becomes a fifth note thanks to the shifting of the harmony.[20] Situated comfortably within the harmonies of the Katrina and the Waves accompaniment, this note sounds even more melodious than it did in relation to the music in the original version, which in turn "popifies" his performance and subverts the torment depicted in the lyrics.[21]

Kembrew McLeod argues that mashups' demonstration of the interchangeability of otherwise disparate source tracks proves Adorno right—pop songs are "simplistic and merely made from easily interchangeable, modular components" (McLeod 2005, 85; see also Adorno 1941). But when it matches such divergent genres, the mashup also clearly demonstrates that chord progression and song form are but two of the many significant pop music parameters, many of which remain jarringly opposed even when they are mashed. For example, a harmonic progression shared by two tracks may present very differently in the context of the instrumentation, sound, melodic elaboration, or performance style. Moreover, similar musical elements may take on different implications depending on their own musical and discursive contexts. It is this multidimensionality of musical parameters and genre expectations that allows listeners to experience mashed sources as at once unexpectedly similar and vastly different.

The experience of something as humorous depends on one's subjective reading, cultural and social knowledge, and affective commitment to what is at stake, but it also depends on the design of the content itself. Mashups generally endorse the key humor trigger of combined incongruity and congruity (some more than others). As we have seen, an obvious form of mashup humor is the blending of disparate genres, especially when they appear to be subverting their tracks' respective extramusical features, such as their subcultural conventions and norms or social stratifications and values. Mashups that do not blend disparate genres may be experienced as less incongruent (and thus not as humorous). In such mashups, the AHA or AH impact weighs more heavily than the HAHA. Nevertheless, even those mashups can evoke a smile, not because they are particularly funny but because of the simple pleasure of the surprise. As DJ Cummerbund put it, "The true focus is a smile. A smile and, like I said before, the ears perking up, listening to something you never heard before." He saw humor (more specifically, "funniness") as a by-product of mashups rather than an essential principle, as did those others who prioritized a mashup's surprise effect and general emotional or aesthetic (AH) impact over laughs. This surprise (or incongruity) is rooted not only in a genre clash but also in the unanticipated musical dialogue that arises between tracks that were not designed to be together but suddenly sound like an "original." Even if combined incongruity and congruity is present in a text, it may still evoke humor in different ways and to different degrees depending on how those aspects are realized. Put differently, it is not only *that* the humor-trigger components of incongruity and congruity are present but also *how* their specific iterations are manifested that shape the listener's experience.

The AHA Impact of Mashups

To Koestler, AHA labels the insight gained from seeing something from a new perspective. During an AHA reaction, that is, one may experience a moment of truth or a flash of illumination (1967, 185–188). I have already touched on the AHA aspect of the HAHA impact of mashups, but I will revisit it here in the context of whether mashups are even still able to produce an experience of genre "violation" or whether we have reached a postgenre era. Next, I turn to another form of AHA impact that mashups can trigger: a rethinking of social issues beyond that of identity politics. Mashups can be framed as political commentaries in which the mashing of sources converges associations and knowledge across a large group of individuals in a way that communicates a political insight.

The Dramatization and Subversion of Genre and Identity Constructions

Koestler's suggestion that bisociation can lead to insights and "a moment of truth" anticipates the thinking of Anton Zijderveld (1982), who regards humorous distortion as a looking-glass through which one's constructed comprehension of the world is self-reflexively displayed. In other words, a humorous response may result from the playful subversion of certain conventions and may be indicative of one's understanding of the world. When a broad audience finds something uniformly humorous, its members typically share a certain amount of knowledge about the content or the (often unspoken) connotations it represents. It is precisely this shared knowledge (or shared "myths") across a large group of individuals that fuels mashup producers in their play with common stylistic and social expectations, categories, and stereotypes. A common form of the AHA impact of mashups, then, arises when their inversion of their sources and emphasis on their differences lead to a HAHA response—a response that is often based on a more-or-less conscious self-reflexive acknowledgment of habitual (and often stereotypical) notions concerning the tracks, as well as their connotations, including their genre expectations, the identity construction of the performers, and the relevant notions of authenticity, as already demonstrated.

McLeod suggests that one goal of the typical mashup is "to undermine, disrupt, and displace the arbitrary hierarchies of taste that rule pop music. Those hierarchies are often gendered, with the 'raw,' 'real' rock representing the masculine and the 'soft,' 'plastic' pop representing the feminine" (McLeod 2005, 84). Such disruption of genre hierarchies was not something the producers themselves mentioned as an underlying motivation, although mashups can certainly be interpreted as doing so. But much has changed since McLeod published his article with respect to taste and notions of subcultural capital in relation to specific genres and genre hierarchies, and mashups may well read differently today (a time when "poptimism" is just as prevalent as "rockism").[22] In contrast to McLeod's interpretation, for example, some critics have interpreted mashups' blending of divergent genres as a rejection of genre boundaries that results from both a bottom-up process and the segregated marketing encouraged by the corporate music industries. So *Salon* journalist Charles Taylor writes, "Mash-ups are a party that takes place both in your head and in your speakers, a fantasy gathering where all sorts of artists kept segregated by radio formats, corporate blandness, snobbishness, the racial and social divides that keep some artists from reaching certain segments of the population—and even death—are brought together to fight it out and, eventually, find harmony. . . . Mash-ups don't so much trash the barriers of high and low that exist in the pop world as simply refuse their existence" (Taylor 2003).

Fifteen years after Taylor suggested that mashups promote a "fantasy gathering" free of genre segregation, Luke Winkie (2018) asserted that rigid genre boundaries belong to a bygone area and that the genre clash accordingly no longer drives the mashup aesthetic for either producer or consumer. If one holds with Taylor and Winkie, then, mashups have promoted their own downfall, and, indeed, Winkie's assumption is based on streaming platforms trending away from traditional genre categorizations.[23] He argues, "That subversiveness applied in the early '00s, when there were still rigidly defined barriers between hip-hop, dance music, and indie rock. But everyone listens to everything now. And while that's certainly a cultural victory, the idea that you're breaking down walls that is so necessary to produce a great mashup—the fundamental belief that Dead Prez and Grizzly Bear deserve to be in the same canon—has been rendered obsolete" (Winkie 2018). As a result, he continues, mashups no longer "catch fire" among their audiences, and the colliding multiverses of mashups are no longer so likely to generate a thrill of excitement.

It may be true that Gen Y (millennials) and Gen Z (the internet generation) have a more distanced relationship to genres than previous generations, which experienced a more fundamental tension between subcultures (as famously described by Dick Hebdige in 1979). Still, I remain convinced that omnivorous tastes need not imply a rejection of the relevance of genre boundaries. As I have already argued, people can exist in numerous genre discourses at once (Hawkins 2002, 151), but they cannot escape them altogether. David Brackett agrees: "While close enough inspection of any text will throw into doubt that it belongs simply to a single genre, so is it also impossible to imagine a genre-less text" (Brackett 2002, 67).[24] It has been well established that humans conceptualize the world in terms of categories and binaries and that the construction of meaning and identity depends on difference and is thus inherently relational. This notion has influentially occupied several structuralists and poststructuralists, including Derrida, who states, "Language, or any code, any system of referral in general, is constituted 'historically' as a weave of differences" (Derrida 1982, 12).[25] As such, differences are often overstated and even illusionary, yet they are also inevitable. Rather than rejecting the existence of genre boundaries, mashups instead often dramatize and highlight these differences, demonstrating that the concept of genre and genre boundaries, as well as the associated stereotypes, are very much alive; otherwise, genre-blending mashups would not be able to trigger an experience of humor in many listeners. Mashups' clash of genres or stereotypes is not a blind reproduction of their notions and categorizations or necessarily a critique of them. Instead, it is a pointed play on notions that identity, genre categories, and authenticity are always constructed by means of differences. Mashups thus highlight the fact that genres and identities are constructs and that these constructs are no less real as constructs; in fact, they make up the world as we know it. Genre-specific habits and dogmas, which arise over time, may be so incorporated into the discourse and understanding of given genres that they resist critical reflection until they are specifically challenged. As Hebdige observes, "Ideology thrives *beneath* consciousness. It is here, at the level of 'normal common sense,' that ideological frames of reference are most firmly sedimented and most effective, because it is here that their ideological nature is most effectively concealed" (Hebdige 1979, 11). When mashups use the genres' own language to self-reflexively comment on the listener's habitual assumptions about them, the cultural and ideological constructedness of those assumptions is exposed.

As mentioned in chapter 3, some mashup producers see themselves as curators introducing listeners to music to which they are not normally exposed. But this is not a matter of converging genres but of joining fan bases or getting people to broaden their repertoire and appreciate music they did not think they would. That is, genre-blending mashups do not reject the existence of genre differences but do reject any notion of them as inherently binary, as well as any assumption that an appreciation of one prevents an appreciation of another.

Daniel Silver, Monica Lee, and C. Clayton Childress (2016) argue in their article concerning genre complexes in popular music that even if traditional genre expectations have been weakened in some ways, they persist in others, including in the work that producers and musicians do when they compose, perform, and mix music, when they find collaborators, and when they self-promote their music and personas: "For instance, if country music airplay and commercial marketing strongly depends on conformity to genre conventions (of dress, speech, lyrical content, and even political orientation), then self-identifying as a 'country' musician will be an important and expected professional statement by a musician aspiring to commercial success in that field" (2016, 3). These researchers also remind us that the consumption of music goes beyond the navigation and choice of music to listen to; it is also about identity formation and interpersonal relationships, which genre categorization can still inform: "Music 'fandom' often involves ethical convictions, political attitudes, styles of sociability, manners, race privilege and protest, and more. . . . To the extent that these are encoded in genre categories, such labels should be relatively sticky forms of social classification" (2016, 3). Moreover, Silver and colleagues suggest that record companies, radio stations, and internet radio also continue to rely on genre categorization in their allocation of resources. Mashup music therefore serves to remind us that the sociohistorical relevance, complexity, and multidimensionality of genre worlds are not so easily abandoned, and that our own (often unconscious) understandings of music as encoded in genre categories abide even in today's otherwise omnivorous popular music landscape. Following Derrida, meaning, after all, is constituted as a fabric of differences, and as such, categorization is fundamental to how we think, even though the categories themselves undergo constant play and negotiation. And this idea that meaning coalesces from what it is not, though often unremarked, can be readily glimpsed in mashups.

But of course, and in response to Winkie's notion that mashups no longer catch fire among audiences that have cultivated omnivorous tastes, it bears remembering that many mashups are not about the blending of genres at all. Whereas these other mashups might not provide a looking glass through which to view our own (often unconscious) understandings of music as encoded in genre categories, they can produce an AHA impact in other ways, including by undercutting the assumption that individual tracks or musical elements are somehow autonomous as opposed to intrinsically tangled in a discourse. Some mashups, moreover, communicate messages that are more explicitly framed as political, as we will see.

The Political AHA Impact of Mashups
Several scholars have engaged with the rhetorical potential of the remix by framing it as an emerging form of media literacy and citizen empowerment or as an effective means of resistance and critique.[26] For example, Virginia Kuhn insists that the remix is not only the "lingua franca [adopted common language] of contemporary life" (2017, 93) but also an effective form of communication with great political potential. Through its polyvocality, its embrace of history, its focus on medium specificity, and its accessibility, the remix is capable of "speaking truth to power" and functioning as "a

championing of the underdog" (87). Similarly, Owen Gallagher argues that remix videos "have the potential to act as tools of resistance against capitalist injustices, raising awareness of social issues, influencing public perception, and offering a vision of an alternative world view" (2018, 132–133). Such comments imply that remix is capable of activating an AHA impact of targeted social awareness that may in turn lead to political action. This rhetorical potential of remixes does not, of course, mean that all remixes are progressive, and they may communicate in more or less explicit ways. When it comes to mashup music, there are very few examples that are explicitly framed as political, and there is surprisingly little to be gleaned from the music videos, interviews, surveys, and general mashup discourse that indicates that this music is typically intended to present a deliberate social critique, save for the times when a listener might discern in it an interrogation of genre boundaries. Interviewee Maya Jacobsen explained, "I think that it's more about getting people amused. And I think that, from the producer side, it's about breaking boundaries [and] creating the unexpected. . . . I haven't felt any political vibe behind it." While acknowledging some exceptions, DJ Schmolli agreed that most mashups are not political but are mainly made for entertainment purposes: "It's the 'wow' effect, and it's the entertainment and fun aspect, not so much like a political or like a society-changing aspect, or something like that." While most of the interviewees agreed with this, the politics of signs transcend intention, as I have demonstrated. As such, the alternative to political or critical need not be apolitical; the distinction instead emerges in the framing, which is, of course, often related to intention.

Examples of mashups that are more explicitly framed as political include DJ Prince's "For What It's Worth Impeach the President (Buffalo Springfield, Honey Drippers)" (2010), which blends political songs to further its message. The Honey Drippers' funk track "Impeach the President" (1973) protests Richard Nixon, and Buffalo Springfield's "For What It's Worth (Stop, Hey, What's That Sound)" (1966) addresses the civil rights protests and disturbances in the wake of the 1966 Sunset Strip curfew riots. By combining the vocals and instrumentals of these two songs (and adding some other tracks as well) and renewing their relevance via a different political context, DJ Prince hoped to share his perspective on what was happening in the United States under President George W. Bush. DJ Schmolli also sometimes merged songs with similar political content. His "Shelter Search" (2017), for example, mashes three songs about the Vietnam War. He also cut up multiple songs into short clips and pasted different lyrics together to create a new narrative from his source tracks. Sometimes he juxtaposed songs that are not political in a way that created a political message or shaped songs about different subjects into a coherent narrative theme. For example, he pointed out that his "Revolution" (2014) is a commentary on the Egyptian Rabaa massacre that took place in Cairo in August 2013—a consequence of the Egyptian security forces' handling of the mass demonstrations against the military coup that removed the first democratically elected president, Mohamed Morsi. Here, he mashed the music and vocals of ten songs with very different lyrics into "one strong message," so that, among others, Black Sabbath sings about "Children of the Grave" (1971) with a revolution on their minds, T-Rex sings about the "Children of the Revolution" (1972), Empire of the Sun sings "We Are the People" (2008) who rule the world, Rihanna (featuring Calvin Harris) sings about standing side by side (from "We Found Love," 2011), and Muse sings about being victorious and resisting those who would bully, degrade, or control us (from "Uprising," 2009). Alongside a video consisting of clips from the songs' original music videos and news reports about the massacre, "Revolution" presents a thematically and structurally coherent narrative about its subject in a compelling manner, as one viewer comment made clear: "Say no more . . . you said it all!"

DJ Earworm took it one step further by using even shorter clips from an even larger number of songs to piece together coherent lyrical narratives that were often politically oriented. He also combined relevant music video clips to support his newly constructed narrative. For example, "No More Gas" (2008) is about overconsumption related to the scenario of running out of gas. In the chorus, Britney Spears sings "Gimme, gimme more, gimme more" (from "Gimme More," 2007) before Ne-Yo takes over, singing, "I just can't stop, I just can't stop" (from "Closer," 2009), and then Rihanna comes in with "no more gas" (a throwaway line from her 2009 song "Disturbia"), and so it goes, all accompanied by a musical montage of the different tracks as well as footage displaying a city street commandeered by cars. "It was more just like social commentary on how we know that we are overconsuming and yet we can't help ourselves," DJ Earworm explained, adding that he wanted to comment on "this helplessness to our urges." He also insisted that almost all of his annual United State of Pop releases try to "capture the zeitgeist of culture." Some are also "strongly political," he added, noting that his 2016 and 2017 versions ("United State of Pop 2016 [Into Pieces]" and "United State of Pop 2017 [How We Do It]") were hugely influenced by Trump. Whereas 2016 "went dark" in its message, 2017 was a more upbeat protest that involved celebrating diversity as well: "You know, 'this is how we do it down in Puerto Rico, this is how we do it all the time in all these places.' It's just an 'up with diversity' and a 'down with hate.' Like, there's the lyrics 'you can hate all the hate if you wanted to,' that kind of stuff." Another recent (and likely related) politically motivated mashup by DJ Earworm was his "Mashional Anthem—50 Songs of America," which he posted on the US Independence Day in 2020. In this megamix, he used clips from fifty songs about the United States. By combining patriotic songs with protests songs (Childish Gambino's "This Is America" [2018], for example, with Kate Smith's "God Bless America" [from the film *This Is the Army*, 1943]) alongside footage of US political and cultural highs and lows, this mashup expresses a sentiment similar to that of Jimi Hendrix's 1969 Woodstock performance of the national anthem: a mixture of "the hopes and fears of a nation" (Clague 2019).

Whereas these mashups are framed as political by reinforcing already articulated messages through their combinations, or by merging lyrics to create a linguistic political message, there are also examples of mashups that explicitly communicate a political message—one that differs from the message of the mashed tracks—by exploring the potential of the signs' intertextual and bisociative transformation.[27] An example of this is DJ Cummerbund's "Blurry in the USA" (2020), which I analyze next.

The AHA Impact of Synergetic, Intertextual, and Double-Coded Messaging

DJ Cummerbund's "Blurry in the USA" mashup combines the instrumentals and footage of Puddle of Mudd's rock ballad "Blurry" (2001) and the vocals and footage of Miley Cyrus's pop hit "Party in the U.S.A." (2009), together with some audiovisual news report clips and short audiovisual extracts from songs by Jay-Z, Randy "Macho Man" Savage, Britney Spears, Ric Flair, and Chase Holfelder. Though the mashup can be interpreted in many ways, the context in which it was posted, together with the associations and connotations that the mashed tracks signify, suggests a very thick message communicated by very few means.

The mashup was posted on June 21, 2020, as the Black Lives Matter protests took off across the United States after a Minneapolis Police Department officer choked a forty-six-year-old African American man to death during an arrest. The mashup starts with Puddle of Mudd's intro to "Blurry" alongside a news report clip stating that the United States "is unraveling for all the world to see" and describing big cities that are "burning in almost unimaginable scenes." After this introduction, which also includes teasers from the music video to Cyrus's "Party in the U.S.A.," Cyrus starts to sing the lyrics to this song, which is about the American dream—in this case, the excitement and wonder of coming to LA, where "everyone is famous," and availing oneself of the surplus of opportunities that the United States has to offer. The original video for this up-tempo and catchy pop tune features a drive-in-theater, pickup trucks and American classic cars, pretty and stylish young women with cowboy boots, and a big American flag behind pouring confetti. As Cyrus sings energetically that it's a party in the U.S.A., the video—replete with several quintessential US symbols—amplifies the almost propagandistic claim that the U.S.A. itself is a party (at least for a young, white, pretty, and talented woman). The mashup, however, reframes the narrative of Cyrus's music video as a vision that is not borne out in reality. The Cyrus-acted protagonist now encounters a burning party in the U.S.A., not the party she dreamed of. During the first verse and prechorus of the mashup, the footage of Cyrus's original video is intermingled with clips from Puddle of the Mudd's official music video, as well as short clips of riots and street demonstrations to supply an ironic undercurrent to the lyrics. This disjunction escalates throughout the remainder of the mashup's video, which includes clips of police brutality, gunfights, tear gas, burning buildings, and people screaming in fear. The mashup thus sets up a stark contrast between a young, white American girl's naive faith in the United States as the land of opportunity, equality and fun, and the harsh reality of racial inequality and an excessively divided country.

The more generally dejected music and video footage by Puddle of Mudd tilts the whole thing toward despair rather than excitement. Moreover, if one is already familiar with "Blurry," the song may come across as a metaphor in the context of the mashup even without hearing its lyrics. It is about the frustration of not being able to take care of a loved one under certain circumstances. As such, the mashup suggests an analogy to the currently widespread frustration in the United States with the institutional failure to prevent racism or facilitate equality. In the middle of the mashup, this dejected political undercurrent is amplified by an audio excerpt of a poignant minor-key version of the national anthem created by Chase Holdfelder in the wake of the Black Lives Matter riots ("'The Star-Spangled Banner' in a Minor Key" [2020]). This version of the anthem forms a musical backdrop to footage of the riots alongside a Donald Trump tweet bragging about "vicious" dogs, "ominous" weapons, and eager Secret Service agents. In the comment section under the video, Holdfelder writes, "The [Black Lives Matter] movement has brought renewed light to a disease that has plagued our nation from the beginning." By merging these songs and media clips and placing them in a new context, the mashup communicates a new message from within—not by the extensive alteration of the texts but by means of recontextualized and clashing connotations and associations.

The repurposing of signs can also be found in some of the mashup's details. The Cyrus protagonist's observation that her nervousness and homesickness in LA fade when the DJ puts on her favorite song by Jay-Z is followed by a clip of the African American rapper snarling, "I got 99 problems but a bitch ain't one" (from "99 Problems" [2003]), which, in this new context, seems to emphasize the racist reality depicted in the mashup's selected news clips. The second times she sings that the DJ puts on her favorite song, she mentions "Britney," which is followed up with a clip of Britney Spears singing, "Oh baby, baby," which many fans will know is followed by the line, "How was I supposed to know that something wasn't right here?" (from ". . . Baby One More Time" [1998]). In the mashup, this sentence comes to represent a retrospective correction of the protagonist's naive attitude about the less pleasant aspects of the United States. When Cyrus sings about the Hollywood sign, the mashup video pivots to an image of it burning—an attack of sorts on American pride. The intermingling of the music and footage of a rock group with that of a pop singer also evokes the stereotypical connotations of these respective genres—rock as confrontational, honest, and reality oriented versus pop as shallow, manufactured, and fantasy oriented—which may in turn echo the contrast between the U.S.A.'s image and its reality.

Montages such as this one make meaning not only by merging symbols and their associations and connotations but also by transforming them in the process. Neither Puddle of Mudd's "Blurry" nor Cyrus's "Party in the

U.S.A." concerns the American political situation as such, yet together, in the context of this mashup, they communicate a strong political message. This reminds us, once again, of Eisenstein, who saw great emotional, intellectual, and political potential in the new "concept" or "quality" that arises in a montage's juxtaposition of its elements (1986, 14). Moreover, the true potential of montage to create unique imaginings lies in its elements' collision (as opposed to amalgamation). The reason the elements collide rather than coalesce is, of course, that they are recognized as originating elsewhere and thus carry with them associations with that context. This is particularly true with samples. As Anne Danielsen points out, with reference to Charles S. Peirce's semiotic theory, samples "carry with them indexical traces of a world outside music and thus act as documentary material within it" (2008, 408).[28] Put differently, a sample is a musical extract already embedded with specific context- and subject-specific associations and connotations, both on the surface and in the details, and these are all the more strongly evoked and put into play if it is the sample itself, rather than an imitation of it, that is recontextualized. By commenting on events from within, sample-based montages inhabit the voices of others to share a message of their own. The juxtaposition and recontextualization of signs, associations, and connotations enable the mashup to mediate a thick message in a short time frame—one that transcends the semantic level of language.

Obviously a mashup like "Blurry in the U.S.A." will be interpreted differently by different listeners, and one might well wonder how much of the meaning discussed above a listener could be expected to absorb. Through insight gleaned from the comment sections under the video, however, it seems as though people have indeed been moved by this mashup:

- "It's almost a perfect transcription of what is happening in America right now. It shows the clash between American Pride vs the no longer silent oppression. Not everything is perfect."
- "Your true Mastery is to make such a complex work look and sound so elegantly easy, as if the pieces of this song (and video) were always meant to be held together in this way. Thank you for this outcry and the simple message: Let's do better."
- "This is a time capsule for history to remember that USA's flag was upside down."

There are numerous similar comments under this particular video, which demonstrate that sometimes a mashup or remix can capture a listener's understanding of the world more specifically and effectively than any other medium.

As I pointed out in the analysis of Bill McClintock's mashup, the AHA and HAHA impacts of mashups are often interrelated, and this is also the case here. That is, "Blurry in the USA" is not completely dark.[29] Interestingly, several of the viewers commented on the effectiveness of combining humor and politics in this case:

- "When a comedian makes you laugh for a while, then suddenly holds a mirror up to society and you're like, "oh, shiiit.""
- "Come for the music, stay for the biting social commentary. God damn, this was art, DJ."
- "I put you in the Dave Chappell, George Carlin category where the most powerful and profound statements are always put most succinctly and poignantly by the ones who can make us laugh the loudest and smile the widest."
- "Simultaneously poignant and hilarious, guffaw inducing and gut wrenching."
- "Started out laughing and ended up depressed, thanks."

The combination of humor, rhetoric, and aesthetics appears to have the potential to reach an audience that traditional political rhetoric might not. This recalls what Limor Shifman, in her study of memes, calls "a new amalgamation of cute cats and hard-core politics" (2014, 119): pop culture, in embracing humor and playfulness, becomes a platform that makes politics more approachable by communicating about it in an accessible and engaging way (136). Henry Jenkins adds, "This is in the end another reason why popular culture matters politically—because it doesn't seem to be about politics at all" (Jenkins 2006, 239).[30]

Moreover, the fact that the relevant AHA impact arises in the context of art indicates the importance of the AH impact to the experience. Useful to this discussion is Prague School scholar Jan Mukařovský's concept of poetic reference, which he defines as "every reference appearing in a text which has a dominant aesthetic function" (1989, 155).[31] The characteristic quality of poetic reference is that it makes the sign itself and its aesthetic function the center of attention, whereas traditional reference does not. As Mukařovský points out, this is not to imply that informational utterance does not have a poetic function or that poetic reference does not communicate; what is involved is instead "a shift, so to speak, in the center of gravity" (157). He explains: "Thus, in poetry, as against informational language, there is a reversal in the hierarchy of relations: in the latter attention is focused above all on the relation, important from the practical point of view, between reference and reality, whereas for the former it is the relationship between the reference of the context incorporating it that stands to the fore" (157). Although one dimension may be stronger than the other, both are still present. In fact, poetic reference introduces a particular kind of referentiality that may be very effective precisely because of its aesthetic function.

When we conceptualize music as a form of poetic reference, its aesthetic function tends to override its communicative function. But even music primarily understood as a source of entertainment and pleasure acts as a means of communication, though it is not always clear exactly what is being communicated. Mukařovský points out that poetic reference often trades the mode of particular (and strong) reference for a more abstract mode—that is, a reference of a higher order. Put differently, it functions as social commentary not by suggesting a causal relation between sign and referent but by "enter[ing] as a global reference into a relationship with the entire world as reflected in the life experiences of persons, either senders or receivers" (1989, 162). As has been demonstrated by a number of popular music scholars, the inversion of signs is a very common feature of popular music more generally, which implies that music that is less associated with politics may still be highly political in its dramatization and interrogation of identity construction, for example. As such, I argue that mashups are indeed political utterances and can evoke an AHA reaction in the listener regardless of whether they are framed, intended, or even interpreted as such. Valuable information about culture lurks in a listener's experience of surprise, humor, and amusement. But the fact that the messaging or reference is a poetic one allows for a more subtle form of AHA—one that often goes almost unremarked.

The AH Impact of Mashups

Koestler does not provide a detailed account of what he means by the "AH" reaction other than noting that it refers to the experience of beauty (1967, 185–188). I here frame beauty, or the AH impact, more broadly in terms of an exclamation of aesthetic appreciation or an affective experience of something artistically or musically pleasant and attractive. Still, several producers described the AH impact of mashups in terms of the key concept of "beauty," including dicksoak: "When I first heard this [particular mashup], I was just blown away. Like, it has such an intense beauty to it that I did in fact find myself kind of moved by it." MsMiep similarly resorted to "beauty": "[One of] my very, very favorite mashups . . . is by PhilRetroSpector, and that is a Morcheeba a cappella over a piece of music by Nick Cave and Warren Ellis from the *Assassination of Jesse James* soundtrack. And that soundtrack is one of my absolute favorite albums. It's so beautiful. And to hear it in a mashup with Morcheeba singing over the top just is, like, to me, one of the most beautiful pieces of music ever. And it's a mashup." PhilRetroSpector tried another strategy to describe aesthetic emotions by referring to how the music manifests physically, as well as how it engages emotionally: "For me it's all about the music, it's all about expression. . . . I would consider music to be the most honest of all art forms. I think you, kind of, connect to it. Automatically it hits you, so as to say, the hair goes up on the back of your neck. Or your ears prick up, or it hits you in the heart, or something like that. I'm not setting out to kind of educate or inform; [instead] I would try to make a piece of music with a twist on it that might resonate, or kind of touch somebody on an emotional level. Definitively. For me it's about texture and tone, and things like that. More than something else." Given the inherently enigmatic nature of aesthetic emotions, empirical accounts seldom pinpoint what it is that causes these positive (or negative) encounters. Yet they are at the heart of what drives people to produce and consume cultural expressions.

Whereas mashup producers such as Poolboy insisted that humor is more important to them than musical enjoyment, most also said that they tried to achieve both, as we saw in chapter 3. For example, DJ Earworm argued that while creating mashups may often be about humor or even about making jokes, the mashups should also function aesthetically to stand the test of time. Several of the mashups mentioned in this book come across particularly successfully as "originals," to use the producers' phrasing (see chapter 3). Oneboredjeu's "Flo Good Inc.—Gorillaz feat. De La Soul vs. Flo Rida feat. T-Pain (mashup)" (2019) and Happy Cat Disco's "₿runo 𝒜ars vs. ℂaravan Palace(24₭ Digger)—Mashup" (2016), mentioned in chapter 3, for example, succeed technically but could also be found on the Billboard charts (if they were not mashups) as musically compelling works in their own right. Yet the fact that mashup producers chose to use familiar samples as compositional building blocks and frame the music as recreational suggests that most of them wanted something more than the sound of an "original" work of art.

Early in this chapter, I tried to capture some of this unique experience of pleasurable beauty in mashup, parody, and other forms of acknowledged appropriations, and specifically montage-based acknowledged appropriations, by turning to the concepts of intertextuality (here understood as contextual transformation), double-codedness, and montage and bisociation. An acknowledged appropriation is usually intended to be conceptualized as a parallel *and* a contrast to its original version—that is, as conceptualized within two different contexts at once. This inner "dialogized hybrid" (Bakhtin 1981) is part of the fascination of and pleasure in the experience. A related concept that comes to mind is Viktor Shklovsky's (1989) notion of "defamiliarization"—that is, when something familiar is somehow made unfamiliar or otherwise twisted. Shklovsky notes that if we have encountered an object repeatedly, we will begin to recognize it but stop truly seeing it as our perception of it becomes habitual and automatic. The beauty or aesthetic effect of defamiliarization, Shklovsky continues, resides in the fact that by escaping our habitual ways of perceiving, we start truly seeing: "And art exists that one may recover the sensation of life; it exists to make one feel things, to make the stone stony" (1989, 278). Defamiliarized content can open one's eyes, ears, and mind to things one has not attended to previously, fortifying the presence of the art in question while prolonging the moment of the experience. Although this ability exists in many forms of art, mashup music's impression of defamiliarization is particularly profound, because the art form keeps its references explicit while simultaneously presenting a new version of them, at once confirming and challenging any existing perception, habitual or otherwise.

To mashup producer Danny Neyman, this repurposing of sources is central: "I feel like the biggest thing that [mashup consumers] get is a different take and perspective on a song. . . . [The mashup] essentially changes the composition of how the song is supposed to be taken and interpreted and gives that perspective to an entirely different audience." DJ Schmolli too emphasized that mashup music is revivifying: "I think people get bored of certain songs they have heard in their original form hundreds of times on the radio or whatever. And they appreciate it if there is this song they really like, [and] now there's a version online that mixes this song with another song from twenty years ago that they liked back then. . . . [It's] refreshing. . . . And people appreciate alternative versions to songs that they like, I think." In line with Shklovsky's description of defamiliarization as disrupting our habitual ways of perceiving things, mashup music encourages listeners to hear something new in the otherwise familiar by highlighting unnoticed aspects of the musical or sociohistorical context—which is where our habits of perception reside, after all—or by leaving something out. This exploration and uncovering of unnoticed aspects of familiar music is engaging for both the listener and the producer, as dicksoak observed: "I guess what drew me to [mashup music] is that, like, you can take something that has already existed, something that's been released, something that's been defined in time, and completely re-contextualize it in whatever way suits you at the moment." The aesthetic impact of the mashup, then, resides both in what it becomes in and of itself *and* what it does to its existing sources.

A mashup that clearly demonstrates this defamiliarization and revivifying function is DJ Poulpi's "No One Knows When the Sky Falls (QOTSA vs Adele)" (2014), in which he combines the vocals from "No One Knows" (2002) by the American rock band Queens of the Stone Age (QOTSA) with the instrumental of Adele's "Skyfall," the title track of the 2012 James Bond film. "Skyfall" contains the typical majestic and richly orchestrated James Bond sound, with John Berry's signature melody line of three rising and then falling intervals of a minor second. In the original version, the generally overblown Bond sound is complemented by Adele's melodic line and rich, deep, powerful diva voice. In the mashup, rocker Josh Homme's distorted chest voice lends the soundtrack an unexpected, eccentric thrill, for several reasons. First, the rhythm of Homme's performance accentuates all four beats of the bar (in contrast to Adele's syncopated phrasing), which, instead of swooping alongside the Bond theme, drives the chorus forward like a march, and the melody line, which lands in the second bar on the accompanying submediant chord's tritonic (or sharp eleventh), introduces dissonance and unresolved harmonic tension. Conversely, when the energetic stoner rock of pulsing bass guitar, crisp guitar riffs, and frenetic drums is replaced by the majestic orchestral arrangement of "Skyfall," the listener reckons anew with the nuances of Homme's voice as a vehicle of not only sheer energy but also a hint of desperation. The Adele arrangement reintroduces the melody and voice of Homme, which reintroduces the music in turn, and the welter of unresolved musical and (vocally) expressive tension evokes in a very different way the fraught life and swashbuckling personality of James Bond.[32]

While most of the interviewed and surveyed producers emphasized the AH impact along with the HAHA, some privileged the AH potential of mashups above the rest. For example, Colatron told us that he built his reputation making emotional, melancholic mashups, and, as mentioned in chapter 3, RaheemD specialized in making "dream collaborations." Rather than evoking a humorous response, the goal of these mashups is to present a different take or perspective on a song. NodaMixMusic said that his niche was to mash tracks that aligned emotionally, including the unhappy vocal tracks of 2Pac: "When I make remixes, I take one depressed guy and another depressed guy. And the depression unites them."[33] He makes music when he is depressed, NodaMixMusic said, and assumes that most of his viewers also feel sad, or depressed, or in love, or hopeless, so that they find comfort in his mashups expressing the same. PhilRetroSpector sees humor as important to most mashups but not his own: "I specifically set out *not* to do that. Like, I would—before I made my first one, I decided I was going to make sad music—and I used to always put this thing at the end of a mixtape, sort of a warning: 'please ensure glass is half empty before listening.' You know? I just didn't want to kind of go with the rest of the current." Several megamix mashups too seem to place the tracks' aesthetic match above anything else.[34] But even here, the mashups' characteristic double-codedness—reinforced by the fact that they are framed as mashups in the first place—makes the aesthetic experience different from that of non-appropriating music.

The Beauty of Synergetic Contrasts
Note that defamiliarization, intertextuality, double-codedness, and bisociation, as well as the combination of congruity and incongruity, all have something in common: they activate the contrasting synergies of the unexpected and familiar, the predictable and novel, and the pleasant and awkward. Scholars (mainly within the field of psychology) have, in fact, associated these aspects of experience with pleasurable aesthetic emotions.[35] For example, Leonard Meyer (1956) and David Huron (2006) argue that especially meaningful moments in music arise from the resolution of schematic expectancy violation. As mentioned in chapter 3, mashup producers likewise point to the surprise element, in all its variety, as key to

mashups themselves and to what attracts listeners to them. While Meyer and Huron emphasize the aesthetic reward of the resolution of expectancy violations, Apter (1982) insists that in circumstances where the context protects the experiencer from any potential physical or psychological harm (as is the case in the art world), one can appreciate expectancy violations in and of themselves, aside from their resolution.[36] In these circumstances, one does not experience expectancy violations as threatening but rather as playful and enjoyable. This distinction is relevant to mashups, which balance expectancy violations and resolutions at the same time. As mentioned previously, the mashup relies on the simultaneous experience of the music *not* making sense (on the connotative level) and *making* sense (on the musical level). The mashup's attraction lies, in other words, in the contrast between something predicted and something unexpected.

Prediction and expectation processes have often been linked to the psychobiological arousal mechanism, which has in turn been linked to preference (that is, increased arousal is often seen as reflecting pleasant affects).[37] This linking has been problematized and even rejected by several scholars since.[38] Yet they still agree that aesthetic emotions can be triggered by certain cognitive mechanisms, including the feeling of simultaneous familiarity and novelty. For example, some scholars have concluded that something understood as novel, unfamiliar, uncertain, complex, inconsistent, and mysterious *and* as familiar, understandable, and meaningful often increases attentiveness or interest and is found to be particularly appealing.[39] Novelty supports interest, excitement, and suspense, and familiarity supports comfort, safety, ease, and contentment. When asked why so many people find mashup music fascinating, Isosine pointed to "the fact that there is an element of familiarity and an element of unpredictability when you listen to a mashup." He then elaborated: "[It] is kinda something that is already inherently accessible, because you already know the song. But, I guess, you're [also] hoping to be surprised in an unexpected way."

A related cognitive mechanism identified by scholars as characteristic of aesthetic appraisal is the combination of positive and negative emotions. For example, Menninghaus and colleagues point out that aesthetic appraisal has a mixed affective nature wherein negative emotions complement positive ones by making the experience more intense, varied, and memorable: "Select unpleasant and affectively negative ingredients [should be understood] as resources that can enrich and altogether deepen positively valent aesthetic emotions, rather than being invariably detrimental to them" (2019, 179).[40] Gérard Genette similarly notes that both positive and negative emotions inform the pleasure of parody, which "stems from the ambiguity of the combination, which is simultaneously nonsensical and whimsically pertinent" (1997 [1982], 47–48). This experience of something as simultaneously nonsensical, strange, and discomforting *and* pleasurable, wonderful, and attractive pinpoints the AH of the mashup. In mashup music, two logics are at play simultaneously, one of which makes sense and the other of which remains incongruent with existing experiences and expectations. As DJ Earworm said, "You don't know whether to laugh or cry, because it's beautiful, but it's ridiculous. And I love that."

But of course, DJ Earworm's description is not only about the mashup's inherent incongruity but also about performing an act of distancing similar to the admission of a guilty pleasure—that is, acknowledging an appreciation of something otherwise thought to be censured by public opinion and, in turn, beneath one's standards. For example, DJ Earworm prefaced that comment as follows: "No one is gonna say, 'This is one of the greatest songs ever written,' but it's super catchy, it's super fun, it's kinda ludicrous. . . . I mean the video is ridiculous, and the concept is just, it's so shallow." This slight frisson of embarrassment also seems to lurk in MsMiep's statement above, where she seems confounded by the fact that what she considers to be one of the most beautiful musical works ever is a mashup. This appreciation with reservations derives from the fact that the mashup interferes with long-established notions of musical value, artistic originality and creativity, and authenticity. I return to this ambivalence regarding mashups' AH impact in chapter 7, where I relate it to the cultural valuation of labor and, in turn, the idea that less labor goes into a mashup than into other forms of art. But before that, I discuss what is at stake for this art form. Having elaborated on its sociocultural significance for the previous three chapters, I next turn to its more problematic aspects, in terms of both its legality and the existential threat that it currently faces due to the copyright-related content moderation of internet platforms.

5 Sampling Ethics and Mashups' Legality

It's like a pirates' code of honor. . . . I didn't pay for the copyright clearances, therefore you shouldn't [pay me] either.
—Adriana A (personal interview)

People say: "Oh, you can evoke the fair use doctrine," or "you can evoke that it's a parody" or so, but I don't know what works or what doesn't work. . . . I was thinking, maybe at some point there should be some legal counseling.
—DJ Faroff (personal interview)

Mashup producers work in the legal margins. Someone sampling from a copyright-protected sound recording (where a copyright exception does not permit the use) must generally seek permission from the rights holders of both the sound recording and the musical work.[1] If what is sampled is an audiovisual recording, the footage in that recording may qualify for copyright separate from both the musical work and the sound recording, and permission must be granted for this use as well. Among the survey respondents, 89 percent said that they did not have permission from the copyright holder or creator of the sound recordings they had sampled in their most recent mashup, as opposed to 8 percent who had cleared some or all of the samples.

Drawing on this survey as well as the interviews, in the first part of this chapter, I elaborate on the reasons the producers gave for why they did not license their samples when creating their mashups, which encompass various practical and economic hurdles. In practice, they insisted, the principal alternative to using unlicensed samples was to stop making mashups. In the second part, I show that mashup sampling is nevertheless governed by its own set of internal ethical guidelines.² Several artists also thought that they did not need to license because permission is already granted to them by copyright law exceptions, and in the third part of the chapter I consider whether this might in fact be the case. Considering the fact that mashups have not been tested in court and that legal evaluations of exceptions are case specific and based on nuanced analysis in which various features are taken into account, I argue that mashup music resides in the legal gray area. I further point out that the internal ethical guidelines of mashup producers, together with the fact that mashups' legality remains untested, clearly disrupt the narrative that has been established about the act of sampling without authorization—that it is synonymous with stealing and erodes both the revenues and the recognition of other hard-working musicians.

Why Mashup Producers Do Not License

If one has obtained permission from the copyright holder to use the protected work in a particular way, the use is lawful under the negotiated conditions. Writing in 2011 and in a US context, Kembrew McLeod and Peter DiCola (2011) demonstrate through their many interviews with sampling musicians and sample-clearance professionals that the process of proactively seeking copyright licensing may not be as straightforward as it seems. They explain that producers of sample-based music sometimes refrain from seeking permission to use copyright-protected material because of the hurdles it involves; for example, they consider it to be too hard or time-consuming to learn the copyright licensing system and track down the relevant copyright holders, or they assume that their request will be rejected or that the fees will be too high. Although the interviews and survey we conducted took place a decade later and in a European as well as a US context, several of these hurdles were seconded by the mashup producers as well.

The first hurdle to licensing samples, the producers explained, is to find out who the copyright holders are, which requires an understanding of how copyright works, including that copyright can be transferred from an author to a corporation, for example. There are at least two types of copyright that apply when one is sampling a recording: that of the musical work and that of the sound recording. The copyright holder in either case is not necessarily the author (here understood as the songwriter or performer/recordist) since the author can transfer these rights to other parties. Often, all or some of the rights related to the musical work are transferred to a publisher, whereas all or some of the rights related to the sound recording are transferred to a record label as part of the contract with that label. This likelihood is not apparent to all mashup producers, some of whom simply assume that the musician or band in question is able to grant permission to use the music. For example, some of the interviewees lamented that they had received permission from an artist whose label later claimed copyright infringement. The challenges in navigating who owns a given track's rights are further complicated by the fact that the two basic rights can be split among multiple parties as well, each of which owns a different percentage of the rights themselves. For example, McLeod and DiCola refer to a sample clearance professional working for Motown who recalled a song that had fifteen copyright coholders, each of whom had a different percentage of the rights (2011, 153). But even when the correct copyright holders have been identified, it is not always clear how to proceed or how to negotiate the conditions for the use.

McLeod and DiCola conclude that a detailed knowledge of the copyright licensing system is basically essential: "Sample clearance often requires an understanding of copyright law; familiarity with record contracts, publishing contracts, and sample-licensing; knowledge of music-industry institutions and relationships with particular individuals within those institutions; and, perhaps most important, common sense about how to conduct licensing negotiations" (2011, 155). Consequently, major labels or artists typically hire an intermediary (such as an experienced music manager or music lawyer). Mashup producers, who generally are not affiliated with a record label, do not have the resources (or are unwilling to commit them) to hire such an intermediary. And they would be hard pressed to acquire all the relevant knowledge and pursue the licensing process for all of those individual samples, especially if they want their mashups to be posted while their sampled sources are (for various reasons) most relevant. One of the anonymous mashup interviewees pointed out, "Younger and younger generations are doing these mashups, and they don't have any sense of how to do things legally. That compass, that legal compass, it's hard to come by. And even when you get older, when you make these mashups, you still have to figure out how you're going to access the people who created the samples and the publishers. They still don't make it easy to find. But we need to get to a point in the future that samples can get approved instantly." The complexity of navigating the system and the large time commitment required are therefore among the reasons that mashup producers do not attempt to license the samples they use.

It is also true that the producers had little faith in striking a reasonable licensing agreement, or any agreement at all. Among the surveyed producers, 7 percent said that they did in fact seek permission to use the samples they mashed but did not receive a response, and some even added that they did not seek permission because they expected to be rejected. Such a sense of resignation was also reflected in some of the interviews. For example, concerning whether he had sought permission to use samples, DJ Faroff stated bluntly: "It's not gonna work. The artists aren't gonna respond. There are many more mashup producers than artists—I mean, you know, Radiohead is not gonna reply to every request for a mashup." This assumption about a lack of response or a rejection is not completely wrong (and it is often not the artist who is the copyright holder in any case). A publisher or a label may reasonably conclude that the process of negotiating a license with a mashup producer does not justify the resources needed if the mashup producer is not willing to pay much. Publishers and record labels are mostly interested only in agreements with significant financial benefits, in terms of either a big buyout or, if the sampling artist has commercial potential, strong royalties.[3] The revenues realized from mashups are negligible, after all, and the licensing fee would presumably be prohibitive given the numerous samples in a single mashup that can be subject to potential licensing. As McLeod and DiCola pointed out, if the sampling artist does not know the right people or have relationships at the companies in question, and if they do not have representatives within the right network, they have little chance of success (2011, 164).

McLeod and DiCola (2011, 153) estimated that typical buyouts for the use of a sample from a sound recording at the time they wrote were ranging from $500 to $1,500, though they also pointed to instances of sample buyouts of $50,000 to $100,000. Several musicians and sample-clearance experts have noted that buyout fees for using samples have increased markedly since the early 1990s, when hip-hop sampling first attracted the attention of the major labels.[4] High licensing fees related to a particular instance of sampling can act as a hindrance to future licensing but can also have a chilling effect in terms of discouraging sampling artists from applying for permission to use samples. The fee is decided on a case-by-case basis, after all, and because this process is inherently unpredictable, people tend to refer to prior instances of licensing and settlements. An example of the latter was one of the first lawsuits in the 1990s hip-hop scene, when De La Soul was sued by the Turtles for using a sample from "You Showed Me" (1968) in the rap group's "Transmitting Live from Mars" (*3 Feet High and Rising*, 1989). The dispute was settled outside of court in favor of the Turtles for a reported $1.7 million (Sanjek 1992, 618). This settlement attracted much attention and caused much moral panic, all the while emboldening copyright holders to demand higher fees for samples and higher settlements. Not unexpectedly, then, 39 percent of the survey respondents said that they did not seek permission because they assumed it would be too expensive. Others added that they had sought permission, but the fee was too high so they gave up. Happy Cat Disco was among the few interviewees who had reached out to a record label for a license, in this case for a Justin Bieber song: "But when I called the record company and they sent me to the PR, they thought I was joking . . . and they told me it was gonna be $5,000 for the [sample] copy. And I said, 'That's the last time I'm gonna call you.' So yeah, it was ridiculous." DJ Prince said that he actually did license a sample that he used in a mashup in 2001 for $22,000. He did not pay the fee himself, since the mashup was already signed to a record label that paid the license fee as well. He added that he otherwise could not have managed to clear the sample.

DJ Poulpi captures the general resignation of the mashup producers: "I never ask [for a license]. Why? Because I don't know where to ask. I don't know how to ask. And my understanding is that if I ask, there are two options: one is, no one will answer; two, they will say no. So, it's better for me to just make it, put it online, and see what happens. I think it's what most people do." As Alan Hui points out, when traditional licensing models do not "provide sampling artists with efficient or effective means to seek permission . . . 'Thou shalt not steal' loses its biblical virtues and morphs into 'thou shalt not use'" (2017, 166).[5] He further argues that a licensing system that is so protective of works that it does not allow for appropriations is counter to one of the purposes of copyright—that is, to promote the creation and distribution of original works (66). The current licensing system is complex and slow but also, more important, reserved in practice for those with commercial success, those who are willing to (and capable of) paying a considerable fee, or those who have representatives who can pay it for them. McLeod and DiCola note that the current licensing system as such pushes other potential applicants into another line of work, the noncommercial sector, or the underground economy (2011, 188). Due to a combination of practical reasons and ethical objections (see below), the latter is not an alternative for mashup producers, who have therefore relocated to the noncommercial marketplace instead. Unfortunately, the platforms' algorithmically driven content moderation means that the noncommercial sector has turned out to be unsafe as well, and perhaps even existentially threatened.

Mashup producers, then, shy away from licensing samples because they assume that it is too expensive and too time-consuming and because they find the licensing system to be too complex. What most of the producers said was that they really wanted a more convenient, efficient, and feasible licensing system that would make licensing both quick and affordable (particularly in light of the large number of samples they needed to clear): "I think what's lacking is being able to convince the labels to really get the sampling [licensing] done quickly. Like, that convenience. Because usually we have convenience for streaming, we have convenience for everything else, but what's missing for us is the labels really giving the 'okay, go' as quickly as possible. And as inexpensively as possible" (anonymous mashup producer). Some of the producers had concrete suggestions for what such a system could look like, but as with the current situation, they felt that except for the option of being monetized on platforms, they were only offered two alternatives: quit making mashups or make them with unlicensed samples.

Sampling Ethics

In fact, 66 percent of the surveyed producers responded that they believed that the posting of mashups at platforms was legal based on the exceptions, or at least that it was in a legal gray area, compared to only 23 percent who responded that they saw it as illegal (11 percent answered that they did not know or checked "other"). Among those who believed that mashups were defensible under copyright law exceptions, the actual knowledge of copyright varied considerably. Many of them referred to the fair use doctrine of the US Copyright Act (including several who were not US residents), but few appeared to understand the complexity of copyright, including the fact that the US Copyright Act may not necessarily apply to their use. Some, such as DJ Earworm, argued for the legality of mashups by mentioning factors relevant to several of the fair use doctrine's four factors (the purpose and character of the use, the nature of the copyrighted work, the amount and substantiality of the portion taken, and the effect of the use upon the potential market):[6] "I do think it's fair use. It's definitely transformative, it's often a parody, the fragments are so short, it does not eat into the appetite for the original."[7] The argument that the fragments are short does not hold true for A+B mashups, of course, and he also acknowledged that some of his mashups would be harder to defend than others. Other producers believed that if the use were transformative or not generating any revenues, it would qualify as fair. DJ Poulpi, for example, said, "I don't know much about copyright, but I understand the concept of fair use. And I really believe that this falls under this category. And I really believe that what I'm doing, as long as I'm not selling it, it's not . . . I'm not feeling like I'm breaking any law, because I'm not doing anything wrong, and I'm not stealing anything from anyone." This quote reflects an observable trend among the producers: the conviction that copyright's fair use doctrine corresponded to their own ethical concept of fairness.

Still, most of the producers found copyright confusing and difficult to understand. DJ Faroff, for example, called for more information regarding the legality of samples and the applicability of the law: "People say, 'Oh, you can evoke the fair use doctrine, or you can evoke that it's a parody,' but I don't know what works or what doesn't work. Maybe that's something you guys are gonna be able to inform us [about]? . . . I was thinking, maybe at some point there should be some legal counseling." Even if it is not fair use, the producers insisted, it is still a fundamentally moral and justifiable practice. Generally they felt that mashup activity was misunderstood and confused with plagiarism or piracy and thus wrongly associated with stealing. As Happy Cat Disco put it, "I'm not going out there just saying, 'Here's the entire catalog of Eminem, please download the whole thing.' No, man, that's not cool. I think we can all agree that it's not cool." DJ Paul V. acknowledged that there are different ways to use samples and argued for limits to what copyright law should protect and, on the flip side, prevent: "I suppose, again, it goes back to, like, do I agree with copyright or whatever. It's like yes, you know, be protective of art, but not to the point where . . . it's just a blanket shutdown of something being presented as art in a different form." Convinced that copyright enforcement was unfortunately ignorant of the difference between plagiarism or piracy and appropriation, the mashup producers felt that their own ethical standards regarding this situation meant more than the law. Regardless of whether the producers saw their mashup activity as illegal or lawful, they operated by the same ethical guidelines for the treatment of the unauthorized samples. Those guidelines emphasize, in turn, that they should not profit from their mashup, and they should always credit the artists that they sample.

Sampling Ethics Rule 1: Do Not Seek Profit from Your Mashups
Ethical rule number 1 among the mashup producers is that their mashups must be noncommercial—that is, they considered it "dodgy" to seek financial gains from their mashups by selling or otherwise monetizing them. This rule was also confirmed by the survey, which found that 82 percent ($n = 72$) of the producers reported that they did not generate any income from their mashups (it is unclear whether the remaining 18 percent, who said that they did generate income from their mashups, also counted indirect income, such as club revenues, subscription patent services such as Patreon, or merchandise). Adriana A explained: "It's like a pirates' code of honor, really, that is what it is. I didn't pay for the copyright clearances, therefore you shouldn't [pay me] either." She added, "I've had some people be like, 'Wow. You should really monetize your website.' And 'The Bootie Mashup website is so popular, you should, you know, Google ads!' Whatever, whatever. And I'm like, 'No! I don't want to do that, because I have other people's copyrighted music posted to this website. And therefore I don't want any advertising on it at all.'" Most of the other producers, including DJ Schmolli, also felt an ethical responsibility to the sampled artists not to profit from their copyrighted music: "Speaking as a musician and artist and songwriter myself, I really want the artists to get paid. I don't want to steal any money from artists. I know a lot of artists and I really support them.... And I don't wanna be the person who takes parts of these songs and releases them with other songs and makes money off it without getting him or her their credits, the revenue or something like that, you know."

It felt like a sacrifice to some of the producers to operate outside the commercial music market without any hope of income from their creative labor or any prospects of being signed to a label or gaining recognition in the market. And this sacrifice, in turn, justified for them the practice of sampling without struggling to pay for permission to do so. As Bring-MeTheMashup put it, "We're not making any money so we shouldn't be spending any money." Nor did they anticipate any improvement to their prospects. As opposed to those few artists whose remixes offered them a way into the commercial music industry, most of the producers remained committed to their commercially renegade work, because mashups were what they wanted to do above all else.

The producers emphasized that mashup music, unlike plagiarism, does not try to trick people into thinking that it is original. They also saw it as an homage of sorts to the sampled artists or, at the very least, as free promotion, as MsMiep pointed out: "I feel that what I'm doing is promoting the other artists. And [the mashup] is another way that makes these artists' work accessible. . . . This is another avenue for someone else to hear the music. So, in a way, 'you're welcome.' Right?" CFLO agreed that it was in the sampled artists' best interests to be mashed and listed a number of old songs that suddenly received a lot of attention thanks to the mashups that sampled them. He then observed that when copyright holders put an end to a mashup that uses their tracks, they do themselves a disservice too: "I think the more [that] people reinterpret your piece, the further your piece spreads, and to discourage that seems counterproductive to business, in my mind. If you're in the music business, you want as many versions out there as possible, I would think. Even if it doesn't stay true to your vision, it still is out there, right?" Mashup producer DJ Farrof, who holds a PhD in economics, agreed with CFLO's economic logic: "It feels like the industry, the labels, are cracking down on mashups because they think it cuts down their profits. Well, that's an empirical question that one can assess. I propose that it actually doesn't, and actually they're losing money by cracking down on mashups, if anything. . . . They always go from the principle that they're just substitutes, right—it's like, 'Oh, we need to prevent mashups.' I'm pretty convinced they're complements. . . . If I listen to . . . [the music of] B-52's mashed with 'Funky Town,' it's like, 'Oh yeah, I haven't heard "Funky Town" for a while, let me just [relisten to it].'" He saw proof that mashups are complementary to their sampled sources in the fact that producers often insert, under the mashup videos, the information about the tracks they have mashed, along with links to the original versions. He then continued his microeconomics analysis: "There are smarter ways to fix this than just to completely strangle and choke and shut down an entire form of art the way they [copyright holders and platform providers] did . . . First, you need to understand what impact [mashup music] has, whether it's even hurting the industry—I don't think it is—and then try to figure out ways of monetizing, you know. . . . I mean, it's all about making money—it's not about the morality of it for the industry, it's about making money."

What DJ Faroff probably did not know when he suggested that copyright holders evaluate the basic economics of mashups via social experiments was that such an investigation had already been carried out and was published soon after the interview. Mike Schuster, David Mitchell, and Kenneth Brown (2019) set out to determine whether unlicensed sampling has an impact on the market for the original in terms of hampering financial gain that would otherwise have accrued to the copyright holders of the sampled material. This claim has long been a key argument in favor of the copyright holders' cases in court (2019, 193–194; see also Beebe 2020). Using Girl Talk's mashup album *All Day* (2010) as a test case and analyzing the sales of its sampled songs, these researchers produced robust and statistically significant data showing that the sales of the sampled songs actually increased after the mashup album's release. In addition to this quantitative argument, the promotional value of sampling is also demonstrated by empirical data such as the fact that a lot of funk music was rediscovered thanks to its sampling by 1980s hip-hop producers.[8] Thanks to the promotional value they recognized in their mashups, several producers called for more collaboration between record labels and "the many talented mashup producers out there," who, as they put it, could make them money for nothing by mashing up songs from their catalogs.

Although the mashup producers seemed to have come to terms with not making any money on mashups, this resignation might be somewhat premature. McLeod and DiCola, for example, are among those who believe that sampling artists should be able to claim compensation for their valuable creative effort: "We believe that the music industry should reward creative labor. . . . To say that copyright owners deserve compensation and that creative labor deserves reward is no answer to the complex issues posed by sampling. Musicians who sample engage in creative labor, too. . . . Samplers and copyright owners alike have legitimate claims to the proceeds from sample-based works. Both groups contribute to the final product. This perspective suggests that a revenue split of 0/100 or 100/0 in all circumstances would be too extreme" (2011, 109). Such an argument is relevant in terms of not only ethical but also legal standards—that is, if the mashup were to fall under a copyright law exception or be considered a copyrightable work in and of itself, the producers would be fully within their rights to claim revenue from it (even if this is something that they do not request or even want).

Sampling Ethics Rule 2: Always Credit the Sampled Artists

Ethical rule number 2 among the mashup producers is that they must always credit the artists from whom they sample. A common argument was that "mashups are not hurting anyone," in terms of both the economics and the attribution and integrity. The mashup producers generally saw their activity more as a way of showing respect toward rather than mocking the artists of the originals, whom they were careful to acknowledge through attribution and the clear signposting of the mashup as a mashup. Along with the rejection of profit, this attribution represented another important ethical guideline for almost all of the producers, as exemplified by BringMeTheMashup: "I one hundred percent think that you should credit the artist that created the music. I think that's absolutely necessary. Because it's not our music that we created. It's our idea that we mash them up." Put another way, they emphasized that the raw material of the mashups is not their own, but that the music that results from the particular juxtaposition and treatment of that material certainly is.

As MsMiep pointed out, this practice of crediting the artists of the original sources distinguishes mashups from many other forms of sample-based music. She then asked rhetorically: "Someone's developed it and made it, and it's beautiful, but why can't you take that and make it beautiful somewhere else?" Simon Iddols, who had experience with making nonmashup music as well, said that he would respond very differently to being sampled depending on whether the sample had been credited: "We always give credit. . . . If someone were using my originals, photos or music or whatever, and it will be a mashup and it will be a nonprofit thing, and if they would give credit, I would be okay with it, because that's the way it works. If somebody were stealing my work and making money with it, that's a different case, and that's the most important rule." McLeod refers to Freelance Hellraiser, who lamented that his Aguilera/Strokes mashup was released as a legitimate single two years after he made it without any credit or profit to him: "It is an interesting thing for him to complain about—the idea that someone is ripping off his own rip-offs" (McLeod 2005, 87). But this makes complete sense if one believes that appropriation and plagiarism are two very different things, as several of the interviewees emphasized as well.

According to that logic, it is also more ethical to use a sample that is long enough to be readily recognized than it is to use an insignificant fragment. This is counter to what McLeod and DiCola suggest: "Musicians' understanding of sample licenses—and assessments of their fairness—reflects a distinction between sampling a large part of a song versus sampling a small amount. As Matt Black told us, 'You can't just take big slices of someone else's work. If so, you should pay. However, if you sample one snare drum off a Rolling Stones record and add 99 percent of the song yourself, you shouldn't pay the Rolling Stones 100 percent of the royalties'" (2011, 155). Yet, when one samples one snare drum sound or a very small amount of music, it is less likely that the musical source will be recognized, which in turn associates the use with outright plagiarism.

Although the artists are credited, of course, the ways in which their music is presented in a mashup may not accord with their own musical vision, and the ways in which their performance appears in the mashup video montage may not be how they want their persona to be staged. The producers responded to this point by noting that they always presented the samples as something new or different rather than as a replacement for the original work: "The artists can disagree with your art [but] it's *your* art at that point; their art has become your art the second you changed it," said CFLO. Poolboy agreed: "Like, when you listen to a mashup, you aren't listening to it instead of the original song—it's a completely different piece of art than the original song. It serves a completely different purpose. It's its own piece of art." In practice, as well, they pointed out that they had almost never experienced any instances of artists objecting to their mashups. In fact, the opposite was often the case. The producers gave several examples of artists—including big names from a broad range of genres, such as Fear Factory, Foo Fighters, Franz Ferdinand, Goldfrapp, Le Tigre, Nickelback, Pixies, Puff Daddy, Radiohead, Snow Patrol, Thin Lizzy, and Yoko Ono—who had tweeted or reposted their mashups as a gesture of approval or endorsed them in the comments section under the mashup videos.

This endorsement from artists meant a lot to the mashup producers. DJ Cummerbund recalled the Foo Fighters even playing his mashup at a concert: "The greatest success I've ever had, besides [the mashup] 'Earth,

Wind & Ozzys' [2017], besides any views, besides anything—Dave Grohl performed my mashup live in Sweden. Live! I freaked out. I was on vacation in Colorado when I got the phone call. And I freaked out. There's no better high than that. Nothing. I mean, I don't do drugs, I don't drink, I don't really do anything like that, but that kind of stuff, that gets me going, man." Several others explained that mashups can represent a way to reach out to artists they admire, and if those artists were to disapprove of a mashup they made, they would take it offline immediately. But while a lot of artists love mashups and do not care about copyright as such, they are usually not the ones who decide about its use. The record labels do. And mashup producers generally felt more alignment with and ethical responsibility toward the artists than toward the copyright holders, whom they saw as motivated by profit alone. While they mostly accepted and occasionally even endorsed copyright holders' monetization of their mashups on online platforms, they regretted that it did not primarily benefit the artists of those songs but rather the copyright holders themselves, and sometimes the platforms.

Although they often alter the mashed sources in humorous ways, almost all the interviewed mashup producers, and the ninety-two producers who took the survey, indicated that they generally mash songs they like, not songs to make fun of: "I genuinely quite enjoy all the music that I make mashups with. . . . I'm trying to think of an example where I've used an artist that I don't enjoy. And I think most of those would have to be in the nonstop pop year-end mixes. . . . So, that's pretty much the only time that I would use samples that I don't enjoy" (Isosine); "Ninety percent of the time it'll be a song that I know I love, and that I know I'll listen to after I make it. . . . Every once in a while, there's a new song out there that everyone's trying to do, so I'll give it a shot. It's never the best" (BringMeTheMashup); "It has to be music that I really like. Because I'm going to spend hours working on it. . . . if I don't love the music, I'm going to just stop doing it" (DJ Poulpi); "We're not trying to make fun of you or mock what you've done, you know—we're trying to exalt and glorify it, really" (Peter, DJ Cummerbund's manager). Diverging from the original artists' musical vision is not synonymous with mocking the artists or their songs or impugning their reputations.

These two ethical guideposts for most of the mashup producers—not seeking to profit from their mashups and always crediting the sampled artists—derive from some combination of personal and collective moral standards and a vague awareness of copyright law exceptions. Interestingly, the producers' convictions about their practice do indeed anticipate several legal rationales for defending certain uses of music as exceptions. These include the facts that their mashups are recognizably different from the original work (there is an absence of confusion); that their sources are credited and otherwise made explicit; that their motive is not harmful and noncommercial; and that their mashups have no substantial effect on the commercial success of the sampled material (their use does not encroach upon the economic prospects of the rights holder).

Copyright Exceptions and Mashup's Legal Status

Several mashup producers believed that mashup sampling needed no justification because they considered their practice to be legal under copyright law exceptions. There are, in fact, several legal exceptions to copyright law exclusive rights that allow for certain uses without authorization in particular circumstances. The exceptions are intended to strike a balance between copyright holders' interests in and rights to intellectual property, on the one hand, and freedom of expression (including freedom of the arts), which no law in a democratic society should curtail, on the other.[9] Together, these rights (copyright itself and the exceptions that safeguard freedom of expression) are intended to foster cultural production and diversity. Copyright is thus understood to represent an economic incentive for the artistic or intellectual creation, while the exceptions allow artists to build on others' expressions within the framework of certain restrictions.

Copyright exceptions are specific to national laws or international treaties and differ somewhat depending on the applicable law. However, there are exceptions that are common to the laws of most countries, which include copying for use that is private; use that is related to teaching or scientific research; quotations for commentary, criticism, or review; and use for the purpose of caricature, parody, or pastiche. With regard to musical sampling in the US and EU contexts, the fair use doctrine of the US Copyright Act and "the purpose of caricature, parody, and pastiche" and "quotation for purposes such as criticism or review" exceptions of the InfoSoc Directive of EU law represent the most relevant content.[10] I elaborate on these exceptions in order to communicate the complexity of the arguments on both ends of the spectrum—from the position of the mashup producers and other remixers, on the one hand, and the position of the copyright holders and platforms, on the other. This discussion further serves as a backdrop for the following chapter's argument: that platforms often undermine exceptions (that are integral to the legal copyright system) and their complexity.

The question of whether a particular use falls under an exception is not straightforward, for several reasons: (1) it is often unclear which law applies; (2) exceptions can be formulated and interpreted differently by courts in different countries; (3) the exceptions interrelate with other relevant legal factors; and (4) judgments on exceptions are made on a case-by-case basis, with few or no relevant precedents, which makes a potential defense unpredictable. Moreover, as I return to in chapter 6, the lack of sufficient tools and resources to account for exceptions at online platforms can make a robust defense redundant (that is, it simply does not matter due to an inadequate, or sometimes even absent, evaluation process).

Before I discuss the likelihood that mashups are defensible under various copyright exceptions, it is important to note that a particular mashup's legality depends on the applicable law. That is, when considering legal matters, the governing law and the jurisdiction to hear the dispute must be settled first.[11] There is no such thing as one transnational copyright law; each country applies its own. Although different international treaties reconcile certain aspects of copyright law between countries,[12] copyright law and its exceptions are not fully reconciled at the international level. It is therefore critical to know what law applies when considering whether a particular use of copyrighted material can be defended under a copyright exception, but this is not always easy to determine. Imagine the following situation, for example. You live in the United Kingdom and are making a mashup that samples an artist from Belgium who has released her music on a UK record label as well as a duo with members in Sweden and Australia that has released its music on a label based in Sweden. You distribute your mashup on a platform based in the United States and make it available there and in several EU countries. Which of these various countries' copyright laws apply here? We presented a similar scenario to the producers we surveyed and asked them the same question. Despite the fact that only 11 percent of the survey respondents admitted that they did not know which country's copyright law applied, they were all clearly confused—for example, most of them (80 percent) insisted that it was the copyright law of the country in which the platform was based that mattered. But the law that governs an internet platform's terms of service is not necessarily the one that governs a potential infringement lawsuit against an uploaded mashup. In fact, the applicable law could be the law of any of the countries to which the mashup was made available (Novović 2019).[13] Consequently, this also means that even if the mashup producer believes that the use can be defended under the US fair use doctrine, it may not matter, assuming the mashup has been made available outside the United States. In addition, what is correct in a legal context may not represent the way things work out in practice. It is no wonder, then, that producers find it difficult to navigate the cross-national copyright landscape of mashups and the internet. Moreover, even when the issue of the applicable law is sorted out, the task of identifying the scope of its exceptions to copyright still remains. Rather than starting down this highly complex path, I instead discuss the most common arguments that have been posed with regard to the legal status of sampling in relation to copyright exceptions, limiting my focus to the exceptions that are most relevant to sample-based music in the US and EU contexts.[14]

EU Law: The Quotation Exceptions
All countries that are part of the EU or the European Economic Area (EEA) must adhere to EU law. Some of the legal instruments set out by EU law—including copyright law as manifested in the InfoSoc Directive—are mandatory for the member states to implement into their national laws, whereas others are not. Article 5 of the InfoSoc Directive allows only two exceptions that might be relevant to the reuse of copyright protected material in art: quotations for purposes such as criticism or review" and "use for the purpose of caricature, parody or pastiche"—each of which requires several specific conditions.[15] This narrow scope was confirmed by the recent DSM Directive (2019) of EU law,[16] which Hui and Frédéric Döhl find surprising: "[The DSM-Directive represents a] missed chance to update EU laws for the digital age of retromania, remix culture, user-generated content, and social media, given that the InfoSoc-Directive limitations and exceptions are the result of a legislative process in the 1990s" (2021, 886). In what follows, I explain the legal conditions of this quotation exception and discuss its relevance to mashups before turning to the parody exception.

The quotation exception, as defined in the EU InfoSoc Directive, is limited to "quotations for purposes such as criticism or review, provided that they relate to a work or other subject-matter which has already been lawfully made available to the public, that, unless this turns out to be impossible, the source, including the author's name, is indicated, and that their use is in accordance with fair practice, and to the extent required by the specific purpose."[17] The sources sampled for mashups are lawfully made available to the public, and the requirement of attribution also seems to be fulfilled by most mashups (but not by all forms of music sampling), as explained in chapters 2 and 3. It is less clear how the requirement of being "in accordance with fair practice, and to the extent required by the specific purpose" might be interpreted in relation to mashups. First, the extent to which the phrase "such as" (in "purposes such as criticism or review") allows for purposes other than criticism or review is highly uncertain. As Hui and Döhl (2021, 871–873) point out, if one interprets it as allowing broader uses (including, for example, artistic expression), it would perhaps not be necessary to mention purposes as a necessary condition since it would potentially be all-inclusive. Second, if review and criticism are meant to be interpreted as the only uses, their respective scopes demand clarification; one might wonder whether art expressing an evaluative or critical stance toward the quoted material or using it to express criticism of some sort would be interpreted in a legal context as a use for the purpose of review or criticism, and furthermore, how much of the material would be justifiable to quote in terms of the requirements of the specific purpose.

The judgments of *Pelham GmbH and Others v. Ralf Hütter and Florian Schneider-Esleben* (2019) and *Spiegel Online GmbH v. Volker Beck* (2019) narrow the legal concept of quotation even further than the InfoSoc Directive by establishing that (1) the material must be quoted with the "intention of entering into dialogue" with the quoted work, which in turn requires the work to be identified;[18] and (2) that the quoted material "cannot be so extensive as to conflict with a normal exploitation of the work or another subject matter or prejudice unreasonably the legitimate interests of the rightsholder"—in short, the quoted material should not conflict with the quoted work.[19] As I argue below while discussing the legal parody concept, most mashup music appears to fulfill these two requirements, as it (1) clearly enters into a dialogue with its sampled tracks (after all, it is intended to be understood as a mashup of prior works) and (2) thus functions as a complement to rather than a substitute for those sampled tracks (it does not conflict with them).

However, Hui and Döhl are leery about the application of the EU concept of quotation to art, including music sampling.[20] As they see it, the review requirement "is less relevant to reuse [in the arts]" and that such "reuse for the purpose of criticism is already (at least partly) covered by parody and caricature under InfoSoc Art.5(3)(k)" (2021, 877). They furthermore interpret the concept of quotation as "using something significantly unaltered" (869), which would exclude the transformative reuse that characterizes most appropriations. They find this concerning:

> This is a challenge especially for contemporary music where deliberate appropriation is widespread for diverse important aesthetical, cultural, and social reasons. The new, post-*Pelham* copyright regime does not suit this musical present. Reusers in the arts, other than financially potent superstar artists and corporations that can afford a license, will have to adjust their artistic practices if parody, caricature, and pastiche, unmodified minor quotations and modifications to the point of unrecognisability will be all that is lawful. Such a new status quo would constitute a huge loss of cultural production, aesthetical diversity and social participation to creators in the countries which now lose their free use provisions.[21] (Hui and Döhl 2021, 886)

Still, there may be hope, given that so far, only one particular way of using samples has been evaluated in EU court and related to the legal quotation concept (the *Pelham* case). Here, German rapper Sabrina Setlur and her team had sampled a two-second sequence from the 1977 track "Metall für Metall" by pioneering electronic music group Kraftwerk in their song "Nur Mir" (1997). The sample was looped and not significantly modified. After a protracted legal process, the case was settled in CJEU with a successful claim, in which the court held that recognizable samples must be authorized, even when they are very short. The judgment, however, also states that recognizable samples of sound recordings *may* qualify as quotation:

> In particular, where the creator of a new musical work uses a sound sample taken from a phonogram which is recognisable to the ear in that new work, the use of that sample may, depending on the facts of the case, amount to a "quotation" . . . provided that that use has the intention of entering into dialogue with the work from which the sample was taken, within the meaning referred to in paragraph 71 above, and that the conditions set out in Article 5(3)(d) are satisfied. However, as the Advocate General stated in point 65 of his Opinion, there can be no such dialogue where it is not possible to identify the work concerned by the quotation

at issue . . . the concept of "quotations," referred to in that provision, does not extend to a situation in which it is not possible to identify the work concerned by the quotation in question.[22]

If recognizable (in the legal sense; see note 23) samples of sound recordings that enter into dialogue with the work from which they were taken may qualify as quotation, there is still hope for mashups.

Surprisingly, the court nevertheless concluded by dismissing the potential legality of virtually any form of sampling: "The phonogram producer's exclusive right under that provision to reproduce and distribute his or her phonogram allows him to prevent another person from taking a sound sample, even if very short, of his or her phonogram for the purposes of including that sample in another phonogram, unless that sample is included in the phonogram in a modified form unrecognizable to the ear."[23] This conclusion, that a sample can be used only if it is "in a modified form unrecognizable to the ear," seems to contradict the notion made in the same judgment that a sample can be considered a quotation, and that in order to do so it must enter into dialogue with the quoted work.[24]

Since the case was settled only recently, its ramifications for the future are still unclear. On the one hand, it may end up establishing that any recognizable samples are denied legality in the EU, given its emphasis on the harmonization of copyright exceptions among the EU member states.[25] On the other hand, this judgment that denies samples may only apply to future cases that are sufficiently similar to this case with regard to sampling, especially since it counterintuitively establishes that a sound sample may in fact be a "quotation" if it has the intention of entering into dialogue with the sampled work. What is considered to be sufficiently similar, including between the *Pelham* case and mashups, is for the EU and EU national courts to decide. Perhaps these courts will eventually come to understand that sampling is far from unitary in nature, in both disposition or form and in function or purpose, and that in several instances of sampling, including mashup sampling, the samples do indeed enter into dialogue with their sources.

EU Law: The Parody Exceptions

An alternative to relying on the legal quotation concept of EU law is to rely on its exception for the purpose of caricature, parody, or pastiche. The InfoSoc Directive does not provide a definition or any constraints for these concepts, though "parody" was clarified by the CJEU in its decision in the *Johan Deckmyn and Vrijheidsfonds VZW v. Helena Vanersteen and Others* (2014) case.[26] The CJEU judgment in *Deckmyn* established that a legal parody must have the following essential characteristics: it must "evoke an existing work, while being noticeably different from it," and it must "constitute an expression of humour or mockery."[27] Furthermore, the application of this exception must be sure to "strike a fair balance between, on the one hand, the interests and rights of the [author or copyright holder of the parodied work], and, on the other, the freedom of expression of the user of a protected work who is relying on the exception for parody,"[28] and "all the circumstances of the case must be taken into account."[29] In what follows, I first discuss the two main requirements of parody in EU law, then consider the legal requirement that it strike a fair balance between interests with regard to both economic exploitation and the interests and rights of the author or copyright holder.

The first requirement—that it must "evoke an existing work, while being noticeably different from it"—resonates with how parody is defined in the field of art (see chapter 2). In both contexts, parody sets out to evoke the original work on which it is based while also displaying a critical distance toward that work. It is an acknowledged appropriation in the sense that it is intended to be experienced on two levels at once—that is, as a new text but one that builds on a prior text. There is thus no confusion about the parody being either an independent original or a mere reproduction of the underlying work (since the concept of parody implies that the underlying work has been significantly transformed). This aspect of parody—the absence of this kind of confusion—is clearly evident in mashup music, especially in that the meaning of the mashup relies on the recognition of the work as a mashup. The A+B mashups explicitly evoke existing work in their use of durable samples from familiar recordings that are edited only subtly, but they are also clearly different from those sources because they significantly transform them by means of their new (musical, lyrical, and social) context and content (certain elements are taken away and others slightly altered). Mashups usually also signal that they are mashups and refer to their sources in their titles and in the information included below the videos. Megamix mashups too evoke existing works through their use of multiple, relatively short samples by keeping those samples long enough to be recognizable and by framing the mashups in a way that reveals the concept and construction behind them (including calling it a "megamix mashup" or "end of year mix," listing all the sources below the video, or adding a disclaimer stating that the track is recreational). Mashups thus seem to meet what legal scholar Sabine Jacques refers to as "the crux" of this requirement: "that the public must be aware they are not being exposed to the original work" (Jacques 2019, 106).

The second requirement—that is must "constitute an expression of humour or mockery"—is more ambiguous. The observation that parody may or may not be mockery, as indicated by the "or" in "humor or mockery," corresponds somewhat to the field of art's understanding of parody as multifunctional.[30] Still, while the CJEU definition limits parody's mockery alternatives to humor, the field of art extends its possibilities beyond both mockery/satire and humor to a broad range of functions, including biting or benign critical commentary (see chapters 2 and 4). As several legal scholars have pointed out, the CJEU judgment in fact fails to clarify what it means by humor, such as whether a parody must possess a humorous intent or produce a humorous effect.[31] If the wording in the judgment implies the former, it is also unclear how this would be measured and validated. If it implies the latter, it is unclear whose experience would be weighted. Would it be, for example, the experience of the relevant judge or an "average consumer," legal scholar Eleonora Rosati wonders (2015, 519). In either case, it would be a highly subjective and unpredictable assessment, complicated by the fact that any experience of humor depends on a wide range of factors, as discussed in chapter 4. Moreover, the lack of clarity concerning what kind of humor is required may lead to ambiguity and inconsistency in the interpretation of the concept. If, for example, humor were to be equated with laughter alone (scornful or otherwise), the parodist might reject their work's association with a humorous intent, having instead intended to evoke a broader spectrum of responses, such as that knowing smile when you are in on the joke or perhaps simply inward, unexpressed amusement. (As mentioned in chapters 2 and 4, this broad spectrum reflects, in fact, how humor is understood by humor scholars, especially when it is a result of the combination of expectancy violation and sense making.)[32] Jacques argues for a more generous understanding of humor in relation to the legal parody concept, one that ranges from "provoking laughter, being playful, paying tribute, to providing positive or negative criticism" (2019, 98–99). She mentions that in legal cases in Australia and Canada, equal weight is already given to humor as critical expression (37), and in several parody cases in France, humor has been interpreted especially broadly—sometimes critical commentary has weighed more heavily than humor,[33] and sometimes humor has been understood as emerging from incongruous juxtaposition and a playful subversion of expectation (although it has not been so broad as to be equated with reworking or transformation; 97–98).[34] Jacques also points out that in recent legal decisions, the humor requirement has primarily served as a supporting rather than a determining factor. She notes that judges tend to be mostly concerned with whether the use in question harms the original author of the work (99).[35]

If the aim is to shrink the gap between the definitions of parody in the fields of law and art, respectively, Jacques's observation is hopeful, since—as several parody scholars pointed out and some of the mashup interviewees confirmed[36]—parody in the field of art is not necessarily intended to be humorous. A liberal understanding of humor would allow for better correspondence between parody in the fields of law and art. Furthermore, mashups may then also be considered an expression of humor, since they generally endorse what humor scholars identify as the key triggers of humor: a combination of incongruity and sense making. Jacques seems to agree with these premises: "It is pertinent that 'humour' in music might not always take the form of traditional ridicule, but may take the form of playful or unexpected juxtapositions, or changes in rhythm or style which break traditional musical rules. Thus, it seems reasonable to presume that there is humour in at least some digital sampling, which derives from the combination of excerpts from earlier recordings which will surprise the audience listening to the sampler's track" (Jacques 2016, 6).

But even if a specific use meets these essential characteristics, it must furthermore strike a fair balance between the author or copyright holder's interests and rights and the freedom of expression of the user of a protected work.[37] Furthermore, "all the circumstances of the case must be taken into account,"[38] which makes the outcome of a particular case unpredictable. Among these additional qualifications, Jacques emphasizes that a parody must not conflict with the normal exploitation of the original work, and it must not harm the moral rights of the author. With regard to the first criterion, she argues that case law has established that what is at stake in the evaluation of exceptions is not so much the commercial nature of the parody but the questions of whether it seeks profit without fair remuneration to the copyright holder, or whether it has a detrimental effect on the economic market for the original—for example, by acting as a substitute for it (114–121). According to Jacques, a parody that generates profit, including by means of platform monetization, may be legally acceptable if it does not in some way replace the original or otherwise either threaten or harm its market (115). On the other hand, any use that gets a "free ride" from the original for the purpose of generating profit will probably not be defensible under a copyright exception (115).

As we saw earlier in this chapter, the interviewed and surveyed mashup producers emphasized that they did not seek profit from their mashups but, on the contrary, considered this an unfair treatment of the artists they sampled. Unlike plagiarism, parody does not narrow the market for the originals on which it is based, because it makes explicit that it is a parodic comment on those works—this absence of confusion also means an absence of competition. Amy Lai maintains that "parodies should be allowed as long as they do not defeat the purpose of the copyright system by harming the incentives of authors" (2019, 46). She further insists that when the work functions as a complement, not a substitution, it does not defeat the purpose of the copyright system. In line with this quality of parody, the mashup producers were always careful to acknowledge the sources of their mashups and saw their music as promoting those original works and potentially increasing their market instead of taking something away from them. This assumption is also supported by the research of Schuster, Mitchell, and Brown (2009), who found that sales of the sampled songs increased after a mashup album's release.

The second relevant criterion Jacques specified concerns moral rights, which are distinct from economic rights: whereas the latter provide the author with exclusive rights to make a copy, make the expression available to the public, and distribute copies of it, the former seek to protect the author's interests with respect to artistic reputation, honor, and dignity (in contrast to the economic rights, the moral rights cannot be transferred to others; Jacques 2019, 167–195). Jacques argues that while the relation between copyright exceptions and moral rights remains largely unexplored, moral rights may, especially in the EU context,[39] be considered additional conditions that the parody must meet (178). The following moral rights are most relevant to parodies: (1) the right of attribution (the paternity right), (2) the right against false attribution, and (3) the integrity right. The first concerns the acknowledgment of an author's claim to authorship (175).

In mashups, as well as parodies more generally, the authors of the original works are acknowledged in terms of both content (establishing recognition) and disclaimers (exposing the track/video as a mashup of prior sources and mentioning the sources in the titles and/or information below the video). In the same way, mashups safeguard the second right; it is very unlikely that the authors of the original works from which the mashups sample would be identified as the authors of the mashups themselves. There is, in other words, no confusion concerning attribution of authorship. As Jacques points out, the integrity right—that is, the requirement that the use in question does not harm the original author's honor or reputation—may appear difficult to reconcile with parody, given that the heart of parody lies in its playful distortion or transformation of prior works (184). Nevertheless, she is able to point to a French parody case (*Tarzoon* [1978]) in which the court held that as long as there was no confusion between the two works, the integrity of the author was not harmed (189).[40] In line with this, Jacques argues, "It seems unlikely that most parodies, even those which are 'near the knuckle,' will undermine the standing of the underlying work, or the original author, because any reasonable observer is aware of how parody operates. [Jacques's explanatory note: 'The parody evolves in a fantasy world separate from the original.'] There is no presumption, for example, that the author of that work has endorsed the parody or countenanced its message" (2019, 191). Of course, she admits, there are limits to this reasoning, for example, if the parody triggers associations with pornography or discrimination (193).

In the end, if the parody were not allowed to transform or comment on a work unless its author approved of the way in which it was done, then the parody exception would be redundant. Still, freedom of expression has its limits, and parody must therefore refrain from serving as an instrument of malevolence. Mashups can certainly present their sources in a manner that their authors and performers would not have endorsed, even though many of the producers expressed respect for those artists and viewed their perhaps transgressive mashups as a kind of playful homage. But distortion beyond the intentions and desires of the authors or performers is not the same as prejudice with regard to their honor, reputation, or dignity.[41] Although mashups, like any other parodies, can cause their audiences to experience the original works differently—perhaps even dismissively—the decisive factor is that they do not do so in the name of the authors or performers but rather as independent comments and interpretations. In this sense, of course, the integrity right is closely related to the rights of attribution and against false attribution.

Mashups appear to meet the criteria set out in relation to the parody exception as defined and treated in EU law, which appears hopeful for a successful defense along these lines if mashups were to be tested in court. Lai (2019) argues that a broad legal definition of parody properly balances the interests of rights holders and users, whereas a narrow definition is harmful to users' freedom of speech while also being unhelpful to those rights holders whose markets remain unharmed. Jacques, however, warns about conflating the parody exception with all forms of appropriation, since this might jeopardize the balance struck between rights holders and users' interests (2019, 18, 25). In an earlier article (2016), she argues that the EU exceptions of quotation and parody are unlikely to apply to most forms of digital sampling. Throughout the article, however, she treats sampling as a single thing instead of acknowledging that while it is one *technique*, it involves a plethora of applications, in terms of both disposition or form and function or purpose (as I demonstrated in chapter 2). This conflation of different sampling practices is symptomatic of much of the literature discussing sampling in relation to copyright law, and it characterizes the CJEU's final conclusion in the *Pelham* case as well. It also perpetuates the unfortunate gap between art and law. Sampling, however, has become the current generation's new language, which is obvious not only from sample-based music but also from the numerous audio-, audiovisual-, and visual remixes, memes, and gifs that flourish on the internet.[42] Consequently, legislators and judges should be encouraged to pay attention to the vocabulary of sampling. With respect to mashup music, I maintain that it should be regarded as a lawful parody (and potentially also a quotation) under EU law and also under the US fair use doctrine, as we shall see.

US Law: The Fair Use Doctrine
Article 107 of the US Copyright Act establishes that the fair use of a copyrighted work is not an infringement of copyright and lists four factors that should be considered when determining whether the use is fair: (1) the "purpose and character of the use" (that is, whether the purpose is nonprofit and noncommercial; whether the use involves criticism, commentary, teaching, and so forth; and whether the use is transformative); (2)

the "nature of the copyrighted work" (that is, whether the used work is published, and whether it is a work of "fiction or fantasy" or factual information [note 56]); (3) the "amount and substantiality of the portion used"; and (4) the "effect of the use upon the potential market for or value of the copyrighted work" (that is, whether it affects the existing or future market of the used work).[43] These four factors should be considered on a case-by-case basis and be balanced against one another. They represent guidance rather than absolute requirements or guarantees, and other factors relevant to the case may also be considered (Beebe 2020, 6–7). This means that a use that does not fulfill all the requirements can still be found to qualify, just as a use that does fulfill all the requirements can fail to qualify (Beebe 2008, 2020). Although the doctrine's openness allows for some flexibility in an ever-changing society, it has also been criticized by several scholars for making legal decisions unpredictable.[44] Happily, case law is clarifying the application of these factors, as well as guiding people as to how they should be weighed against one another; accordingly, as Barton Beebe (2008, 2020), Matthew Sag (2012), and Pamela Samuelson (2009), among others, have pointed out, the fair use doctrine is more coherent and predictable than is often assumed. I next discuss the four factors in relation to case law and academic interpretations, as well as to mashups.

Factor 1: The "Purpose and Character of the Use" In his empirical study of US fair use decisions, Beebe (2020) argues that the first fair use factor—the purpose and character of the use—is itself almost decisive for the court's ultimate determination. He therefore divides it into three subcriteria: (1) the transformativeness inquiry, (2) the commercial/noncommercial inquiry, and (3) the good or bad faith inquiry.[45]

The first subcriterion, transformativeness, has been a key issue in legal fair use cases in recent decades (Beebe 2020; Netanel 2011) and has also been at the core of scholarly arguments about the scope of fair use.[46] In an influential article from 1990, Judge Pierre N. Leval argued that the transformativeness of a work should weigh heaviest in a fair use analysis and encouraged courts to make it so:

> I believe the answer to the question of justification turns primarily on whether, and to what extent, the challenged use is *transformative*. The use must be productive and must employ the quoted matter in a different manner or for a different purpose from the original. A quotation of copyrighted material that merely repackages or republishes the original is unlikely to pass the test; in Justice Story's

words,[47] it would merely "supersede the objects" of the original. If, on the other hand, the secondary use adds value to the original—if the quoted matter is used as raw material, transformed in the creation of new information, new aesthetics, new insights and understandings—this is the very type of activity that the fair use doctrine intends to protect for the enrichment of society. (Leval 1990, 1111; italics in original)

This emphasis on transformativeness is later reflected in several fair use cases, including *Feist Publications, Inc. v. Rural Telephone Service Co.* (1991), *Castle Rock Entertainment v. Carol Publishing Group* (1998), and *Campbell v. Acuff-Rose Music* (1994).[48] The opinion in *Campbell* states that "the goal of copyright, to promote science and the arts, is generally furthered by the creation of transformative works," and that "the central purpose of this investigation is to see, in Justice Story's words, whether the new work merely 'supersede[s] the objects' of the original creation . . . or instead adds something new, with a further purpose or different character, altering the first with new expression, meaning, or message. It asks, in other words, whether and to what extent the new work is 'transformative.'"[49] Beebe (2020) finds that of the seventy-eight core legal opinions after *Campbell* that found transformativeness, fair use was supported in all but three of them.[50] Throughout the previous chapters, I have demonstrated the various ways in which mashups are transformative in terms of textual content and meaning. Mashups always alter the tracks by filtering out certain elements, modifying others, and changing their musical and social context. Though the portions taken can be substantial and the alterations can be (apparently) subtle, they are never verbatim copies of the original.

Also related to the "purpose" factor is parody, which has long been established by case law as a legitimate fair use purpose. Beebe (2020) refers to parody as a subset of fair use. He found that of the twenty-six cases that the court explicitly defined as parody, all but three were determined to be fair use (he adds that the last time a legally defined parody failed to be considered fair use in US court was in 1988). Whereas parody had in previous cases been defined quite broadly, the 1994 *Campbell* case set a new precedent for defining parody: as "the use of some elements of a prior author's composition to create a new one that, at least in part, comments on that author's works."[51] As such, "a parody needs to mimic an original to make its point, and so has some claim to use the creation of its victim's (or collective victims') imagination."[52] This definition is quite similar to that of EU law, in the sense that the parody has to evoke a work while remaining different from it, but the *Campbell* definition, in contrast to the EU *Deckmyn* case, does not limit the comment requirement to one expressing humor or mockery. According to these criteria, there should be no doubt that mashups qualify as parody, and Beebe (2020) observes that although transformative uses nearly always qualify as fair uses, parodies, more than transformative works more generally, "are especially privileged under factor one and the overall four-factor fair use analysis," which should be good news for mashups.

The second subcriterion of the first fair use factor (the purpose and character of the use) concerns whether the use is commercial in nature, so that, as stated by case law,[53] an affirmative answer to this question would be harder to defend than a negative one. This notion was nuanced by the *Campbell* case, which held that the commercial factor is not necessarily determinative and may weigh less if the use is transformative.[54] Relatedly, in the *Blanch v. Koons* (2006) case, the appropriator, Jeff Koons, made a substantial profit from his use, but it was still found to qualify as fair.[55] While acknowledging that the issue of commerciality is often invoked in courts' fair use analyses, Beebe points out that several commentators and courts (including the US Supreme Court in *Campbell*) have been dismissive of this inquiry "primarily on the ground that nearly all expression in our culture is produced for profit or is otherwise income-producing in some sense" (2008, 602–603). Regardless of the weight given to this subcriterion, mashups generally do not bring in any income, except in the sense that some of the producers also work as DJs and a few maintain separate crowdfunding sites (such as Patreon), either of which might earn income. Law professor Rebecca Tushnet argues that since freely shared remixes do not participate in the "money economy" but are instead created with no hope of monetary compensation, they should have a "special fair use treatment" (Tushnet 2010, 3).

The third subcriterion of the first fair use factor is what Beebe calls the "bad faith inquiry," and it refers to issues such as fairness, propriety, and an equitable rule of reason. According to Beebe's empirical analysis of US fair use court cases, this subfactor has not played a significant role in comparison to the other factors, except in cases where the court explicitly found that the use was undertaken in bad faith (2008, 607–608; 2020). Mashups would likely not be recognized as such.

Factor 2: The "Nature of the Copyrighted Work" The second factor of the fair use doctrine—the nature of the copyrighted work—concerns whether the given use copies from a published or unpublished work and whether it is a creative work "of fiction or fantasy" or a "factual" work.[56] According to Beebe's empirical analysis, this factor has a minimal effect on the overall fair use test. It consists of two subcriteria, the first of which was clarified in *Harper & Row v. Nation* (1985), which held simply that "the scope of fair use is narrower with respect to unpublished works."[57] The second was clarified in *Campbell*, which explained that creative works of "fiction or fantasy" are "closer to the core of intended copyright protection than others, with the consequence that fair use is more difficult to establish when the former works are copied."[58] Still, several uses of the former (which I understand to mean cultural expressions) have been considered fair.[59] While mashups indeed do sample from creative works, then, this second fair use factor does not pose much of a challenge because mashup sources are almost always published.

Factor 3: The "Amount and Substantiality of the Portion Used" The third factor—the amount and substantiality of the source—concerns how much of the copyrighted work is used. When more is used, a fair use defense is less likely. This could mean trouble for mashups, which usually use quite robust samples; even their shorter samples are "substantial" in that they are typically the "heart" of the tracks that contain them. Yet the amount or substantiality of the source portion used is often considered in relation to the requirements of the new work's purpose, and this has also been established by US case law, which has allowed for the use of a considerable amount of copyrighted material based on this reasoning.[60] This inclination to accept relatively substantial use of the source work when the first factor is fulfilled is also confirmed by Beebe's systematic analysis of US case law, which shows several instances of uses involving the copying of entire works that have been determined to be fair, as well as several instances of uses of the heart of the plaintiff's work (2008, 615–616; 2020).[61] As long as the parody is recognized as such, the amount can be justified as necessary for its purpose, which by nature requires some level of copying. As Jacques points out, if too little is used, the parody may fail to evoke the original in question, and if too much is used, it may fail to be recognized as a parody and instead be confused with the original (2019, 102).

Factor 4: The "Effect of the Use upon the Potential Market for or Value of the Copyrighted Work" The fourth factor—the effect of the use upon the potential market for or value of the copyrighted work—is, according to Beebe (2020), the most emphasized factor after the first one. This is an economically oriented factor whose impact is strongly informed by the other three factors (Beebe 2020). For example, the *Sony Corp. of America v. Universal City Studios, Inc.* (1984) case established that commercial use is likely to harm the potential future market of the original work.[62] This conclusion was later referred to in *Campbell*, which also considered its relation to the first fair use factor by clarifying that "no 'presumption' or inference of market harm that might find support in *Sony* is applicable to a case involving something beyond mere duplication for commercial purposes."[63] It thus established that a transformative use is not thought to harm the potential market of the original since it functions as a complement and not a substitution: "[When] the second use is transformative, market substitution is at least less certain, and market harm may not be so readily inferred. Indeed, as to parody pure and simple, it is more likely that the new work will not affect the market for the original in a way cognizable under this factor, that is, by acting as a substitute for it ('supersed[ing] [its] objects'). . . . This is so because the parody and the original usually serve different market functions."[64] The case also clarified that what is relevant is not whether the use is commercial per se or whether it might harm the market for its source due to "the very effectiveness of its critical commentary"; what matters is only "the harm of market substitution."[65] The opinion furthermore stated that although the potential market also encompasses that which could be developed by the original work through licensing, the unlikelihood that the use would be granted such license—the most likely scenario for mashups—disassociates the use from the notion of a potential licensing market.[66] Few mashups are commercial, and they do not make direct inroads on the current or potential market of the original works because they function as complements rather than substitutes. Given their exposure of their sources—in terms of content, disclaimers, and accreditation—they are more likely to increase and expand the original works' market than to harm it.[67]

As the four-factor analysis of mashups demonstrated, it would appear that they should be readily defensible under fair use. Yet as Patricia Aufderheide and Peter Jaszi emphasize in their thorough study of fair use, it is not copyright law that hinders appropriative creativity but rather a misunderstanding of the scope and meaning of the US fair use doctrine (2018, xi). In order to rectify such confusions, they compress the fair use factors into a test consisting of two questions: (1) Was the use of copyrighted material for a different purpose from the original? (2) Was the amount of material taken appropriate to the purpose of the use? (25). They continue: "If the answer to these basic questions is yes, then a court these days—if ever asked—would likely find a use fair. . . . [J]udges and juries have overwhelmingly rejected claims of infringement and supported fair users when they carefully employed this reasoning to make their decisions. This is hardly surprising, given the long history of the fair-use doctrine and its strong constitutional roots" (25). Mashups definitely pass this test. Aufderheide and Jaszi seem to agree, noting that remix and mashup artists on YouTube often believe they are infringing copyright even though most of them are simply exercising their fair use rights without realizing it (20). They further argue that the recombination of copyrighted material to create something new is fair use, and that remixes and mashups have been identified as such in the Code of Best Practice in Fair Use for Online Video (169).

Yet researchers have also remarked on the fact that music sampling seems to represent a notable exception to an otherwise positive trend regarding fair use defenses.[68] And it remains true that only one out of the total of three cases in US courts concerning musical sampling, or, more precisely, the use of a sound recording section, were considered fair use. The first relevant case, *Grand Upright Music, Ltd. v. Warner Bros. Records Inc.*, was settled in 1991 in US district court.[69] Grand Upright Music Limited filed a copyright infringement suit against Biz Markie for having sampled a sequence with the piano riff from the British songwriter Gilbert O'Sullivan's song "Alone Again (Naturally)" from 1972 and using it in his 1991 track with the same name, "Alone Again." Judge Kevin Thomas Duffy famously started his opinion with the biblical admonition, "Thou shalt not steal," before claiming that Biz Markie was liable for theft. The artist was ordered to pay $250,000 in damages and to pull the album from the market (Wang 2013). Fair use was not taken into consideration. The second case, *Bridgeport Music, Inc. v. Dimension Films*, was settled fourteen years later (2005), this time in a court of appeals.[70] The hip-hop group N.W.A. sampled a two-second guitar-riff (consisting of three tones) from Funkadelic's "Get Off Your Ass and Jam" and looped it throughout much of their 1991 track, "100 Miles and Runnin." Funkadelic's lawsuit was directed toward Dimension Films, which had used N.W.A.'s song in a film. The court of appeals concluded as follows: "Get a license or do not sample."[71] This case established that no de minimis exception would apply to sound recordings; even a small part of a sound recording represents something of value.[72] This ruling contradicted many hip-hop producers' and music lawyers' understandings of copyright law, and McLeod and DiCola cite the music lawyer Dina LaPolt's rueful admission in this regard: "I would advise my clients before *Bridgeport* if they used a little snippet of a recording that was de minimis, 'That's fine; we don't have to clear it.' . . . But now I can't say that anymore" (McLeod and DiCola 2011, 142). Fair use was not considered in this case either.

The only successful defense in a sampling case settled in US court is *VMG Salsoul v. Ciccone* (2016). The Salsoul Orchestra filed a copyright infringement suit against Madonna and others for having sampled a 0.23 second (that is, a quarter of a second long) segment of horns from their "Ooh, I Love It (Love Break)" from 1983 and using it in her 1990 track "Vogue." In contrast to *Bridgeport*, the court held that this use was in fact de minimis—that is, they believed that a general audience would not recognize the brief snippet in "Vogue" as originating from "Love Break," so the use did not constitute infringement.[73] This was, however, a district court decision (that is, a lower court ruling) and thus set no legal precedent. There have been several court cases concerning music infringement more generally, including the recent successful fair use defense involving the hip-hop artist Drake,[74] but these have concerned the use of a musical work and not a recording specifically; for example, Drake was sued for using the musical work and not the sound recording, for which he had obtained a license.[75]

Notably, the two sampling cases that resulted in successful claims of infringement involved hip-hop music, and both uses were remarkably dissimilar to the way mashups work. As such, there remains cause for optimism regarding mashups' potential fair use defense. But since there are currently no precedent cases for mashup music or for sample-based parodies more generally, the situation remains unpredictable.

The Legality of Mashups

The reasons for mashup producers' belief that their mashups could be defended as fair use, parody, or another exception, or that their use of copyrighted samples is otherwise justifiable, were as follows: (1) the mashup is transformative and thus counts as new work and not piracy (or consuming another's music without paying for it); (2) the sources are made explicit, thus making the use distinct from plagiarism (or stealing other's work and pretending that it is your own); (3) it is noncommercial and generates no direct income for the producer; (4) the producer always credits the originators; and (5) the mashup does not take either profit or integrity away from the mashed artists (because it does not replace the original music) but rather serves to promote them. As demonstrated, there is much correlation between mashup producers' practice and sampling ethics and the requirements of the most relevant exceptions of EU and US law. Still, one cannot leap from this acknowledgment to the conclusion that mashups are legal or most likely so. Although I believe that mashups have a strong defense, their legality remains untested territory, and there is no clear-cut answer to this question in the letters of the law or in legal judgments, given that legal evaluations of exceptions are case specific and based on nuanced analysis in which various features are taken into account. The most accurate answer to the question of whether mashups are legal is that copyright law is complex and the outcome of exception evaluation is highly unpredictable. Mashups thus reside in the contested area of copyright law that is often referred to as the legal gray area.[76]

It is critical that the gray area is not simply assumed to be illegal; the alternative may be just as true. If one eliminates all uses that have not been tested in court as unqualified for defense under copyright exceptions, the intended purpose of those exceptions is lost, as they would no longer serve to balance copyright holders' interests in and rights to intellectual property with the right to freedom of expression. They would instead function only as instruments for fostering certain segments of cultural diversity. Appropriation is historically, culturally, politically, and aesthetically significant. Appropriation is also at the heart of democracy in terms of the cultural participation, dialogue, and critical thinking it involves, and it is thus rooted in the fundamental right of freedom of expression. As Jacques points out, if copyright is applied either too restrictively or too broadly, it will lose its justification (2019, 158). In contrast to scholars who argue for major copyright reform,[77] I believe a more feasible and fruitful avenue for change would be as follows:

- To clarify and modify the general understanding of copyright exceptions to make it both more predictable and more inclusive with regard to acknowledged appropriation without diluting those exceptions;[78]

- To acknowledge that sampling is not one thing in terms of its disposition/form and function/purpose but instead a broad and multifunctional artistic field.

With respect to one's interpretation of the exceptions and one's understanding of sampling, I believe that the benefit of the use in question should be weighed against its disadvantages and that mashups arguably have a good case.[79] Since mashup music does not feed on others' music in a cannibalistic way, I do not find it to harm the original artists economically or in terms of integrity. Instead, it offers a complement: an alternative interpretation that both prolongs and pluralizes the original musical experience.

The efficacy of copyright exceptions depends, of course, on users' inclination to rely on them, and this can be improved with a clearer conception and consensus regarding the scope of the exceptions. However, the efficiency and meaning of the exceptions also depends on users' *ability* to rely on them, which, as I explain in the next chapter, is not a given.

Mashup Producers as Thieves and Copyright Activists?

Society has often framed the act of using nonlicensed samples as stealing. The most cited example is probably the first US court judgment against sampling (*Grand Upright*), in which sampling artist Big Markie received a reprimand for theft ("Thou shalt not steal").[80] The concept of stealing, of course, indicates not only that something is unlawful but also that it is unethical and damaging to those who are being stolen from. Such assumptions are quite common, though they do not reflect how mashup artists regard their own practice. David Sanjek writes, "Samplers should apply for the appropriate licenses, respect the rights of copyright holders, and be respected in turn as equal creators" (1992, 621). He thus represents the common view that sampling feels disingenuous with regard to the artists who are being sampled in the sense that the sampling artists help themselves to musical material into which others have already put so much work, time, and money. As demonstrated, mashup producers do not agree with this position. Taking into consideration the mashup producers' ethical guidelines, emphasis on licensing hurdles, and conviction that their unauthorized use is either legal or otherwise justifiable, I argue that mashup sampling does not fit into the narrative that has often been associated with sampling artists: they are not dismissive of other hard-working artists' efforts and rights to acknowledgment, and their practices cannot be equated with selfish erosion or subversive stealing. Such assumptions fail to recognize the important differences between, on the one hand, acknowledged appropriation and illegal file sharing, and, on the other hand, acknowledged appropriation and plagiarism. Whereas illegal file sharing is about acquiring and sharing complete files for the purpose of consumption, acknowledged appropriation takes a piece of a file and transforms it to make an artistic commentary. And whereas plagiarism feeds on others' music in a cannibalistic way, acknowledged appropriation offers an addendum of sorts. Moreover, the assumption that sampling is stealing takes for granted that any act of sampling is illegal, a conclusion that is highly uncertain, as we have seen.

Somewhat surprising, the framing of sampling as stealing, as Judge Duffy proclaimed, has been perpetuated by the mashup artists themselves. One of the most vital mashup organizations, Bootie Mashup, fronts itself with the skull and crossbones, and its name, recalling the many "bootie" mashup club nights around the world, indicates not only that these artists initially called their music "bootlegs" but also that the activity might well be illegal.[81] Whereas John Shiga (2007, 95) relates this branding to Dick Hebdige's (1979) notion of the "self-consciously subversive bricolage" of British youth cultures in the 1970s, it can also be seen as a tactic that simply responds to an imposed identity. According to Adriana A, the reason the scene perpetuates the skull and crossbones logo is because the music is banned from the internet and remains largely an underground phenomenon: "I mean, even though sonically there's nothing all that underground about it—it's, like, 'okay, yeah, I got it; I know what a mashup is'—you can't just, like, go on iTunes, or go on Spotify, or go on Pandora or any other platform, and just easily find mashups. . . . And then at other platforms like YouTube, where it's mostly user-generated content, mashup gets [attention]—sometimes there'll be stuff that lasts, and then sometimes it gets pulled down for copyright issues. So, there's still this—there's a skull and crossbones in the Bootie logo for a reason." More than indicating something the producers believe is wrong, then, the skull and crossbones may simply symbolize their endorsement of what others believe is wrong. As to whether mashups are copyright infringement, Adriana A responded, "I mean, I kinda have to say, 'no, I don't believe that.' Otherwise, my entire career has been horrible, right? . . . I mean, what kind of horrible person *steals* music from other people? I believe in fair use. And I believe that all art is derivative in some form or another. And as long as one isn't, like, really profiting off the backs of other people's work, I think that mashups for the most part should fall under the category of fair use or parody. Especially if, you know, you're not selling these in stores. You know, most mashup producers make the track and put it online, and they're not, like, really making money off of it." As Aufderheide, Tijana Milosevic, and Bryan Bello, among others, have pointed out, the music industry discourse that frames sampling as stealing often leads toward cultural practices self-identifying as illegal or piratical even when they are not (2015, 2016).

The metaphorical language of "stealing," "theft," "piracy," and "killing" has been used in a landslide of campaigns against free file sharing. For example, there have been several "Respect Copyright" campaigns within the sectors of music and film that have framed unauthorized use as a criminal act, such as the "Piracy. It's a Crime." label featured on numerous DVDs internationally from 2004 to 2007. This campaign, developed by the Motion Picture Association in collaboration with the Federation against Copyright Theft and the Intellectual Property Office of Singapore, began with the admonition, "You wouldn't steal a car," then depicted a man committing various kinds of theft, including the unauthorized copying and distribution of films. "Who Makes Movies" was another Motion Picture Association campaign of the early 2000s that featured footage of movie industry workers describing how piracy had affected them personally. The music industry has conducted similar campaigns, including the British Phonographic Industry's 1980s Home Taping Is Killing Music campaign, which featured the image of an audio cassette, crossbones, and "And It's Illegal." In 2007, the Norwegian branch of the International Federation of the Phonographic Industry launched a similar international campaign, Piracy Kills Music, that also featured a skull with eyes made out of headphones and a nose made out of a mini-jack cable. The backdrop of the latter campaign was the threat that the industry faced at the turn of the century when websites such as Napster started to offer free downloading of music via peer-to-peer sharing of MP3 audio files.[82] Putting an end to the piracy of file sharing is, of course, not the same as putting an end to the transformative and often parodic use of unauthorized samples, but the distinction can be lost on the public. As such, several scholars point out that this metaphorical language shapes public perception and policy decisions in a dramatic way.[83] Everyone knows that stealing a car is wrong, and if sampling is like stealing a car, then it is wrong too.

Part of the confusion of illegal file sharing with sampling activity is that mashups have been used in relatively high-profile virtual demonstrations to front the case for free file-sharing, including, most notably, the Grey Tuesday campaign in 2004 organized by the nonprofit activist organization Downhill Battle. As mentioned in chapter 1, this digital protest involved the *Grey Album* (2004), a mashup album by Danger Mouse, which Capitol Records required to be removed from the internet. Downhill Battle took up the case by encouraging websites to make the album available as a free download, which enabled its digital distribution to continue despite the injunction of Capitol Records. As Sam Howard-Spink (2005) points out, Downhill Battle capitalized on the *Grey Album*'s mainstream attention and then consolidated its political relevance by making it an occasion to protest the copyright regime's stifling of musical innovation and endorse file sharing. Howard-Spink therefore persists in describing mashups as "political statements," and in a way they are, but primarily because they have been framed as such by others. Ellis Jones (2021b) points out that while several early mashup scholarship of the mid- to late 2000s frames mashups as a disruption of cultural power (and specifically as a "battle of ICT's [Information and Communications Technology] liberatory potential versus music industries' property hoarding"), the producers themselves were "rarely at the frontline of digital activism in the mid-2000s"—that is, they were not "the emergent techno-dilettantes that online and then mainstream media coverage tended to present them as." Referring to early mashup scholar Philip A. Gunderson (2004), who describes Burton as a "cultural prophet" who promotes "the unrestricted sharing of digital copies without originals," Paul Harkins and I (2012) point out that Burton himself did not express any allegiance to file sharing (see also chapter 1).

Some scholars, including Owen Gallagher, see the remix as a political act: "an anti-establishment statement that defies the law and challenges the exclusive rights of copyright holders" (Gallagher 2018, 5). While this may be the perspective of several remix artists, we did not find this position to be common among mashup producers; the interviewees instead simply saw either copyright law or copyright enforcement as unfortunately ignorant of the difference between plagiarism or piracy and appropriation. The freedom to create and distribute remix appropriations is more specific, and responds to a different argument, than the freedom to borrow or take someone else's music. This conviction was also behind several producers' belief that their mashups would be defensible via fair use doctrine or other copyright exceptions. As Aufderheide and Jaszi point out, the difference between a belief in free use and a belief in fair use was somewhat obscured in the early 2000s, thanks to scholars and activists (including John Perry Barlow, Lawrence Lessig, and Siva Vaidhyanathan) who presented free use, or a parallel system such as the Creative Commons, as the only feasible pathway for remixes, rather than pointing to fair use as a possible solution to safeguarding the thriving of remix culture (2018, 53–56). Aufderheide and Jaszi warn that such polarized activism, which has propelled the view of appropriating artists as pirates and anarchists, may have the opposite of its intended effect, in the sense that artists who are most likely exercising their right to fair use start to believe that they are acting illegally (70–71), which might in turn lead to self-regulation. The authors regard the current situation as more hopeful than that, however, thanks to the contribution of several scholars and interest groups to the creation of codes of best practices for fair use; to users who exercise these rights respectfully; and to a juridical shift toward more nuanced fair use analysis with more attention to transformativeness (74–75, 80).

Because the producers generally believed that their mashups could be defended under fair use, their impression that their music is treated unfairly informs their argument less against copyright law than against copyright regulation—that is, against the copyright holders' (in most cases, the record labels) enactment of copyright law, including via the online distribution platforms. Most of the producers, including Poolboy, did not express a resistance to the law but lamented instead that the law is often abused: "Copyright law should protect when what somebody is doing with another person's art is preventing that person's art from taking off, or it's in some way damaging that person's art. Mashups don't do that. . . . So, I think that copyright, when it comes to that, is just being abused. It's just being abused by the labels and stuff. . . . We can't do anything to fight the copyright law, so they can just abuse it all they want." But, of course, whereas most of the mashup producers did not regard themselves as activists, their continuous practice of distributing their music can be interpreted as, if not intentional disobedience, at least a subtle act of activism against appropriation restrictions, including what many of them perceived as commercially motivated restrictions enforced in the name of the copyright law.

6   How Platform Moderation Affects Mashup Producers

> I think maybe 70 percent of my YouTube videos were removed. . . . So at some point you just kind of lose a little bit of the motivation. . . . There's always this gamble—it's like, "I hope it's not gonna be taken down," because you've spent hours producing something, putting all of your heart and mind into it, and then it's taken down. It's quite frustrating. Especially when it's taken down by the algorithm, you know, automatically, where [the platforms] just run it and they take it down. Which is painful.
> —DJ Faroff (personal interview)

In 2011, Kembrew McLeod and Peter DiCola wrote: "What is also interesting about mash-ups is that—with a few notable exceptions—their creators have not incurred the legal wrath of copyright holders. They are largely tolerated or ignored by the mainstream music industry, and since the turn of the millennium thousands of individuals have posted and shared their mashups without consequence" (2011, 176). The experiences of the interviewed and surveyed mashup producers suggest that if this were once the case, it is certainly not so any longer. Of the survey respondents, 87 percent reported that their mashups had been blocked or taken down from a platform due to copyright infringement claims, and 57 percent indicated that their mashup accounts on various platforms had been terminated for the same reason. McLeod and DiCola's quotation might reflect a certain faith in the democratic promise of the internet that was prevalent at their time of writing, but it is also a testament to the fact that the policies of these platforms regarding copyright-related content moderation have changed dramatically over the past decade. They did, however, anticipate the development of copyright moderation: "Still, the media gatekeepers of the future might use audio fingerprinting to help copyright holders sniff out samples in songs and enforce their copyrights, perhaps too aggressively. New technology and fear of litigation could combine to lead music distributors to require the licensing of *all* samples—regardless of fair use, the *de minimis* doctrine, and other legal limits on copyrights. This would exacerbate the current inefficiencies of the sample clearance system" (2011, 185). This development, and its implications for mashup producers, is the focus of this chapter.

Several scholars have already addressed the current tension between remix and content moderation, but as Tarleton Gillespie and colleagues also pointed out, we need more thorough study of the impact of content moderation on specific user groups (Gillespie et al. 2020). By examining the impact of platforms' content moderation on mashup creativity, I hope that this chapter will contribute toward this end and complement other scholarly studies on the effects of copyright restrictions on creativity. I also hope that the empirical findings I present here will provide insight into how notice and takedown systems, and the content moderation that extends them, operate in practice.[1] By "platforms," I am specifically referring to online services hosting user-generated content (such as YouTube, SoundCloud, and Facebook), and by "content moderation," I am referring to copyright-related moderation in particular and not to any broader implications (including, for example, the moderation of hate speech, racism, terrorism, or child pornography).

This chapter consists of four parts. The first part discusses the transition that took place during the decades up to and after the turn of the new millennium, when the prospects for the music industry's ability to control its copyrighted content went from weakened to significantly strengthened and, conversely, when sample-based music lost much of its promise as an art form. This transition happened in two successive phases, the first of which involved a tension between hip-hop artists and copyright holders, and the second of which involved a tension between mashup producers (and other remix and sample-based artists) and platforms' content moderation. The second part delves deeper into the development of current content moderation systems and addresses some concerns about their design and use in the context of sample-based music (as well as their potential benefits). The third part discusses mashup producers' experiences with content moderation, including its effect on their distribution choices, the ways in which they make mashups, and their overall motivation to create this music. I conclude by addressing the pending fate of mashups and the puppeteers who design and decide that fate.

From a Thriving to a Threatened Remix Culture

The act of sampling has gone from thriving to threatened, then back to thriving, and then, once again, to threatened. The copyright regime has followed a directly inverse (and obviously related) path in relation to sampling. In what follows, I describe music sampling's checkered history and successive threats.

Hip-Hop versus Copyright Holders

The first bloom of sampling activity is associated with the hip-hop scene's "golden era" between 1987 and 1992, when it was common practice to use potentially hundreds of samples on any given album. For example, Public Enemy's production team, the Bomb Squad, embraced a dense form of sampling in which they constructed the music out of multiple brief snippets from other music recordings, as well as other sounds such as speeches or sirens. During the 1980s, copyright had not been an issue, but as hip-hop gained commercial success, it started to attract attention from copyright holders, resulting in litigation warnings and lawsuits.[2] In 1991, the first US judgment against sampling took place in a US district court after Grand Upright Music Limited filed a copyright infringement suit against rapper Biz Markie for having sampled a sequence from O'Sullivan's song "Alone Again (Naturally)" (1972) in "Alone Again" (1991) (*"Grand Upright"*).[3] (This was the court case mentioned in chapter 5, in which Judge Duffy started his opinion with "Thou shalt not steal.") The case had huge ramifications in terms of spurring an already increasing tendency among copyright holders to file lawsuits against music sampling while also encouraging a pro-licensing orientation among hip-hop artists.

During the 1990s, the sampling activity of the hip-hop music scene markedly decreased, and the strictures imposed by copyright holders, which made it economically unviable for most hip-hop artists to sample other recordings legitimately, forced a fundamental aesthetic change. Some hip-hop producers started to recreate the samples in question by hiring musicians to mimic or replay (interpolate) the sequence—a measure that required royalties to go to the copyright holders of the songs but not of the recordings—or to make something new sound like a sample. Others obscured their samples to avoid ready recognition by playing them backward, chopping them up and rearranging them, layering them with other sounds, changing their tempo or pitch, or distorting their sound. Still others started to sample lesser-known recordings or recordings with less resourced copyright holders. Aside from certain exceptions involving producers signed to major labels who could sample from the affiliated label's catalog, most hip-hop producers changed their sampling practices as described or stopped using samples altogether.[4] Copyright enforcement clearly did not suffocate hip-hop music as such, but it did restrain one of its once-fundamental components: sampling, or, more specifically, what Siva Vaidhyanathan (2003, 143) would call "signifying samples" (samples that refer to prior recordings). As such, hip-hop changed its shape, as indicated by De La Soul's Trugoy: "I think for me personally hip-hop lost a little bit of its feel because of it. You know, when you can't sample, I think it definitely loses a big part of what hip-hop is" (quoted in McLeod and DiCola 2011, 191). Whereas optimism concerning the prospects for sample-based music fell during the 1990s, it would revive at the start of the new millennium with the emergence of an interactive internet and the accompanying remix culture.

Remix versus Content Moderation
After having barely overcome the threat of infringement accompanying sample-based music, the music industry faced another threat at the turn of the century when websites such as Napster started to offer free (and unlawful) downloading of music via the peer-to-peer sharing of MP3 audio files. Peer-to-peer file sharing certainly made it easier for sampling artists to acquire music to sample, but sampling's second bloom first and foremost took place in the context of the internet platforms hosting user-generated content.

Whereas the first phase of the internet was server centered and featured mostly static websites, its second stage—the so-called Web 2.0—was characterized by dynamic websites and increased user participation, including the ability of the public to upload content and provide feedback or participate in conversations in comment sections. Such platforms hosting user-generated content included Myspace (2003), Facebook (2004), Vimeo

(2004), YouTube (2005), Twitter (2006), and SoundCloud (2007). With the emergence of these platforms, a new generation of consumers was promptly framed by scholars as embracing its new technological prowess to appropriate and combine the cultural texts surrounding it into ever-proliferating remixes.[5] For many scholars, journalists, and artists and consumers in the early 2000s, the buzzword of "participatory culture" was grounded in a euphoric belief that Web 2.0 was a communal and collaborative space free of commercial market constraints, copyright control, and other traditional gatekeepers (Dijck 2013; Gillespie 2018). One of the reasons for this impression was that the platforms' initial strategy of reliance on self-regulation and community-supported surveillance of activity fell short as the number of users and amount of uploaded content exploded. This tremendous growth gave the impression of cyberspace being a free-for-all.

In the same vein, with regard to music that depended on unlicensed sampling, the internet was celebrated as a means of bypassing the gatekeepers of the music industry, allowing producers to develop a new digital take on the enduring practice of musical recycling. The changed strategy for music sampling was striking: contrary to the hip-hop producers, who had resigned themselves to using obscure and very short samples or no samples at all, the mashup producers, whose music now started to circulate on the internet, sought out durable and only subtly edited samples from highly recognizable popular mainstream recordings. However, the initial image of Web 2.0 as egalitarian and unregulated would soon start to show cracks as it became evident that its platforms were not unaffected by commercial interests and that uploaded content was not safe from being regulated and controlled. The explosion in users and uploaded content pushed several platform providers to seek alliances with other corporations, including agreements with major copyright holders and rights enforcement organizations (REOs). Some were also acquired by commercial firms; for example, YouTube, founded in 2005, was acquired by Google in 2006, and Myspace, founded in 2003, was acquired by News Corporation in 2005. The platforms generally shifted from primarily hosting amateur content to including more professional content, and from being an ad-free environment to relying on advertisements linked to content, after which they split the revenue with the copyright holders of that content (Dijck 2013; Kim 2012). In line with this trajectory of development and under economic and legal pressure from media corporations,[6] several platforms started to implement more substantial content moderation measures in order to prevent copyright-infringing content from circulating, including measures that relied on the automated identification and handling of content.

Prior to the installment of content moderation, the large-scale infringement taking place on these platforms, such as the reposting of unaltered and entire commercial tracks, had led to significant declines in revenue for copyright holders and, by extension, songwriters and artists, among others (Urban and Quilter 2006; U.S. Copyright Office 2020). This indicates that copyright infringement is in fact a huge problem that should not be taken lightly. Algorithmic content-identification technology remedies this situation, particularly given that manual human moderation is ineffective, unprofitable, and slow. Nevertheless, in addition to removing content that unmistakably infringes, it also demonstrably removes content that is *not* infringing, as well as content whose legality is not clear-cut—that is, content that resides in the gray area of copyright law (which is created by its limitations and exceptions; see Urban, Karaganis, and Schofield 2016). As an example of gray-area material, mashup music has been afflicted by platforms' blockings and takedowns. As such, sampling is once again threatened, this time not only by copyright holders' enforcement of copyright restrictions but also by the actual workings of platform moderation. While the source of this threat also carries some hope for the future of sample-based music in terms of its potential to offer a more efficient way to license samples (more on this below), this potential does not contribute to safeguarding the viability of copyright exceptions. Before turning to the impact of platform content moderation on mashup producers, I provide a more detailed description of its development and discuss the challenges that arise for these systems when they seek to accommodate copyright exceptions. I also point to the potential of content moderation for streamlining licensing procedures, though this is a less than complete solution.

Pros and Cons of Content Moderation for Sampling

As a result of the rapid growth of the internet and thus also digital piracy, concern arose regarding the liability of internet platforms in terms of their hosting of infringing third-party content (content uploaded by others). In 1998, after a series of law cases and the adoption of the WIPO Internet Treaties,[7] the US Digital Millennium Copyright Act (DMCA)[8] implemented a "safe harbor" for online service providers (OSPs)—that is, an immunity from liability under certain conditions. These conditions include that the OSP "does not have actual knowledge that the material . . . is infringing" and "is not aware of facts or circumstances from which infringing activity is apparent."[9] Upon obtaining any such knowledge or awareness—for example, receipt of a valid notice from a copyright holder—the platform must "act expeditiously to remove, or disable access to, the material."[10] The DMCA is thus often referred to as a "notice and takedown system" (Wu 2008, 623) and as a compromise between copyright holders and platform providers with regard to copyright infringement (Urban et al. 2016, 1). The DMCA also creates a legal incentive for OSPs to take reasonable steps to notify the alleged infringer upon removal of the content and to forward a valid counternotice from the alleged infringer to the claimant.[11] A similar regime protecting platforms from secondary liability (which assumes legal responsibility for the actions of another party) was implemented in the European Union's e-Commerce Directive (ECD) in 2000.[12] Importantly, within both the DMCA (US) and the ECD (EU), the responsibility for identifying infringing content is placed upon the copyright holder, not the platform.

As a consequence of the adaptation of these safe harbor provisions, platforms implemented notice and takedown systems using the DMCA or ECD as a framework. But the DMCA and ECD were, of course, designed for the internet's quieter phase. With the dramatic growth of Web 2.0, including the emergence of social media platforms and other platforms hosting an enormous amount of user-generated content, copyright holders found it exceedingly challenging to monitor content to detect infringement and therefore insisted that the platforms take a more active role in moderating content than that required by the DMCA and ECD.[13] This evolving tension between platforms and copyright holders was particularly pressing in the United States, since most of the major content-sharing platforms (including Facebook, Myspace, Twitter, Vimeo, and YouTube) and many major media corporations (including Sony Music, Universal Music Group, Viacom, and Warner Music Group)—copyright holders on an enormous scale—were based there and used the US Copyright Act as their governing law. This situation received public attention in 2007 via the billion-dollar lawsuit between Viacom—a major American media conglomerate—and Google-owned YouTube (*Viacom International Inc. v. YouTube, Inc.*).[14] Viacom sued YouTube for being liable for the infringement of thousands of

Viacom's copyrighted works, to which YouTube responded that it had met the DMCA's "safe harbor" requirement to implement a notice and takedown regime. Viacom asserted that YouTube did not qualify for the statutory safe harbor provision since it, among other things, "had 'actual knowledge' and were 'aware of facts and circumstances from which infringing activity [was] apparent,' but failed to 'act[] expeditiously' to stop it."[15] A district court ruled in favor of the defendant, deciding that YouTube qualified for the DMCA's safe harbor and that a general knowledge, as opposed to knowledge of specific cases, did not impose on YouTube the responsibility to monitor infringements.[16]

In the early 2000s, several major copyright holders and their REO agents started to use software "bots" to spot infringing use of their or their representatives' content, resulting in several platforms receiving takedown notices on a massive scale (Urban et al. 2016, 31).[17] As a consequence, these platforms implemented automated measures that allowed them to handle copyright notices more efficiently. Several platforms also implemented another system that was parallel to the takedown and notice system involving algorithmic content-identification technology designed to manage large-scale copyright infringement (and thus mitigate legal threats).[18] So although the legal regimes of DMCA and ECD placed the onus to identify infringement on copyright holders and not platforms, the platforms developed tools to do this as well in order to avoid being sued by the copyright holders (and perhaps also to benefit from them economically in other ways). This technology is now in common use at platforms hosting user-generated content even though it goes beyond the statutory requirements of the DMCA and ECD.[19] For example, the major music and video platforms hosting user-generated content (including Facebook, SoundCloud, Vimeo, and YouTube) all rely on algorithmic content-identification technology.[20]

Content-identification technology works by scanning the platforms' abundant content for matches to reference files supplied to the platforms by the copyright holders. If a match between this data set and the uploaded content is found, the detected content will next be treated according to the relevant copyright holder's request. For example, YouTube's Content ID (the name of its content moderation system) works as follows: if the technology detects content that matches the digital fingerprints[21] of any of the platforms' reference files provided by the copyright holders, the video gets a Content ID claim. It will next be handled according to a default moderation rule set by the relevant copyright holder, including either allowing or denying access to the content. YouTube's help page explains these two alternatives in more detail: "Copyright owners can set Content ID to block uploads that match a copyrighted work they own the rights to. They can also allow the claimed content to remain on YouTube with ads. In such cases the advertising revenue goes to the copyright owners of the claimed content" (Google n.d.-c). The latter option of monetizing the content has been endorsed by some stakeholders for "creat[ing] an entirely new revenue stream for the music industry by allowing rightsholders, if they wish, to leave fan videos up and earn revenue from them" (Michael Petricone from the Consumer Technology Association, as quoted in U.S. Copyright Office 2020, 23). Copyright holders can also choose to track the content's viewership statistics, potentially for promotional purposes.[22] Several smaller copyright holders, however, are not eligible for YouTube's Content ID (or similar content moderation systems at other platforms); access to Content ID requires an agreement involving certain eligibility criteria, including that the copyright holders "own exclusive rights to a substantial body of original material that is frequently uploaded by the YouTube creator community" (Google n.d.-a; n.d.-f).

While YouTube's Content ID system may lead to blocking, content can also be removed (instead of just blocked) if a copyright holder submits a valid legal takedown request based on assumed infringement of their content. Note that these are two parallel systems: one (the takedown system) required by law and the other (the algorithm-based detection system) a semivoluntary initiative of the platforms. If the platform receives a valid takedown request from a copyright holder (the takedown system), it will give the uploader a so-called strike on their account; after three strikes on the same account, that account is closed and its content removed (Google n.d.-b).[23] YouTube, like other hosting platforms, also offers an option for the targeted user to submit a formal counternotice in response to a takedown or copyright takedown strike, as well as an option to contest a claim of the platform's detection measures (in this case, Content ID; Google n.d.-g, Google n.d.-b; more on this below).

The implementation of such extensive content-moderation systems does not jibe with these platforms' early image of a willing participant in a hands-off, noncommercial environment that promoted liberating and inclusive user participation. Instead, it clearly reflects the interdependence of platforms and copyright holders, or, as Stuart Cunningham, David Craig, and Jon Silver put it, the "increased interpenetration of very different, often clashing industry cultures" (Cunningham et al. 2016). From the copyright holders' perspective, agreements with platforms, including access to tools that allow them to block material without submitting formal notices, have improved their control over their content. Moreover, platforms providing monetization as an option (such as Facebook, SoundCloud, and YouTube) have also improved the copyright holders' compensation situation.[24] From the platforms' perspective, their agreements with copyright holders and their implementation of automatic content moderation have, in the context of YouTube being sued by Viacom, forestalled costly litigation from copyright holders for hosting infringing content as well as ensured legal distribution of commercial content that has become central to their ongoing viability. Moreover, it is in the platforms' interest to remain attractive distribution choices for all kinds of artists, which encourages their initiatives to ensure that artists receive compensation for the use of their copyrighted content.

Clearly, copyright-related content moderation has significant advantages but also significant limitations.[25] I do not discuss these in general but rather focus on the pros and cons for sample-based music in particular. First, I unpack the reasons that content moderation presents an existential threat to sample-based music by pointing out that its procedural steps do not guarantee adequate accommodation of copyright exceptions and that it also often eliminates the gray area of copyright. Next, I show how content moderation nevertheless offers some hope for that same music in terms of providing for more efficient licensing procedures (though it does not solve the issues related to copyright exceptions and gray-area content).

Content Moderation's Insufficient Accommodation of Copyright Exceptions

Empirical investigations suggest that numerous blocks and takedowns have occurred in cases that are questionable in terms of the underlying claim's enforceability in court.[26] For example, one of the most comprehensive studies of the accuracy of takedowns, conducted by Jennifer M. Urban and colleagues, found that nearly a third of the takedown requests sent to the platform by a copyright holder (or their agent) were of questionable validity, including targeted content that did not match the identified infringed content at all and content with characteristics weighed favorably toward fair use (2016, 2, 11–12).[27] The number of questionable takedowns of content with the potential for a fair use defense would be even higher if content blocked by measures beyond formal copyright takedowns were counted (such as content blocked by YouTube's Content ID), especially if one included gray area material as well.[28]

Much creative content falls within the gray area of copyright in which its legality is not clear-cut, thanks to copyright's exceptions and limitations. As Tim Wu points out, given its legal uncertainty, such content can, on the one hand, be described as "tolerated use"[29] or "mass infringement," and, on the other hand, as "fully legal exploitation of the fair use doctrine" (Wu 2008, 621). The problem with the latter description is that one cannot know for sure whether this really is the case, since "the contours of fair use for causal infringement has not been and may never be well mapped out" (621). This notion also applies to other copyright exceptions beyond the fair use doctrine of the US Copyright Act, which is the jurisdiction to which Wu refers. Yet the fact that content residing in this gray area (including mashups) potentially qualifies for protection under copyright law's exceptions makes platforms' frequent removal of it problematic.

The main reason for faulty blockings and takedowns is the automated nature of the identification of infringing content by both platforms and copyright holders and the automated nature of the submission and handling of takedown notices, as well as the handling of platforms' content-identification matches according to default rules set by the relevant copyright holder. Given the complex nature of fair use and other copyright exceptions, automated detection and decision making are ill suited to dealing with content that potentially qualifies for such defenses. Although some minor copyright holders and smaller platforms rely on the human review and handling of content and complaints, the major ones rely primarily on automated measures.[30] Several copyright holders and platform providers have stressed that automation is critical to coping with the massive scale of infringement and notices.[31] Within this automated environment, human review is largely sacrificed. Yet most of the copyright holders and platform providers that were interviewed and surveyed by Urban and colleagues (2016)[32] described various safeguards to limit mistakes, including supplementing the automated systems with periodic manual human review of detected content.[33] Some copyright holders also explained that they limited automatic searches to title or artist matching to avoid detecting mashups and parodies, for example, or used manual review for borderline cases, such as fan work (34–35), and some platform providers explained that they also ask copyright holders to evaluate potential fair use or other exceptions before submitting a notice (43). Still, the copyright holders and platform providers alike admitted that most decisions happen without human intervention and that mistakes are therefore inevitable, including complaints about content that would obviously qualify for fair use (40). Moreover, the high number of questionable takedowns suggests that current safeguards to avoid this are insufficient.

To remedy potential wrongful blockings and takedowns, most platforms also offer users the option of contesting such decisions. YouTube states, "Automated systems like Content ID can't decide fair use because it's a subjective, case-by-case decision that only courts can make. While we can't decide on fair use or mediate copyright disputes, fair use can still exist on YouTube. If you believe that your video falls under fair use, you can defend your position through the Content ID dispute process. This decision shouldn't be taken lightly" (Google n.d.-d). In the case of YouTube, a dispute of a Content ID claim is followed by the claimant copyright holder's reconsideration of whether the claim should be released or upheld. The user can appeal the latter outcome as well, but it remains the copyright holder's decision in the end. Several scholars have found this procedure to be problematic; since the dispute or appeal is considered not by an independent apparatus but by the claimant (usually a private corporation), there is no guarantee that the decision is unbiased or legally enforceable.[34] At any time, the copyright holder can bypass this process and submit a formal copyright takedown request to remove the video in question, which also results in a copyright strike on the user's account (Google n.d.-g). Users may thus choose not to contest a Content ID claim for fear of accumulating strikes that could lead to the termination of their accounts, or they may be intimidated by the possibility of being subjected to a copyright infringement suit (as we will see below, this scenario reflects the thinking of several of the interviewees for this study).

Disputing a copyright takedown request requires the user to submit a formal counternotice, a different process from Content ID, and is anchored in the DMCA Directive. A counternotice is, like a Content ID complaint, handled by the claimant copyright holder but with the potential outcomes being to either restore the content or file a lawsuit. Although counternotices are meant to restore content that is legitimately claimed to having been faultily removed, empirical research suggests that this option is rarely used (Seng 2014; Urban and Quilter 2006; Urban et al. 2016; and U.S. Copyright Office 2020). Out of the many platform providers that Urban and colleagues interviewed and surveyed, only one of them reported receiving more than a handful of counternotices per year (Urban et al. 2016, 44). An obvious reason for this low rate of counternotice is the situation's various chilling effects, especially when it comes to content that potentially qualifies for a fair use defense or other copyright exception.[35] Aufderheide and colleagues have done extensive empirical studies indicating that many users do not understand their right to utilize, or claim protection under, copyright law's exceptions.[36] This lack of awareness derives not simply from a lack of effort but also from the crippling conviction that any form of unauthorized use is an instance of infringement—a conviction largely inculcated by corporations' legal threats and litigations, as well as their rhetoric framing unauthorized use as "piracy" and "stealing" (see the discussion in the previous chapter). Aufderheide adds, "Even when they are familiar enough with fair use to employ it in remix, when they are challenged with a takedown notice, most makers do not challenge with a counter-takedown after seeing a forbidding legal notice that makes them wonder if they were right" (2015, 271). Urban and colleagues similarly report that the platform providers they interviewed and surveyed regarded the counternotice procedure as limited in practice with regard to protecting the targeted users, since users often had little knowledge of copyright law and feared the risk of copyright liability or liability for misrepresentation; they also added that the language in a formal notice was "really threatening" (2016, 44–45).

In the end, the inclusion or exclusion of a user's content on a platform is in the hands of the relevant copyright holders and platform. While platforms have an interest in including material for commercial reasons as well as to sustain their user group and reputation for being democratic, the risk of being sued by copyright holders for failing to remove infringing material is, according to several platform providers, decisive in their handling of disputes between users and copyright holders (Urban et al. 2016). Yet there are also several examples of platforms strongly opposing copyright holders' handling of content and working hard to find solutions that would benefit users.[37] One such solution is monetization, to which I turn next.

Platforms' Novel Form of Licensing

Several of the platforms' content moderation systems allow for a new and more effective licensing model through the option of monetizing content (Hui 2021a, 2021b). As discussed in the previous chapter, the lack of an efficient licensing model has always been an obstacle to sample-based music (McLeod and DiCola 2011; Vaidhyanathan 2003). Contrary to traditional licensing, through which permission is granted prior to distribution, licensing via monetization happens after distribution. More precisely, such a licensing system relies on an already struck agreement between the copyright holder and the platform—one that is tailored to allow for case-specific or collective license (tolerated use) and case-specific or collective revocable license (rejection via blocking or takedown) of content. If the use is tolerated, a potential share of the revenue from ads or subscriptions functions in practice as licensing royalties. As Alan Hui (2017, 164) points out, monetization can be understood as a form of so-called collective licensing, one that relies not on the negotiation between users and copyright holders but instead on an agreement between copyright holders and platforms.[38]

The benefit of monetization is that it removes several of the licensing hurdles discussed in the previous chapter. For example, in place of a transaction cost (the fee that the user must pay for permission to use), the copyright holder shares the revenue of the use with the platform (Hui 2017; Wu 2008). It also solves the problem of drawn-out procedures that, together with the barrier of transaction cost, can make licensing an unfeasible option. More important, monetization might mean that more of the content residing in the gray area of copyright would be tolerated by platforms (although it provides no such guarantee). Wu (2008, 632–633) points out that the type of ex post licensing system that monetization represents is valuable when the volume of harmless infringement or gray-area instances is large and the value for licensing the usage is low (that is, when a conventional licensing would probably not bring with it considerable revenue).[39] This is because the potential alternatives would be that licensing is not realized due to the low revenue value, or that the uncertain legality of the content hinders users from creating, and distributers from distributing, the content. Hui adds that monetization, which encourages tolerated use, can further create a "feedback loop to fair use": "Tolerated uses establish over time what is a 'reasonable and customary' use, which the US Supreme Court recognized is likely to be fair use" (Hui 2017, 197).[40]

Recently renewed agreements between copyright holders and platforms that arrived after several years of negotiation and litigation have secured for copyright holders a larger percentage of the advertisement and subscription revenues from monetized content. This presumably increases their incentive to allow sample-based content to stay up rather than blocking or removing it even when the samples are not authorized; that is, the economic revenue gained from monetizing it may be greater than the gains from denying its availability on a platform.[41] According to Google, more than 90 percent of all Content ID claims result in monetization rather than blocking or takedown (Google 2018, 14). While this rate indicates an improved situation for sampling artists, that remaining 10 percent translates to a considerable amount of content that is not being monetized, given the total number of Content ID claims. And it also remains the case that several sampling artists refer to blocking and takedown as an everyday experience, and one that has had significant impact on their practice.

Copyright holders' willingness to monetize unauthorized remixed content is, moreover, unpredictable at best. As long as platforms do not use extensive "staydown" filters, copyright holders have few other options, as the alternative is that the blocked or taken-down content is reuploaded on the same or an alternative platform (the so-called whack-a-mole problem).[42] If such a staydown option were to become widespread, the scenario could play out differently. Some have understood various forms of staydown options as being encouraged by the Digital Single Market (DSM) Directive adopted by the European Parliament in 2019, in which its article 17 removes the limited liability of platforms operating in the EU for hosting infringing content (more on this directive and its potential implications in the next chapter).[43] For example, Hui (2021a) argues that this new directive forces platforms operating in the EU to either strike licensing agreements or remove copyright-infringing content and ensure that it is not reuploaded. There is, in other words, no option for ignoring content without monetizing it. On the one hand, then, copyright holders' incentives to block or take down instead of tolerating and monetizing may be stronger, given that stricter control mitigates the risk that the content is subsequently reuploaded. On the other hand, the revenue that copyright holders earn from monetizing mashups and remixes can be a substantial part of their total platform compensation, which incentivizes them to allow such content to stay up. This ambiguity makes copyright holders' future moves in terms of monetization and takedowns highly unpredictable. And even if they were to trend toward licensing mashups and other sample-based music via agreements and monetization, the situation would still have significant downsides, including the fact that not all platforms offer monetization, and even at those that do, it is currently not available to all copyright holders (who are instead limited to submitting copyright takedown requests).[44]

Although monetization suggests some cause for optimism regarding the prospects for getting samples more efficiently licensed, it is not a sufficient solution for content that potentially qualifies for fair use or other exceptions. First, monetization undermines the purpose of copyright exceptions. That is, copyright holders still have the power to determine the public's level of access to this content, whereas copyright exceptions are designed to be outside of copyright holders' control. As Rebecca Tushnet (2014) points out, if the content moderation systems that platforms use allow for transformative uses to exist only at the mercy of copyright holders, platforms may impinge on artists' freedom of expression since copyright holders could remove content that criticizes their work or that they otherwise find unacceptable. Second, the copyright holder of a sample used in a work may end up earning revenue from it even if the use qualifies for an exception or qualifies for copyright itself. While this is something that mashup producers seem to accept, copyright holders have no legal rights to exploit copyrightable elements or content that qualifies for exceptions (Tushnet 2014, 1461). Third, involuntary monetization—which is what these instances are because it happens without the consent of the one who has made the content—is, as Tushnet points out, problematic due to the fact that it may harm cultural expressions that flourish outside the commercial market and are not made for material gain as such (Tushnet 2008). Owen Gallagher, a remix creator himself as well as a scholar, adds that remixers may not wish their work to realize any material gain and may thus feel marginalized or dismissed by this arrangement (2018, 205). Even if monetization can (at best) mitigate the existential threat that mashups and other sample-based expressions currently face, that is, the problem persists; content moderation in practice often overrides copyright exceptions.

Mashup Producers' Experience with Blockings and Takedowns

So how does the development of platforms' content moderation systems affect the mashup producers? Among the ninety-two mashup producers surveyed for this study, 96 percent of them reported that their mashups had been identified by platforms as using copyrighted material. Upon this detection, 82 percent had experienced blockings or takedowns, and 53 percent had had a mashup account permanently terminated. Among the thirty interviewed mashup producers, blockings, takedowns, and account deletions were also described as an everyday experience. In fact, only a handful of the producers said that they had not had an issue with content moderation, whereas most of them described it as detrimental to their mashup activity. I first report on the producers' various views of the monetization of their mashups, then turn to their descriptions of their negative experiences with content moderation more generally. Finally, I present their perspectives on the roles of both copyright holders and platforms with respect to platforms' content moderation.[45]

The Producers' Experiences with Monetization

About one in six of the interviewed producers said that they had not had that much trouble with blockings and takedowns.[46] Some said that most of their mashups had been spotted by the platforms' content identification technology but remained up. DJ Schmolli pointed to monetization as a common reason for this tolerated use: "Most of the time there's not a problem because it gets monetized for the original right holders." The number of mashups currently available on platforms may indicate a widespread practice of tolerated (if monetized) use and/or that the platforms' content identification technology misses a lot of content.[47]

Most of the interviewed producers, including DJ Schmolli, raised no objections to copyright holders' monetizing their mashups: "I have no problem at all that the original artist earns money with their songs I used in my mashups. That's absolutely fair and good enough."[48] BringMeTheMashup agreed: "I'm 100 percent okay with copyright ID, when it comes to saying you put an ad on the video, and then the artist and the label gets a quantity off those ads. I think that's perfectly fine." Isosine admitted, albeit reluctantly—probably due to the mashup scene's code of honor about not seeking any revenue from mashups (see chapter 5)—that he thought it would be fairer if the mashup producer were to receive a small percentage of the revenue as well:

> I think fair would be that, if you were making a transformative derivative work of a copyrighted piece, that it should be non-commercial. But is that fair? I don't know actually. Because some mashups take quite a lot of work [to produce], and

so obviously there's a lot of hours of labor involved. But it might involve a copyrighted sample so I don't know how that would be—like, how you would've come up with a fair system like that. Because if you make it non-commercial then none of this work is monetizable [for the mashup producer]. But that sucks, because a lot of work goes into making these, and people should be paid for their editing. . . . But I do not know what would be fair. There are so many problems with that question for me.

Still, although the current situation is more in line with a 0/100 percent revenue split, the producers preferred to go without compensation rather than continue to fear that a mashup, or their whole mashup account, could be taken down at any time. Kap Slap said: "The main thing is, like, being able to do something like that, and get it out there for people to listen to. . . . I don't care about the money. Are you kidding me? Take all my money from the mashups and the mixes." Adriana A agreed and called for the system of monetization to be the default rather than one option among several: "I wish I could not have to worry every time we post a mashup to YouTube that it might get taken down. And with all the new [monetizing] systems in place, I as a producer don't really make any money, but the artists still get their money. I would even be okay with that. But nobody wants to deal with that legal headache, I don't think." As indicated by these two last quotes, while a handful of the interviewed producers were not overly concerned about content moderation, most of them found the experience of having their mashups frequently blocked or taken down, and the uncertainty as to whether and when this would happen, to be detrimental to their motivation to make and distribute mashups.

Frustration and Resignation Caused by Blockings and Takedowns
When asked whether he had ever experienced a takedown or a termination of a mashup account, Isosine answered: "Yeah, so many mashups have been blocked . . . it kinda sucks. 'Cause they were quite big videos, so I'm a little bit sad about that." BringMeTheMashup had a similar experience: "I've had two YouTube channels shut down for copyright. At least five SoundCloud channels shut down. Vimeo shut down. And then Facebook has taken down videos. Instagram has taken down videos." DJ Faroff (quoted in the chapter's epigraph) guessed that around 70 percent of his mashups had been taken down, and DJ Surda reported that half of his mashups had been banned worldwide. Most of the other producers interviewed for this study gave descriptions like the four mentioned here.

Adriana A recalled aspects of the way in which the mashup scene shifted from benefiting from platform distribution to being threatened by it: when producers began posting mashups online, individuals as well as dedicated mashup websites started to receive cease-and-desist letters. With the emergence of platforms hosting user-generated content, SoundCloud was a popular distribution platform among mashup producers until it increased its content moderation: "SoundCloud was great for a while! And then it stopped being great, and people's accounts started getting deleted like crazy," said Adriana A. Many of the producers said the same thing about SoundCloud, and the survey data showed that it had many more "former users" than "current users." When SoundCloud increased its content moderation, producers moved on to other platforms, including Facebook, Hearthis, Twitter, Vimeo, and YouTube, but met with the same fate. Adriana A lamented: "You post your mashups to Facebook, and then next thing you know your account is blocked. You can't get in, because some record company or publisher sent a nasty letter. You know, same thing with YouTube. So, there's literally almost no safe platform for mashups in 2019 [the year of the interview]."

Given that there remain several instances of tolerated use, producers do continue to upload content on major hosting platforms such as Facebook, SoundCloud, Twitter, and YouTube to try to reach a large audience. But the fear that their mashups or accounts may suddenly disappear stays with them always: "I wish I would not have to worry every time we post a mashup to YouTube that it might get taken down. . . . People get the music out there, but you literally always run a risk no matter where you put it," said Adriana A. Whereas a takedown sometimes happens during an upload but before the mashup is published, other times it may happen later. Once a mashup has been successfully uploaded, there is no telling when or whether a blocking, strike, or takedown may happen, even months or years later, which is partly thanks to the ongoing possibility of an update to either the platforms' databases or the algorithms of content-identification technology. This fraught situation has had a profound impact on producers' motivation to distribute or even create mashups.

One reason that the mashup producers were frustrated that content moderation sometimes prevented them from sharing their mashups publicly was that there are no other outlets for them. In fact, 56 percent of the surveyed producers indicated that content moderation had made them less motivated to produce mashups, and this lack of motivation was also reflected in the interviews. CFLO recalled his reaction to a specific takedown:

> I was sad, because I put two or three months' worth of work—yeah, it was insane, it was insane. And I had, like, it was getting on its way to going viral, like, naturally, organically. And it was going up, and then it was gone. And only I could log in and see it, but no one else could. Because, like, my account still could, and then eventually it was just gone on my account—I couldn't even [access it]. And then my whole account was gone. And I had paid for the yearly subscription. So, I was like a pro user paying a hundred dollars a year, and my account was gone. And it just turned me off to the whole . . . I was like, "Yo, if you guys aren't gonna support me, why would I wanna direct views to your website," you know.

Kap Slap similarly explained that content moderation has made him truly frustrated and unmotivated: "The downside is the industry prevents me being able to do what I'm best at in the world. And make money from that. Or get that out to people. . . . So, the time and effort that goes into making something cool like that, it's not worth it anymore to do. Because if I spend a couple of days on that one mashup, making it really cool, who's gonna see it? Where would I put it? No one can see that. . . . That work is going completely unrecognized, and therefore, where is the motivation for me to do it?"

DJ Poulpi pointed out that when takedowns are done retroactively, the links that the mashup may have received from other channels, websites, or media coverage become defunct, and all the work of promotion on the mashup is wasted. When mashups are taken down, producers also lose any related comments, likes, and play numbers, which are quite important to them. But most detrimental of all was the loss of subscribers and other followers. BringMeTheMashup, who had had two YouTube accounts terminated, insisted that his current YouTube account would have been a lot bigger if not for his past. He recalled, "All those followers were gone. Because I had two strikes at one point, I made a backup channel at that point. So, I was like, 'Hey, I have a secondary channel just in case this one goes down. Go here.' And maybe like 5 to 10 percent ended up doing it. So, when the channel got shut down, most of those followers were completely gone. Almost fifty thousand people completely gone." As Poolboy pointed out, it takes a lot to attract users to a platform they are not otherwise part of, meaning that they may not care enough to follow a producer there. According to DJ Schmolli, it can take years to build up the same number of followers as before an account was terminated. Kap Slap had an experience like Bring-MeTheMashup: "Man, [the takedown] has been my battle—the bane of my existence ever since the beginning. . . . So, for the first three years of my mashup career, if not more than that, I got like five million plays, a million downloads, fifty thousand followers. It got deleted outright. Just because of mashup copyright infringement. . . . So, I had to start fresh. Completely from scratch." Having to begin again, over and over, and build up a new base of subscribers and followers can clearly be a frustrating experience.

CFLO believed that the mashup community had been diluted because of content moderation. Adriana A, who has a broad mashup network thanks to the Bootie website and clubs that she co-organizes, agreed: "There are a few people in our community who are like, 'Screw this! Fuck it! I'm retiring. I can't deal with it anymore.' And like, 'What's the point of making mashups if every time I post it to Facebook, to YouTube, to SoundCloud, it gets taken down?' You know, so it's very frustrating. It has definitely had an effect on the community." Such resignation was also reflected in the survey, in which 9 percent reported that they had stopped making mashups because their music had been taken down by platforms or they were too concerned about infringing on content. Among the interviewees, almost a third said that they had more or less stopped producing mashups or stopped distributing them on platforms because of content moderation.[49] NodaMixMusic explained that his frustration and fatigue over takedown issues, and the associated threat and risks had led him to produce non-sample-based music instead of mashups. Colatron and DJ Schmolli said that they had already started to grow tired of making mashups and that the lack of outlets and hassles with takedowns pushed them all the way to retirement. Colatron explained: "There was nowhere to have this outlet, and there was a sense of, well, everything I've done for ten years is just gone overnight. So, okay, let's call it a day. Plus, to be fair, I was just—it was becoming more of a hassle to actually do it, you know. I wasn't enjoying it as much as I had been." To others, including DJ Poulpi, content moderation was the primary reason for giving up: "YouTube tends to block a lot of my tracks. And I used to have a SoundCloud account; it got closed after too many copyright claims. I used to have a hearthis.at account; it got closed because of too many copyright claims. It's one of the reasons why I've been doing fewer and fewer mashups. At some point a few years ago, I stopped making mashups completely. And one of the main reasons was these copyright problems."

Several of those who had not stopped producing them, including CFLO, had nevertheless stopped distributing them on platforms:

> Now when I make a mashup, I don't even put it on SoundCloud. Because if I put it on SoundCloud, I get another strike, then all my views go away. I mean, it's all just screwed up now—there's no real outlet. And, like, you can't put it on Spotify, because it's not an original production. . . . There's no avenue to get it on Apple Music. . . . So I make 'em, but I don't put them out anywhere. If I do, I give them directly to other DJs, but I don't put them where, like, you could find it. And that's only because I risk losing my account. Not that I'm worried about any legal repercussions. . . . The ones that I know, everyone sort of stopped. I know guys who still make them, but, yeah, no one posts them. . . . And I feel like it's sad that these algorithms have limited the platforms and have discouraged access to the artists.

DJ Faroff and DJ Prince were also among those who explained that while they still make mashups for their own pleasure, they have stopped distributing them on hosting platforms. DJ Prince said that it can be extremely tough to lose one's mashup, together with all its comments and followers, and DJ Faroff similarly described the experience as "a little bit of a heartbreak." Isosine believed that such demotivating experiences will hinder newcomers from making mashups as well: "I can imagine for, you know, someone that's starting out, or really just wants to do this for fun, but then their friends can't view their mashups because they're taken down. Yeah, that totally sucks. It makes you feel like, 'should you even do this anymore?' Which is, I don't know—that totally sucks. Because most people just do it for fun. And I don't see the harm in doing it." If some artists have stopped producing mashups or at least stopped posting them, others have developed various ways of bypassing algorithmic and manual detections, as we will see below.

Content Moderation's Impact on Distribution

The interviewees noted that content moderation had significantly affected their distribution choices, and this was also reflected in the survey, in which 81 percent of respondents said that content moderation had "to a great extent" or "somewhat" affected where they distributed their mashups. One way of dealing with the fear or hassle associated with content moderation, they explained, is to turn to private mashup forums. Some producers had also built their own platforms using a customized SoundCloud clone script (that is, a third-party, ready-made clone script of SoundCloud) to create a safe space for themselves. One of the founders of this tailored Sound-Cloud clone (who wished to remain anonymous) explained the motivation behind it:

> It came about because a lot of mashup producers were sick of the constant takedowns and account deletions. . . . It was made by the mashup community for the mashup community. But because the community is diverse, and many of us make other types of music, we haven't branded the site as just a mashup site. Our users are mostly mashuppers but we welcome all types of music, remixes, originals, and DJ mixes. We've never had the goal of being the next SoundCloud—we just want a small corner of the internet to do our thing in peace, legally. . . . We're coming up on three years of [this platform's existence] and haven't removed music for copyright infringement in that time.

This platform obviously does not use content moderation, which makes it safer for the producers to host their mashups there, although the platform itself is vulnerable to termination, which is why I am not using its name. In fact, it was initially terminated but survived when its administrators changed its server and domain name to a Canadian option (because they assumed that Canadian law would then apply and believed that this copyright law was more permissive than UK or US law). Whereas several of the producers seemed grateful to have such a "free space," most of them also lamented that posting mashups at the site limits the exposure of their mashups to their mashup peers. Although this website is open to all and despite public invitations to the site, it does not have a large audience, and its content does not show up on a Google search; instead, it is kept underground. The same applies to the private mashup forums. To some, including DJ Surda, "safety is better than popularity because if it's taken down it's no use anyway." To others, the public exposure of the mashup matters more than its safety, and they therefore continue to host their mashups on big media sites such as YouTube. Unlike platforms with a smaller user base, the play counts, likes, and followers grow organically on such major platforms via the sharing of links and algorithmic structuring of content according to search keywords and similarities among tracks.

Kap Slap expressed a common view that instead of relying exclusively on traditional outlets such as the major hosting platforms, producers have to self-maintain, in the sense of finding creative ways to distribute their mashups. In addition to mashup forums and a customized platform, some producers have turned to alternatives such as satellite radio, podcasts, and personal websites; one even said that he played his mashups during video game live streaming. Such alternative outlets, of course, are less exposed to content moderation, but they are also less exposed to potential audiences. Some producers have decided to play their mashups only at clubs and festivals due to the hassle and fear associated with content moderation.[50] While this provides them with an audience, it is a very local one, and it also allows only for music, not for video (at least in the traditional club setting).

Others persist in the risky venture of posting on the major platforms but hedge their bets using test mixes, cross-posting, and linking options. In terms of the first strategy, DJ Earworm explained that he uploaded test mixes on a secret and private (invisible) account before posting them on his website to see if they triggered algorithmic detection. DJ Schmolli said that he did the same thing because his mashups were detected 90 percent of the time during these tests, but at least it did not lead to strikes against him. Another common strategy was to upload the mashups on different platforms at the same time, so that if one is taken down, the others might remain accessible.

An alternative distribution workaround is for producers to post a teaser segment of a mashup at their main mashup accounts on a major platform with links leading to the full-length version of the mashup, which is hosted at another account on the same platform or on a smaller platform, a personal website, or even a Dropbox or Google Drive account. The teaser can be a trailer or short excerpt from the main mashup, a manipulated version of it, or an image representing the mashup. Happy Cat Disco explained that at first, he used to open a new account to post his mashups every time his existing account had reached two strikes, thus avoiding the third strike that would terminate the present account. But then he eventually turned to the strategy of having one primary hub with links to other accounts: "I got sick of sending out letters to my followers, like, 'Hey, check out my new channel!' I got tired of it. So, what I did, because they have a three-strike policy, is I opened a new account every time I released three songs. Get three songs out, open a new account." But as Tom Boates Everybody observed, such linking can undermine a smooth audience experience of the mashup; moreover, the linked content will not be captured by algorithms that recommend content based on streaming of other content, which in turn hurts the promotion of the mashup.

Content Moderation's Impact on Aesthetics

Content moderation affects producers beyond their distribution choices. Among the surveyed producers, 66 percent said that it had also changed mashup music in terms of its content and sound. The interviewees indicated that they sometimes tried to bypass detection by altering the mashup content itself. Because of the opacity concerning exactly how the algorithms work, a lot of folk theories regarding how to bypass such automated detection circulated among the mashup producers and resulted in various approaches. Most of these approaches were the result of much trial and error. As DJ Earworm put it: "I keep on hacking it away until they [the algorithms or human moderators] say yes." Few were certain that their approaches were working but tried them nevertheless because someone said that they worked or because they had avoided a takedown after tailoring their content in a certain way. While some of the producers were actually reluctant to give away their bypass tactics, most were resigned to the fact that the algorithms were constantly advancing and would probably figure them out anyway.

One workaround involved inserting five to thirty seconds (the requisite time differed according to the producer) of introduction with silence, talking, or sounds before the mashup started, on the assumption that detection algorithms and human moderators always work from the beginning of the track or video. Maya Jacobson pointed out that this tactic came with a cost, in that the beginning of the mashup was also the aspect of it that needed to attract potential listeners.

Another frequently mentioned tactic was to alter the content itself. In terms of a video, for example, this could mean mirroring or flipping the original, editing its colors or size, or scaling it differently. DJ Faroff admitted that this could compromise the mashup's aesthetic quality: "It looks a little weird but the reason I did it is because that way the machine, the bot, would not recognize it; it would not match the video with existing [data]." Isosine was also hesitant about workaround techniques that compromised his aesthetic principles: "It's such a hassle to deal with the content detection. 'Cause I find myself—I mean, some videos are brutal because I'll have to do ten-plus edits of the video to try to evade copyright detection. And sometimes I'm asking myself if this is even worth it."

In terms of the audio, the producers said that they sometimes layered several tracks to make them harder to detect individually, or they altered the pitch or tempo of the mashed tracks or warped their audio signals in other ways. Danny Neyman explained: "The more warped you can make a song sound, almost the better to avoid copyright. So as opposed to pro pitching or transposing, which is when you keep it in the original pitch but you change the key, you could not be as stringent with the material so it makes more of a warped sound. . . . Doing something like that helps to avoid detection. Also changing the bpm a lot really works, because when YouTube has its AI trying to detect a song, it tries to detect it as the song itself. The more you can change the song from the original material, the more it diverges from that, the less likely it will be detected." Other producers simply insisted that the algorithms would detect the music no matter what they did, and no tactic was worth compromising their aesthetic vision. Raheem D explained: "Back in the day I used to pitch my music [to avoid detection]. I don't really do that too much anymore, because I feel like it affects the quality of the overall mashup, and the sound. But I know a lot of people that would make their mashups sound like [Alvin and] the Chipmunks or they'd slow it down a lot as well so the [stretched] wavelengths don't look the same. So those are things that people would do to try and avoid copyright [detection]." Isosine seconded Raheem D's skepticism about altering the audio: "In the same sense with the video, you can alter the audio with some effects, but it kind of doesn't sound very good if you have to alter it so much. So that's part of the reasons I mostly don't bother anymore. . . . I don't actively go out of my way to have [content moderation] impact the creative process at all. I just kinda do it, and if it gets blocked, then, well, it's blocked. But I still enjoyed making it."

Although not all the producers were willing to alter the content itself, several had become very aware of how they were using samples and what sources they were sampling. Some believed that if the duration of the sample was limited, it would bypass detection, and some also believed that the exact time span threshold varied according to the record label that would be responsible for the takedown. They also believed that some labels' catalogs were safer to sample from than others (small, independent labels were considered safer than Universal or Warner, for example), or that the sampling of some artists (including Taylor Swift, Ariana Grande, and Madonna) was more vulnerable to blocking and takedown than the sampling of others. Some also believed that new releases were more prone to takedown because the label feared that the mashup would ruin its promotion plans, whereas others believed that new releases were less prone to takedown because the labels wanted to have as much attention paid to the tracks as possible.

Such content-related bypass tactics imply that content moderation has a certain impact on the mashup aesthetic itself, along the lines of how the hip-hop aesthetic was altered because of copyright enforcement. While some researchers have found that internet content is sometimes designed to attract the attention of algorithms to boost its popularity,[51] the interview and survey data demonstrate that content is sometimes designed to avoid the attention of algorithms in order to sustain a public life for the producer.[52] Although most of the producers admitted to having used such tactics at some point, relatively few were willing to compromise on aesthetics, as DJ Schmolli explained: "I'm not gonna hold it back, or alter it, or cut things out, just to [avoid takedowns or strikes]. And that's the most important thing, because I see it somehow as art, and I wanna get my art across. No famous artists want to take things away from their art just to make it accessible to more people, I think." Many of them would rather stop the production or distribution of their mashups, or both, than compromise their aesthetic vision.

Mashup Producers' Experiences with Disputing Blockings or Takedowns
Earlier in this chapter I voiced the concern that users would not challenge blockings or takedowns due to certain chilling effects, and this turned out to be true for the mashup producers in this study as well. Only 41 percent of the surveyed producers had ever contested a mashup blocking or takedown, and 71 percent of those said that their dispute had been unsuccessful.[53] Similarly, few of the interviewees had ever contested blockings or takedowns of their mashups. Their reasons all recall the chilling effects mentioned above.

First, they were afraid that a dispute would draw attention to their accounts that could lead to strikes and eventually termination. DJ Faroff added, "So again, there are all these urban myths among mashup producers—'Oh, if you dispute, then they can remove your entire channel.'" He continued by saying that while he was not sure a dispute would result in such a scenario, the possibility played into his reluctance: "I would be too scared."

A couple of interviewees said that they did not contest blockings or takedowns because they thought that content moderation was fundamentally fair, in that mashups did infringe copyright or that the platforms, as private entities, had every right to decide what should or should not be included on them. Other interviewees pointed to their lack of legal knowledge or, at minimum, their inability to back up their counternotice in court. For example, CFLO recalled a time when he considered filing a counternotice: "But they've set it up so that it seems really like you're vouching, like they could take you. . . . It makes it sound like you're signing it, like it's a legal agreement, and they're like, 'Hey, if you're gonna dispute this, are you able to back that up in court?' And I was like, you know, twenty. And I'm like, 'No, like, I can't—I don't know enough about the law to really say one way or another.'" DJ Cummerbund wanted nothing to do with litigation: "We get the messages all the time, that our mashups are taken down and everything like that. Never fight it, because it is what it is. . . . Yeah, we're not ready to get into that kind of legal battle. You know, we can't afford that."

Isosine spoke for those who did not dispute because they assumed that it would not help: "You can try to reject or appeal a notice, but really, at the end of the day, you don't have any say. 'Cause if you do that, it's just gonna be blocked again in a few days when someone says no." Raheem D also lamented that if a copyright holder and a user disagreed, a platform like YouTube was always going to take the label's side. Poolboy added, "I can't think of a time that any of the big platforms have ever taken the side of the content creators. I don't think there are any, like [not] YouTube, Twitter, Facebook, [or] SoundCloud. I can't think of anyone [saying], 'I felt like SoundCloud really had my back on this one.'" CFLO, who remained convinced that mashups would be protected under the US fair use doctrine, expressed a similar sentiment along with a distrust in the system:

> I understand. For them, when they have millions upon billions of things posted, it's in their best interest to just purge it from their system, but . . . I think there's enough gray area in the fair use clause. . . . I think there is some interpretation in there that's about whether or not you've created a new piece of work. And I think you have. Not that I'm saying you should monetize it, but I think they shouldn't be able to take it away. You have created something new. I feel like if it wasn't new then they could take it away. But if it is new and they still take it away, then they're contradicting themselves. And you don't have the capacity or the . . . when they flag you and you dispute it, there's no [real] dispute process, like someone who's like, "Oh, you're right, this is actually fair use." No one's looking out for the mashup artists. . . . It seems like an uphill battle and we're not in a position to gain any ground.

CFLO's comment concerns not only the platforms' dispute and counternotice procedures but also their content moderation systems more generally, which he sees as the ultimate problem. As I will show below, he was not the only one who felt this way.

The Puppeteers of Mashups' Pending Fate

Mashup producer Danny Neyman believed that platforms' content moderation was fair in terms of the need to detect copyright infringement. What he thought was unfair was the platforms' punishment and retribution for using copyrighted content in creative ways. Several others, including Isosine, also condemned the platforms' treatment of mashup producers, which they found quite brutal: "It's a very heavy-handed way of dealing with copyright infringement. Especially on a level that's not very severe. Because it's a transformative work that was created for people to enjoy the music, not to replace the music that it samples."

Others agreed with Danny Neyman that the degree of punishment was extreme but added that the decision-making process behind blocking content in the first place was equally flawed. Often this objection related to the human/algorithm divide, in that the producers saw their art indicted by an algorithm, not a careful legal analysis. CFLO explained:

> I don't think [that copyright holders are involved in the process] at all. I think the algorithm does it, and they just take it away. I don't think there's anyone moderating it. . . . It's an algorithm that's responsible for being, like, "This is wrong, this is wrong," but, like, I think it's up to interpretation if it's really wrong. The content filtration could be like, "This is using this element," but you can't have it until someone judges, in my opinion, whether it's being used improperly or not. But it's in their best business interest to just take it off the platform, because they don't want to deal with the legal repercussions. So, I feel like it forced a lot of artists off those platforms, and I think the community has suffered because of that.

With so much at stake, producers shared a lot of understandable frustration that the fate of their work rested with an automated rather than a human intervention. Adriana A felt that algorithms had shifted the balance of power against the producers:

> These were issues that we were dealing with in 2003. And it kind of felt like it went away. . . . Like, it was just a losing battle for the record companies; they can't go after everybody. . . . And then it also sort of seemed like record companies started to care less—like, they started to realize, "Oh! Okay, so these mashups are

actually not necessarily a bad thing. If one goes viral or gets popular it actually is good." . . . Like, especially, say, a legacy artist who hasn't had a hit in years and then suddenly there's all this free advertising for their music, because it got remade into, like, a derivative work. You know, suddenly they're pop-culturally relevant again. So, I think record companies sort of recognized that, and kind of like laid off. But now, with technology, they don't have to have teams of people doing this—they have bots that do this. And so in 2019, you know, you're not fighting against a lawyer; you're fighting a bot! You know? These crazy algorithms find your copyrighted music, and no questions are asked. Nope, it's gone. . . . And now it's . . . even worse than what it was in the early days of mashup culture.

She pointed out that producers do not even receive a letter explaining the situation, only a message saying "it recognizes copyrighted material, therefore you can't post this." And, she explained, whereas mashup producers used to look at cease-and-desist letters from copyright holders as a badge of honor[54]—"They noticed me! They know who I am!"—they do not feel the same about takedowns. There is no honor in being detected by an algorithm.

Clearly, then, content moderation has had important ramifications for the exposure of mashups that have led in turn to various tactics to bypass detection. It has therefore indirectly affected the producers' creative process and aesthetic results, as well as their distribution choices. Blockings, takedowns, and account terminations have also undermined producers' motivation to distribute or even create mashups, thus hurting the mashup scene as a whole.

In their frustration with content moderation, most of the producers held the copyright holders responsible, rather than the platforms, for both the implementation of the system in the first place and the blockings and takedowns that too often resulted from it. This assignment of responsibility to the copyright holders can be understood in light of the way in which sampling artists have been constrained by copyright holders historically, including the numerous legal threats (and some lawsuits) and unreasonably high fees directed at 1990s hip-hop producers for sample licensing and infringement settlements (see chapter 5). Several scholars have long insisted that commercial interests have taken advantage of the legal vagueness and ambiguity around user rights in ways that have expanded the copyright monopoly and damaged creative and culturally valuable art expressions.[55] For example, in their discussion of sampling licensing, McLeod and DiCola state, "At this point, we hand off the sampling quandary to the music business, with its informal and formal practices that guide its decisions. From our research, we know what their answer will be regarding copyright limitations: the default setting is total protection for samples. As we have demonstrated, individuals and organizations within the mainstream music industry typically ignore the existence of fair use, the *de minimis* threshold, and other exceptions to copyright protection" (2011, 259). Similarly, Aram Sinnreich (2013) argues that the media cartels' long exploitation of copyright law under the aegis of "fighting piracy" has had detrimental implications for free speech and, in turn, democratic society. In a less polemic fashion, Sabine Jacques (2019, 43) argues that instead of being a means of fostering cultural diversity, the primary function of copyright over the past fifty years has been to protect the industry's economic interests—society's unbalanced activation of copyright has significantly constrained and impaired cultural production. Vaidhyanathan similarly states that strong copyright protection has pushed the general conception of copyright toward the exercise of excessive control over use and further notes that "copyright myths have had as much power as copyright law" (2003, 5). The myths about copyright can have as much impact as the law itself, in that they may convince the public that the laws are more far-reaching than they actually are. This misconception causes the chilling effects that inhibit users from exercising their rights or even trying to create cultural expressions that might well reside in the contested area of copyright law.

The ways in which platforms' content moderation has been designed leaves copyright holders with a huge responsibility to act in good faith and accommodate copyright exceptions when they are flagging content and instructing platforms about how to respond to detected matches of their copyrighted works. Yet the responsibility is not on the copyright holders alone; in fact, the platforms' content moderation has promoted this enduring tension, given the enormous cultural power that platforms wield in today's society. However, most of the interviewed and surveyed producers still saw platforms as relatively neutral mediators or even victims of economic negotiations. Tom Boates Everybody and others looked at it from a business perspective and sympathized with the need to take the side of the major copyright-holder corporations: "I can just say as a design product person in a tech startup community, if I were them it would be like, you know, I would have to guess it was probably 5 percent or less of their listener base was mashups. So, I'd rather focus my attention on the

95 percent, you know, instead of going through all these legal loopholes that have to do with, like, country by country rules. So much headache for 5 percent of the user base. Like, why bother?" Some saw the platforms' implementation of algorithmic content moderation as necessary in order to prevent lawsuits or platform closure: "At the end of the day, YouTube is not trying to do any evil, although there are some things that we can all question about YouTube. But a lot of times what YouTube does, especially with copyright, is in response to labels really pushing them to. They are forcing YouTube. YouTube doesn't necessarily want to do this, but they have to do this" (anonymous mashup producer). Poolboy shared a similar view: "It's sad, but also, I understand. It's not like they can magically stand up to the labels. I think that people try to villainize them . . . like a villain that just hates its creators, when, really, they're put in a headlock by these, like—by literally not making money—and then they get hit by more and more lawsuits. They can't really do anything. So, of course, they aren't gonna care about mashups. . . . They just need money." Still, he believed that in preventing such content from being distributed, the platforms were dismissing the very reasons for their own existence:

> They don't care about copyright-infringing content—they have no reason to want them on the site, or they don't realize that they want them on the site because they don't realize how big of a part it is in their audience. So, like, all they see is a lawsuit from a label and they panic, and they will just delete everything on the website. What SoundCloud wants is legitimate musicians; they want, like, label musicians posting their stuff, their completely original stuff, and for them to be treated like they were an iTunes or a Spotify, when in reality the reason people use SoundCloud is that they can't get [their content posted] on iTunes and Spotify. . . . They'll delete everything copyright infringing and they'll sit and wonder why the hell no one's on their website.

According to Poolboy, platforms are digging their own graves for economic reasons and out of the fear of litigation.

Despite the mashup producers' general if not unanimous opposition to copyright moderation, they seemed to be more forgiving of the platforms than of the copyright holders. The producers saw the platforms in a catch-22 situation—they wanted to accommodate copyright exceptions but feared litigation and loss of revenue—and the platforms saw themselves that way too, according to Urban and colleagues: "Several [online service providers] view their measures as compromise positions designed to head off stronger rightsholder demands" (2016, 57). If we accept this perspective, one alternative to CFLO's belief that platforms do not care about keeping copyright-infringing content on their sites is that they *do* care, which is partly why they have negotiated comprehensive licensing agreement with the major labels. Yet although platforms have a long history of fronting themselves as neutral intermediaries[56] and several platforms still cultivate an image of a hands-off mediator of content, they are not neutral. Over the years, it has become increasingly evident that platforms are often caught between the demand of their co-creative community to provide an open space for free speech and their consumers' and various stakeholders' interests, as well as the conflicting logics involved in sustaining their images as open communities and avoiding litigation and following the money. As Gillespie (2018) argues, content moderation is essential to what they do and part of what defines them, and the political and economic nature of mediating related conflicts has simply made neutral moderation impossible. Given that the major platforms are pivotal forums for expression in today's society, they exercise considerable power and influence in shaping the contemporary and future cultural sphere when they moderate content.

What is troubling, then, is not platform content moderation per se, which is necessary for many good reasons. It is instead the fact that the current moderation systems of the major hosting platforms cannot handle copyright exceptions, and thus often undermine the legal gray area of copyright.[57] Certainly the development of a system that could handle a huge amount of content while also accommodating copyright exceptions is challenging and perhaps unrealistic. Yet systems that cannot accommodate copyright exceptions and thus disrupt the careful balance ensured by the law between property rights and users' rights simply generate extended and privatized copyright enforcement on an enormous scale and with an enormous impact. Even if an alleged infringer should prove to have a strong case in court, what matters more is the platforms' extrajudicial procedure in the first place, the outcome of which relies on how the relevant copyright holder and platform evaluate or treat the case. This situation in turn harms individuals and their creative expressions as well as whole types or genres of expression, including mashups and sample-based music more generally.

Whereas sample-based music's early threat resulted in a change of direction for hip-hop in terms of its aesthetics, the current threat is existential, even though it results from nothing more than platforms' and copyright holders' negotiations over respective responsibilities. While mashup producers are certainly not passive victims—some of them have resigned themselves to their fate, but others are always eager to find workarounds for the hindrances they face—they are not able to adapt to sampling restrictions in the same way that hip-hop producers could. Unlike 1990s hip-hop music, in which sampling was one of several components and the sound of the samples was often just as important as their referential function, mashup music fundamentally depends on samples in and of themselves, and especially their intertextual referentiality. As such, mashups are extremely vulnerable to sampling restrictions: obscuring or avoiding widely known samples is simply not an alternative for mashup producers, because mashups would then cease to be mashups.

7 Authorship and Ownership in the Age of Remix and Takedowns

Rather than propose potential solutions to or remedies for the problems I have addressed, this concluding chapter is intended to spur critical reflection by discussing some fundamental questions related to the three main topics of this book: art, copyright, and platform regulation.

- If it were an all-or-nothing situation, what kinds of cultural expressions would we choose to either preserve or erase from our culture?
- What role do we want copyright to have when it comes to incentivizing and regulating culture, and on what premises?
- What cultural and juridical power should private corporations be allowed to wield in the name of their internal policies?

I tie these questions to the various arguments I have made throughout this book.

Art and Ideological Hierarchies

When grappling with the first question—If it were an all-or-nothing situation, what kinds of cultural expressions would we choose to either preserve or erase from our culture?—our answers will tend to be informed by our various aesthetic ideologies, which are in turn informed by the cultural hegemony of a given time and context.

Lawrence Lessig articulates a likely concern of many regarding the topic of this book: "But why should anyone care about whether remix flourishes, or even exists? What does anyone gain, beyond a cheap laugh? What does a society gain, beyond angry famous people?" (Lessig 2008, 76). Though mashups are valued, encouraged, and kept alive by millions of people, they have remained familiar targets for the various tyrannies of "good taste." For example, John Shiga refers to *Mixmag* columnist Pete Tong, who, while acknowledging that some mashups are "very clever," nevertheless describes them as "musical fast food" (Shiga 2007, 104; Tong 1999, 7). Likewise, Liam McGranahan refers to *SF Weekly* journalist Garrett Kamps's description of the process of making mashups: "Uploading tracks into ready-made programs that conveniently do the work of syncing up the two songs for you." He then continues, "It takes little or no musical talent to make mashups this way, which explains why the trend is so popular—and why it has become so saturated with crap" (McGranahan 2010, 46; Kamps 2004). In his study of the mashup and what he sees as its "apolitical irony," Michael Serazio similarly asks rhetorically:

> In this "ultimate expression of remix culture," this "highest form of recontextualization," does the mash-up aesthetic and movement amount to anything more than "in-jokes for music geeks" (Cruger [2006])? Is there a real cause here, beyond irony—a genuine call to arms towards *something* rather than a simple wink-wink, tongue-in cheek prank about *nothing*? I would argue that the mash-up is *bricolage* for its own sake; as a definitive generational statement, it hesitates to espouse anything more than detached, wry commentary, which actually may be apropos. . . . I would concur with Angelica Madeira that "music is empowering not only because of the explicit political ends it is able to serve, but also because it formulates the yearnings and values for an entire generation" (Balliger [1995] 17). I remain uncertain what exactly, in the end, the mash-up really has to say. (Serazio 2008, 91–92, italics in original)

Nor is music critic Simon Reynolds particularly enthusiastic about them: "Mash-ups mash the history of pop like potatoes, into indistinct, digital-data-grey pulp, blood-sugar blast of empty carbohydrate energy, flava-less and devoid of nutritional value. For all their aura of mischief and cheeky fun, mash-ups exude pathos. This is a barren genre—nothing will come from it" (2011, 360).

Despite their dedication to and enthusiasm about mashups, several of the mashup producers themselves expressed some reservation about this music, framing it as a kind of "guilty pleasure" (see chapter 4). This may be their way of acknowledging that mashups (and mashup activity) are distinctively different from, and thus not comparable to, other forms of music (and musical activities). An ironic approach to the music may also be a way of creating a space where one is allowed to enjoy something one should not without sacrificing any cultural capital or compromising one's preferred ideology. Pierre Bourdieu (1984) has famously pointed out that the hierarchies of ideology, or the grand cultural narratives about value and taste, are neither natural nor individual but rather socially and historically constructed. Aesthetic judgment, he argues, results from the need to display social difference and gain cultural capital. To indicate that something is one's "guilty" pleasure (instead of just pleasure) is, in other words, to react with a defensiveness and judgmentalism that says more about the discourse surrounding the music—including standards and expectations regarding value and taste—than about the actual autonomous feelings about the music in question.[1] However, the notion that musical tastes, values, and expectations are socially constructed does not make a person's reservations about that music or his or her preferred ideology any less real or true.

In the popular music discourse, particularly that of rock music, "good" music and "true" musicianship are often framed as the fruits of diligence and labor.[2] This emphasis on labor—on technical proficiency achieved through hard work alone—within the rock discourse was, for example, part of the reason why early punk was dismissed by the mainstream industry (Laing 2015). This ideology runs much deeper than the rock discourse, though, which is evident from the fact that an artistic expression is often labeled a "work" or an "artwork" and has been so for a very long time.[3] An artwork that evidently does not result from time-consuming and labor-intensive diligence is, conversely, often described as cheap, fake, or otherwise unworthy of serious attention and appraisal.

In her study of the gimmick, Sianne Ngai (2017, 2020) links the distrust or rejection of an obvious reduction of labor in art to the Protestant work ethic—and, more important, to the significant ramifications (and thus fundamental distrust) of capitalism's exchange of actual human labor for more efficient machines and techniques of production that increase economic productivity. Ngai points out that conceptual art, including sampling and random art, in which the idea weighs heavier than the method of production is particularly vulnerable to rejection on the basis of its deskilled labor (Ngai 2020, 54, 94). She furthermore suggests that when art is associated with leisure activities, it is more vulnerable to being dismissed since this alignment indicates that it is not the result of hard work. This emphasis on hard work is also tangled with ethics, which is evident in John Locke's labor theory of property. Locke (2015 [1689]) argues that property and its reward are justified by the labor used to produce the material goods; it is the labor put into it that gives it value, and awarding property therefore also incentivizes labor in turn. Although Locke's theory of value and property has been much debated and variously interpreted (especially in relation to his principle of acquisition—that is, the proviso that individual property ownership should be limited so that enough is left in common for others), its emphasis on labor has joined with alternative theories to inform the justification of copyright law.[4]

Related to the core value of labor is "originality," especially in relation to the notion of the creative (and pointedly unformulaic) "genius" who makes art almost from scratch (I will return to the notion of genius later). Like Ngai, who relates certain forms of art criticism to a fundamental distrust of capitalist processes, Theodor W. Adorno (1941) famously explained his own dismissal of formulaic or standardized music as rooted in a distrust of those processes. That is, he frames this music as the product of capitalistic forces that encourage, and manufacture a demand for, serial production to increase profits. As such, formulaic or standardized music is labeled as inappropriately seductive in its exploitation of music for greedy purposes and simultaneous enticement of the unsuspecting into believing that what is "bad" or unintelligent music is instead "good" (and desirable) music. This music is also rendered dismissible due to the related conviction that creating something "original" requires more effort (in terms of both time and thought) than using "templates." As most forms of popular music today follow some kind of formula, this last verdict may seem to hold less water. Yet as Simon Frith points out, "formula criticism" still rears its head as a means of either criticizing or legitimizing musical genres, and what is regarded as formulaic is furthermore confoundingly genre dependent: "Minor variations in boy band music are taken to be insignificant; minor variations in rural blues guitar tunings or madrigal polyphonics are of great aesthetic importance" (Frith 2004, 20). Such genre-dependent formulaic critiques clearly depend on real insight (or lack thereof) into the musics in question. Whereas Kamps (2004) describes mashups as simply the result of automated processes produced by "ready-made programs," the mashup producers' descriptions of the process of making them represents an alternative narrative (see chapter 3), in which nuances within the parameters of key, tempo, harmony, rhythm, sound, structure, lyrics, and video are critical. And whereas those with only a brief or superficial encounter with mashup may regard it as presenting few intellectual or creative challenges, others who have engaged with it deeply and thoroughly may celebrate its enormous intellectual and creative potential. Formulaic critique, that is, seldom emerges from within the genre in question and is furthermore always relative; as such, it is ill suited to informing an argument for or against a music's value, although it continues to do so.

Authenticity, or the notion of sincerity, is also related to the value of labor. For example, Andrew Goodwin states that the new music technologies, including sampling, "place authenticity and creativity in crisis, not just because of the issue of theft, but through the increasingly automated nature of their mechanism" (1990, 262). But the notion of authenticity can actually be related to divergent ideologies, since it may take many forms, including expressing genuine personal emotions, messages, or experiences; being true to a tradition or genre; or standing up for one's convictions.[5] After all, authenticity is, as Allan F. Moore puts it, always "ascribed, not inscribed. . . . Whether a performance is authentic, then, depends on who 'we' are" (2002, 210). For example, mashups shamelessly embrace the manipulated and fabricated by relying on nothing but samples; as such, they can be experienced as inauthentic. Yet as Lawrence Grossberg points out, the act of revealing the truth about one's nature can generate its own sort of self-justification and consequently be experienced as authentic, or as authentic inauthenticity (1992, 226). As emphasized through this book, mashup producers stay loyal to their own premises, and there are no truths hidden from the audience in their works.

Mashup producers are an easy target for critique or dismissal from the perspective of an ideology that emphasizes labor and originality: their music relies primarily on samples; they are trying to make the most out of as little as possible; they work with production parameters that are often invisible (such as tweaking the sound of the tracks to make them match); and they emphasize that this is something they do in their leisure time. And, as mentioned in chapter 5, such a rejection of sample-based music or remixes may also arise from the ethical conviction that this work subtracts from (or feeds off) either the profit, the reputation, or the aesthetic vision of the author (despite the fact that such assumptions may not prove out). Although the emphasis on labor in the popular music discourse does explain some amount of reservation concerning mashups (and sample-based music and remixes more generally), this music is also celebrated and justified by people who rely on other ideologies with less emphasis on labor. Still, it seems as though a rock ideology lurks beneath the surface of not only the outside reception of this music but also the very mashup scene that would appear to dismiss it by celebrating mashups. Some of the mashup producers expressed a certain reluctance about their work by framing it as a guilty pleasure, but others, including NodaMixMusic, went even further: "There is nothing unique about this thing that I do. But people found it interesting, and they still listen to it." Poolboy echoed this sentiment, saying that some mashup producers in fact aspire to make "actual music" as well, and that when making mashups, "you almost feel like you're making music in a way." When confronted with his unspoken assumption that mashup is not actual music, he answered, "I'm very supportive of, like, if it's art, it's art. . . . [Still,] I say 'almost' because I feel bad giving myself the credit of like making a song when I feel like I just, it took me like thirty minutes to make this, you know? And I think there's also, there's almost this guilt when you make stuff and you get credit for it. There's this guilt because, like, 'I could have put more effort into this. I could have made something more original.' You almost feel like you aren't being original, so that's why I think I say 'almost.'" Although some form of self-recrimination is present in any art practice, it is perhaps particularly common in musical practices that clearly disrupt the values associated with the typical rock ideology. As Kiri Miller (2012, 97–119) observes in her study of players of the *Guitar Hero* and *Rock Band* video games, abiding assumptions concerning the nature of authenticity in music tend to generate complicated and ambiguous views about one's own creativity and musicality. Most of the producers, of course, defended their practice, but several of them did so in alignment with the rock ideology by pointing to the great skill that is required to make mashups (often with reference to the mixing process; see chapter 3).[6] The mantra of hard work might even explain some mashup producers' attraction to mashup music itself, as it provides them with challenges that require both diligence and skill.

In the end, though, should the value of labor really be critical to art's sociocultural significance and support? "The crucial question," Dick Hebdige asserts, "has to do with which specific ideologies, representing the interests of which specific groupings and classes, will prevail at any given moment. . . . We must ask which groups . . . have how much say in defining, ordering and classifying out the social world" (1979, 14). There are no self-evident reasons for why an ideology of labor should determine which forms of art we choose to support or condemn. But when certain ideologies become institutionalized, in terms of education and awards, legal enforcement, and the work of various cultural gatekeepers (including social media platforms), some forms of art may appear worthier of our support than others. As such, these cultural mechanisms of artistic hierarchy evoke Antonio Gramsci's theory of cultural hegemony, wherein cultural institutions serve to enforce the hegemony by convincing people that one ideology and its values and norms is somehow more "natural" or legitimate than another—that it is, in short, a matter of common sense to abide by its convictions.[7] But whereas Gramsci saw cultural hegemony as the result of the ruling capitalist class's attempt to establish and maintain its power, value formation and hegemonic ideologies can result from other complex historical and social patterns and mechanisms as well. It remains critical, in any case, to question why we support certain art forms rather than others.

An alternative to the aesthetic ideology emphasizing labor, skill, and the unformulaic is the one underpinning explicitly intertextual forms of art. This ideology has deep roots in the aesthetics of montage, collage, readymades, curatorial creativity, and parody and is reflected in sample-based music, remix, and mashups as well. As mentioned in chapters 2, 3, and 4, the value of these kinds of artworks lies less in the effort of making them than in the ideas behind them, as well as the functions or experiential effects they trigger. Scholar and art curator Nicolas Bourriaud, for example, discusses the aesthetic principles of appropriation, or what he calls "postproduction," using Marcel Duchamp's artworks as his illustration: "When Duchamp exhibits a manufactured object (a bottle rack, a urinal, a snow shovel) as a work of the mind, he shifts the problematic of the 'creative process,' emphasizing the artist's gaze brought to bear on an object instead of manual skill. He asserts that the act of choosing is enough to establish the artistic process, just as the act of fabricating, painting, or sculpting does: to give a new idea to an object is already production. Duchamp thereby completes the definition of the term *creation*: to create is to insert an object into a new scenario, to consider it a character in a narrative" (Bourriaud 2005, 12). Bourriaud then notes that the central question within the ideology of post-production is not "what can we make that is new?" but "how can we make do with what we have?"—it is a "matter of seizing all the codes of the culture, all the forms of everyday life, the works of the global patrimony, and making them function" (8). This ideology was also articulated by several mashup producers; Kap Slap, for example, suggested that there are two types of creativity: "There is, like, the raw oil well of creativity that comes out, and then there's people who have composite creativity, which is like me, and like Weird Al Yankovic. Same idea, where it's essentially taking these other things and making a commentary about it that is a little more high-level." He associates his own mashup activity with the latter: "I am the refinery. I go on top. I take that [raw oil], I turn it into gasoline, to kerosene, to propane." With respect to the functions or experiential effects triggered by these kinds of works, one of the aspects that is valued within this ideology is art's ability to defamiliarize the habitual—that is, to foster the experience of something as at once familiar and new. Another aspect that is valued is art's ability to trigger divergent associations in a way that produces a productive oscillation that can, in turn, result in an experience of humor, critical reflection and enlightenment, and artistic attraction and pleasure (see chapter 4).[8]

Another ideology that is present in the discourse of mashup and remix culture is democratic cultural participation, which emphasizes two core values: a low threshold for cultural participation and intrinsic motivation. The first core value—that cultural participation should not be restricted to a certain few—does not imply that this ideology favors or is favored by amateurs; it also applies to those who work to professional ends but choose not to enter the commercial sector of the industry. This leads us to the second core value, that the motivation must be primarily intrinsic (or what I described in chapter 3 as paratelic or autotelic)—people operating according to this ideology participate in cultural activities for the love of doing so rather than for material gain. While this ideology is clearly present in the contexts of remix and mashup (see especially chapters 3 and 5), it is also present in contexts where people play an instrument just for fun; where they join a local choir or corps; where they play music video games such as *Guitar Hero* or *Rock Band*;[9] where they sing together at social occasions such as football events, religious ceremonies, or national celebrations; or where they perform karaoke at a club or party, to mention but a few. This equally deep-rooted ideology is often associated with folk culture. Richard Carlin (2004, 175), for example, observes that folk music rejects the notion that art should be reserved for a talented few and promotes instead art that represents the "voice of the people." It also sometimes dovetails with the ideology underpinning explicitly intertextual artworks. For example, Henry

Jenkins (2006) points to the tendency of folk cultures to democratically respond to the content of mass culture by appropriating and transforming it. Intrinsically motivated cultural participation has always been part of daily life, as has the practice of appropriating and transforming content. But technological developments in recent decades have extended both tendencies drastically by making the means of production and distribution accessible to a larger group of people (see chapter 1). These new technological means of distribution have also made this large and integral part of culture more visible, refuting any persisting claim that people in their everyday lives exclusively value professional and commercial expression.

The ideology of democratic cultural participation resonates with the opposition to neoliberal capitalism informing Adorno's skepticism of standardized forms and Ngai's interrogation of the artistic emphasis on labor; after all, it rejects both professionalization (see Butler 2019) and material profit as artistic motivations. Rebecca Tushnet (2008, 110) argues that such creative activities are valuable because they contribute to cultural diversity by providing content that distinguishes itself from what is produced for the commercial market. These expressions are often unplanned and spontaneous; they dare to move beyond the expected (thanks to their "freedom to be bad"), and they dare to challenge the status quo (because they do not seek material gain). There is also an educative component to these low-barrier activities, which means they can even enable the development of new talent (113–115). Tushnet concludes, "If we value expressive diversity, as copyright doctrine routinely suggests, we should not attempt to assimilate everything into the profit-seeking sphere, even if it were possible to do so" (117).

In contrast to Tushnet, who endorses a low-level threshold for cultural participation, Andrew Keen (2006) is skeptical about Web 2.0's reinforcement of grassroots creativity, fearing that the talented will be suffocated by the masses. "If you democratize media," he writes, "then you end up democratizing talent. The unintended consequence of all this democratization, to misquote Web 2.0 apologist Thomas Friedman, is cultural 'flattening.'" With regard to Keen's concern, I believe that talent will always be valued and sought after in society, as was evident from the mashup producers' emphasis on getting feedback from their peers before posting their mashups and from their clear distinction between what they saw as good and bad mashups (see chapter 3). The democratization of cultural participation combined with the enhanced display of noncommercial activity (via internet platforms) has surely contributed a large amount of what many would regard as inferior material, but that is not all there is. As Lessig notes, "There's good and bad remix, as there's good and bad writing. But just as bad writing is not an argument against writing, bad remix is not an argument against remix" (2008, 81). And as I argued in chapter 3, the social value of creative endeavors cannot be measured solely in terms of the end result but must also be located in the process of creation itself.[10] The process of making art on its own can lead to a sense of belonging and contributing to society in a meaningful way; it can build communities, networks, and friendships; it can provide an escapist and liberating feeling of distraction (through absorption and fun) from one's otherwise messy life; it can feel empowering, since creative participation—where one takes control rather than is controlled—allows one to make the world one's own; it can be intellectually stimulating in its encouragement to overcome or make the most out of given challenges and restrictions; and, not least, it can induce the meaningful and exciting feeling of having fun—on one's own and together with others. If we take away all the forms of mashup and remix activity that are currently flourishing on the internet, we also take away the means through which a number of people accomplish all these ends, as well as a large proportion of those cultural expressions that offer an alternative to the commercial market.

Mashup producers, I have argued, seem to adhere to all the aesthetic ideologies presented above, although the emphasis varies. For example, some make a mashup in less than an hour, whereas others take weeks; some are primarily motivated by external factors such as the prospect of being recognized as a versatile producer, whereas others are primarily intrinsically motivated. In society as a whole, however, a hierarchy of aesthetic ideologies remains in place despite an ongoing emphasis on cultural diversity. For example, the creative activities and expressions with the strongest support in terms of both legal protection and institutional compensation are professional and commercial ones. But can we not also support those creative activities that are located on the outskirts of this established marketplace, at least in terms of allowing them to exist? The question of what cultural expressions we would choose to either preserve or erase from our culture is actually a question of what we want from culture in the first place. If culture is supposed to offer people meaningful experiences, we should acknowledge that what engages people—what people find meaningful in relation to creative expression—is quite diverse and multifaceted.

The Gap between Legal Reasoning and Artistic Practice

One objection to supporting mashups and remixes is, of course, that this art is against the law. And whereas I am convinced, following my scrutiny of mashups, mashup producers' stated intentions, and the legal exceptions of EU and US law (see chapter 5), that most mashups are not illegal but instead have a strong legal justification, some people think otherwise. But even if they were proven to be illegal, my second question still warrants critical consideration: What role do we want copyright to have when it comes to incentivizing and regulating culture, and based on what assumptions?

The twentieth and twenty-first centuries have seen the profound strengthening of the legal rights and enforcement power of authors and copyright holders.[11] According to Siva Vaidhyanathan, among others, this development has been propelled by the influence of large corporations' drive toward market control (in terms of protecting intellectual "property") rather than the desire to promoting creativity and furthering the public good (2003, 116). This, he argues, has harmed the public sphere by depriving it of culturally valuable and important voices (2003, 6–7). As a reaction to the strengthened rights and reinforced power of copyright holders, a countermovement developed in the early 2000s that campaigned for "free culture." This countercapitalist ideology is oriented toward the free flow of information rather than the proprietary and commercial marketplace.[12] Fronting ideas of free culture, influential law professor and political activist Lessig used remix as the poster child for this movement, a gesture also taken up by others, including the activist group Downhill Battle, which used Danger Mouse's mashup album (*The Grey Album*) as a test case for free use (see chapters 1 and 5). The proliferation of remix spurred optimism among producers and scholars who shared the view that abiding copyright law and practice did not reflect cultural developments in the digitized era.[13] Several of those who continue to share this view have rejected copyright altogether, including any faith in copyright exceptions such as the US fair use doctrine.[14] Lessig, for example, developed the alternative legal system Creative Commons, an open license system wherein a copyright holder makes his or her work or sound recording available with minimal restrictions. This possibility of voluntarily reserving only certain rights has been promoted as a reasonable step forward by several scholars (including Yochai Benkler 2006, 455–456; and James Boyle 2008, 192), while others remain skeptical. For example, Joanna Demers laments that if this stands as "the only model of corporate-sanctioned transformative appropriation, remixing will remain a permissions-based activity wherein the copyright holder approaches transformers, not vice versa" (2006, 146). Given the fact that well-known artists seldom use such open licenses,[15] this model does not help mashup producers much either, as they are drawn to contemporary or classic sources that are well known to a broad group of listeners.

As mentioned in chapter 5, Patricia Aufderheide and Peter Jaszi (2018) have reservations about the free culture movement (including Creative Commons) and scholars' dismissal of copyright law more generally. Such approaches, they argue, contribute to undermining copyright exceptions by implying that the practices they use as cases (such as remix) are necessarily in conflict with the law (55–56). Instead of helping users to understand their rights and thereby encouraging their art, such activist approaches, they claim, make users believe that what they do is illegal and that copyright law is their worst enemy (63–64). In a sense, the free culture discourse has, despite its constructive intentions, bolstered the conception that appropriation based on sampling is stealing and that producers are pirates, activists, or even anarchists (68–71). Instead, Aufderheide and Jaszi argue, these producers deserve to be acknowledged and represented as responsible individuals who act within their own rights (71). They further observe that if free culture were to be realized, it would be just as unfair as current practices but in the other direction, with copyright holders losing all their rights to users (61). A better way to ensure that copyright actually balances the interests of copyright holders with freedom of expression (including freedom of the arts; see chapters 5 and 6) is to educate people about copyright exceptions and make sure that these exceptions are not undermined in practice or in court (71). This book takes a similar stance by arguing that much mashup music and other forms of remixes have a legal justification under the parody exception (and potentially the quotation exception) in EU law and under fair use in US law—a justification that is jeopardized by platforms' content moderation, among other things.

Copyright, of course, is important to artists as well. For one thing, it supports their creative practice financially. I must therefore clarify that the argument for taking copyright exceptions seriously does not represent an indictment of copyright law in general or artists' right to earn money on their work. It merely insists that this right should not exclude the right of users to create acknowledged appropriations and make them public. Arguments such as that of Keen, who maintains that "user-generated media are destroying our economy, our culture, and our values" (2008, 144), do not seem to distinguish between plagiarism, piracy, and acknowledged appropriation, which are vastly different practices. As I have argued throughout this book, acknowledged appropriations complement rather than replace the works they use as their sources. And they do so while crediting the authors of the recycled works and furthermore making explicit that this is the user's interpretation of those works (see the discussion of sampling ethics in chapter 5; see also chapters 2 and 3). As such, acknowledged appropriations do not harm either the economic or moral rights of those whose work they appropriate. An objection based on the opinion that the acknowledged appropriation goes against the original intent and vision for the artwork is not legitimate in a democratic society, as Jacques and colleagues point out: "To participate in a democratic society, citizens must be able to accept or reject, via ridicule or parody, the messages, cultural values, attitudes, or other forms of behavior that constitute their society" (2018, 288). The question of compensation is a related though different debate that I will not go into here; my argument for the moment is simply that acknowledged appropriations such as mashups and parody more generally should be allowed to (publicly) exist. Copyright law currently makes room for both types of art via its exceptions, and this fact should be acknowledged and endorsed by judges, lawyers, and expert witnesses in court, as well as by legislators and others with the power to affect the law. Moreover, it should also be acknowledged by copyright holders and their representatives, who use their power in the name of the law. It is often neither copyright law nor judges who represent the main barrier for remix creativity but rather private actors (including platforms and major copyright holders such as the big record labels) that put their own interpretation of the law into practice via the regulation of culture. These practices in turn exercise an unhelpful influence on how the law is perceived by the public, the artists themselves, expert witnesses, lawyers and judges in court, and legislators. Furthermore, copyright has become more and more tilted toward the copyright holder at the expense of the appropriating artist. As such, we must ask again: On what premises should copyright incentivize and regulate culture?

Elsewhere in this book I have argued that the law and legal enforcement, whether they are functioning as a cultural promoter or a gatekeeper, must be sufficiently informed by artistic practice, but this does not always seem to be the case. Other scholars have pointed out that there is insufficient alignment between the fields of art and law. Such discussions have mainly been centered around the concept of authorship. For example, Martha Woodmansee and Jaszi argue that copyright, which was institutionalized by government and court at the start of the eighteenth century,[16] is based on the Romantic notion of authorship that dominated at that time and was itself based on the notion of "possessive individualism" associated with early capitalism in England (1994, 2–6). The Romantic notion of authorship rests on the idea that the author is a genius expressing novel ideas stemming from an inner self; authorship, then, is solipsistic, intuitive, and original (Toynbee 2012, 133).[17] This notion does not reflect the way in which creativity is actually exercised or realized, and it has garnered much criticism, most notably from those poststructuralist thinkers who argue that the author is a socially constructed figure and a function of discourse (Foucault 1979 [1969]), and furthermore a capitalist notion that reduces works to commodities (Barthes 1967).[18] Woodmansee and Jaszi further argue, "Law has missed out on the contemporary 'critique of authorship'—the impulse, especially in literary studies, to put in question the naturalness and inevitability of Romantic ideas about creativity" (1994, 8). They conclude, "Western copyright laws—and the international copyright system derived from them—are at once too broad and too narrow: they tend to deny or marginalize the work of many creative people while providing such intense protection to the works they cover that reasonable public access to these later works is frustrated" (10–11).

The claim that copyright law is based on a fleeting nineteenth-century notion of authorship that also influences cultural regulation in other ways has in turn been problematized. Scholars have questioned its historical validity and pointed to equally strong influences on the development of copyright law such as institutional practices and technological developments (Saunders 1992), as well as neoliberal thinking (Bently 2008).[19] Lionel Bently notes that copyright's treatment of authorship does not always mirror the Romantic notion of authorship—that is, the test of originality does not account for artistic quality, and copyright can also attribute authorship to nonhuman actors (1994, 981). Still, even if we acknowledge that copyright is formed and reformed based on multiple factors and does not naively treat authorship as the consequence of a genius creating art ex nihilo, there remains an unfortunate gap regarding the concept of authorship between the fields of law and art in certain specific cases including sampling and parody.

As mentioned in earlier chapters, legal cases often treat sampling as a single thing instead of recognizing its plethora of uses and functions in different contexts. This tendency appears in the *Grand Upright* sampling case from 1991, wherein Judge Duffy associated the act of sampling with theft; in the *Bridgeport* sampling case from 2005, wherein the court of appeals concluded, "Get a license or do not sample"; and in the *Pelham* sampling case from 2019, wherein the court made the sweeping claim that the phonogram producer's exclusive rights prohibit anyone else from taking any sound sample at all (see chapter 5).[20] If those who filled these courtrooms had been adequately informed about the many ways in which sampling is done and the various purposes and functions it serves, they might have recognized that some forms of sampling may well be plagiarism but others are quite clearly parodies or other forms of acknowledged appropriation and that these are vastly different practices.

Mireille van Eechoud initiated the Humanities in the European Research Area (HERA) project Of Authorship and Originality with the aim of exploring how humanities research can and should affect law and legal interpretation. In one of the project's main publications, *The Work of Authorship*, she concludes that the interpretation of copyright law should be informed by in-depth analysis of specific instances of production provided by scholars from the humanities, and especially those pursuing empirical studies. This, she argues, would foster richer legal reasoning and have a "real impact on the quality of law and legal interpretation" (Eechoud 2014, 14–15, 8). Eechoud further notes, "One might be forgiven to think that, being concerned with (the study of) regulating creative practices, legal scholars of copyright as well as policymakers are deeply interested in how works get made, how authors operate. But there is remarkably little in the way of academic publications and policy documents to show that this is in fact so" (7).[21] If legal judgments about sampling are to resonate with empirical and theoretical insights from the field of art, the question of whether a specific case is infringement must acknowledge that a sample may be transformed by its contextual displacement even if its formal features are unchanged. Too often in previous court cases concerning musical infringement the validity of the claim has been tested via a comparison of the excerpt's structural and sonic similarity to the original source. This is, in fact, the standard approach of the forensic musicologists, who often serve as expert witnesses in such copyright cases.[22] For example, the forensic musicologists Durand Begault, Heather Heise, and Christopher Peltier (2014) have called for these formalistic comparisons to become the main method used in the forensic analysis of music, as they believe that "expert opinions based merely on subjective impression or from 'golden ear' analysis are pseudo-scientific and not objectively based" (1). A formal comparative analysis of the excerpt and its source that is based on "a series of structured categorizations" should, according to them, ensure "a consistent, replicable, and objectively verifiable means of determining whether or not a recorded piece of music has been misappropriated" (1). While such formalized categorizations and analytical criteria may be useful to some legal cases concerned with music, they do not inform the debate over whether a particular use of a sample constitutes copyright infringement. As discussed throughout this book, and as pointed out by Julia Kristeva and Roland Barthes, among others (see chapter 4), transformativeness transcends that which can be gleaned from the representational or "writerly" level of a given work. That is, a sample can be exactly the same as the original at the representational or writerly level yet be completely different by virtue of its transformation from one context to another.[23] Such tests are blind to the potential for subsequent originality in the use of existing work. While forensic musicologists often have backgrounds in the humanities rather than the law, methods such as these manifestly overlook intertextual insights and thus (unintentionally) sustain the gap between law and art.

Nor is it easy to reconcile the concepts of parody in the fields of art and law, respectively. As discussed in chapter 2, art scholars generally define parody as an acknowledged appropriation that displays an ironic critical distance to the parodied work(s). Parody here is multifunctional and does not necessarily involve mockery; while it may well be satirical, it may also be a benign joke or commentary. Its key features of incongruity and irony combined with sense making often trigger a humorous response, but parody is not necessarily experienced as, or intended to be, humorous as such. The core of the parody is that which lies outside the representation itself; it is the sum of the divergent associations that the parody sets into motion that makes it an effective and valuable aesthetic and communicative resource. In EU law, as discussed in chapter 5, a work that qualifies as parody must "evoke an existing work, while being noticeably different from it" and "constitute an expression of humour or mockery."[24] There is thus a potential, though not inevitable, conflict between the ways in which parody is defined in EU law and in the arts due to several factors. Although the fields of law and art agree that parody should evoke an existing work (point 1), they might disagree on whether the new work is noticeably different from that which it parodies, especially if it is the work's meaning that has been changed, not its representational features. That is, if a recycled work is not textually altered, an evaluation of it in a legal context might reject it as parody even if people from the field of art celebrate it as such in their recognition that the work is transformed due to its recontextualization alone. It is thus not the letter of the law but the restriction of its implications that can create a gap between the two fields. The subsequent legal requirement (point 2) clearly differs from how parody is understood in the field of art, which acknowledges mockery and humor as potential functions of parody but actually emphasizes parody's irony and multifunctionality instead. Still, it all depends on how the work's humor is evaluated within the field of law—that is, whether the legal determination of the work's humor relies on humor scholars' notion that humor should be interpreted rather broadly (such as emphasizing incongruity)[25] or whether it depends entirely on a few individuals' experiences of the work or the parodist's articulation of their intent, in which the notion of humor might be limited to the incitement of laughter. Ultimately, if the humor requirement of the legal concept of parody implies an acknowledged appropriation that displays ironic, critical difference from the parodied work, then the legal definition of parody might correspond to the way in which parody is understood in the field of art. On the other hand, the way in which a given work is interpreted by legal stakeholders may also serve to narrow the concept of parody, which in turn narrows parody's future definitions, cultural circulation, and creation.

Although we must acknowledge that the law remains a domain distinct from the arts, with its own concepts and definitions, we should not underestimate the power that law and legal enforcement have with respect to incentivizing, discouraging, or abating artistic practice. This power contributes in turn to the establishment and maintenance of the hegemony and persuasiveness of certain cultural ideologies, as discussed above. One of the purposes of copyright is to facilitate the flourishing of art and culture, and it does so via incentives and rewards, but if there is insufficient communication between the two fields, these means can lead to overprotectiveness and barriers to artistic practice. The ways in which copyright has been enacted in recent decades suggest that it tends to foster some forms of creative expression while rejecting others, despite their deep historical roots and significant (and obvious) social value. Whereas the law still has room for several forms of acknowledged appropriation (including mashups) via its exceptions, they may be excluded because of a lack of artistic insight into, and thus a narrow legal interpretation of, concepts such as transformativeness and parody. It is the interpretation, not the law itself, that is the greatest hurdles for mashups and other remixes, through initiatives such as internet platforms' content moderation measures.

The Positional Power of Private Actors

In chapter 6, I argued that content moderation presents a major threat to sample-based music, as it does not adequately accommodate copyright exceptions and thus often eliminates gray-area content. I reported on mashup producers who explained that platforms' content moderation has restricted their creative choices and directed where and how they distribute their mashups, as well as affected their overall motivation to produce this music. Valuable archives of comments and likes are lost upon the termination of a producer's account, they explained, and several felt that they had been forced off their preferred platform and banished to less visited sites. The chilling effects of content moderation had also led some of them to stop creating or sharing mashups altogether. This situation prompts critical reflection regarding the third question I posed above: What cultural and juridical power should private corporations be allowed to wield in the name of their internal policies?

The urgency of this trend toward the removal or monetization of content at the expense of the appropriate application of copyright exceptions is underscored by the Digital Single Market (DSM) Directive adopted by the European Parliament in April 2019. As briefly mentioned in chapter 6, this directive considerably narrows the immunity from legal responsibility of the EU platforms (or more precisely "online content service providers") who host third-party, copyright-infringing content.[26] Prior to this ruling, platforms were not held responsible for hosting infringing content unless they were notified of infringement by copyright holders and did not act to remove that content (see chapter 6, note 42). Now, EU platforms can be sued for hosting content that infringes on others' works even when they are not notified of this infringement. The only exception to this rule is if the content is licensed, which may, for example, happen via monetization. EU member states were required to implement the DSM Directive by June 21, 2021; as of this writing, it remained too early to understand the directive's implications, including the extent to which it would affect non-EU-based platforms. Still, the directive clearly leaves platforms and platform users in a tricky situation with respect to content that resides in the legal gray area.

Given the massive amount of content uploaded onto platforms every day, they are simply unable to evaluate gray-area content on a case-by-case basis. The DSM Directive's narrowing of their immunity from liability thus seems to offer EU platforms four options when it comes to what they do about gray-area content: (1) they can remove it all to ensure that they are not breaching the law and implement staydown filters to ensure that it is not reuploaded (for more on staydown filters, see chapter 6); (2) they can ignore it and hope that they are not sued if it turns out that the content is determined to be illegal; (3) they can try to secure a large-scale licensing agreement via the monetization of gray-area content with major copyright holders (see chapter 6 for an explanation of how this works); or (4) they can try to develop algorithms to detect content that most likely falls under copyright exceptions.

None of these options are particularly promising. The first option could, in a worst-case scenario, mean the death of remixes on the relevant platforms, which would change the internet as we know it and make the contemporary cultural environment much poorer for a significant number of people. Happily, article 17(7) of the DSM Directive insists that member states ensure that users are able to rely on the relevant copyright exceptions when uploading their content into online content-sharing services.[27] This presumably gives platforms an incentive to allow or put back content that falls within the contested area of copyright, which would in turn tilt them toward the second option mentioned: ignoring gray-area content. However, their fear of secondary liability makes this alternative less palatable. After all, it was this fear, coupled with their commercial interests, that led them to the costly and resource-intensive step of developing internal content-moderation measures in the first place (see chapter 6). The third option—to monetize the content and split the revenues with the copyright holder—would allow gray-area content to stay up while meeting the requirement of Article 17 of the DSM Directive. Yet as I argued in chapter 6, monetization of this content is a top-down strategy (outside the purview of the creator of the content) that treats the content as infringement even when it is not and dismisses the fact that it might not even need permission. As such, it undermines the purpose of copyright exceptions—that is, to preserve freedom of expression by ensuring that certain forms of content are outside the control of copyright holders. Moreover, platforms' and copyright holders' colonization of gray-area content—sharing the revenue that it brings in but not with the producer of the content—is problematic for ethical as well as legal reasons: if the use qualifies for copyright itself, it is the creator of the content that should profit from it, not the copyright holder of the sampled content, and that creator may not even want the content to be commercial in the first place.[28] And if monetization were the only feasible option for meeting the requirements of the DSM Directive, it could even lead to an unfortunate state of monopolism: few platforms have the resources to use content-moderation technology, and even when they do, not all copyright holders qualify for it (see chapter 6), meaning that a few major platforms (such as YouTube and Facebook) and a few major copyright holders (such as the big music labels) would end up dominating the market (see also Tushnet 2019).

While these first three alternatives are not especially helpful to either platforms or creators, the fourth alternative—to develop algorithms to detect gray area content—is even worse. As argued in chapter 6, the sheer amount of content makes a case-by-case review impossible, and even if the number of human content moderators who supplement the platforms' automated content moderation were to increase dramatically, this still would not allow platforms to review cases individually. The task of determining whether the unauthorized use of material is an instance of infringement will thus always be assigned first and foremost to algorithms, however ill suited to it they are. For example, using machine-learning identification technology to detect parodies is enormously challenging due to the complex task of finding applicable features. Content matching, for example, does not recognize how the material is being used or for what purposes; it cannot identify the specific sociocultural meanings in which parody is enmeshed. Likewise, technology that bases its detection on metadata (such as titles, descriptive information, and comments) will tend to generate incorrect matches, including false positives—videos that are parody in name only—and false negatives—dismissing a true parody for not being so.[29] Though there are numerous ways to design algorithms and humans retain a crucial role in the process of designing them, machine-learning technology is not capable of identifying a parody's web of texts, contexts, and connotations like a human interpreter can. Content moderation thus risks reducing parody to its representational and paratextual features alone, ignoring the critical impact of context and that which exists beyond the representational level.

Of course, I am not suggesting that platforms should treat each individual case of gray-area content with the same amount of time and resources that a court would. But they need to be in dialogue with the fields of both law and art to find solutions that protect content from being infringed while sustaining the effectiveness of copyright exceptions. Fundamentally, they must be able to distinguish between content that uses copyrighted material in a (textually or contextually) transformative way and that which does not. While this distinction does not guarantee a successful defense of the content under the parody or quotation exceptions in EU law or the fair use doctrine in US law, it at least acknowledges the possibility of such a defense. This should in turn qualify the content for immunity from blocking and takedown (unless a court considers it infringement). The fact that platforms currently represent a nexus through which numerous members of society communicate among themselves also means that they have an inappropriate opportunity to influence the premises of our debates and principles of freedom of expression (including freedom of the arts). Being banned from the major platforms, that is, sometimes means being banned from the cultural public sphere.[30] In contrast to a court proceeding, content moderation does not bring with it the same guarantee of unbiased treatment, transparency, and public and juridical oversight.[31] And as Vaidhyanathan reminds us, if private interests carry the day, copyright could be misused as an instrument to censor culturally valuable expressions rather than serve the public good (2003, 184). It is therefore crucial to maintain the efficacy and thus relevance of copyright exceptions in the context of platform regulation—we must ensure that the role of the law in society, including copyright law's careful balancing act between property rights and freedom of expression, is not subverted by private contracts.

As I have tried to demonstrate throughout this book, the current situation is complex and not easily resolved due to the many competing and legitimate interests and rights involved in it. Yet it is far too important and consequential to be ignored. Especially concerning is that a given cultural expression's fate (survival or destruction) resides with a simple rule programmed into an algorithm designed by a private corporation. An algorithm should not have this power. While I acknowledge that the public sphere cannot be freed from commercial interests and that private actors can operate with their own sets of policies and rules, we should be mindful that those actors have a responsibility to serve the social ambitions of democratic participation and, as Rosemary J. Coombe (1998) emphasizes, that government must sustain the balance between private property and freedom of expression. Though the platforms are private, their hegemonic power to regulate culture is not a private matter.

The case presented in this book represents a much more profound challenge that we currently face regarding how we regulate and preserve culture. That is, there is more at stake than the simple survival of mashups and other forms of parody in the age of remix, and there is more to problematize than the content moderation practices of platforms. We find ourselves at a political crossroads where long-established art forms are facing dramatic technological changes in terms of both the mode of production and distribution and the ways in which they are regulated. What governments, private institutions and actors, legislators, scholars, everyday users and producers, and other stakeholders do next will have far-reaching consequences. To that end, it is in everyone's best interest to communicate early and often across the fields of art, law, and media to refine and sustain the diverse perspectives and cultural expressions that a democratic society deserves.

Appendix: Notes on MASHED Interview and Survey Methods

Ellis Jones and Ragnhild Brøvig
University of Oslo, May 2020

This document provides further information on the interview and survey methods used in the research project MASHED: Mashup Music, Copyright, and Platform Regulation. MASHED consists of Ragnhild Brøvig (project leader), Alan Hui and Ellis Jones (postdocs), Irina Eidsvold-Tøien, Miloš Novović, and Elisabeth Staksrud (researchers), and Eirik Jacobsen and Øyvind Skjerdal (research assistants). Vemund Hegstad Alm, Ole Kristian Bekkevold, Oskar Holldorff, and Solveig Wang also worked as research assistants for defined periods to perform specific tasks. The project is funded by the Research Council of Norway through FRIPRO (project 275441) and through its Centres of Excellence scheme (RITMO, project 262762), and it is based at the University of Oslo. Since the research team will be drawing on interview and survey material as a shared central resource, we have compiled this document to provide additional context regarding the methodological choices. This document is not intended to replace methods sections in other publications (which will be tailored to fit their purpose) but rather to complement them.

Research Population

The project's central research ambition to understand mashup producers' experiences with mashups, copyright, and online platforms provided the orienting justification for seeking data from this population. For the purposes of this study, we define mashups as musical productions that are primarily based on generally recognizable samples of existing musical recordings. The definition of *mashup producer* is also based on this definition of *mashup*. While we sought mashup producers from anywhere in the world, we had a particular interest in European and US producers, since the project seeks to consider the legality of mashups in the context of European and US law and to explore the producers' perspectives on the legality of their own mashups and the ways in which mashups are regulated in the name of the law.

Sample Selection

The sample of producers we approached satisfied various criteria of diversity in order to represent a broad range of contributions to the mashup scene. We considered aspects including location, background, age, and gender (although some aspects of the identity of practitioners were not necessarily known to us). We also sought to assure diversity in the participants' choice of distribution platform, mashup style, level of popularity, and extent of current involvement in mashups (that is, a blend of theoretical sampling and diversity sampling). Some efforts to produce a diverse sample were more successful than others. For example, the mashup scene is predominantly male, and we struggled to locate and communicate with female producers. The project's focus on US and European law influenced the interview sample in terms of the producers' location: fourteen resided in the European Union (then including the United Kingdom), fourteen resided in the United States, and two resided elsewhere.

The survey was open to anyone who self-defined as a mashup producer based on the definition above. Initial screening questions confirmed this status while ensuring that the respondents were over eighteen years old. We recruited respondents largely via social media (primarily Twitter), as well as personal messages to mashup producers and posts on mashup and remix online forums. We also relied on word-of-mouth recruitment via trusted copractitioners; these were helpful in drawing attention to the survey publicly over Twitter and Reddit, as well as privately via messages and within closed groups. We remained aware that the nature of online sharing can result in the overrepresentation of specific "hubs" within the scene—that is, groups of friends or acquaintances—and lower representation of other groups that we did not reach.

Themes and Methods

The interview guide contained questions about the music that the interviewees made; the scene and community of which they were a part; their perspectives on the music industries and copyright, as well as online platforms and their regulatory systems; and their experiences with and responses to these systems. (The interview guide is available from the MASHED project website: https://www.uio.no/ritmo/english/projects/mashed/mashups-copyright/.) The choice to format these interviews as semistructured allowed for the conversations to expand to other areas, including the producers' perspectives on social structures, industries, institutions, and their life courses more generally. When coding the interview transcriptions, we combined our preestablished codes with unanticipated ones that emerged through a thematic analysis of the data (Braun and Clarke 2006). Thematic analysis acknowledges that the themes of the interview guide may not be the same as those revealed by the patterning of responses across the data set and insists that the themes reported should be supported by the data.

The survey questionnaire (also available on the project's website), which used the online survey service JISC, covered similar themes but framed its questions in ways intended to generate a more overall picture of the mashup scene, including quantitatively (for example, a quantification of the frequency with which producers experienced takedowns). We prepared, analyzed, and presented the survey results using SPSS (Statistical Package for the Social Sciences).

Interview Medium

We conducted most of the interviews via online video calls to allow us to reach mashup producers across several continents. Approximately one-third of the interviews were face-to-face. We concur with Valeria Lo Iacono, Symonds, and David Brown (2016) that the advantages of using Skype (or its equivalents) outweigh the limitations. Two interviews were text only, in accordance with the practitioners' preferences, using the private direct-messaging system on Twitter. These interviews offered less time for deep reflection since the conversations were more measured and formal via text.

Participant Safeguarding

As part of an informed consent process, we made the aims of the project clear and comprehensible to the (potential) participants. Along with providing a description of the project in the written consent form they had to sign, we outlined it at the beginning of the interviews and invited any questions they might have. This effort to establish informed consent was also a primary motivation for the creation of two project videos, made in collaboration with filmmaker Joshua Perrett, which accessibly outlined the purposes of both the project and the survey for the research participants. Both before and after the data collection process, we maintained the project Twitter account with which we initially reached out to the producers in an effort to remain available beyond the formal, institutional context of the university websites and emails.

The interviewees could choose to be quoted anonymously or by their artist pseudonyms (that is, their "stage names" or production aliases). Julia Downes, Maddie Breeze, and Naomi Griffin (2013) have suggested that in research on DIY cultures specifically (which arguably include mashup), "removing identifiable information can undermine participant labour, power and agency," and that "the explicit naming of participants can become a moral and ethical obligation." The vast majority of the participants chose to be referred to by their pseudonyms, and we are pleased to be able to attribute the many illuminating reflections to them directly. Some of the interviewees pointed out that they were taking a risk, but a necessary one, in providing us with information. Mashup producer Kap Slap said, "I'm a little reluctant to tell you all this. . . . But it's a risk you gotta take to inform people about this." We have therefore tried to mitigate the risks of naming individuals (even using pseudonyms) in certain contexts. A related concern involved divulging the strategies producers use to avoid or mislead content ID systems—strategies that are crucial to their continued capacity to make and distribute mashups. One important consequence of this risk management is that in the published accounts, we have removed the names of some mashup-specific websites since we feared that the publications might otherwise have drawn undue and unwanted attention to them.

Responses to the survey were anonymous, a decision we made largely to fulfill our responsibilities under the EU General Data Protection Regulation (or GDPR). We recoded some demographic information to maintain participant anonymity; for instance, responses relating to nationality and country of residence were recoded to larger geographical regions. Any identifying material provided by respondents in free-text answers was removed.

The interviews and survey followed the ethical guidelines set out by the National Committee for Research Ethics in the Social Sciences and the Humanities (NESH) and the Norwegian Centre for Research Data (NSD).

The data from the interviews and survey are treated according to the data management plan developed during the project's startup, including safe storage. The interviewees were asked to sign informed-consent forms, and all requests for confidentiality have been honored.

Relationship between Interview and Survey

The use of both survey and interview material—combining, as it does, quantitative and qualitative approaches—corresponds to the sphere of mixed-methods research. However, unlike much mixed-methods work, we give epistemological primacy to a "qualitative-interpretivist" approach rather than a "quantitative-experimental" one (Howe 2004). Instead of positioning the measurable data as the most "meaningful" aspect of the project, we looked to interview material and free-text survey responses for ontological depth regarding the producers' experiences and used the survey data to gain an overview of, and situate the interview data within, the broader mashup context. The overarching methodological approach of the project is in keeping with a critical-realism paradigm in which statistics and other quantitative findings simply "quantify certain characteristics of a structure or object" and therefore act primarily as "descriptive summaries rather than predictive tools" (Zachariadis, Scott, and Barrett 2013, 862). Critical realism also helps to clarify why the copresence of qualitative and quantitative data does not constitute an epistemological clash, since, in this approach, "methods are seen to be redescriptive devices uncovering alternative views of objects of analysis in order to compare their relative standing (and therefore the validity of the findings produced) as well as allowing them to mutually inform each other" (877). Another consideration related to the simultaneous use of interviews and surveys is that due to the survey being anonymous, we cannot be sure of the precise extent of overlap between the samples. However, given our awareness of where the survey was circulated, we feel confident that the two sources of data supply a meaningfully coherent representation of the same actors, institutions, and phenomena.

Reflection on Methodological Limitations

One limitation of the project is that our decision to focus on mashup producers gives us insight into their individual motivations but not the motivations of other actors. For example, we do not have interview or survey data reflecting perspectives from the music industries (including rights-holders). We have generally drawn on trade press and existing scholarship to gain insight into those perspectives. Initial plans to also interview and/or survey representatives of online platforms did not come to fruition.

References

Braun, Virginia, and Victoria Clarke. 2006. "Using Thematic Analysis in Psychology." *Qualitative Research in Psychology* 3 (2), 77–101.

Downes, Julia, Maddie Breeze, and Naomi Griffin. 2013. "Researching DIY Cultures: Towards a Situated Ethical Practice for Activist-Academia." *Graduate Journal of Social Science* 10 (3).

Howe, Kenneth R. 2004. "A Critique of Experimentalism." *Qualitative Inquiry* 10 (1), 42–61.

Lo Iacono, Valeria, Paul Symonds, and David H. K. Brown. 2016. "Skype as a Tool for Qualitative Research Interviews." *Sociological Research Online* 21 (2), 1–15.

Zachariadis, Markos, Susan Scott, and Michael Barrett. 2013. "Methodological Implications of Critical Realism for Mixed-Methods Research." *MIS Quarterly* 37 (3), 855–879.

Notes

Chapter 1

1. Over the past twenty years, the study of remix has evolved into a research field of its own. Important books and dissertations include, among many others, Aufderheide and Jaszi 2018; Boone 2011; Borschke 2017; Burgess 2007; Church 2022; Gallagher 2018; Gunkel 2016; Jenkins 2006; Laderman and Westrup 2014; Lessig 2008; McGranahan 2010; Navas 2012; Navas, Gallagher, and Burrough 2015, 2018, 2021; and Sinnreich 2010, 2013. This list excludes several important works on remix (including articles and book chapters), as well as works on hip-hop and EDM, that also represent significant contributions to the field.

2. Not without reason have several scholars and journalists referred to remix as the "defining feature" (Gibson 2005, 118) and "dominant aesthetics" (Manovich 2013, 267) of contemporary culture and as "part of how our culture operates and relates to itself" (Howard-Spink 2005).

3. See, for example, Hutcheon 2000 and Rose 1993.

4. This definition of parody relies in part on Linda Hutcheon's definition of it as "a form of repetition with ironic critical distance, marking difference rather than similarity" (2000, xii). For a more detailed discussion of parody and mashup music, see chapters 2 and 3.

5. Works that do address this current threat include Aufderheide 2015; Aufderheide and Jaszi 2018; Birk 2015; burrough and Erickson 2015; Coleman and Anthoney 2020; Gallagher 2013, 2015, 2018; Gillespie et al. 2020; Jacques 2019; Jacques et al. 2018; and Tushnet 2014, 2019; as well as the output of the research group MASHED (including Brøvig-Hanssen and Jones 2021; Hui 2021a, 2021b; and Jones 2021b).

6. For a range of broad definitions of mashup, see, for example, Cefrey 2008; Gunkel 2008, 504; Harrison and Navas 2018, 195–197; Horwatt 2008a; O'Brien and Fitzgerald 2006, 1–2; Sonvilla-Weiss 2010, 8; and Tough 2010, 205–206.

7. According to the survey we conducted with ninety-two mashup producers, 46 percent of respondents reported that they primarily made A+B mashups; 49 percent said that they did a combination of A+B mashups and megamixes; and 5 percent said that they made only megamixes.

8. For an overview of the development of the term *remix*, see, for example, Borschke 2017; Church 2022; Frosio 2021; Gunkel 2016; and Navas 2012, 2018.

9. This club night was initially called "Kind of the Boots," before it was rebaptized "Bastard" (Howard-Spink 2005; McGranahan 2010, 11; and Shiga 2007, 94).

10. According to McSlzy as well as the mashup producers interviewed by Liam McGranahan (2010, 17), the GYBO conversations sprawled beyond mashups to include politics, news events, and sports, which contributed to strengthening the feeling of community on the website.

11. In addition to numerous mashups (or "bootlegs")—including works by Freelance Hellraiser, Frenchbloke, Girl Talk, Girls on Top (aka Richard X), Kurtis Rush, Osymyso, McSleazy (aka McSlzy), Soulwax (aka 2ManyDJs), and Soundhog—the compilation also contained official releases that were considered relevant to the scene (probably because of their liberal use of sampling), including tracks by the Avalanches, Coldcut, Eric B. and Rakim, John Oswald, Kid606, The KLF, M/A/A/R/S, Negativland, and DJ Shadow. For more on the Boom Selection website and CD, see, for example, Boom Selection n.d.; McGranahan 2010, 12; Orlando Weekly 2002; and Plagenhoef 2003.

12. For the complete track list, see Discogs n.d.

13. The MTV documentary *MTV: Ultimate Mashup-Ups: Jay Z vs. Linkin Park* was released in November 2004. For more on the Linkin Park/Jay-Z mashup collaboration, see Huhn 2005 and Wiederhorn 2020. See also Robson 2021 for McSlzy's memories of contributing to the *MTV Mash* show.

14. For more on this contest, see Gunkel 2008, 490–491; Huhn 2005; and Sherwin 2004.

15. In addition to several UK mashup producers, certain established artists (including DJ Shadow, Grandmaster Flash, and Daft Punk) also contributed to this game's development (McGranahan 2010, 14).

16. In an attempt to move beyond the traditional binary of producer and consumer, Axel Bruns (2009) introduced the words *produser* (producer/user) and *produsage*, echoing Alvin Toffler's (1980) portmanteaus *prosumer* (producer/consumer), and *prosumption*, which were later adopted by George Ritzer and Nathan Jurgenson (2010), among others. Leadbeater and Miller further emphasized the omnipresence of so-called pro-ams, which they defined as "amateurs who work to professional standards" (2004, 12). Aram Sinnreich (2010) and Jean Burgess (2007) further noted

that within this "configurable" or "vernacular" culture, it is not only the traditional cultural binary of amateur/professional or artist/audience that is blurred but also the related binaries of art/craft, original/copy, underground/commercial, private/public, and ordinary/spectacular (content).

17. See, for example, Bourriaud 2005; Bruns 2009; Gunkel 2016; Jenkins 2006; Laderman and Westrup 2014; Lessig 2008; Manovich 2001; Navas 2012; Navas, Gallagher, and Burrough 2015; Rosa, Clifford, and Sinnreich 2021; and Sinnreich 2010.

18. According to McGranahan, while Girl Talk is often introduced as a mashup producer, his association with mashups is problematic on both sides: several of his peers consider him an outsider, and Girl Talk has also distanced himself from the scene in interviews (2010, 14–15).

19. See, for example, Berry 2008; Dijck 2013; Gillespie 2018; Guertin 2012; and Wu 2018.

20. For a description of Mashuptown, see, for example, Boone 2011, 82, 164.

21. The survey shows that among the ninety-two producers who responded, 17 percent of them started to produce mashups between 1999 and 2004, 37 percent between 2005 and 2010, and 44 percent between 2011 and 2017. While this summary may, of course, say more about the group taking the survey than about the scene at large, it does show that many people started producing mashups during the second decade of the millennium as well.

22. A cease-and-desist order is a standard procedure whereby a copyright holder or their attorney sends a notification letter to the assumed infringer with a demand that the infringement stop. It is often interpreted as a warning involving the possibility of resorting to the judicial system.

23. The a cappella version of the *Black Album* was released by Roc-a-Fella as an invitation to remix and reuse Jay-Z's tracks.

24. Sam Howard-Spink (2005) reports that the file-sharing tracking company Big-Champagne estimated that over 100,000 copies of the album were downloaded that day. For more on Grey Tuesday, see also Jones 2021b and Rambarran 2013.

25. 17 U.S.C. § 512.

26. Articles 12–15 of the Electronic Commerce Directive (ECD). Directive 2000/31/EC of the European Parliament and of the Council of June 8, 2000, on Certain Legal Aspects of Information Society Services, in Particular Electronic Commerce, *Official Journal* L178 (2000).

27. I carried out the interviews together with Ellis Jones and Alan Hui; they were transcribed by Eirik Jacobsen, Oskar Holldorff, and Ole Kristian Bekkevold. Ellis

Jones (in the lead) and I carried out the survey, with helpful advice from Elisabeth Staksrud as well as input from the other members of MASHED.

28. I have chosen not to name these various subcommunity platforms due to the risk of their potential entanglement in copyright issues.

29. The survey showed that 64 percent of the producers reported that they were currently active in areas of music other than mashups (as DJs or musicians and as professionals or hobbyists), and the interviews also revealed that several of the producers of the later mashup generation had a music background as well. For example, DJ Cummerbund pointed to his master's degree in music and experience playing music his entire life; Isosine said that he played several different instruments and considered music production as a career before he started producing mashups; and DJ Poulpi described a background playing classical piano and performing in metal and rock bands.

30. The MASHED project that I initiated and led for three years involved fellow scholars Alan Hui, Ellis Jones, Irina Eidsvold-Tøien, Miloš Novović, and Elisabeth Staksrud, as well as research assistants Eirik Jacobsen and Øyvind Skjerdal. Vemund Hegstad Alm, Ole Kristian Bekkevold, Oskar Holldorff, and Solveig Wang also worked as research assistants for shorter periods to perform specific tasks.

31. Links to the mashup examples that I mention throughout this book can be found on the MASHED website at a page dedicated to this book (although there is, of course, no guarantee that these links will continue to be functional). See https://www.uio.no/ritmo/english/projects/mashed/mashups-copyright/.

Chapter 2

1. See, for example, Ayers 2006; Boone 2011; Fairchild 2017; Guertin 2012; Howard-Spink 2005; Katz 2012; Levay 2005; McLeod 2005; and Serazio 2008.

2. See, for example, Adams 2015, Boone 2013, Holm-Hudson 1997, McLeod 2005; and Roseman 2007.

3. See, for example, Adams 2015; Brøvig-Hanssen and Harkins 2012; Cruger 2003; and McLeod 2005.

4. Typologies of intertextual practices within the field of popular music have also been proposed by several scholars, including Boone 2013; Lacasse 2007, 2018; Ratcliffe 2014; Sewell 2013; and Williams 2014.

5. Although typologies can provide a basis for comparison and otherwise aid the analysis of music relying on prior music, they remain problematic in that their validity relies on the relevance of their selected features, and there are almost always some features that are excluded as well. In addition, different sets of features will

lead to different groupings, depending on what one determines to be most relevant feature-wise. Another challenge with typologies is that there are usually cases that can be assigned to several categories at once and cases that do not fit into any category at all. Finally, since typologies consist of constructed categories based on various features, the categories are often given names that require further explanation, meaning that the reader of a text using a typology must learn the typology in question in order to understand the analysis. If a typology is to be useful, then, it must be firmly established, which is why I limit myself here to the typology of parody, satire, homage, pastiche, and plagiarism while discussing the variables of appropriations independently.

6. See, for example, Burns and Lacasse 2018; Hawkins 2002; and Turner 2016.

7. For a similar discussion of these two different meanings of intertextuality, see, for example, Allen 2011; Echard 2018; Klein 2004; and Mai 1991.

8. For other examples, see Howard 1974; Metzer 2003; and Williams 2014.

9. See also Sinnreich 2010, 124, for the same notion.

10. See, for example, Burkholder 1994; Goodman 1974; Holm-Hudson 1997; Howard 1974; Katz 2004; Lacasse 2000; Metzer 2003; and Williams 2014. To several scholars, a musical quotation necessitates the recognition of its reference; this recognition, David Metzer argues, forms the crux of the musical quotation (2003, 6–7). Others regard it as an ontological criterion, in which the quotation marks are either concealed or exposed; V. A. Howard (1974), for example, posits that a quotation only requires containment; it does not cease to be a quotation if it is not recognized as such. To him, similarity to and the familiarity of the source are only symptoms of the quotation's presence, not that which defines it. Moreover, as Amanda Sewell (2013, 3) points out in her critique of David Sanjek's (1994, 348–351) typology of sampling, recognition is a criterion that is difficult to quantify.

11. *Appropriation* is from the Latin *appropriare*, which means "to make one's own" (Navas, Gallagher, and burrough et al. 2018, 15).

12. Another related term is *adaptation*, and these terms are sometimes used interchangeably. However, as Julie Sanders (2015, 35–36) points out, whereas both often signal a relationship to an existing source that demands a "reading alongside," adaptation involves a generic shift, such as turning a book into a film or a film into a video game, whereas appropriation does not.

13. In his discussion of musical appropriations, Boon distinguishes between appropriation in its broadest sense, arguing that "all musical experience involves and is constituted by appropriation," and appropriation in a narrower sense—that is, "what we might call the secondary, more literal appropriations of 'other people's sounds'" (Boon 2007, 7). Boon's distinction further evokes Jeanette Bicknell's differentiation

of "coincidental similarities" between works and "deliberate evocations" of specific works (and, we might add, styles) (2001, 185).

14. This quote by Mikhail Bakhtin, often cited in isolation, represents a rather reductive description of his much broader notion of the concept of intertextuality, as well as Julia Kristeva's notion of her own term, *intertextualité* (see more below). Still, as Michael L. Klein points out, intertextuality is often used in scholarly contexts (including the discipline of musicology) synonymously with influence and the poietic connections between works, in terms of both assumed and documented influence (2004, 11–12). It has also been used with regard to the inevitable linking of texts when one experiences music (see, for example, Middleton 2000, 61). This take on intertextuality is also related to Gérard Genette's "transtextuality," which he defines as "all that sets the text in a relationship, whether obvious or concealed, with other texts" (1997, 1).

15. Related to this variable is Burkholder's distinction between "borrowing" and "allusion," wherein the latter points to "general repertoires and archetypes or even to the styles of individual composers as a closely related but different phenomenon" (1994, 863). Robert Hatten similarly distinguishes between "strategic referentiality," which asserts and plays with a text's individuality (that is, a specific work) and the style in which the text is enmeshed, and "stylistic intertextuality," which refers to "strategies which have lost their individuality" (Hatten 1985, 70). Spicer (2009, 353–354) applies Hatten's concepts to the field of popular music. Theodore Gracyk likewise differentiates between "general" and "specific intertextuality" (2001, 58–59).

16. For a discussion of the definition of sampling, see, for example, Harkins (2019) and Kvifte (2007). Inspired by Nelson Goodman's (1968) terms *allographic* and *autographic works*, Lacasse distinguishes between "allosonic" and "autosonic quotations," in which the former implies that musicians are reperforming a specific musical reference (as in cover songs), whereas the latter refers to the physical copying of a musical reference (as in sampling) (2007, 38–39; 2018, 26). In the context of this book, I prefer to distinguish between re-created or performed and sampled forms of appropriation, because these descriptors are more intuitive than allosonic and autosonic and, in addition, quotation is itself an ambiguous term (see note 10 in this chapter).

17. For the notion of sound, see, for example, Brøvig-Hanssen and Danielsen (2013).

18. I here refer to the terminology of Charles S. Peirce, in which "index" describes "a sign which refers to the Object that it denotes by virtue of being really affected by that Object" (Peirce 1960, 143).

19. Gallagher points out the importance of recognizing medium specificity and considers sampling to be the most characteristic feature that distinguishes remixes from other intertextual practices: "The ability to sample by cutting, copying, and pasting is one of the defining traits of new media that enables much of its potential

and it is the primary means by which remixing can occur. Prior to the possibilities enabled by digital technologies, the acts of sampling and remixing were much more cumbersome and limited activities. Above all other traits, sampling is the fundamental property that makes remix what it is and separates it from several other forms of intertextual practices" (Gallagher 2018, 31).

20. My perspectives here differ from that of Navas, Gallagher, and burrough and colleagues (2018, 18), who reserve *appropriation* for instances "when we can recognize the pieces the artist has used."

21. I here rely on Gérard Genette's distinction between text (understood in the narrow sense) and "paratext"—that is, titles, illustrations, prefaces, and book covers (1997, 3–4)—instead of the common distinction between text and context, to indicate that I regard both types of information as integral to the work or text (understood in its broader sense; see also chapter 4). The clues outside of the "narrow" text can also be signaled "metatextually"—that is, through critical commentaries related to the text, for example (3–4).

22. Whereas Sabine Jacques (2019, 10) writes that parody, as opposed to pastiche, is based on one work only, this view is not shared by other parody authorities. Linda Hutcheon, for example, gives several examples of parodies that rely on more than one work (see, for example, Hutcheon 2000, 7, 46, 60, 67).

23. Marion Hestholm defines the concept of montage as incorporating "works that openly display their compoundness, either by presenting contrasts and disjunctions in the musical continuum or by displaying a multiplicity of references within a more or less fragile continuity" (2010, 14). As she points out, *montage* and *collage* have often been used interchangeably, though a montage is often associated with film theory—partly thanks to the Soviet film director and scholar Sergej Eisenstein's theorization of the concept—and the "temporal relationships among things in motion," as opposed to collage, which is sometimes defined as the "spatial relationships among static objects" (Hestholm 2010, 24). See also Cook 2006, 121–122, for a similar notion.

24. Despite this emphasis on editing as a creative act resulting in a collision of sources, Eisenstein still sees the film as a coherent whole in and of itself (Harrah 1954, 172). He adds that the collision of sources does not always result in such an amalgamation but can also generate "the sensation of duality" (Eisenstein 1986, 15).

25. While mashup music as a whole is evaluatively open, the information from this study's interviews and survey with mashup producers suggests, as I discuss in the following chapter, that most mashups tilt toward the homage end of the spectrum rather than the satirical end. Still, this does not mean that they are received along these lines.

26. For thorough discussions of the mixtape, see, for example, Boon 2010, 53–57, and Lacasse and Bennett 2018.

27. Plagiarism stems from the Latin *plagiarus*, which means "kidnapper." For a thorough discussion of plagiarism, see Dyer 2007, 25–32.

28. Although the concept of "ironic critical distance" is introduced by Hutcheon (2000), the same phenomenon has been discussed by several other parody scholars as well, as I explain later.

29. Though some scholars refer to these types as different "genres" (see, for example, Hutcheon 2000 and Jacques 2019) and others refer to them as different "techniques" (see, for example, Chambers 2010), I here choose to refer to them as "types," because I find both of the alternatives too limited, in that a parody may be manifested across musical genres and produced by means of various techniques.

30. The Greek *parōidia* ("para") means counter, against, along, or beside, and "ode" means chant, song, or poem (see, for example, Genette 1997, 10, and Hutcheon 2000, 32).

31. See, for example, Rose 1993.

32. See, for example, Chambers 2010, 17; Hutcheon 2000, 60; and Rose 1993, 83, 90.

33. For a discussion of the notion of repetition and difference, see, for example, Deleuze 1994 [1968]; Gates 1988; Jones 1971; and Kierkegaard 1983 [1843].

34. Amy Lai similarly states, "Not only is the presence of comic intent highly subjective, but an overemphasis on this element also risks overlooking parody's other valuable functions" (2019, 36).

35. For a discussion of the similarities between sampling/mashups and other techniques and works in the Middle Ages, see McLeish 2013.

36. Whereas Lawrence Kramer (2004, 113) and Asbjørn Ø. Eriksen (2016, 244) interpret "Golliwog's Cakewalk" as a satirical jest at the expense of the culturally inflated movement of Wagnerism, Martelly (2010) reads it as a commentary on the clash between the painful history of enslaved and colonized people and white bourgeois leisure, in which the Golliwog doll carries racist undertones in its trivialization of this history.

37. For an analysis of "Mission: Impossible Theme/Norwegian Wood" (1968) by Alan Copeland, see, for example, Brøvig-Hanssen and Harkins 2012.

38. Kembrew McLeod (2005, 81) also mentions "The Flying Saucer" by Buchanan and Goodman as a potential mashup predecessor, but as I pointed out in my study with Harkins (Brøvig-Hanssen and Harkins 2012, 92), this early example of a pop montage, also known as a break-in record, actually anticipates music medleys more than mashups because the incongruous juxtapositions of various recordings unfold in linear time without any superimposition (they are separated by clips from a spoof news bulletin about the threat of spacemen landing in a US city). Even a

megamix mashup consists of samples that are aligned atop each other, not strictly successively.

39. I have not even mentioned Charles Ives's music, which is characterized by its explicit juxtapositions of heterogeneous material; see, for example, Burkholder 1985.

Chapter 3

1. The question regarding whether rules guide practice or practice gradually solidifies into rules recalls the chicken-or-the-egg causality dilemma (for causality dilemmas between practice and norms, theory, or structures, see Bourdieu 1977). Although I will not delve into this question here, it is important to note that while most of the interviewed and surveyed mashup producers shared these underlying aesthetic principles, there will always be exceptions, and the empirical data also suggest that there were various and sometimes contradictory ways of realizing these principles, as I demonstrate below.

2. Other scholarly encounters with the aesthetic principles of mashups include the works of Christine E. Boone (2011) and Liam McGranahan (2010). Boone's research, however, relies primarily on her own analysis and interpretation, as well as the instruction manual by Jordan Roseman (2007) (aka DJ Earworm) concerning how to construct a mashup (2011, 123 fn.14), which generates a slimmer account than those that otherwise characterize the subfield, as demonstrated here (though her work is still full of analytical insight). McGranahan's research is based on interviews with eleven mashup producers conducted in 2008 and 2009 (2010, 239). There are several overlaps between his findings and mine, though they also differ in important ways. Also different is his interpretation and organization of his findings; for example, he emphasizes recognizability, whereas I regard it more as a matter of exposing the fact that mashups are appropriations, and he emphasizes genre clash, whereas I see it instead as one of several manifestations of ironic distancing. Aram Sinnreich, whose research is also based on interviews with mashup producers, is not overly concerned with their underlying aesthetic principles but points out that mashup producers emphasize "recognizability as an essential element of the mashup style," that their mashups' appeal is often related to their mixture of scenes and cultures, and that the producers see mashup talent as amounting to more than the possession of technical skills (2010, 114, 132, and 165).

3. In the survey, 80 percent of respondents indicated that the title of their most recent mashup was related to the samples they used in it, and 84 percent further confirmed that they had listed the samples in their track's description.

4. In alignment with the interview results, 87 percent of the survey respondents indicated that, in their most recent mashup, they used samples from songs that they expected most listeners to know.

5. In the survey, 87 percent of respondents indicated that the samples in their most recent mashup were long enough to be readily recognized. See Boone 2011, 40–41, for an exception to this tendency, which she refers to as a "mosaic form of making mashups" and as "paint palette mashups."

6. See Renzo 2021 for a discussion of an exception to this tendency.

7. Music philosopher Jeanette Bicknell similarly notes that the source of a musical quotation need not be recognized for it to be conceptualized as a quotation; it can also be aesthetically effective so long as it is signaled as a quotation (2001, 190). She further insists there is an auditory equivalent of quotation marks and that familiarity with the source is only one of several ways in which those quotation marks are manifested. Another form of manifestation takes place via the listener's "musical literacy"—that is, the competence or knowledge that is often tacit and intuitively acquired, such as one's recognition of the stylistic differences between the primary composition and the quoted material (187).

8. Software programs offering the ability to do vocal and instrumental extraction include Adobe's Audition Center Channel Extractor, Prosoniq's sonic WORX Isolate, and Audionamix's ADX Trax Pro. Software programs enabling AI-based extractions include the online platforms PhonicMind, RX7, and Xtrax.

9. See Boone 2011, 132, and Brøvig-Hanssen 2016, 274–275, for similar notions.

10. See https://www.djprince.no/mixingtips.aspx.

11. Mixed in Key was developed by Yakov Vorobyev; see Vorobyev and Coomes 2012.

12. As Anne Danielsen (2006, 43) explains, the concept of groove encompasses a rhythmic pattern that often consists of several layers forming a fabric of sorts wherein the individual rhythmic components are all in dialogue with one another.

13. Listen, for example, to his mashup "Justin Timberlake vs. 1980's (Can't Stop The 80's)" (2016).

14. The survey respondents added comments in the open survey fields to the effect that mashups should "sound like an original track with effective mixing and mastering" or otherwise display "a solid overall production," "excellent technical quality," "effective mixing and mastering," or a "coherent sound." One of the respondents wrote, "Mastering is a very crucial part of creating a great mashup. I spend hours tirelessly focusing on reverb, delays, EQing, and compressors to create a smooth track."

15. See, for example, his mashup "Rock of Ages" (2012), which illustrates this point.

16. On the notion of social authorship, see, for example, Bennett 2018; Frosio 2021; Guertin 2012; and Toynbee 2001.

17. One example of the ways in which various tracks can be cut up and pasted together to make a coherent lyrical narrative in terms of the call-and-response technique is the mashup "Never Be Afraid to Be Who You Are (Glee vs. Westlife vs. Oasis vs. Cat Stevens)" (2013) by Elastic Productions. The track is part of the compilation album *Bootie Gay Pride!* (2013), curated by Adriana A, and it consists of the Glee cast's cover version of REO Speedwagon's 1984 hit "Can't Fight This Feeling" (2009), Westlife's "Flying without Wings" (1999), Oasis's "Wonderwall" (1995), and Cat Stevens's "Father and Son" (1970). For examples of DJ Earworm's complex constellations of lyrics, see, for example, Yunek, Wadsworth, and Needle 2020.

18. DJ Earworm is here referring to his mashup "If I Were a Free Fallin' Boy (Tom Petty & Beyoncé)" (2016).

19. Listen, for example, to his "Bruno Mars x Ariana Grande x Snoop Dogg x Justin Timmerlake*—24k Magic $igns (Mashup)" (2016). For another example of a mashup in which it sounds as though the artists are singing together in the studio and in which the mashed artists together perform a lyrical message that makes sense (and that comments on these artists' breakup), see AnDyWuMusicland's "Selena Gomez, Justin Bieber—Lose You To Love Me / Sorry (Mashup)" (2019).

20. See, for example, Adamusic's "Katy Perry—The Megamix" (2017) and Isosine's "Ed Sheeran & Sia—Luster" (2015).

21. For more on vaporwave, see, for example, Alm 2021; Born and Haworth 2018; Koc 2017; and Tanner 2016. For more on Simpsonwave, see Church and Feller 2021.

22. The mashup consists of the following tracks: The Weeknd featuring Daft Punk's "I Feel It Coming" (2016); 2Pac's "How Do You Want It" (1996); Michael Jackson's "Human Nature" (1982); Notorious B.I.G.'s "Dead Wrong" (1999) and "Come On" (1999); Eazy E's "Hittin Switchs" (2002); 50 Cent's "In Da Club" (2003); Dr. Dre featuring Snoop Dogg's "Nuthin' but a G Thang" (1992); and MC Hammer's "Have You Seen Her" (1990).

23. For a discussion of various production ideals that emphasize a transparent versus opaque mixing paradigm, see Brøvig-Hanssen 2018 and Brøvig-Hanssen and Danielsen 2016.

24. As Boone notes, there should be a clash at the level of meaning but not at the musical level: "If the concept of clash carries a negative charge when it appears under the basic constructive principles, that same concept is valorized at the level of meaning, especially with respect to genre. It is instructive that the mashup community employs the term clash for both genre and key, yet in one case embraces its effect but in the other case rejects it" (2011, 150). See also Brøvig-Hanssen and Harkins 2012 and Church 2022 (chapter 3) for a similar point.

25. See, for example, Adams 2015; Boone 2013; McGranahan 2010; and Sinnreich 2010.

26. "We Are Number One" from *LazyTown* has appeared in several memes and remixes. For an analysis of another remix using this song, see Brøvig-Hanssen and Sinnreich 2019.

27. The mashup's video footage is a clip from a performance of 4'33" accompanied by Eminem's evocation of a protagonist who is "nervous [but] looks calm," who "keeps forgetting what he wrote down," who was "playin' in the beginning [but whose] mood [has] all changed," and so forth. The (presumed) pianist ultimately concludes his Cage performance while Eminem assures him, "You can do anything you set your mind to, man."

28. The survey demonstrated that genre clash is still important to most producers, at least for some of their mashups (66 percent indicated that mashing tracks from different musical genres is either "somewhat" or "to a great extent" important to them, 16 percent indicated that it varies, and 18 percent indicated that it was of "very little" importance or "not [important] at all"). The survey also revealed, as mentioned in chapter 2, that 46 percent of the respondents generally make A+B mashups, 49 percent do a combination of A+B mashups and megamix mashups, 4 percent only make megamix mashups, and 1 percent said "other" (mashing up to five whole tracks instead of vocal and instrumental versions). This breakdown indicates that while several producers do see the clashing of genres as important, it is more important to an A+B mashup than to a megamix mashup.

29. See, for example, pomDeter's mashup "Raining Single Ladies" (2016).

30. See Brøvig-Hanssen 2019b for a further analysis of these two mashups; see also Gallagher 2018 for a description of his ragaman7 work.

31. For more on the concept of defamiliarization, see chapter 4.

32. McGranahan (2010, 21) comes to a similar conclusion after interviewing several mashup producers: "The ability to create within set limitations is a skill that is valued by the mashup community." Richard L. Edwards likewise includes mashup music among the examples of what he calls "restrictive remixes," whereby its producer's main focus is on exploring the potential of the "constrained recombinatorics" of the samples (2014, 32).

33. The Prince tribute compilation was released the same day he died; the Bowie tribute was released the day after he died; the Whitney Houston one was released two days after she died; and the tribute to Michael Jackson was released a couple of months after he died.

34. See, for example, Lieberman 1977; Nachmanovitch 1990; and Sutton-Smith 1997.

35. He is here referring to his mashup "Call Me Greyhound (Kap Slap Bootleg)—Swedish House Mafia ft. Carley Rae Jepsen" (2012).

36. Jaakko Stenros notes that several theorists have problematized this assumption and points to several examples of forced play (2015, 72–76). For an example of involuntary play, see Áine Mangaoang's (2018) discussion of a Filipino detention center that compelled prisoners to dance to Michael Jackson's "Thriller" while being filmed, after which the video went viral on YouTube.

37. The intrinsically motivated mind-set has been assigned other names as well, including "playful mindset," "play spirit," or simply "play" (see, for example, Caillois 2001; Gadamer 2003; Lieberman 1977; and Sutton-Smith 1997). Other times, playfulness is reserved for the state of mind whereas play is reserved for the activities or events (see, for example, Stenros 2015).

38. For other works using Certeau's theory of strategies and tactics as a resource for understanding remix, see Brøvig-Hanssen and Sinnreich 2019; Jenkins 1992; and Manovich 2013.

39. Their use of unauthorized samples can also be seen as an oppositional tactic, an aspect to which I return in chapter 5.

40. Play activities have also been assigned many other functions. See Stenros 2015 for an overview of play theory and the functions ascribed to play.

Chapter 4

1. As Richard Dyer points out, the examination of art's aesthetic and political value does not necessarily involve an assumption that the art form that is under scrutiny "is by definition either profound or trivial, progressive or reactionary, a good or a bad thing" (Dyer 2007, 137). Of course, it can be all these things, but that should not prevent us from trying to illuminate some of its attraction.

2. For a thorough discussion of how theories of intertextuality relate to the theories of Saussure and Bakhtin, see Allen 2011. For a discussion of the role of semiotics/semiology and intertextuality in remix and music studies, see, for example, Burns and Lacasse 2018; Gallagher 2018; Klein 2004; and Tagg 1987. For a discussion of Michel Foucault's related notion of genealogy and how this can inform the analysis of popular music, see Burns, Woods, and Lafrance 2015.

3. See, for example, Allen 2011, 68, and Klein 2004, 109.

4. For a similar notion, and with reference to Gates's concept, see Robert Walser's (1995) analyses of Miles Davis's jazz performances. For example, Walser states, "Davis is signifyin' on all of the versions of the song he has heard; but for his audience, Davis is signifyin' on all of the versions each listener has heard. What is played is played up against Davis's intertextual experience, and what is heard is heard up against the listeners' experiences" (173). Later: "The melody of 'My Funny Valentine' was so familiar to his audience that Davis did not need to state it before signifyin' on it" (174).

5. Apter's description of make-believe synergies also evokes Brian Sutton-Smith's (2001) notion of "imaginary worlds." Sutton-Smith problematizes the labeling of imaginary worlds as "unreal" in his examination of play: "Now that we realize that human cultures are built out of imagination and fantasy, not just out of physical discoveries, the present duality of the mundane and the virtual is more appropriate" (195). Sutton-Smith's distinction between the mundane and the virtual, in turn, recalls Deleuze's distinction between the virtual and the actual in *Difference and Repetition* (1994 [1968]), and both scholars insist that the virtual is just as real as the actual/mundane (similar to the imaginary and "real" or "[that which is] the case" to which Apter refers).

6. See Church 2022, chapter 3, for an interesting discussion (but one I do not delve into here) of how incongruity in mashups can also be related to the ideas of Kenneth Burke (the contemporary American rhetorician) and particularly his concepts of "perspective by incongruity" and "exorcism by misnomer."

7. See, for example, Oring 2008.

8. As John Morreall emphasizes, these three theories are not exhaustive and there are several accounts of humor that do not fit easily into one of these alone, including the theories of Henry Bergson, Sigmund Freud, and Emmanuel Kant.

9. See Brøvig-Hanssen 2016, 2019a, and Brøvig-Hanssen and Harkins 2012.

10. According to Attardo (2008, 108), Raskin's SSTH theory resonates with the incongruity theory, because oppositions are, by definition, incongruous.

11. See also Attardo and Raskin 1991, Gleitman 1991, Raskin 1985, and Suls 1972, among others.

12. Some humor scholars allow for different forms of distribution of incongruity and sense-making in the experience of something as humorous (see, for example, Attardo et al. 2002, Oring 1989, Rothbart 1976, Rothbart and Pien 1977, and Veatch 1998). Other scholars, however, have restricted this sense making to achieving resolution, arguing that what we enjoy about humor is not the incongruity in itself but the resolution that follows it (see, for example, Suls 1972). In parody, the entire design relies on the simultaneous violation and fulfillment of expectations. For example, in mashups, the incongruity and the sense making do not occur in successive phases but simultaneously, which makes the notion of resolution less applicable if resolution implies a linear process in which a discord or discrepancy has transitioned to a concord.

13. Several scholars have discussed the role of humor in popular music specifically, and incongruity, or the combination of incongruity and sense making, has often been identified as crucial in this context as well (see, for example, Kitts and Baxter-Moore 2019 and Turner 2016).

14. See, for example, Morreall 1986 and Raskin 2008.

15. See also note 24 in chapter 3.

16. For similar treatments of genre as discourse, including notions about how divergent value claims have contributed to form divergent notions of authenticity within genres, see, for example, Brackett 2016; Frith 1998; Grossberg 1992; Holt 2007; Keightley 2001; Lena 2017; Middleton 2006; Moore 2002; and Negus 1999.

17. On the notion of "cock rock," see Frith and McRobbie 1990 (1978), who coined the term. See also Auslander 2004 and Frith 1981.

18. See also Hawkins 2018. Related to genderplay is camp, understood as (often humorous) queer critique (see, for example, Moore and Purvis 2018). For example, Jarman's (2018) analysis of lip-syncing as potential camp has much in common with mashups' potential genderplay; here, divergent identity constructions of voice and face are made to appear unified—a flamboyant female vocal may, for example, appear to be produced by a masculine and heteronormative male body. This is a form of camp genderplay that functions as both entertainment and a critique of a normative or hegemonic heterosexuality discourse.

19. The "5" here means neither major nor minor, a typical condition for power chords.

20. In the original version, Araya sings an A note that is accompanied by an A5 chord. In the mashup version, this A5 chord is replaced by a Dm, which turns his original root note into the fifth note in the latter chord.

21. For related notions involving another mashup—Isosine's "Justin Bieber vs. Slipknot—Psychosocial Baby" (2011), which combines Slipknot's "Psychosocial" (2008) with Justin Bieber's "Baby" (2010), see Brøvig-Hanssen 2016.

22. For a discussion of poptimism and rockism, see, for example, Sanneh 2004.

23. See also Krogh 2020; Rossman 2012; and Silver, Lee, and Childress 2016.

24. Relatedly, Walser channels Fredric Jameson (1982, 322), who insists that genre is a fruitful analytical category despite its inevitable fluidity: "Discourses are formed, maintained, and transformed through dialogue; speakers learn from and respond to others, and the meanings of their utterances are never permanently fixed, cannot be found in a dictionary" (Walser 2014, 29). See Hawkins and Richardson 2007 and Lacasse 2018 for similar notions.

25. Other relevant theories include Benjamin Lee Whorf's principle of linguistic relativity (in short, differences between linguistic structures shape how their speakers perceive and conceptualize the world), Roman Jakobson's theory of structural linguistics and phonology (that is, his theory of consonants and vowels), and Claude Lévi-Strauss's theory of structural anthropology (cultural systems and the

human mind are based on binary oppositions). For an overview of these structuralist notions of categorization and difference, see Apter 1982, 137–139.

26. See, for example, Boon 2010, 2021; Church 2022; Gallagher 2018; Guertin 2012; Horwatt 2008b; Kuhn 2021; and McIntosh 2011.

27. For examples of other mashups framed as political, see, for example, Gallagher 2018 and McGranahan 2010.

28. Peirce's (1960) notion of sign as index—which he differentiates from sign as icon and sign as symbol—points to a causal connection between the sign and its referent, thus transcending both likeness and convention. For a similar point regarding sampling, see Gallagher 2018, 123–125.

29. In addition to the humor that arises from the mashup's bizarre juxtaposition of tracks and their transformation therein, several other potential humor triggers are inserted as well. These include, for example, clips from Puddle of Mudd frontman Scantlin's acoustic cover (or imitation) of Nirvana's legendary unplugged version of "About a Girl" (1989), which he performed live for the American broadcasting company Sirius XM in January 2020, only to see the video go viral because so many listeners savaged his performance.

30. Lawrence Lessig similarly points out, "For anyone who has lived in our era, a mix of images and sounds makes its point far more powerfully than any eight-hundred-word essay in the *New York Times* could" (2008, 74). This is why several scholars, including Paolo Peverini, view remix "as one of the most popular methods of media activism" (2015, 335). Martin Butler argues that the political dimension of humor, which often appears in musical parodies on the internet (including shreds and spoofs), illuminates "the *social* significance of popular music, even—or rather, especially—when it seems to be 'just funny'" (2019, 321).

31. For another discussion of the relevance of Mukařovský's concept to sample-based music, see Danielsen 2008.

32. See Brøvig-Hanssen 2019b for a more thorough analysis of this mashup.

33. Listen, for example, to his mashups "2Pac feat. Eminem—In The Air" (2018) and "2Pac—Gave You My Heart—[Sad Love Song]" (2017).

34. For mashups whose AH impact is likely to be more salient to the listener than their HAHA impact, see, for example, PhilRetroSpector's "Beatles vs Coldplay: Jude'll Fix It" (2008) and "Pixies vs Goldfrapp vs Puccini—Monkey Gone To Opera" (2010); Isosine's "Billie Eilish, Khalid, Jeremy Lim, Anna Toth, Banks, Kendrick Lamar—sometimes i need to be alone" (2019) and "Taylor Swift vs. Nine Inch Nails—Shake It Off (The Perfect Drug)" (2015); and Reborn Identity's "The Smiths vs Lana Del Rey 'This Charming Video Game' (mashup)" (2012).

35. Winfried Menninghaus and colleagues define "aesthetic emotions" as personal, subjective experiences related to felt pleasure or displeasure and to the liking or disliking of a given artistic expression. They further argue that aesthetic emotions differ from art-represented emotions (such as music that expresses sadness or happiness) and art-elicited emotions (such as the ability of sad music to evoke the conforming emotion of sadness in the listener) as they transcend such mechanisms and are discrete, "full-blown" feelings categorically different from other kinds of feelings (2019, 185).

36. See also note 12 in this chapter, which addresses the related topic of divergent notions regarding resolution in humor.

37. See, for example, Berlyne 1971, 1974.

38. See, for example, Neiss 1988 and Silvia 2006.

39. See, for example, Menninghaus et al. 2019; Scherer 2001; and Silvia 2006.

40. This notion evokes Immanuel Kant, who stated that pleasurable aesthetic emotions often result from a combination of attraction and repulsion in relation to the subject in question (Kant 2001 [1790], 91–92). In his development of the concept of defamiliarization, Shklovsky (1989) refers to Aristotle, who saw *wonder* as significant to aesthetics, so that poetic language, for example, should appear "strange and wonderful." A similar argument is also found in the works by Barthes, where he distinguishes between what he calls "pleasure" and "bliss": "Text of pleasure: the text that contents, fills, grants euphoria; the text that comes from culture and does not break with it, is linked to a *comfortable* practice of reading. Text of bliss: the text that imposes a state of loss, the text that discomforts (perhaps to the point of a certain boredom), unsettles the reader's historical, cultural, psychological assumptions, the consistency of his tastes, values, memories, brings to a crisis his relation with language" (Barthes 1975b, 14). However, contrary to central theories of aesthetic emotions, Barthes understands these two different kinds of emotions (one positive and one negative) to be evoked at different times rather than working together in a suspended state.

Chapter 5

1. The law distinguishes between a musical "work" and a "sound recording" (in US law) or "phonogram" (under EU law) as different expressions that qualify for different kinds of protection. From a musical perspective, this division of rights may seem odd due to the fact that contemporary sound recordings are today seldom recordings *of* compositions but are instead the primary texts themselves (see, for example, Gracyk 1996). But in a legal context, a sound recording is considered to be separate from a work, although the work is obviously an inseparable part of it.

2. Some of the findings in this section are also discussed in Brøvig-Hanssen and Jones 2021. The ethical guidelines of the mashup community differ considerably from the "sampling ethics" that Joseph Schloss (2004, chapter 5) identifies among hip-hop artists, including that one cannot sample material that has been recently used by someone else (quite common among mashup producers) and that one cannot sample recordings one respects (often reversed in mashups). This supports the argument that sampling is far from a single thing but rather a whole field of practice.

3. See, for example, Demers 2006 and McLeod and DiCola 2011.

4. See, for example, McLeod and DiCola 2011, 27, and Vaidhyanathan 2003, 133.

5. Hui (2017) here refers to the *Grand Upright* case in which Judge Duffy started his opinion with a biblical admonition: "Thou shalt not steal" (*Grand Upright Music, Ltd. v. Warner Bros. Records Inc.*, 780 F. Supp. 182. (S.D.N.Y. 1991), 183).

6. 17 U.S.C. § 107.

7. As I will return to later in this chapter, *transformative* is a term often used in relation to the fair use doctrine of the US Copyright Act. Law professor Rebecca Tushnet describes it as "the extent to which a new work or use adds new meaning or message to an original work" (Tushnet 2017, 185).

8. See, for example, Demers 2006; McLeod and DiCola 2011; and Vaidhyanathan 2003.

9. For the EU context, see recital 3 of the Information Society Directive (InfoSoc Directive), Directive 2001/29/EC of the European Parliament and of the Council of 22 May 2001 on the harmonization of certain aspects of copyright and related rights in the information society, *Official Journal* L167 (2001). For the US context, see U.S. Const. art. I, § 8, cl. 8. amend. I. See also Lai 2019, 14–20, for an account of the natural right to freedom of expression (and parody) as fundamental to a democratic society.

10. 17 U.S.C. § 107; *InfoSoc Directive*, art. 5(3)(d),(k).

11. The field of law dealing with these issues is known as private international law (see Novović 2019).

12. The most widely adopted international agreement is the Berne Convention, a treaty signed by 180 countries that guarantees the protection of literary and artistic works. Other treaties include the WIPO Copyright Treaty and WIPO Performance and Phonograph Treaty, the Rome Convention, and the Agreement on Trade-Related Intellectual Property Rights (or TRIPS Agreement).

13. The plaintiff cannot pick the applicable law; the court has the task of figuring out which law is applicable. Yet, the plaintiff can choose where they want to sue,

as long as it is a country in which the damage took place or the infringer resides. The rules currently make it clear that the court should apply its own law—a Norwegian court will, for example, apply the Norwegian copyright act. This means that the plaintiffs are de facto choosing the law, even though in theory they cannot (Novović 2019).

14. I will not treat the exceptions of the British Copyright Act, since England exited the EU in 2020 and is, at the time of writing, operating with the same copyright act as it did before the exit, which was aligned with EU law.

15. InfoSoc Directive, art. 5(3)(d),(k).

16. Copyright in the Digital Single Market Directive, 2019, Article 17(7) (Directive 2019/790 of the European Parliament and of the Council of 17 April 2019 on copyright and related rights in the Digital Single Market and amending Directives 96/9/EC and 2001/29/EC, *Official Journal* L130 (2019)).

17. InfoSoc Directive, art. 5(3)(d).

18. Pelham GmbH and Others v. Ralf Hütter and Florian Schneider-Esleben, ECJ, case no. C-476/17 (2019), para. 73.

19. Spiegel Online GmbH v. Volker Beck, ECJ, case no. C-516/17 (2019), para. 79.

20. For a broader interpretation of the EU legal concept of quotation, see, for example, Bently and Aplin 2020 and Maier and Jütte 2017.

21. Several European countries have long operated, at a national level, with so-called free use provisions, meaning that copyright-protected material may be reused without license if it creates a new independent work of artistic expression. As such, it is reminiscent of the fair use doctrine of the US Copyright Act. According to Hui and Döhl (2021), three copyright decisions of the Court of Justice of the European Union (CJEU) settled in 2019 were game changers with respect to free use, as they categorically established that member states cannot introduce free use provision that exceed the exceptions and limitations recognized in EU law's InfoSoc Directive article 5. This means that the relevant countries have in practice lost their free use provisions, and Hui and Döhl thus strongly argue for including them in future EU copyright directives. For similar arguments, see also Engman 2020, 130; Jütte 2020, 80; and Rosati 2020, 267.

22. *Pelham*, paras. 72–74.

23. *Pelham*, para. 87. In the same paragraph, the court also states that samples used "in a modified form unrecognizable to the ear" may not be considered reproductions. Hui (2019) further points to the ambivalence of the phrase "unrecognizable to the ear," as it is unclear whose ear is indicated: Is it, for example, the expert's or layman's ear? Might it also include an "ear" informed by algorithmic detection tools?

Similarly, it is also uncertain how the court would evaluate "recognizability"—recognizability for whom or what and under which circumstances?

24. *Pelham*, paras. 72–74.

25. *Pelham*, paras. 65, 77, 81, 87; InfoSoc Directive, arts. 2–4.

26. *Johan Deckmyn and Vrijheidsfonds VZW v. Helena Vandersteen and Others*, ECJ, case C-201/13 (2014). To Sabine Jacques, the fact that neither the Opinion of the Advocate General nor the legislators of the *Deckmyn* case found it necessary to distinguish among the terms *caricature*, *parody*, and *pastiche* implies that they should be treated as one exception (that is, as the legal concept of parody) rather than three (2019, 27–28). Others have argued that pastiche and comedy simply remain untested concepts (see, for example, Hudson 2017).

27. *Deckmyn*, para. 33.

28. *Deckmyn*, paras. 27, 34.

29. *Deckmyn*, para. 28.

30. See, for example, Hutcheon 2000 and Rose 1993.

31. See, for example, Jacques 2019, 19, and Rosati 2015, 518–519.

32. See, for example, Attardo and Raskin 1991 and Raskin 1985.

33. See, for example, the French *Peanuts* case from 1977 (TGI Paris, 19/01/1977, RIDA, 1977, n°92, p. 167, Peanuts).

34. See, for example, TGI Paris, 3e ch., 1/04/1987, cah. Dr. d'auteur 1998, n°1, 16, and TGI Evry, 9/07/2009, RG n°09/02410 confirmed Paris, 18.02.2011, RB 09/19272, Propr. Int. 2011 n°39 p. 187, Saint-Tin.

35. Jacques points out, however, that it remains to be seen how humor will be weighted after *Deckmyn* (2019, 99).

36. See, for example, Hutcheon 2000, 20. For the mashup producer's relation to humor, see chapter 4.

37. *Deckmyn*, paras. 27, 34.

38. *Deckmyn*, para. 28.

39. The legal protection of moral rights differs depending on the legal tradition, so that authors under the civil law tradition (represented by several European countries) have stronger support than authors under the common law tradition (represented by the United States and Canada, for example). See Jacques 2019, 167–195.

40. TGI Paris, 03/01/1978, D., 19790, p. 99 obs. Desbois.

41. While arguing for copyright exceptions for parody based on the principle of freedom of speech, Lai emphasizes that "international courts have agreed in principle that freedom of expression must be guaranteed not only for the dissemination of expressions, information, and ideas that are favorably received or considered inoffensive or indifferent, but also for those that shock, disturb, or offend the state or any member of the population" (2019, 27).

42. Owen Gallagher observes: "Remix culture has become pervasive in society and remix practice is now as commonplace as traditional authorship was, prior to the development of digital technologies. Remixing is an extension of how people read, write, and interact with culture in the digital age" (2018, 243). He further argues that because of this pervasiveness, it should be "explicitly legalized" (243).

43. 17 U.S.C. § 107.

44. See, for example, Carroll 2007; Lessig 2004; Netanel 2008; and Vaidhyanathan 2003.

45. In an article from 2004, Madison reviewed fair use cases from 1841 onward and found that a common consideration in fair use analyses, and in relation to the first factor, was whether the use was typical for common practice within the users' social context. This consideration is, however, not mentioned in Beebe's (2020) more updated study of US fair use cases.

46. See, for example, Aufderheide and Jaszi 2018; Samuelson 2009; and Tushnet 2008.

47. Joseph Story was Supreme Court justice in *Folsom v. Marsh*, 1841, and his summary notion on how to understand fair use has been very influential (*Folsom v. Marsh* 9 F. Cas. 342 (C.C.D. Mass. 1841)).

48. Feist Publications, Inc., v. Rural Phone Service Co., 499 U.S. 340 (1991); Castle Rock Entertainment v. Carol Publishing Group, 150 F.3d 132 (2nd Cir. 1998); and Campbell v. Acuff-Rose Music, Inc., 510 U.S. 586 (1994).

49. *Campbell*, 580(b).

50. Beebe (2020) points out, however, that the impact of the transformativeness factor on the treatment of the other factors varies, and so a finding of transformativeness does not necessarily result in a successful fair use defense.

51. *Campbell*, (n 199) 580.

52. *Campbell*, (n 199) 580–581.

53. See, for example, *Sony Corp. of America v. Universal City Studios, Inc.*, 464 U.S. 417 (1984), and *Harper & Row, Publishers, Inc. v. Nation Enterprises*, 471 U.S. 539 (1985).

54. *Campbell*, 579.

55. Blanch v. Koons, 467 F.3d 244 (2d Cir. 2006).

56. *Harper & Row*, 563 ("The law generally recognizes a greater need to disseminate factual works than works of fiction or fantasy").

57. *Harper & Row*, 564.

58. *Campbell*, 586. See also *Feist*.

59. See, for example, Aufderheide and Jaszi 2018; Beebe 2020; and Jacques 2019.

60. Examples include Elsmere Music, Inc. v. National Broadcasting Co., 482 F. Supp. 741 (S.D.N.Y. 1980) (n 50); Fisher v. Dees 794 F.2d 432 (9th Cir. 1986), 438; *Sony* (n 14); and *Campbell* (n 12). See also Jacques 2019, 110–112. As Jacques reminds us, such legal reasoning does not imply that anything goes regarding the original, which has also been emphasized by the US courts (Henley v. DeVore, 733 F. Supp. 2d 1144 (C.D. Cal. 2010)).

61. See also Reese 2015 for a similar finding.

62. "Actual present harm need not be shown. . . . What is necessary is a showing by a preponderance of the evidence that some meaningful likelihood of future harm exists. If the intended use is for commercial gain, that likelihood may be presumed. But if it is for noncommercial purpose, the likelihood must be demonstrated" (*Sony*, 451).

63. *Campbell*, 591.

64. *Campbell*, 591, brackets in original.

65. *Campbell*, 593. Beebe shows, however, that lower courts often cite *Sony* instead of *Campbell* in this regard (2020).

66. *Campbell*, 591.

67. For similar arguments, see, for example, Cherry 2011, 518; Harper 2010, 434; and McLeod 2005, 163.

68. See, for example, Aufderheide and Jaszi 2018, 98; Hui 2017, 149; Samuelson 2009, 2578; and Tushnet 2004, 582.

69. *Grand Upright*.

70. Bridgeport Music, Inc. v. Dimension Films, 410 F. 3d 792 (6th Cir. 2005).

71. Cherry 2011.

72. *Bridgeport*, 802. *De minimis* is Latin for "pertaining to minimal things" and is used to indicate that "the law does not concern itself with trifles" (Legal Dictionary, n.d.).

Notes 259

73. VMG Salsoul, LLC v. Ciccone, 824 F.3d 871 (9th Cir. 2016).

74. Drake was sued for having used a spoken-vocal sequence of jazz musician Jimmy Smith in his "Pound Cake/Paris Morton Music 2" (featuring Jay-Z) from the album *Nothing Was the Same* (2013).

75. Estate of Smith v. Graham, 799 F.App'x 36 (2nd Cir. 2020).

76. See Eidsvold-Tøien 2021 for a similar argument.

77. See, for example, Gallagher 2018; Lessig 2004; McLeod 2005; and Vaidhyanathan 2003.

78. For a similar approach, see, for example, Aufderheide and Jaszi 2018; Cherry 2011; and Jacques 2019.

79. For a similar perspective on mashups and law, see, for example, Golosker 2012 and Simpson-Jones 2010.

80. *Grand Upright*, 183.

81. An early example of such an approach is that of John Oswald, who labeled his sample-based music "plunderphonic" (see, for example, Holm-Hudson 1997 and Oswald 2006).

82. For an analysis of such campaigns, see, for example, David and Whiteman 2015.

83. See, for example, Gallagher 2018; Guertin 2012; Logie 2006; Patry 2009; and Sinnreich 2013.

Chapter 6

1. For important studies on the former, see, for example, Aufderheide and Jaszi 2018; Aufderheide, Milosevic, and Bello 2015; Demers 2006; McLeod and DiCola 2011; and Sinnreich 2013. On the latter, see, for example, Seng 2014; Urban and Quilter 2006; and Urban, Karaganis, and Schofield 2016.

2. The first US lawsuit against sampling happened in 1986, when Jimmi Castor filed a copyright infringement suit against Def Jam, claiming that the Beastie Boys, in "Hold It Now, Hit It" (*Licensed to Ill*, 1986), sampled the phrase "Yo, Leroy!" from "The Return of Leroy Pt. 1" (1977). The dispute was settled out of court in Castor's favor, but it caused much confusion and fear among hip-hop producers and spurred other lawsuits against music sampling, including the one against De La Soul in 1989 mentioned in the previous chapter, in which the hip-hop group allegedly had to pay $1.7 million to the Turtles (see, for example, Sanjek 1992, 618).

3. Grand Upright Music, Ltd. v. Warner Bros. Records Inc., 780 F. Supp. 182 (S.D.N.Y. 1991).

4. In the 1990s, the assumption persisted that de minimis sampling was allowed, but even this changed following a later judgment against sampling—Bridgeport Music, Inc. v. Dimension Films, 410 F.3d 792 (6th Cir. 2005)—that concluded that de minimis did not apply to sound recording ("Get a license or do not sample"; see previous chapter). For other discussions of the impact of copyright enforcement on the hip-hop scene, see, for example, Demers 2006; McLeod and DiCola 2011; and Vaidhyanathan 2003.

5. See, for example, Bruns 2009; Jenkins 2006; Lessig 2008; and Sinnreich 2010.

6. See, for example, Viacom Int'l., Inc. v. YouTube, Inc., 676 F.3d 19 (2nd Cir., 2012) and UMG Recordings, Inc. v. Myspace, Inc., 526 F. Supp. 2d 1046 (C.D. Calif., 2007).

7. See U.S. Copyright Office 2020, 13–18. The World Intellectual Property Organization (WIPO) was established in 1967 and is a global forum for intellectual property services, policy, information, and cooperation. It currently has 193 member states (see WIPO n.d.-a). The "WIPO Internet Treaties" consists of the WIPO Copyright Treaty and the WIPO Performances and Phonogram Treaty. These treaties "set down international norms aimed at preventing unauthorized access to and use of creative works on the Internet or other digital network" (WIPO n.d.-b).

8. 17 U.S.C. § 512.

9. 17 U.S.C. § 512 (c)(1).

10. 17 U.S.C. § 512 (c)(1).

11. 17 U.S.C. § 512 (g).

12. Electronic Commerce Directive (ECD), 2000, Articles 12–15. (Directive 2000/31/EC of the European Parliament and of the Council of 8 June 2000 on Certain Legal Aspects of Information Society Services, in Particular Electronic Commerce, *Official Journal* L178 (2000)). The most notable difference between the DMCA and the ECD regimes is that the ECD does not provide a legal incentive to notify the alleged infringer upon blocking or removal of content or to provide counternotice procedures, although some member states have introduced the latter (Urban et al. 2016, 22).

13. For thorough discussions of platforms' implementation of notice and takedown systems, see Urban et al. 2016 and U.S. Copyright Office 2020.

14. Viacom Int'l, Inc. v. YouTube, Inc., 718 F. Supp. 2d 514 (S.D.N.Y. 2010).

15. *Viacom*, 718 F. Supp. 2d 514 (S.D.N.Y. 2010).

16. Viacom appealed but the decision was partly upheld by court of appeals and sent back to the district court (*Viacom*).

17. According to Jennifer M. Urban and colleagues (2016, 10), this automation generated hundreds of thousands or even millions of requests.

18. See Urban and colleagues' (2016) descriptions of what they call "DMCA Auto" and "DMCA Plus."

19. Although the DMCA and the ECD require platforms seeking immunity from liability to remove or disable access to material after obtaining actual knowledge or certain awareness of infringement or, in the DMCA context, a valid takedown notice, the use of content-identification technology is not mentioned by either.

20. Some platforms rely on in-house technology—YouTube's "Content ID" is the best known—whereas others rely on the technology of specialized data/tech companies that often operate across multiple platforms. For example, Facebook, SoundCloud, and Vimeo currently use Audible Magic's content-identification services (Audible Magic n.d.).

21. Fingerprint-based technology differs from hash-based technology in that it is able to identify inexact matches (Urban et al. 2016, 57–58). See also Google n.d.-e.

22. See, for example, Google n.d.-a.

23. At YouTube, a strike expires after six months if no further strikes are received (Google n.d.-b). SoundCloud has a similar policy in which it "permanently terminate[s] accounts that have reached more than two active strikes" (SoundCloud n.d.-a). See also SoundCloud n.d.-b.

24. Some copyright holder spokespeople have lamented that the compensation provided by ad and subscription revenue for the distribution of their content is low (see, for example, Kafka 2016 and Ingham 2019), but it is still better than not being compensated at all.

25. See, for example, Gillespie et al. 2020.

26. See, for example, Gillespie 2018; Urban et al. 2016; and Urban and Quilter 2006.

27. The project examined a sample of 1,800 takedown requests from a data set of 108.3 million takedowns over a six-month period using the Lumen database, in which most takedowns relate to Google Web Search. These takedowns were manually reviewed and coded (Urban et al. 2016, 10). The requests that did not match the identified infringed content at all made up 4.2 percent, translating to approximately 4.5 million notices out of the total data set of 108.3 million. The requests that targeted content with characteristics weighed favorably toward fair use made up 7.3 percent, translating to approximately 8 million notices across the total datset.

28. Urban and colleagues (2016) examined only content being removed via formal copyright takedowns, not content blocking, which belongs to a system outside of formal takedown requests, as explained above.

29. "Tolerated use" is a term Wu coins for "infringing usage of a copyrighted work of which the copyright owner may be aware, yet does nothing about" (Wu 2008, 619).

30. The Lumen study conducted by Urban and colleagues (2016) suggests that 98.9 percent of the 1,800 takedown requests they examined were submitted using automated measures (Urban et al. 2016, 82). They further explain that platforms receiving an unmanageable number of notices also turn to automated measures: "The vast majority of infringement claims DMCA Auto and DMCA Plus OSPs receive are not substantively reviewed—either by the senders, who rely largely on title matches and similar proxies to identify copyrighted material, or by the recipient OSPs, which can, at best, triage small percentages of notices for human review. . . . Unable to evaluate every takedown request or fail to act on valid ones without risking their safe harbor protection, OSPs may take down material even where there is doubt about the substance of the claim" (54). See Urban et al. 2016 and U.S. Copyright Office 2020 for thorough descriptions of the automated nature of the infringement detection and handling by copyright holders (and their agents) and platforms.

31. See, for example, Urban et al. 2016, 97 and U.S. Copyright Office 2020, 79–80.

32. Urban and colleagues' study is based on "close to three dozen survey responses and in-depth interviews with OSPs [Online Service Providers] and major copyright holders" (2016, 25).

33. Urban and colleagues report that the largest human reviewer team among the platforms in their study consisted of thirty full-time positions (2016, 36). This number of manual reviewers may have increased by this writing, but given the sheer amount of content being blocked and removed every minute on the major platforms and the legal competence needed to make legitimate decisions in borderline cases, an increase still would not eliminate the problem of faulty blockings or removals (although it would surely help).

34. See, for example, Gillespie 2018; Meyers 2009; Nunziato 2014; Urban and Quilter 2006 and 2016; and Zimmerman 2014. Even if the decision is taken in good faith, copyright owners may not have the legal competence to evaluate whether the content qualifies for a copyright exception, since this is a highly complex matter and is decided in a court case by case.

35. Owen Gallagher reports on a similar situation for remix producers more generally (see Gallagher 2018, 238–239).

36. See, for example, Aufderheide et al. 2013, 2015, 2018.

37. See, for example, Hui, 2017, 2021a; Urban et al. 2016; and U.S. Copyright Office 2020. See also the debates related to the European Digital Single Market Directive and the Digital Services Act.

38. "Collective licensing" refers to a relatively common agreement struck between copyright owners and copyright collecting agencies (also referred to as copyright societies or collective management organizations). Copyright collecting agencies license use on behalf of the copyright holders that they represent, meaning that a

Notes 263

user needs only a single license to use multiple copyrightable works. This enables, for example, radio stations, streaming platforms, shopping malls, and clubs to play music without seeking separate permission for each track being played. The benefit of collective licensing is that it effectively and promptly makes a large amount of copyrighted content available to a large group of consumers and does so with reduced transaction costs (see Hui 2017, 167).

39. Wu argues for the legal development of an ex post licensing regime in which "use of the property is 'safe,' or not illegal, until the owner takes some action—typically, complaining or issuing notice. At that point, continued use becomes illegal, but, importantly, usage up to that point is excused" (2008, 622). This suggested regime would contrast on a legal basis with the current one, in which a copyright holder can claim that the use of unauthorized content is infringement without giving a warning. The difference is crucial because legal use may be more palatable to all than presumed illegal but tolerated use (640).

40. Hui here refers to *Harper & Row v. Nation*, which established that "the fair use doctrine was predicated on the author's implied consent to 'reasonable and customary' use" (Hui 2019, 197; Harper & Row, Publishers, Inc. v. Nation Enterprises & Row, 471 U.S. 539 (1985)). See also note 45 in chapter 5.

41. This double reward of content identification and monetization, benefiting both major labels and sampling artists, has been promoted by the platforms themselves. For example, in its announcement of its deal with Universal Music Group (UMG) in January 2016, SoundCloud stated that the agreement would allow artists signed to UMG to earn revenue from their tracks distributed on the platform and create "a sustainable ecosystem" for user-generated remixes (SoundCloud 2016). This presumed win-win situation has also been recognized by major labels including Warner Music Group (WMG), which in November 2014 stated the following when announcing that it was the first major music group to forge a partnership with SoundCloud: "The landmark partnership will create new commercial and promotional possibilities for WMG's roster of established and emerging recording artists as well as songwriters signed to WMG's music publishing arm, Warner/Chappell Music. Further, the deal includes innovative licensing terms that will provide WMG and its artists greater ability to manage the availability of content, while providing a path towards delivering additional revenue from user-generated mixes and mash-ups of WMG music" (Warner Music 2014).

42. Several copyright holders have addressed this problem with the suggestion that platforms should implement a "staydown" option—that is, an automatic filter (using, for example, hash-based or fingerprint-based matching) that prevents previously taken-down content from being subsequently reuploaded on the given platform or across platforms (U.S. Copyright Office 2020, 181, 186–193, and Urban et al. 2016, 55–62; see also Kafka 2016). In contrast, Urban and colleagues strongly discourage any future legal requirement for such staydown options (2016, 140).

They also report that platforms have expressed reluctance about adopting such a practice, especially with regard to inexact matches, since it risks the occurrence of mistaken takedowns, including takedowns of material that potentially qualifies for fair use (60).

43. Copyright in the Digital Single Market Directive, 2019, Article 17. See also Kuczerawy 2020 and U.S. Copyright Office 2020, 63.

44. For stakeholders' complaints about this fact, see U.S. Copyright Office 2020, 43–44, fn. 220.

45. The empirical findings I present here are also discussed in Brøvig-Hanssen and Jones 2021.

46. In the survey, 27.6 percent of respondents reported that their mashups had rarely or never been subject to any kind of "notice-and-takedown" procedure, although it is uncertain whether they distinguished between notice-and-takedown procedures and other forms of copyright claims, such as Content ID claims. Only 4.4 percent reported that their mashups had never been identified by any online platform as using copyrighted material.

47. Some copyright holders, including Sony Entertainment Music, have complained that YouTube's Content ID fails to capture a significant amount of infringing content (U.S. Copyright Office 2020, 44, fn. 224).

48. This relatively positive attitude toward monetization does not reflect the perspective of all remixers, including remixer and scholar Gallagher, referred to previously in this and other chapters (see Gallagher 2018, 205).

49. Among the surveyed producers, 17 percent reported that they no longer made mashups. Of those, 9 percent said that it was because of the platforms' removal of their mashups or copyright infringement concerns. The remaining 8 percent gave other reasons, such as that their taste in music had changed or they had lost interest in making mashups, they had less free time, or they did not feel as though people were interested in what they were making.

50. Playing at clubs and festivals does not raise the same legal issues as posting remixes on the internet, since most such venues rely on collective licensing (see note 38 in this chapter).

51. See, for example, Bishop 2018; Bucher 2012; and Nieborg and Poell 2018.

52. See also Brøvig-Hanssen and Jones 2021. Miles C. Coleman and Mark Anthoney (2020) call such instances of composing mashups specifically to avoid "copyright bots" and takedowns "machinic enculturation."

53. In contrast to these findings, Gallagher reports that his remix videos (including mashups) have always been reinstated after he has filed a counternotification if the video in question made a strong case for fair use (2015, 476; 2018, 205).

Notes 265

54. Liam McGranahan (2010, 208) found the same among those he interviewed in 2006.

55. In addition to those mentioned below, see, for example, Aufderheide and Jaszi 2018; Berry 2008; Boon 2021; Boyle 1997; Coombe 1998; Lessig 2008; McLeod 2007; Netanel 2008; and Vaidhyanathan 2003.

56. See, for example, Dijck 2013; Gillespie 2018; Jones 2021; and Kim 2012.

57. For a similar argument, see also Brøvig-Hanssen and Jones 2021 and Hui 2021b.

Chapter 7

1. As Deena Weinstein points out, although the judgment of music as "bad" can certainly appear to derive primarily from the music's inherent qualities, the concept of "bad music" is not about music at all (2004, 307).

2. For a discussion of the rock discourse's emphasis on labor, diligence, and talent—as well as how this emphasis is rather more flexible in the context of pop music—see, for example, Auslander 2008, 73–127; Frith 1998; Keightley 2001; Middleton 2006, 199–246; and Moore 2002.

3. For a discussion of the work concept, see Goehr 2007.

4. For a discussion of the various theories used to understand and justify copyright, including Locke's labor theory of property, see, for example, Biron 2014. See also Gallagher 2018, 207–209, which discusses Locke's theory in the context of remix.

5. For a discussion of some of the diverse reasons for experiencing something as authentic, see, for example, Middleton 2006, 199–246; Moore 2002; and Weisethaunet and Lindberg 2010.

6. David Gunkel points out that the value of skill is also emphasized in several remix scholars' justifications of this art form (2016, 100).

7. For a brief introduction to Gramsci's theories, see Hall 1977.

8. As Lori Burns, Alyssa Woods, and Marc Lafrance put it, creative innovation may also be traced to the creation of a dialogical space between references, "allowing for multiple musical voices and subjectivities to interrelate in a complex intertextual dialogue" (Burns, Woods, and Lafrance 2015, 31).

9. See Miller 2012 for a study of the social value of "playing along" with interactive digital media, including *Guitar Hero* and *Rock Band*.

10. As Antoine Hennion points out, "The object is not 'the music,' a given, that could be isolated from the activity; it is what arises with it, through it" (Hennion 2005, 140).

11. See Vaidhyanathan 2003 for a robust elaboration of this development.

12. See, for example, O'Dwyer 2015, 323–324. See also the influential manifesto by digital rights activist John Perry, founder of the Internet activist group Electronic Frontier Foundation, titled "A Declaration of the Independence of Cyberspace" (1996).

13. See, for example, Lessig 2004, 2008.

14. For a discussion of the free use movement and different scholars' approaches to it, see Aufderheide and Jaszi 2018, 54–56, 66–69. Owen Gallagher takes a middle position with respect to free use and copyright protection, insisting that "by expanding the fair use provision to explicitly exempt non-commercial remixes from infringement status, the abuse of copyright law to censor and wrongfully remove remixes from the web can be prevented" (2018, 255). Still, he regards this as but a short-term improvement and argues that a longer-term improvement would be "to either replace copyright entirely with an alternative system for the digital age (i.e., R2P), or allow copyright to remain in existence, but have it focus solely on the regulation of physical media, while R2P law simultaneously concentrates solely on protecting digital media content" (2018, 255). (R2P [Right-to-Profit] is his proposed system whereby exclusive rights are limited to profit, including the right to sell, rent, or lease; see Gallagher 2018, 245–249.)

15. Another example of open license is the GNU General Public License.

16. Via the Statute of Anne, a copyright act passed by the Parliament of Great Britain in 1710.

17. For an overview of the Romantic notion of authorship, see, for example, McIntyre 2012 and Woodmansee 1994.

18. Other critics of Romantic authorship include Howard S. Becker, who argues, "Art worlds rather than artists make art" (1982, 198–199); Bourdieu (1993), who sees art as a field of production according to habitus; and Mikhail Bakhtin, Jacques Derrida, and Julia Kristeva, mentioned in chapter 4, who argue that a text is never isolated but always draws on prior texts.

19. For an overview of this debate, see Bently 1994 and Lavik 2014.

20. *Grand Upright Music, Ltd. v. Warner Bros. Records Inc.*, 780 F. Supp. 182. (S.D.N.Y. 1991); *Bridgeport Music, Inc. v. Dimension Films*, 410 F.3d 792 (6th Cir. 2005); and *Pelham GmbH and Others v. Ralf Hütter and Florian Schneider-Esleben*, ECJ, case no. C-476/17 (2019).

21. See Coombe 1998, 7, for a perspective like Eechoud's.

22. Forensic musicology arose in response to the fact that courts often turn to musicologists when in doubt as to how to resolve legal cases concerning music. One of

the issues facing forensic musicology is whether a particular song qualifies as copyright infringement—a question that is highly relevant to sample-based music such as mashups.

23. As Mark Katz puts it, "Sampling is most fundamentally an art of transformation. A sample changes the moment it is relocated" (2004, 174). See also Brøvig-Hanssen 2019b on the notion of "contextual transformation."

24. Johan Deckmyn and Vrijheidsfonds VZW v. Helena Vandersteen and Others, ECJ, case no. C-201/13 (2014), para. 33.

25. As mentioned in chapter 4, humor scholars point to the combined features of incongruity and sense making as key humor triggers, which allows for some overlap between the two fields' understandings of humor vis-à-vis parody.

26. Copyright in the Digital Single Market Directive, 2019, article 17.

27. Copyright in the Digital Single Market Directive, 2019, article 17(7). The European Commission explains, "Article 17(7) stipulates that, when online content-sharing service providers cooperate with rightholders under article 17(4) to avoid unauthorised content, such cooperation shall not result in the unavailability of works and other subject matter uploaded by users, which do not infringe on copyright and related rights" (Communication from the Commission to the European Parliament and the Council: Guidance on Article 17 of Directive 2019/790 on Copyright in the Digital Single Market, 4 June 2021, COM(2021) 288 final. Available at https://eur-lex.europa.eu/legal-content/EN/TXT/?qid=1625142238402&uri=CELEX%3A52021DC0288).

28. See also Gallagher 2018, 205, and Tushnet 2008 and 2014.

29. For a study on the extent to which metadata can be used in machine learning to detect parodies, see Weese, Murphy, and Knight 2017.

30. This is especially true if "staydown" filters, which prevent removed content from being reuploaded, become more common (see chapter 6).

31. For similar observations regarding platforms' biased and opaque treatment of content, see, for example, Gillespie 2018; Meyers 2009; Nunziato 2014; Urban and Quilter 2006; and Zimmerman 2014.

References

Adams, Kyle. 2015. "What Did Danger Mouse Do? The Grey Album and Musical Composition in Configurable Culture." *Music Theory Spectrum* 37 (1), 7–24.

Adorno, Theodor W. 1941. "On Popular Music." *Studies in Philosophy and Social Science* 9 (1), 17–48. https://doi.org/10.5840/zfs1941913.

———. 1997 [1970]. *Aesthetic Theory*. London: Continuum.

Allen, Graham. 2011. *Intertextuality*. New York: Routledge.

Alm, Vemund H. 2021. "'As Though It Was the Internet Spitting Back What We've Been Feeding into It': Vaporwave—En musikksjanger i internetts tidsalder." Master's thesis, University of Oslo.

Apter, Michael J. 1982. *The Experience of Motivation: The Theory of Psychological Reversals*. Cambridge, MA: Academic Press.

Aquilante, Dan. 2005. "Mash Bash: Amster Jam Gets Headliners Mixed Up." *New York Post*, August 14. https://nypost.com/2005/08/14/mash-bash-amster-jam-gets-headliners-mixed-up/.

Attardo, Salvatore. 2008. "A Primer for the Linguistics of Humor." In *The Primer of Humor Research*, edited by Victor Raskin, 101–156. Berlin: Mouton de Gruyter.

Attardo, Salvatore, Christian F. Hempelmann, and Sara Di Maio. 2002. "Script Oppositions and Logical Mechanisms: Modeling Incongruities and Their Resolutions." *Humor: International Journal of Humor Research* 15 (1), 3–46. https://doi.org/10.1515/humr.2002.004.

Attardo, Salvatore, and Victor Raskin. 1991. "Script Theory Revis(it)ed: Joke Similarity and Joke Representation Model." *Humor: International Journal of Humor Research* 4 (3–4), 293–347. https://doi.org/10.1515/humr.1991.4.3-4.293.

Audible Magic. n.d. https://www.audiblemagic.com/.

Aufderheide, Patricia. 2015. "Copyright and Fair Use in Remix: From Alarmism to Action." In *The Routledge Companion to Remix Studies*, edited by Eduardo Navas, Owen Gallagher, and xtine burrough, 270–282. New York: Routledge.

Aufderheide, Patricia, Jan Lauren Boyles, and Katie Bieze. 2013. "Copyright, Free Speech, and the Public's Right to Know: Journalists and Fair Use." *Journalism Studies* 14 (6), 875–890. https://doi.org/10.1080/1461670X.2012.739320.

Aufderheide, Patricia, and Peter Jaszi. 2018. *Reclaiming Fair Use: How to Put Balance Back in Copyright*. Chicago: University of Chicago Press.

Aufderheide, Patricia, Tijana Milosevic, and Bryan Bello. 2015. "The Impact of Copyright Permissions Culture on the US Visual Arts Community: The Consequences of Fear of Fair Use." *New Media and Society* 18 (9), 2012–2027. https://doi.org/10.1177/1461444815575018.

Auslander, Philip. 2004. "I Wanna Be Your Man: Suzi Quatro's Musical Androgyny." *Popular Music* 23 (1), 1–16. https://doi.org/10.1017/S0261143004000030.

———. 2008. *Liveness: Performance in a Mediated Culture*. London: Routledge.

Ayers, Michael D. 2006. "The Cyberactivism of a Dangermouse." In *Cybersounds: Essays on Virtual Music Culture*, edited by Ayers, 127–136. New York: Peter Lang.

Bakhtin, Mikhail. 1971 [1929]. "Discourse Typology in Prose." In *Readings in Russian Poetics: Formalist and Structuralist Views*, edited by Ladislav Matejka and Krystyna Pomorska, 176–196. Cambridge, MA: MIT Press.

———. 1981 [1975]. *The Dialogic Imagination: Four Essays*. Edited by Michael Holquist. Translated by Caryl Emerson and Michael Holquist. Austin: University of Texas Press.

———. 1984 [1963]. *Problems of Dostoevsky's Poetics*. Translated by Caryl Emerson. Minneapolis: University of Minnesota Press.

———. 1986 [1979]. *Speech Genres and Other Late Essays*. Edited by Caryl Emerson and Michael Holquist. Translated by Vern W. McGee. Austin: University of Texas Press.

Balliger, Robin. 1995. "Sounds of Resistance." In *Sounding Off! Music as Subversion/Resistance/Revolution*, edited by Ronald B. Sakolsky and Fred Wei-han Ho, 13–26. New York: Autonomedia.

Barlow, John Perry. 1996. "A Declaration of the Independence of Cyberspace." Davos, Switzerland. https://www.eff.org/cyberspace-independence.

Barthes, Roland. 1967. "The Death of the Author." *Aspen* 5+6, 3.

———. 1975a. *S/Z: An Essay*. Translated by Richard Miller. New York: Hill and Wang.

———. 1975b. *The Pleasure of the Text.* Translated by Richard Miller. New York: Hill and Wang.

———. 1977. *Image, Music, Text.* Translated by Stephen Heath. London: Fontana Press.

———. 1981. "Theory of the Text." In *Untying the Text: A Post-Structuralist Reader*, edited by Robert Young, 31–47. London: Routledge and Kegan Paul.

Beattie, James. 1971. "An Essay on Laughter, and Ludicrous Composition." In *Essays*, 583–705. New York: Garland.

Becker, Howard. 1982. *Art Worlds.* Berkeley: University of California Press.

Beebe, Barton. 2008. "An Empirical Study of U.S. Copyright Fair Use Opinions, 1978–2005." *University of Pennsylvania Law Review* 156 (3), 549–624.

———. 2020. "An Empirical Study of U.S. Copyright Fair Use Opinions Updated, 1978–2019." *New York University Journal of Intellectual Property and Entertainment Law* 10 (1), 1–39.

Begault, Durand, Heather Heise, and Christopher Peltier. 2014. "Forensic Musicology: An Overview." Paper presented at the 54th International Audio Engineering Society Conference.

Benkler, Yochai. 2006. *The Wealth of Networks: How Social Production Transforms Markets and Freedom.* New Haven: Yale University Press.

Bennett, Joe. 2018. "Songwriting, Digital Audio Workstations, and the Internet." In *The Oxford Handbook of the Creative Process in Music*, edited by Nicolas Donin. Oxford: Oxford University Press.

Bently, Lionel. 1994. "Review Article: Copyright and the Death of the Author in Literature and Law." *Modern Law Review Limited* 57 (6), 973–986.

———. 2008. "R. v. The Author: From Death Penalty to Community Service." *Columbia Journal of Law and the Arts* 32 (1), 1–110.

Bently, Lionel, and Tanya Frances Aplin. 2020. *Global Mandatory Fair Use: The Nature and Scope of the Right to Quote Copyright Works.* Cambridge: Cambridge University Press.

Berio, Luciano. 1986. *Sinfonia; Eindrücke.* New Swingle Singers, Orchestre National de France. Erato Records.

Berlyne, Daniel. 1971. *Aesthetics and Psychobiology.* New York: Appleton-Century-Croft.

———. 1974. *Studies in the New Experimental Aesthetics: Steps toward an Objective Psychology of Aesthetic Appreciation.* Washington, DC: Hemisphere.

Berry, David M. 2008. *Copy, Rip, Burn: The Politics of Copyleft and Open Source*. London: Pluto Press.

Bicknell, Jeanette. 2001. "The Problem of Reference in Musical Quotation: A Phenomenological Approach." *Journal of Aesthetics and Art Criticism* 59 (2), 185–191.

Billi, Mirella. 1993. *Il Testo Riflesso: La Parodia Nel Romanzo Inglese*. Naples: Liguori.

Birk, Mette. 2015. "The Panoptic of Ethical Video Remix Practice." In *The Routledge Companion to Remix Studies*, edited by Eduardo Navas, Owen Gallagher, and xtine burrough, 246–257. New York: Routledge. https://doi.org/10.4324/9781315879994.

Biron, Laura. 2014. "Creative Work and Communicative Norms: Perspectives from Legal Philosophy." In *The Work of Authorship*, edited by Mireille van Eechoud, 19–44. Amsterdam: Amsterdam University Press.

Bishop, Sophie. 2018. "Anxiety, Panic and Self-Optimization: Inequalities and the YouTube Algorithm." *Convergence: The International Journal of Research into New Media Technologies* 24 (1), 69–84. https://doi.org/10.1177/1354856517736978.

Bloom, Harold. 1973. *The Anxiety of Influence: A Theory of Poetry*. Oxford: Oxford University Press.

Bogost, Ian. 2016. *Play Anything: The Pleasure of Limits, the Uses of Boredom, and the Secret of Games*. New York: Basic Books.

Boom Selection. n.d. *Boom Selection*. http://web.archive.org/web/20060205042359/http://boomselection.info/.

Boon, Marcus. 2007. "On Appropriation." *New Centennial Review* 7 (1), 1–14. https://doi.org/10.1353/ncr.2007.0024.

———. 2010. *In Praise of Copying*. Cambridge, MA: Harvard University Press.

Boone, Christine E. 2011. "Mashups: History, Legality, and Aesthetics." PhD diss., University of Texas at Austin. https://repositories.lib.utexas.edu/bitstream/handle/2152/ETD-UT-2011-05-3311/BOONE-DISSERTATION.pdf;sequence=1.

———. 2013. "Mashing: Toward a Typology of Recycled Music." *Music Theory Online* 19 (3), 1–14.

———. 2021. "Popular Song Remixed: Mashups, Aesthetic Transformation, and Resistance." In *The Routledge Handbook of Remix Studies and Digital Humanities*, edited by Eduardo Navas, Owen Gallagher, and xtine burrough, 417–429. New York: Routledge.

Born, Georgina, and Christopher Haworth. 2017. "From Microsound to Vaporwave: Internet-Mediated Musics, Online Methods, and Genre." *Music and Letters* 98 (4), 601–647. https://doi.org/10.1093/ml/gcx095.

Borschke, Margie. 2017. *This Is Not a Remix: Piracy, Authenticity and Popular Music.* New York: Bloomsbury Academic.

Bourdieu, Pierre. 1977. *Outline of a Theory of Practice.* Cambridge: Cambridge University Press.

———. 1984. *Distinction: A Social Critique of the Judgment of Taste.* London: Routledge.

———. 1993. *The Field of Cultural Production: Essays on Art and Literature.* Edited by Randal Johnson. Cambridge: Cambridge University Press.

Bourriaud, Nicolas. 2005. *Postproduction: Culture as Screenplay; How Art Reprograms the World.* New York: Lukas and Sternberg.

Boyle, James. 1997. *Shamans, Software, and Spleens: Law and the Construction of the Information Society.* Cambridge, MA: Harvard University Press.

———. 2008. *The Public Domain: Enclosing the Commons of the Mind.* New Haven: Yale University Press.

Brackett, David. 2002. "(In Search of) Musical Meaning: Genre, Categories, and Crossover." In *Popular Music Studies*, edited by David Hesmondhalgh and Keith Negus, 65–84. London: Arnold.

———. 2016. *Categorizing Sound: Genre and Twentieth-Century Popular Music.* Berkeley: University of California Press.

Bradley, Catherine A. 2018. *Polyphony in Medieval Paris: The Art of Composing with Plainchant.* Cambridge: Cambridge University Press.

Breihan, Tom. 2005. "AmsterJam Gets AmsterSlammed? AmsterDAMN!" *Village Voice*, August 22. https://www.villagevoice.com/2005/08/22/amsterjam-gets-amsterslammed-amsterdamn/.

Brod, Doug. 2002. "The Best Bootlegs in the World Ever Album Review." *Entertainment Weekly*, March 17. https://ew.com/article/2002/05/03/best-bootlegs-world-ever/.

Brøvig-Hanssen, Ragnhild. 2016. "Justin Bieber Featuring Slipknot: Consumption as Mode of Production." In *Music and Virtuality*, edited by Sheila Whiteley and Shara Rambarran, 266–281. Oxford: Oxford University Press.

———. 2018. "Listening *To* or *Through* Technology: Opaque and Transparent Mediation." In *Critical Approaches to the Production of Music and Sound*, edited by Samantha Bennett and Eliot Bates, 195–210. New York: Bloomsbury Academic.

———. 2019a. "Humor's Role in Mashups and Remixes." In *On Popular Music and Its Unruly Entanglements*, edited by Nick Braae and Kai Arne Hansen, 189–207. London: Palgrave Macmillan.

———. 2019b. "Mixing with Quotations: Mashups and Contextual Transformation." In *The Art of Record Production: Creative Practice in the Studio*, edited by Simon Zagorski-Thomas, Katia Isakoff, Sophie Stévance, and Serge Lacasse, 50–65. New York: Routledge.

Brøvig-Hanssen, Ragnhild, and Anne Danielsen. 2013. "The Naturalised and the Surreal: Changes in the Perception of Popular Music Sound." *Organised Sound* 18 (1), 72–81. https://doi.org/10.1017/S1355771812000258

———. 2016. *Digital Signatures: The Impact of Digitization on Popular Music Sound*. Cambridge, MA: MIT Press.

Brøvig-Hanssen, Ragnhild, and Paul Harkins. 2012. "Contextual Incongruity and Musical Congruity: The Aesthetics and Humour of Mash-Ups." *Popular Music* 31 (1), 87–104.

Brøvig-Hanssen, Ragnhild, and Ellis Jones. 2021. "Remix's Retreat? Content Moderation, Copyright Law and Mashup Music." *New Media and Society* (published online June 27), 1–19. https://doi.org/10.1177/14614448211026059.

Brøvig-Hanssen, Ragnhild, and Aram Sinnreich. 2019. "Do You Wanna Build a Wall? Remix Tactics in the Age of Trump." *Popular Music and Society* 43 (5), 535–549. https://doi.org/10.1080/03007766.2019.1650990.

Bruns, Axel. 2009. *Blogs, Wikipedia, Second Life, and Beyond: From Production to Produsage*. New York: Peter Lang.

Bucher, Taina. 2012. "Want to Be on the Top? Algorithmic Power and the Threat of Invisibility on Facebook." *New Media and Society* 14 (7), 1164–1180. https://doi.org/10.1177/1461444812440159.

Bürger, Peter. 1984. *Theory of the Avant-Garde*. Minneapolis: University of Minnesota Press.

Burgess, Jean E. 2007. "Vernacular Creativity and New Media." PhD diss., Queensland University of Technology. https://eprints.qut.edu.au/16378/.

Burkholder, Peter J. 1985. *Charles Ives: The Ideas behind the Music*. New Haven: Yale University Press.

———. 1994. "The Uses of Existing Music: Musical Borrowing as a Field." *Notes* 50 (3), 851–870. https://doi.org/10.2307/898531.

Burns, Lori, and Serge Lacasse, eds. 2018. *The Pop Palimpsest: Intertextuality in Recorded Popular Music*. Ann Arbor: University of Michigan Press.

Burns, Lori, and Alyssa Woods. 2019. "Humor in the 'Booty Video': Female Artists Talk Back through the Hip-Hop Intertext." In *The Routledge Companion to Popular Music and Humor*, edited by Thomas M. Kitts and Nicolas Baxter-Moore, 310–320. New York: Routledge.

Burns, Lori, Alyssa Woods, and Marc Lafrance. 2015. "The Genealogy of a Song: Lady Gaga's Musical Intertexts on *The Fame Monster* (2009)." *Twentieth-Century Music* 12 (1), 3–35. https://doi.org/10.1017/S1478572214000176.

burrough, xtine, and Emily Erickson. 2015. "Going Crazy with Remix: A Classroom Study by Practice via Lenz v. Universal." In *The Routledge Companion to Remix Studies*, edited by Eduardo Navas, Owen Gallagher, and xtine burrough, 453–460. New York: Routledge.

Butler, Martin. 2019. "Of Shreds, Spoofs, and Participatory Cultures: Parodies of Popular Music Videos in Web 2.0 Contexts." In *The Routledge Companion to Popular Music and Humor*, edited by Thomas M. Kitts and Nicolas Baxter-Moore, 321–328. New York: Routledge.

Caillois, Roger. 2001. *Man, Play and Games*. Translated by Meyer Barash. Champaign: University of Illinois Press.

Carroll, Michael. 2007. "Fixing Fair Use." *North Carolina Law Review* 85 (4), 1087–1090.

Cefrey, Holly. 2008. *Career Building through Music, Video, and Software Mashups*. New York: Rosen Publishing.

Certeau, Michel de. 1984. *The Practice of Everyday Life*. Berkeley: University of California Press.

Chambers, Robert. 2010. *Parody: The Art That Plays with Art*. New York: Peter Lang.

Cherry, Daniel. 2011. "Blanch It, Mix It, Mash It: A Fair Use Framework for the Mashup." *Thomas M. Cooley Law Review* 28 (3), 495–524.

Christensen, Ralf, Henrik Moltke, and Andreas Johnsen. 2007. *Good Copy Bad Copy*. Copenhagen: Rosforth.

Church, Scott H. 2022. *Turntables and Tropes: A Rhetoric of Remix*. East Lansing: Michigan State University Press.

Church, Scott H., and Gavin Feller. 2021. "Internet Memes as Remixes: *Simpsons* Memes and the Swarm Archive." In *The Routledge Handbook of Remix Studies and Digital Humanities*, edited by Eduardo Navas, Owen Gallagher, and xtine burrough, 259–272. New York: Routledge.

Clague, Mark. 2019. "50 Years Ago, Jimi Hendrix's Woodstock Anthem Expressed the Hopes and Fears of a Nation." *The Conversation*, August 14. http://theconversation.com/50-years-ago-jimi-hendrixs-woodstock-anthem-expressed-the-hopes-and-fears-of-a-nation-120717.

Coleman, Miles C., and Mark Anthoney. 2020. "Machinic Enculturation, Copyright Bots, and the Aesthetics of Composing Mashups for Machines." *Journal of Aesthetics and Culture* 12 (1), 1831841. https://doi.org/10.1080/20004214.2020.1831841.

Cook, Nicholas. 2006. "Uncanny Moments: Juxtaposition and the Collage Principle in Music." In *Approaches to Meaning in Music*, edited by Byron Almén and Edward Pearsall. Bloomington: Indiana University Press. https://muse.jhu.edu/book/9044.

Coombe, Rosemary J. 1998. *The Cultural Life of Intellectual Properties: Authorship, Appropriation, and the Law*. Durham: Duke University Press.

Covach, John. 1991. "Dahlhaus, Schoenberg, and the New Music." *In Theory Only* 12 (1–2), 19–42.

———. 1995. "Reviewed Works: *A History of Western Musical Aesthetics* by Edward Lippman; *Perspectives on Musical Aesthetics* by John Rahn." *Music Theory Spectrum* 17 (2), 275–282. https://doi.org/10.2307/745875.

Cruger, Roberta. 2003. "The Mash-up Revolution." *Salon*, August 10. https://www.salon.com/2003/08/09/mashups_cruger/.

Csikszentmihalyi, Mihaly. 2008. *Flow: The Psychology of Optimal Experience*. New York: Harper and Row.

Cunningham, Stuart, David Craig, and Jon Silver. 2016. "YouTube, Multichannel Networks and the Accelerated Evolution of the New Screen Ecology." *Convergence: The International Journal of Research into New Media Technologies* 22 (4), 376–391. https://doi.org/10.1177/1354856516641620.

Danielsen, Anne. 2006. *Presence and Pleasure: The Funk Grooves of James Brown and Parliament*. Middletown, CT: Wesleyan University Press.

———. 2008. "The Musicalization of 'Reality': Reality Rap and Rap Reality on Public Enemy's *Fear of a Black Planet*." *European Journal of Cultural Studies* 11 (4), 405–421. https://doi.org/10.1177/1367549408094980.

David, Matthew, and Natasha Whiteman. 2015. "'Piracy' or Parody: Moral Panic in an Age of New Media." In *The SAGE Handbook of Intellectual Property*, edited by Matthew David and Debora Halbert, 451–469. London: Sage. https://doi.org/10.4135/9781473910027.n26.

Deleuze, Gilles. 1994 [1968]. *Difference and Repetition*. Translated by Paul R. Patton. London: Athlone Press.

Demers, Joanna. 2006. *Steal This Music: How Intellectual Property Law Affects Musical Creativity*. Athens: University of Georgia Press.

Dennett, Daniel. 1996. *Kinds of Minds: Towards an Understanding of Consciousness*. New York: Basic Books.

Dentith, Simon. 2000. *Parody*. New York: Routledge.

Derrida, Jacques. 1976 [1967]. *Of Grammatology*. Translated by Paul R. Patton. London: John Hopkins University Press.

———. 1982 [1972]. *Margins of Philosophy*. Translated by Alan Bass. New York: Harvester Wheatsheaf.

Dijck, Jose van. 2013. *The Culture of Connectivity: A Critical History of Social Media*. Oxford: Oxford University Press. https://doi.org/10.1093/acprof:oso/9780199970773.001.0001.

Discogs. n.d. "The Best Bootlegs in the World Ever." *Discogs*. https://www.discogs.com/Various-The-Best-Bootlegs-In-The-World-Ever/release/479099.

Downhill Battle. 2004. "Grey Tuesday: Free the Grey Album." *Downhill Battle*. February 24. http://downhillbattle.org/greytuesday/.

———. n.d. *Downhill Battle*. http://downhillbattle.org/.

Dyer, Richard. 2007. *Pastiche*. New York: Routledge.

Echard, William. 2018. "Someone and Someone: Dialogic Intertextuality and Neil Young." In *The Pop Palimpsest: Intertextuality in Recorded Popular Music*, edited by Lori Burns and Serge Lacasse, 169–189. Ann Arbor: University of Michigan Press.

Edwards, Richard L. 2014. "Remixing with Rules: Constraint and Potential in Restrictive Remixes." In *Sampling Media*, edited by David Laderman and Laurel Westrup, 31–42. Oxford: Oxford University Press. https://doi.org/10.1093/acprof:oso/9780199949311.003.0003.

Eechoud, Mireille van. 2014. "Introduction." In *The Work of Authorship*, edited by Mireille van Eechoud, 7–18. Amsterdam: Amsterdam University Press.

Eidsvold-Tøien, Irina. 2021. "Parodirettslig vakuum i norsk rett." In *Festskrift til Jørgen Blomquist*, edited by Morten Rosenmeier, Thomas Riis, Jens Schovsbo, and Henrik Udsen, 87–130. Copenhagen: Ex Tuto Publishing A/S.

Eisenstein, Sergej. 1977. *Film Form*. New York: Harcourt.

———. 1986. *The Film Sense*. London: Faber and Faber.

Engman, Adrian. 2020. "Exceptions and Limitations to Copyright: Is There Any Scope for National Diversity?" *Nordiskt Immateriellt Rättsskydd* 2020 (1), 127–138.

Eriksen, Asbjørn Ø. 2016. "A Taxonomy of Humor in Instrumental Music." *Journal of Musicological Research* 35 (3), 233–263. https://doi.org/10.1080/01411896.2016.1193418.

Fairchild, Charles. 2017. "The Emergence and Historical Decay of the Mash Up." *Journal of Popular Music Studies* 29 (4), e12246, 1–12. https://doi.org/10.1111/jpms.12246.

Foucault, Michel. 1979 [1969]. "What Is an Author?" Translated by Josué V. Harari. In *Textual Strategies: Perspectives in Post-Structuralist Criticism*, edited by Josué V. Harari, 141–160. Ithaca: Cornell University Press.

Frith, Simon. 1981. *Sound Effects: Youth, Leisure, and the Politics of Rock*. London: Constable.

———. 1998. *Performing Rites: On the Value of Popular Music*. Cambridge, MA: Harvard University Press.

———. 2004. "What Is Bad Music?" In *Bad Music: The Music We Love to Hate*, edited by Christopher J. Washburne and Maiken Derno, 15–37. New York: Routledge.

Frith, Simon, and Angela McRobbie. 1990 [1978]. "Rock and Sexuality." In *On Record: Rock, Pop, and the Written* Word, edited by Simon Frith and Andrew Goodwin, 371–389. New York: Routledge.

Frosio, Giancarlo. 2021. "A Brief History of Remix: From Caves to Networks." In *The Routledge Handbook of Remix Studies and Digital Humanities*, edited by Eduardo Navas, Owen Gallagher, and xtine burrough, 19–35. New York: Routledge.

Gadamer, Hans Georg. 2003. *Truth and Method*. New York: Continuum.

Gallagher, Owen. 2013. "The Assault on Creative Culture: Politics of Cultural Ownership." In *The Participatory Cultures Handbook*, edited by Aaron Alan Delwiche and Jennifer Jacobs Henderson, 86–96. New York: Routledge.

———. 2015. "Occupy/Band Aid Mashup: 'Do They Know It's Christmas?'" In *The Routledge Companion to Remix Studies*, edited by Eduardo Navas, Owen Gallagher, and xtine burrough, 471–479. New York: Routledge.

———. 2018. *Reclaiming Critical Remix Video: The Role of Sampling in Transformative Works*. New York: Routledge.

Gates, Henry Louis, Jr. 1988. *The Signifying Monkey: A Theory of African-American Literary Criticism*. Oxford: Oxford University Press.

Gaylor, Brett. 2008. *RiP: A Remix Manifesto*. Toronto: Kinosmith.

Genette, Gérard. 1997 [1982]. *Palimpsests: Literature in the Second Degree*. Lincoln: University of Nebraska Press.

Gibson, William. 2005. "God's Little Toys: Confessions of a Cut and Paste Artist." *Wired* January 7, 2015. https://www.wired.com/2005/07/gibson-3/.

Gillespie, Tarleton. 2018. *Custodians of the Internet: Platforms, Content Moderation, and the Hidden Decisions That Shape Social Media*. New Haven: Yale University Press.

Gillespie, Tarleton, Patricia Aufderheide, Elinor Carmi, Ysabel Gerrard, Robert Gorwa, Ariadna Matamoros-Fernández, Sarah T. Roberts, Aram Sinnreich, and Sarah Myers West. 2020. "Expanding the Debate about Content Moderation: Scholarly Research Agendas for the Coming Policy Debates." *Internet Policy Review* 9 (4). https://doi.org/10.14763/2020.4.1512.

References

Givan, Benjamin. 2015. "'The Star-Spangled Banner' and 'God Save the King': Glenn Gould's Quodlibet." *Musicology Now*, July 4. https://musicologynow.org/the-star-spangled-banner-and-god-save-the-king-glenn-goulds-quodlibet/.

Gleitman, Henry. 1991. *Psychology*. New York: Norton.

Goehr, Lydia. 2007. *The Imaginary Museum of Musical Works: An Essay in the Philosophy of Music*. Oxford: Oxford University Press.

Golosker, Vera. 2012. "The Transformative Tribute: How Mash-Up Music Constitutes Fair Use of Copyrights." *Hastings Communications and Entertainment Law Journal* 34 (3), 381–402.

Goodman, Nelson. 1968. *Languages of Art: An Approach to a Theory of Symbols*. New York: Bobbs-Merrill.

———. 1974. "On Some Questions Concerning Quotation." *Monist* 58 (2), 294–306.

Goodwin, Andrew. 1990. "Sample and Hold: Pop Music in the Age of Digital Reproduction." In *On Record: Rock, Pop, and the Written Word*, edited by Simon Frith and Andrew Goodwin, 258–273. New York: Routledge.

Google. n.d.-a. "How Content ID Works. YouTube Help." Accessed 7 January 2020. https://support.google.com/youtube/answer/2797370?hl=en.

———. n.d.-b. "Copyright Strike Basics. YouTube Help." Accessed 7 January 2020. https://support.google.com/youtube/answer/2814000?hl=en.

———. n.d.-c. "What Is a Content ID Claim? YouTube Help." Accessed 7 January 2020. https://support.google.com/youtube/answer/6013276?hl=en.

———. n.d.-d. "Frequently Asked Questions About Fair Use. YouTube Help." Accessed 7 January 2020. https://support.google.com/youtube/answer/6396261?hl=en.

———. n.d.-e. "What Is a Reference? YouTube Help." Accessed 7 January 2020. https://support.google.com/youtube/answer/107004.

———. n.d.-f. "Qualify for Content ID. YouTube Help." Accessed 7 January 2020. https://support.google.com/youtube/answer/1311402?hl=en&ref_topic=9282364.

———. n.d.-g. "Dispute a Content ID Claim. YouTube Help." Accessed 7 January 2020. https://support.google.com/youtube/answer/2797454?hl=en.

———. 2018. "How Google Fights Piracy." Accessed 7 January 2020. https://storage.googleapis.com/gweb-uniblog-publish-prod/documents/How_Google_Fights_Piracy_2018.pdf.

Gracyk, Theodore. 1996. *Rhythm and Noise: An Aesthetics of Rock*. Durham: Duke University Press.

———. 2001. *I Wanna Be Me: Rock Music and the Politics of Identity*. Philadelphia: Temple University Press.

Grossberg, Lawrence. 1992. *We Gotta Get Out of This Place: Popular Conservatism and Postmodern Culture*. New York: Routledge.

Guertin, Carolyn. 2012. *Digital Prohibition: Piracy and Authorship in New Media*. London: Bloomsbury.

Gunderson, Philip A. 2004. "Danger Mouse's Grey Album, Mash-Ups, and the Age of Composition." *Postmodern Culture* 15 (1). https://doi.org/10.1353/pmc.2004.0040.

Gunkel, David J. 2008. "Rethinking the Digital Remix: Mash-ups and the Metaphysics of Sound Recording." *Popular Music and Society* 31 (4), 489–510. https://doi.org/10.1080/03007760802053211.

———. 2016. *Of Remixology: Ethics and Aesthetics After Remix*. Cambridge, MA: MIT Press.

Hall, Stuart. 1977. "Culture, the Media and the 'Ideological Effect.'" In *Mass Communication and Society*, edited by James Curran, Michael Gurevitch, and Janet Woollacott, 315–348. London: Arnold.

Harkins, Paul. 2019. *Digital Sampling: The Design and Use of Music Technologies*. New York: Routledge.

Harper, Emily. 2010. "Music Mashups: Testing the Limits of Copyright Law as Remix Culture Takes Society by Storm." *Hofstra Law Review* 39 (2), 405–445.

Harrah, David. 1954. "Aesthetics of the Film: The Pudovkin-Arnheim-Eisenstein Theory." *Journal of Aesthetics and Art Criticism* 13 (2), 163–174. https://doi.org/10.2307/425910.

Harrison, Nate, and Eduardo Navas. 2018. "Mashup." In *Keywords in Remix Studies*, edited by Eduardo Navas, Owen Gallagher, and xtine burrough, 188–201. New York: Routledge.

Hatten, Robert S. 1985. "The Place of Intertextuality in Music Studies." *American Journal of Semiotics* 3 (4), 69–82. https://doi.org/10.5840/ajs1985345.

Hawkins, Stan. 2002. *Settling the Pop Score: Pop Texts and Identity Politics*. Aldershot: Ashgate.

———. 2016. "Remembering Sheila Whiteley." *Popular Music* 35 (1), 118–121. https://doi.org/10.1017/S0261143015000847.

———. 2018. "Performative Strategies and Musical Markers in the Eurythmics' 'I Need a Man.'" In *The Pop Palimpsest: Intertextuality in Recorded Popular Music*, edited by Lori Burns and Serge Lacasse, 252–270. Ann Arbor: University of Michigan Press.

Hawkins, Stan, and John Richardson. 2007. "Introduction." In *Essays on Sound and Vision*, edited by John Richardson and Stan Hawkins, 13–23. Yliopistopaino: Helsinki University Press. https://www.academia.edu/241893/Essays_on_Sound_and _Vision_co_edited_with_John_Richardson_2007_.

Hebdige, Dick. 1979. *Subculture: The Meaning of Style*. London: Methuen.

Heidegger, Martin. 1962 [1929]. *Being and Time*. Translated by John Macquarrie and Edward S. Robinson. New York: Harper and Row.

Hennion, Antoine. 2005. "Pragmatics of Taste." In *The Blackwell Companion to the Sociology of Culture*, edited by Mark D. Jacobs and Nancy W. Hanrahan, 131–144. Oxford: Blackwell.

Hestholm, Marion. 2010. "Fragments, Flights, and Forms: Montage as a Constructive Principle of Twentieth-Century Music." PhD diss., University of Oslo.

Holm-Hudson, Kevin. 1997. "Quotation and Context: Sampling and John Oswald's Plunderphonics." *Leonardo Music Journal* 7, 17–25. https://doi.org/10.2307/1513241.

Holt, Fabian. 2007. *Genre in Popular Music*. Chicago: University of Chicago Press.

Horwatt, Elijah. 2008a. "A Taxonomy of Digital Video Remixing: Contemporary Found Footage Practice on the Internet." In *Cultural Borrowings: Appropriation, Reworking, Transformation*, edited by Iain Robert Smith, 76–91. London: Scope.

———. 2008b. "New Media Resistance: Machinima and the Avant-Garde." *Cineaction!* 73–74, 8–14.

Householder, Fred W. 1944. "Π ΑΡΩ ΙΔ ΙΑ." *Classical Philology* 39 (1), 1–9.

Howard, V. A. 1974. "On Musical Quotation." *Monist* 58 (2), 307–318.

Howard-Spink, Sam. 2005. "Grey Tuesday, Online Cultural Activism and the Mash-Up of Music and Politics." *First Monday* Special issue no. 1. https://doi.org/10.5210 /fm.v0i0.1460.

Hudson, Emily. 2017. "The Pastiche Exception in Copyright Law: A Case of Mashed-Up Drafting?" *Intellectual Property Quarterly* 2017 (4), 346–368.

Huhn, Mary. 2005. "Mash-Up Mania: Odd Couple Genre-Benders Make Beautiful Music Together." *New York Post*, January 8. https://nypost.com/2005/01/08/mash-up -mania-odd-couple-genre-benders-make-beautiful-music-together/.

Hui, Alan. 2017. "99 Problems But a Riff Ain't One: How Sampling Helps Copyright Promote Originality." PhD diss., Australian National University. https://openre search-repository.anu.edu.au/handle/1885/141160.

———. 2019. "Norwegian Copyright Limitations and Exceptions Following Pelham v Hütter." Paper resented at the Market, Innovation, Competition Group, Faculty of Law, University of Oslo, December 12.

———. 2021a. "Emerging Frontiers: Platform Regulation of Mashups in and Beyond an EU Context." In *The Present and Future of Music Law*, edited by Tony Rigg and Ann Harrison, 64–81. New York: Bloomsbury Academic.

———. 2021b. "Mashup Music as Expression Displaced and Expression Foregone." *Internet Policy Review* 10 (4). https://doi.org/10.14763/2021.4.1604.

Hui, Alan, and Frédéric Döhl. 2021. "Collateral Damage: Reuse in the Arts and the New Role of Quotation Provisions in Countries with Free Use Provisions after the ECJ's Pelham, Funke Medien, and Spiegel Online Judgments." *International Review of Intellectual Property and Competition Law* 52, 852–892. https://doi.org/10.1007/s40319-021-01084-4

Huizinga, Johan. 1955. *Homo Ludens: A Study of the Play-Element in Culture*. Boston: Beacon Press.

Huron, David. 2006. *Sweet Anticipation: Music and the Psychology of Expectation*. Cambridge, MA: MIT Press.

Hutcheon, Linda. 1994. *Irony's Edge: The Theory and Politics of Irony*. London: Routledge.

———. 2000. *A Theory of Parody: The Teachings of Twentieth-Century Art Forms*. Urbana: University of Illinois Press.

———. 2006. *A Theory of Adaptation*. London: Routledge.

Ingham, Tim. 2019. "What Happens If Google Buys the World's Biggest Music Company?" *Rolling Stone*, March 15. https://www.rollingstone.com/music/music-features/what-happens-if-google-buys-the-worlds-biggest-music-company-807891/.

Jacques, Sabine. 2016. "Mash-Ups and Mixes: What Impact Have the Recent Copyright Reforms Had on the Legality of Sampling?" *Entertainment Law Review* 3 (1), 1–15.

———. 2019. *The Parody Exception in Copyright Law*. Oxford: Oxford University Press. https://doi.org/10.1093/oso/9780198806936.001.0001.

Jacques, Sabine, Krzysztof Garstka, Morten Hviid, and John Street. 2018. "An Empirical Study of the Use of Automated Anti-Piracy Systems and Their Consequences for Cultural Diversity." *Scripted* 15 (2), 277–312. https://doi.org/10.2966/scrip.150218.277.

Jameson, Fredric. 1982. "Towards a New Awareness of Genre." *Science Fiction Studies* 9 (3), 322–324.

Jarman, Freya. 2018. "Watch My Lips: The Limits of Camp in Lip-Syncing Scenes." In *Music and Camp*, edited by Christopher Moore and Philip Purvis, 95–117. Middletown, CT: Wesleyan University Press.

References

Jenkins, Henry. 1992. *Textual Poachers: Television Fans and Participatory Culture*. New York: Routledge.

———. 2006. *Convergence Culture: Where Old and New Media Collide*. New York: New York University Press.

Jones, Ellis. 2021a. *DIY Music and the Politics of Social Media*. New York: Bloomsbury Academic and Professional. http://public.eblib.com/choice/PublicFullRecord.aspx?p=6416243.

———. 2021b. "The Role of Mashup Music in Creating Web 2.0's Democratic Promise." *Convergence*, 1–17. https://doi.org/10.1177/1354856520983758.

Jones, LeRoi. 1971. "The Changing Same (R&B and New Black Music)." In *The Black Aesthetic*, edited by Addison Gayle, 112–125. New York: Doubleday.

Jütte, Bernd J. 2020. "Forcing Flexibility with Fundamental Rights: Questioning the Dominance of Exclusive Rights." In *EU Internet Law in the Digital Era*, edited by Tatiana-Eleni Synodinou, Philippe Jougleux, Christiana Markou, and Thalia Prastitou, 79–98. Cham: Springer. https://doi.org/10.1007/978-3-030-25579-4_4.

Jütte, Bernd J., and Henrike Maier. 2017. "A Human Right to Sample—Will the CJEU Dance to the BGH-Beat?" *Journal of Intellectual Property Law and Practice* 12 (9), 784–796. https://doi.org/10.1093/jiplp/jpx096.

Kafka, Peter. 2016. "Here's Why the Music Labels Are Furious at YouTube. Again." *Vox*, April 11. https://www.vox.com/2016/4/11/11586030/youtube-google-dmca-riaa-cary-sherman.

Kamps, Garrett. 2004. "Monster Mash Up." *SF Weekly*, May 12. http://www.sfweekly.com/2004-05-12/music/monster-mash-up/1.

Kant, Immanuel. 2001. *Critique of the Power of Judgment*. Translated by P. Guyer and E. Matthews. Cambridge: Cambridge University Press.

Kassabian, Anahid. 2013. *Ubiquitous Listening: Affect, Attention, and Distributed Subjectivity*. Berkeley: University of California Press.

Katz, Mark. 2004. *Capturing Sound: How Technology Has Changed Music*. Berkeley: University of California Press.

———. 2012. *Groove Music: The Art and Culture of the Hip-Hop DJ*. Oxford: Oxford University Press.

Keen, Andrew. 2006. "Web 2.0: The Second Generation of the Internet Has Arrived, It's Worse Than You Think." *Weekly Standard*, February 14.

———. 2008. *The Cult of the Amateur: How Blogs, MySpace, YouTube, and the Rest of Today's User-Generated Media Are Destroying Our Economy, Our Culture, and Our Values*. New York: Doubleday.

Keightley, Keir. 2001. "Reconsidering Rock." In *The Cambridge Companion to Pop and Rock*, edited by Simon Frith, Will Straw, and John Street, 109–142. Cambridge: Cambridge University Press.

Kierkegaard, Søren. 1983 [1843]. "Repetition: A Venture in Experimenting Psychology by Constantin Constantius." In *Fear and Trembling; Repetition*. Translated by Howard V. Hong and Edna H. Hong, 125–131. Princeton: Princeton University Press. https://www.degruyter.com/document/doi/10.1515/9781400847198-009/html.

———. 1987 [1843]. *Either/Or*. Princeton: Princeton University Press.

Kim, Jin. 2012. "The Institutionalization of YouTube: From User-Generated Content to Professionally Generated Content." *Media, Culture and Society* 34 (1), 53–67. https://doi.org/10.1177/0163443711427199.

Kitts, Thomas M., and Nicolas Baxter-Moore, eds. 2019. *The Routledge Companion to Popular Music and Humor*. New York: Routledge.

Klein, Michael L. 2004. *Intertextuality in Western Art Music*. Bloomington: Indiana University Press.

Klinger, Eric. 1971. *Structure and Functions of Fantasy*. New York: Wiley-Interscience.

Koc, Alican. 2017. "Do You Want Vaporwave, or Do You Want the Truth?: Cognitive Mapping of Late Capitalist Affect in the Virtual Lifeworld of Vaporwave." *Capacious: Journal for Emerging Affect Inquiry* 1 (1), 57–76. https://doi.org/10.22387/CAP2016.4.

Koestler, Arthur. 1964. *The Act of Creation*. London: Hutchinson.

———. 1967. *The Ghost in the Machine*. New York: Macmillan.

Kramer, Lawrence. 2004. *Opera and Modern Culture: Wagner and Strauss*. Berkeley: University of California Press.

Kristeva, Julia. 1969. *Sēmeiōtikē: Recherches pour une sémanalyse*. Paris: Seuil.

———. 1980. *Desire in Language: A Semiotic Approach to Literature and Art*. Translated by Leon S. Roudiez, Thomas Gora, and Alice Jardine. New York: Columbia University Press.

———. 1984. *Revolution in Poetic Language*. Translated by Margareth Waller. New York: Columbia University Press.

Krogh, Mads. 2020. "Context Is the New Genre." *Norsk medietidsskrift* 27 (3), 1–15. https://doi.org/10.18261/ISSN.0805-9535-2020-03-05.

Kuczerawy, Aleksandra. 2020. "From 'Notice and Takedown' to 'Notice and Stay Down': Risks and Safeguards for Freedom of Expression." In *Oxford Handbook of Online Intermediary Liability*, edited by Giancarlo Frosio, 523–543. Oxford: Oxford University Press. https://doi.org/10.1093/oxfordhb/9780198837138.013.27.

Kuhn, Virginia. 2017. "Remix in the Age of Trump." *Journal of Contemporary Rhetoric* 7 (2/3), 87–93.

———. 2021. "Production Plus Consumption: Remix and the Digital Humanities." In *The Routledge Handbook of Remix Studies and Digital Humanities*, edited by Eduardo Navas, Owen Gallagher, and xtine burrough, 70–79. New York/Oxon: Routledge.

Kvifte, Tellef. 2007. "Digital Sampling and Analogue Aesthetics." In *Aesthetics at Work*, edited by Arne Melberg, 105–128. Oslo: Unipub.

Lacasse, Serge. 2000. "'Listen to My Voice': The Evocative Power of Vocal Staging in Recorded Rock Music and Other Forms of Vocal Expression." PhD diss., University of Liverpool.

———. 2007. "Intertextuality and Hypertextuality in Recorded Popular Music." In *Critical Essays in Popular Musicology*, edited by Allan F. Moore, 35–58. Aldershot: Ashgate. https://doi.org/10.5949/liverpool/9780853238256.003.0003.

———. 2018. "Toward a Model of Transphonography." In *The Pop Palimpsest: Intertextuality in Recorded Popular Music*, edited by Lori Burns and Serge Lacasse, 9–60. Ann Arbor: University of Michigan Press.

Lacasse, Serge, and Andy Bennett. 2018. "Mix Tapes, Memory, and Nostalgia: An Introduction to Phonographic Anthologies." In *The Pop Palimpsest: Intertextuality in Recorded Popular Music*, edited by Lori Burns and Serge Lacasse, 313–329. Ann Arbor: University of Michigan Press.

Laderman, David, and Laurel Westrup, eds. 2014. *Sampling Media*. Oxford: Oxford University Press.

Lai, Amy. 2019. *The Right to Parody: Comparative Analysis of Copyright and Free Speech*. Cambridge: Cambridge University Press.

Laing, Dave. 2015. *One Chord Wonders: Power and Meaning in Punk Rock*. Oakland, CA: PM Press.

Lavik, Erlend. 2014. "Romantic Authorship in Copyright Law and the Uses of Aesthetics." In *The Work of Authorship*, edited by Mireille van Eechoud, 45–94. Amsterdam: Amsterdam University Press.

Leadbeater, Charles, and Paul Miller. 2004. *The Pro-Am Revolution: How Enthusiasts Are Changing Our Society and Economy*. London: Demos.

Legal Dictionary. n.d. "De Minimis." *Legal Dictionary*. Accessed July 31, 2021. https://legaldictionary.net/de-minimis/.

Lelièvre, F. J. 1954. "The Basis of Ancient Parody." *Greece and Rome* 1 (2), 66–81.

Lena, Jennifer C. 2017. *Banding Together: How Communities Create Genres in Popular Music*. Princeton: Princeton University Press.

Lessig, Lawrence. 2004. *Free Culture: The Nature and Future of Creativity*. New York: Penguin Books.

———. 2008. *Remix: Making Art and Commerce Thrive in the Hybrid Economy*. New York: Penguin Books. https://doi.org/10.5040/9781849662505.

Leval, Pierre N. 1990. "Toward a Fair Use Standard." *Harvard Law Review* 103 (5), 1105–1136. https://doi.org/10.2307/1341457.

Levay, William J. 2005. "The Art of Making Music in the Age of Mechanical Reproduction: The Culture Industry Remix." *Anamesa: An Interdisciplinary Journal* 3 (1), 21–41.

Lieberman, Josefa N. 1977. *Playfulness: Its Relationship to Imagination and Creativity*. New York: Academic Press.

Locke, John. 2015 [1689]. *Two Treatises of Government*. Denham Springs, LA: Cavalier Classics.

Logie, John. 2006. *Peers, Pirates, and Persuasion: Rhetoric in the Peer-to-Peer Debates*. Anderson, SC: Parlor Press.

Lozano, Kevin. 2016. "What the Hell Is Simpsonwave?" *Pitchfork*, June 14. https://pitchfork.com/thepitch/1188-what-the-hell-is-simpsonwave/.

Madison, Michael. 2004. "A Pattern-Oriented Approach to Fair Use." *William and Mary Law Review* 45 (4), 1525–1690.

Mai, Hans-Petter. 1991. "Bypassing Intertextuality: Hermeneutics, Textual Practice, Hypertext." In *Intertextuality*, edited by Henrich F. Plett, 30–59. Berlin: de Gruyter.

Mangaoang, Áine. 2018. "Here Lies Love and the Politics of Disco-Opera." In *The Routledge Companion to Popular Music Analysis*, edited by Ciro Scotto, Kenneth M. Smith, and John Brackett, 347–363. New York: Routledge. https://doi.org/10.4324/9781315544700-24.

Manovich, Lev. 2001. *The Language of New Media*. Cambridge, MA: MIT Press.

———. 2013. *Software Takes Command*. New York: Bloomsbury Academic.

Martelly, Elizabeth de. 2010. "Signification, Objectification, and the Mimetic Uncanny in Claude Debussy's 'Golliwog's Cakewalk.'" *Current Musicology*, no. 90, 7–34. https://doi.org/10.7916/D8X63KSZ.

McGranahan, Liam. 2010. "Mashnography: Creativity, Consumption, and Copyright in the Mashup Community." PhD diss., Brown University. https://repository.library.brown.edu/studio/item/bdr:11071/PDF/.

McIntosh, Jonathan. 2011. "A History of Subversive Remix Video before YouTube: Thirty Political Video Mashups Made between World War II and 2005." *Transformative Works and Cultures* 9 (June). https://doi.org/10.3983/twc.2012.0371.

McIntyre, Philip. 2012. *Creativity and Cultural Production*. New York: Palgrave Macmillan.

McLeish, Claire E. A. 2013. "'The Future Is Medieval': Orality and Musical Borrowing in the Middle Ages and Online Remix Culture." Master's thesis, University of Western Ontario.

McLeod, Kembrew. 2005. "Confessions of an Intellectual (Property), Danger Mouse, Mickey Mouse, Sonny Bono, and My Long and Winding Path as a Copyright Activist-Academic." *Popular Music and Society* 28 (1), 79–93. https://doi.org/10.1080/03007760042000300981.

———. 2007. *Freedom of Expression: Resistance and Repression in the Age of Intellectual Property*. Minneapolis: University of Minnesota Press.

McLeod, Kembrew, and Peter DiCola. 2011. *Creative License: The Law and Culture of Digital Sampling*. Durham: Duke University Press.

Menninghaus, Winfried, Valentin Wagner, Eugen Wassiliwizky, Ines Schindler, Julian Hanich, Thomas Jacobsen, and Stefan Koelsch. 2019. "What Are Aesthetic Emotions?" *Psychological Review* 126 (2), 171–195. https://doi.org/10.1037/rev0000135.

Metzer, David. 2003. *Quotation and Cultural Meaning in Twentieth-Century Music*. Cambridge: Cambridge University Press.

Meyer, Leonard B. 1956. *Emotion and Meaning in Music*. Chicago: University of Chicago Press.

Meyers, Brette G. 2009. "Filtering Systems of Fair Use? A Comparative Analysis of Proposed Regulations for User-Generated Content." *Cardozo Arts and Entertainment Law Journal* 26 (3), 935–956.

Middleton, Richard. 2000. "Work-in(g)-Practice: Configurations of the Popular Music Intertext." In *The Musical Work: Reality or Invention?*, edited by Michael Talbot, 59–87. Liverpool: Liverpool University Press.

———. 2006. *Voicing the Popular: On the Subjects of Popular Music*. New York: Routledge.

Miller, Kiri. 2012. *Playing Along: Digital Games, YouTube, and Virtual Performance*. Oxford: Oxford University Press. https://doi.org/10.1093/acprof:oso/9780199753451.001.0001.

Mitchum, Rob. 2002. "2 Many DJs: As Heard on Radio Soulwax, Pt. 2; Album Review." *Pitchfork*, August 29. https://pitchfork.com/reviews/albums/8228-as-heard-on-radio-soulwax-pt-2/.

———. 2005. "Be Your Own Harry Smith." *Pitchfork*, February 28. https://pitchfork.com/features/article/5975-be-your-own-harry-smith/.

Moore, Allan F. 2002. "Authenticity as Authentication." *Popular Music* 21 (2), 209–223. https://doi.org/10.1017/S0261143002002131.

———. 2016. *Song Means: Analysing and Interpreting Recorded Popular Song*. New York: Routledge.

Moore, Christopher, and Philip Purvis, eds. 2018. *Music and Camp*. Middletown, CT: Wesleyan University Press.

Moore, George E. 2005. *Principia Ethica*. New York: Barnes and Noble.

Morreall, John, ed. 1986. *The Philosophy of Laughter and Humor*. Albany: State University of New York Press.

———. 2008. "Applications of Humor: Health, the Workplace, and Education." In *The Primer of Humor Research*, edited by Victor Raskin, 449–478. Berlin: Mouton de Gruyter. https://doi.org/10.1515/9783110198492.449.

Morse, Phil. 2011. "DJ Earworm Interview: 'I Prefer to Call Myself a Data Jockey.'" *Digital DJ Tips*, February 18. https://www.digitaldjtips.com/2011/02/dj-earworm-interview-i-prefer-to-call-myself-a-data-jockey/.

Morson, Gary S. 1981. *The Boundaries of Genre: Dostoevsky's "Diary of a Writer" and the Traditions of Literary Utopia*. Austin: University of Texas Press.

Mukařovský, Jan. 1989 [1938]. "Poetic Reference." In *Semiotics of Art: Prague School Contributions*, edited by Ladislav Matejka and Irwin R. Titunik, 155–163. Cambridge, MA: MIT Press.

Nachmanovitch, Stephen. 1990. *Free Play: Improvisation in Life and Art*. New York: Tarcher.

Navas, Eduardo. 2012. *Remix Theory: The Aesthetics of Sampling*. New York: Springer.

———. 2018. "Remix." In *Keywords in Remix Studies*, edited by Eduardo Navas, Owen Gallagher, and xtine burrough, 246–258. New York: Routledge.

Navas, Eduardo, Owen Gallagher, and xtine burrough, eds. 2015. *The Routledge Companion to Remix Studies*. New York: Routledge.

———, eds. 2018. *Keywords in Remix Studies*. New York: Routledge.

———, eds. 2021. *The Routledge Handbook of Remix Studies and Digital Humanities*. New York: Routledge.

Navas, Eduardo, Owen Gallagher, and xtine burrough, in collaboration with contributors. 2018. "Appropriation." In *Keywords in Remix Studies*, edited by Eduardo Navas, Owen Gallagher, and xtine burrough, 14–22. New York: Routledge.

Negus, Keith. 1999. *Music Genres and Corporate Cultures*. London: Routledge.

Neiss, Rob. 1988. "Reconceptualizing Arousal: Psychobiological States in Motor Performance." *Psychological Bulletin* 103 (3), 345–366. https://doi.org/10.1037/0033-2909.103.3.345.

Netanel, Neil W. 2008. *Copyright's Paradox: Property in Expression/Freedom of Expression*. Oxford: Oxford University Press.

———. 2011. "Making Sense of Fair Use." *Lewis and Clark Law Review* 15 (3), 715–771.

Ngai, Sianne. 2017. "Theory of the Gimmick." *Critical Inquiry* 43 (2), 466–505. https://doi.org/10.1086/689672.

———. 2020. *Theory of the Gimmick: Aesthetic Judgment and Capitalist Form*. Cambridge, MA: Belknap Press of Harvard University Press.

Nieborg, David B., and Thomas Poell. 2018. "The Platformization of Cultural Production: Theorizing the Contingent Cultural Commodity." *New Media and Society* 20 (11), 4275–4292. https://doi.org/10.1177/1461444818769694.

Novović, Miloš. 2019. "Fighting European Copyright Tourism: Lessons from Defamation Laws." *European Review of Private Law* 27 (5), 949–971.

Nunziato, Dawn C. 2014. "The Beginning of the End of Internet Freedom." *Georgetown Journal of International Law* 45 (2), 383–410.

O'Brien, Damien, and Brian Fitzgerald. 2006. "Mashups, Remixes and Copyright Law." *Internet Law Bulletin* 9 (2), 17–19.

O'Dwyer, Rachel. 2015. "A Capital Remix." In *The Routledge Companion to Remix Studies*, edited by Eduardo Navas, Owen Gallagher, and xtine burrough, 323–332. New York: Routledge.

Oring, Elliott. 1989. "Between Jokes and Tales: On the Nature of Punch Lines." *Humor: International Journal of Humor Research* 2 (4), 349–364. https://doi.org/10.1515/humr.1989.2.4.349.

———. 2003. *Engaging Humor*. Urbana: University of Illinois Press.

———. 2008. "Humor in Anthropology and Folklore." In *The Primer of Humor Research*, edited by Victor Raskin, 183–210. Berlin: Mouton de Gruyter. https://doi.org/10.1515/9783110198492.183.

Orlando Weekly. 2002. "Review: Boom Selection_Issue 01." *Orlando Weekly*, September 19. https://www.orlandoweekly.com/Blogs/archives/2002/09/19/review-boom-selection_issue-01-2314908.

Oswald, John. 2006. "Bettered by the Borrower: The Ethics of Musical Depth." In *Audio Culture: Readings in Modern Music*, edited by Christoph Cox and Daniel Warner, 131–137. New York: Continuum.

Patry, William F. 2009. *Moral Panics and the Copyright Wars*. Oxford: Oxford University Press.

Peirce, Charles S. 1960. *Collected Papers of Charles Sanders Peirce. Vol. 2: Elements of Logic*. Cambridge, MA: Belknap Press of Harvard University Press.

Peverini, Paolo. 2015. "Remix Practices and Activism: A Semiotic Analysis of Creative Dissent." In *The Routledge Companion to Remix Studies*, edited by Eduardo Navas, Owen Gallagher, and xtine burrough, 333–345. New York: Routledge.

Phillips, Dom. 2002. "Smells Like Teen Booty." *Guardian*, February 27. http://www.theguardian.com/culture/2002/feb/27/artsfeatures.

Plagenhoef, Scott. 2003. "Boom Selection_Issue 01; Album Review." *Stylus: The Needle and the Damage Done*, January 9. http://stylusmagazine.com/review_ID_1111.html.

Rambarran, Shara. 2013. "99 Problems" But Danger Mouse Ain't One: The Creative and Legal Difficulties of Brian Burton, 'Author' of The Grey Album." *Popular Musicology Online*, no. 3.

Raskin, Victor. 1985. *Semantic Mechanisms of Humor*. Dordrecht: Reidel.

———, ed. 2008. *The Primer of Humor Research*. Berlin: Mouton de Gruyter.

Ratcliffe, Robert. 2014. "A Proposed Typology of Sampled Material Within Electronic Dance Music." *Dancecult: Journal of Electronic Dance Music Culture* 6 (1), 97–122.

Reese, Anthony J. 2015. "How Much Is Too Much?: Campbell and the Third Fair Use Factor." *Washington Law Review* 90 (1), 755–813.

Renzo, Adrian. 2021. "Exploring Remix Process: The Case of the Megamix." In *The Routledge Handbook of Remix Studies and Digital Humanities*, edited by Eduardo Navas, Owen Gallagher, and xtine burrough, 500–512. New York: Routledge.

Reynolds, Simon. 2011. *Retromania: Pop Culture's Addiction to Its Own Past*. London: Faber and Faber.

Ricoeur, Paul. 1991. "Appropriation." In *A Ricoeur Reader: Reflection and Imagination*, edited by Mario J. Valdés, 86–98. London: Harvester Wheatsheaf.

Rimmer, Matthew. 2005. "The Grey Album: Copyright Law and Digital Sampling." *Media International Australia Incorporating Culture and Policy* 114 (1), 40–53.

Ritzer, George, and Nathan Jurgenson. 2010. "Production, Consumption, Prosumption: The Nature of Capitalism in the Age of the Digital 'Prosumer.'" *Journal of Consumer Culture* 10 (1), 13–36. https://doi.org/10.1177/1469540509354673.

Robson, Grant J. 2021. "MTV: Memoirs of a Minor MTV DJ." April 11. https://grantjrobson.com/mtv-memoirs-of-a-minor-mtv-dj/.

Rosa, Fernada R., Maggie Clifford, and Aram Sinnreich. 2021. "The More Things Change: Who Gets Left Behind as Remix Goes Mainstream?" In *The Routledge Handbook of Remix Studies and Digital Humanities*, edited by Eduardo Navas, Owen Gallagher, and xtine burrough, 36–52. New York: Routledge.

Rosati, Eleonora. 2015. "Just a Laughing Matter? Why the Decision in Deckmyn Is Broader Than Parody." *Common Market Law Review* 52 (2), 511–529.

———. 2020. "Round-Up of CJEU Copyright Decisions in 2019." *Journal of Intellectual Property Law and Practice* 15 (4), 264–275. https://doi.org/10.1093/jiplp/jpaa020.

Rose, Margaret A. 1993. *Parody: Ancient, Modern, and Post-Modern*. Cambridge: Cambridge University Press.

Roseman, Jordan. 2007. *Audio Mashup Construction Kit*. Hoboken, NJ: Wiley.

Rossman, Gabriel. 2012. *Climbing the Charts: What Radio Airplay Tells Us About the Diffusion of Innovation*. Princeton: Princeton University Press.

Rothbart, Mary K. 1976. "Incongruity, Problem-Solving and Laughter." In *Humor and Laughter: Theory, Research, and Applications*, edited by Anthony J. Chapman and Hugh C. Foot, 37–54. Piscataway, NJ: Transaction Publishers.

Rothbart, Mary K., and Diana Pien. 1977. "Measuring Effects of Incongruity and Resolution in Children's Humour." In *It's a Funny Thing, Humour*, edited by Anthony J. Chapman and Hugh C. Foot, 211–213. Oxford: Pergamon Press. https://doi.org/10.1016/B978-0-08-021376-7.50042-5.

Ruch, Willibald. 2008. "Psychology of Humor." In *The Primer of Humor Research*, edited by Victor Raskin, 17–100. Berlin/New York: Mouton de Gruyter. https://doi.org/10.5167/uzh-6447.

Sag, Matthew. 2012. "Predicting Fair Use." *Ohio State Law Journal* 73 (1), 47–92. https://doi.org/10.2139/ssrn.1769130.

Samuelson, Pamela. 2009. "Unbundling Fair Uses." *Fordham Law Review* 77 (5), 2537–2621.

Sanders, Julie. 2015. *Adaptation and Appropriation*, 2nd ed. New York: Routledge.

Sanjek, David. 1992. "'Don't Have to DJ No More': Sampling and the 'Autonomous' Creator." *Cardozo Arts and Entertainment Law Journal* 10 (2), 607–624.

———. 1994. "'Don't Have to DJ No More': Sampling and the 'Autonomous' Creator." In *The Construction of Authorship: Textual Appropriation in Law and Literature*, edited by Martha Woodmansee and Peter Jaszi, 343–361. Durham: Duke University Press.

Sanneh, Kelefa. 2004. "The Rap against Rockism." *New York Times*, October 31. https://www.nytimes.com/2004/10/31/arts/music/the-rap-against-rockism.html.

Saunders, David. 1992. *Authorship and Copyright*. New York: Routledge.

Scherer, Klaus R. 2001. "Appraisal Considered as a Process of Multilevel Sequential Checking." In *Appraisal Processes in Emotion: Theory, Methods, Research*, edited by Klaus R. Scherer, A. Schorr, and T. Johnstone, 92–120. Oxford: Oxford University Press.

Schloss, Joseph G. 2004. *Making Beats: The Art of Sample-Based Hip-Hop*. Middletown, CT: Wesleyan University Press.

Schopenhauer, Arthur. 1957. *On Human Nature: Essays, Partly Posthumous, in Ethics and Politics*. Translated by Thomas B. Saunders. Crows Nest, Australia: Allen and Unwin.

Schuster, Mike, David Mitchell, and Kenneth Brown. 2019. "Sampling Increases Music Sales: An Empirical Copyright Study." *American Business Law Journal* 56 (1), 177–229. https://doi.org/10.1111/ablj.12137.

Seng, Daniel. 2014. "The State of the Discordant Union: An Empirical Analysis of DMCA Takedown Notices." *Virginia Journal of Law and Technology* 18 (369), 1–59. https://doi.org/10.2139/ssrn.2411915.

Serazio, Michael. 2008. "The Apolitical Irony of Generation Mash-Up: A Cultural Case Study in Popular Music." *Popular Music and Society* 31 (1), 79–94. https://doi.org/10.1080/03007760701214815.

Sewell, Amanda. 2013. "A Typology of Sampling in Hip-Hop." PhD diss., Indiana University. https://hcommons.org/deposits/item/hc:18431.

Sherwin, Adam. 2004. "Just Steal My Greatest Hits, Says Bowie." *Times*, April 26. https://www.thetimes.co.uk/article/just-steal-my-greatest-hits-says-bowie-q0p3x7r38fh.

Shifman, Limor. 2014. *Memes in Digital Culture*. Cambridge, MA: MIT Press.

Shiga, John. 2007. "Copy-and-Persist: The Logic of Mash-Up Culture." *Critical Studies in Media Communication* 24 (2), 93–114. https://doi.org/10.1080/07393180701262685.

Shklovsky, Viktor. 1989. "Art as Technique." In *The Critical Tradition: Classic Texts and Contemporary Trends*, edited by David H. Richter, 774–784. New York: St. Martin's Press.

Silver, Daniel, Monica Lee, and C. Clayton Childress. 2016. "Genre Complexes in Popular Music." *PLoS One* 11 (5), 1–23. https://doi.org/10.1371/journal.pone.0155471.

Silvia, Paul J. 2006. *Exploring the Psychology of Interest*. Oxford: Oxford University Press.

Simpson-Jones, Katie. 2010. "Unlawful Infringement or Just Creative Expression: Why DJ Girl Talk May Inspire Congress to Recast, Transform, or Adapt Copyright." *John Marshall Law Review* 43 (4), 1067–1096.

Sinnreich, Aram. 2010. *Mashed Up: Music, Technology, and the Rise of Configurable Culture*. Amherst: University of Massachusetts Press.

———. 2013. *The Piracy Crusade: How the Music Industry's War on Sharing Destroys Markets and Erodes Civil Liberties*. Amherst: University of Massachusetts Press.

Smith-Laing, Tim. 2018. *An Analysis of Jacques Derrida's Structure, Sign, and Play in the Discourse of the Human Sciences*. London: Macat Library.

Sonvilla-Weiss, Stefan. 2010. "Introduction: Mashups, Remix Practices and the Recombination of Existing Digital Content." In *Mashup Cultures*, edited by Stefan Sonvilla-Weiss, 8–23. Vienna: Springer-Verlag.

Soulwax. n.d. *Soulwax*. Accessed January 7, 2020 https://www.kevinenjoyce.com/soulwax/detail.php?idrls=39Rls2c5d41106&hideparent=true.

SoundCloud. n.d.-a. "How Do Copyright Strikes Work?" Accessed January 7, 2020. https://help.soundcloud.com/hc/en-us/articles/360005032554-How-do-copyright-strikes-work-.

———. n.d.-b. "Copyright Methods and Notifications." Accessed January 7, 2020. https://help.soundcloud.com/hc/en-us/articles/115003452067-Copyright-methods-and-notifications.

———. 2016. "Announcing Our Partnership with Universal Music Group." January 13. https://blog.soundcloud.com/2016/01/13/announcing-our-partnership-with-universal-music-group/.

Spicer, Mark. 2009. "Strategic Intertextuality in Three of John Lennon's Late Beatles Songs." *Gamut: Online Journal of the Music Theory Society of the Mid-Atlantic* 2 (1).

Stenros, Jaakko. 2015. "Playfulness, Play, and Games: A Constructionist Ludology Approach." PhD diss., Tampere University. https://trepo.tuni.fi/bitstream/handle/10024/96986/978-951-44-9788-9.pdf?sequence=1&isAllowed=y.

Strauss, Neil. 2002a. "Spreading by the Web, Pop's Bootleg Remix." *New York Times*, May 9. https://www.nytimes.com/2002/05/09/business/spreading-by-the-web-pop-s-bootleg-remix.html.

———. 2002b. "Music: The Year in Review—the Critics/the 10 Best Albums; Somber Anthems, Loose-Limbed Funk." *New York Times*, December 29. https://www.nytimes.com/2002/12/29/arts/music-year-review-critics-10-best-albums-somber-anthems-loose-limbed-funk-536890.html.

Stravinsky, Igor. 2003 [1947]. *Poetics of Music: In the Form of Six Lessons.* Cambridge, MA: Harvard University Press.

Suits, Bernard. 1967. "What Is a Game?" *Philosophy of Science* 34 (2), 148–156. https://doi.org/10.1086/288138.

———. 2005 [1978]. *The Grasshopper: Games, Life and Utopia.* Peterborough, ON: Broadview Press.

Suls, Jerry M. 1972. "A Two-Stage Model for the Appreciation of Jokes and Cartoons: An Information-Processing Analysis." In *The Psychology of Humor: Theoretical Perspectives and Empirical Issues*, edited by Jeffrey H. Goldstein and Paul E. McGhee, 81–100. New York: Academic Press. https://doi.org/10.1016/B978-0-12-288950-9.50010-9.

Sutton-Smith, Brian. 1997. *The Ambiguity of Play.* Cambridge, MA: Harvard University Press.

———. 2001. "Emotional Breaches in Play and Narrative." In *Children in Play, Story, and School*, edited by Artin Göncü and Elisa L. Klein, 161–176. New York/London: The Guilford Press.

Tagg, Philip. 1987. "Musicology and the Semiotics of Popular Music." *Semiotica* 66 (1/3), 279–298.

Tanner, Grafton. 2016. *Babbling Corpse: Vaporwave and the Commodification of Ghosts.* Ridgefield: Zer0 Books.

Taylor, Charles. "2003. A Love Song to Bastard Pop." *Salon*, August 10. https://www.salon.com/2003/08/09/mashups_taylor/.

Toffler, Alvin. 1980. *The Third Wave.* New York: Bantam Books.

Tong, Pete. 1999. "Pete Tong's Essential July." *Mixmag*, July.

Tough, David. 2010. "The Mashup Mindset: Will Pop Eat Itself?" In *Play It Again: Cover Songs in Popular Music*, edited by George Plasketes, 205–212. London: Ashgate.

Toynbee, Jason. 2001. "Creating Problems: Social Authorship, Copyright and the Production of Culture." *Pavis Papers in Social and Cultural Research* 3, 1–31.

———. 2012. "Music, Culture, and Creativity." In *The Cultural Study of Music*, edited by Martin Clayton, Trevor Herbert, and Richard Middleton, 102–112. New York: Routledge.

Trier, Lars von, and Thomas Vinterberg. 1995a. *Dogme 95 Manifesto.* http://www.dogme95.dk/dogma-95/.

———. 1995b. *Vows of Chastity.* http://www.dogme95.dk/the-vow-of-chastity/.

Turner, Katherine L. 2016. *This Is the Sound of Irony: Music, Politics and Popular Culture.* New York: Routledge.

Tushnet, Rebecca. 2004. "Copy This Essay: How Fair Use Doctrine Harms Free Speech and How Copying Serves It." *Yale Law Journal* 114 (3), 535–590. https://doi.org/10.2307/4135692.

———. 2008. "User-Generated Discontent: Transformation in Practice." *Columbia Journal of Law and the Arts* 31 (June), 101–120.

———. 2010. "Hybrid Vigor: Mashups, Cyborgs and Other Necessary Monsters." *I/S: A Journal for Law and Policy* 6 (1), 1–12.

———. 2014. "All of This Has Happened Before and All of This Will Happen Again: Innovation in Copyright Licensing." *Berkeley Technology Law Journal* 29, 1447–1488.

———. 2017. "Architecture and Morality: Transformative Works, Transforming Fans." In *Creativity without Law: Challenging the Assumptions of Intellectual Property*, edited by Kate Darling and Aaron Perzanowski, 171–200. New York: New York University Press.

———. 2019. "Content Moderation in an Age of Extremes." *Journal of Law, Technology and the Internet* 10 (1), 1–19.

Tynyanov, Yury N. 1975 [1921]. "Dostoevsky and Gogol." In *Twentieth-Century Russian Literary Criticism*, edited by Victor Erlich, 102–116. New Haven: Yale University Press.

Urban, Jennifer M., Joe Karaganis, and Brianna L. Schofield. 2016. *Notice and Takedown in Everyday Practice*. UC Berkeley Public Law Research Paper 2755628. http://www.ssrn.com/abstract=2755628.

Urban, Jennifer, and Laura Quilter. 2006. "Efficient Process or Chilling Effects: Takedown Notices under Section 512 of the Digital Millennium Copyright Act." *Santa Clara High Technology Law Journal* 22 (4), 621–693.

U.S. Copyright Office. 2020. "Section 512 of Title 17: A Report of the Register of Copyrights." https://www.copyright.gov/policy/section512/section-512-full-report.pdf.

Vaidhyanathan, Siva. 2003. *Copyrights and Copywrongs: The Rise of Intellectual Property and How It Threatens Creativity*. New York: New York University Press.

Veatch, Thomas C. 1998. "A Theory of Humor." *Humor: International Journal of Humor Research* 11 (2), 161–215. https://doi.org/10.1515/humr.1998.11.2.161.

Vergo, Peter. 1989. "The Reticent Object." In *The New Museology*, edited by Peter Vergo, 41–59. London: Reaktion Books.

Vorobyev, Yakov, and Eric Coomes. 2012. *Beyond Beatmatching: Take Your DJ Career to the Next Level*. Mixed In Key. https://mixedinkey.com/book.

Walser, Robert. 1995. "'Out of Notes': Signification, Interpretation, and the Problem of Miles Davis." In *Jazz among the Discourses*, edited by Krin Gabbard, 165–188. Durham: Duke University Press. https://doi.org/10.2307/j.ctv1220nbh.

———. 2014. *Running with the Devil: Power, Gender, and Madness in Heavy Metal Music*. Middletown, CT: Wesleyan University Press.

Wang, Oliver. 2013. "20 Years Ago Biz Markie Got the Last Laugh." *NPR*, May 6. https://www.npr.org/sections/therecord/2013/05/01/180375856/20-years-ago-biz-markie-got-the-last-laugh.

Warner Music. 2014. "Warner Music Group and SoundCloud Announce Groundbreaking Partnership." November 4. https://www.wmg.com/news/warner-music-group-and-soundcloud-announce-groundbreaking-partnership-20036.

Weese, Joshua L., Jessica C. Murphy, and Kim B. Knight. 2017. "Parody Detection: An Annotation, Feature Construction, and Classification Approach to the Web of Parody." In *Data Analytics in Digital Humanities*, edited by Shalin Hai-Jew, 67–89. Cham: Springer. https://doi.org/10.1007/978-3-319-54499-1.

Weinstein, Deena. 2004. "Rock Critics Need Bad Music." In *Bad Music: The Music We Love to Hate*, edited by Christopher J. Washburne and Maiken Derno, 294–310. New York: Routledge.

Weisethaunet, Hans, and Ulf Lindberg. 2010. "Authenticity Revisited: The Rock Critic and the Changing Real." *Popular Music and Society* 33 (4), 465–485. https://doi.org/10.1080/03007761003694225.

Wiederhorn, Jon. 2020. "16 Years Ago: Linkin Park Team with Jay-Z on 'Collision Course.'" *Loudwire*, November 30. https://loudwire.com/linkin-park-jay-z-collision-course-album-anniversary/.

Williams, Justin A. 2014. "Theoretical Approaches to Quotation in Hip-Hop Recordings." *Contemporary Music Review* 33 (2), 188–209. https://doi.org/10.1080/07494467.2014.959276.

Winkie, Luke. 2018. "What Ever Happened to the Mashup Artist?" *The A.V. Club*, April 18. https://music.avclub.com/what-ever-happened-to-the-mashup-artist-1825338050.

WIPO. n.d.-a. "Inside WIPO." Accessed January 7, 2020. https://www.wipo.int/about-wipo/en/.

———. n.d.-b. "WIPO Internet Treaties." Accessed January 7, 2020. https://www.wipo.int/about-wipo/en/.

Woodmansee, Martha. 1994. *The Author, Art, and the Market: Rereading the History of Aesthetics*. New York: Columbia University Press.

Woodmansee, Martha, and Peter Jaszi. 1994. "Introduction." In *The Construction of Authorship: Textual Appropriation in Law and Literature*, edited by Martha Woodmansee and Peter Jaszi, 1–13. Durham: Duke University Press.

Wu, Tim. 2008. "Tolerated Use." *Columbia Journal of Law and the Arts* 31 (4), 617–636.

———. 2018. *The Curse of Bigness: Antitrust in the New Gilded Age*. New York: Columbia Global Reports.

Yunek, Jeffrey S., Benjamin K. Wadsworth, and Simon Needle. 2020. "Perceiving the Mosaic: Form in the Mashups of DJ Earworm." *Music Theory Spectrum* 43 (1), 19–42. https://doi.org/10.1093/mts/mtaa016.

Zijderveld, Anton C. 1982. *Reality in a Looking-Glass: Rationality through an Analysis of Traditional Folly*. Abingdon: Routledge and Kegan Paul.

Zimmerman, Diane. 2014. "Copyright and Social Media: A Tale of Legislative Abdication." *Pace Law Review* 35 (1), 260–285.

Žižek, Slavoj. 2006. "Philosophy, the 'Unknown Knows,' and the Public Use of Reason." *Topoi* 25 (1–2), 137–142.

Index

A+B mashups, 5, 68, 73, 77, 155
A+D, 9–10
Aaliyah, 78
Acid, 12
Acknowledged appropriation, 39, 45–46, 54, 55, 81, 132, 155, 171, 221
Activision, 12
Adele, 133
Adorno, Theodor W., 104, 117, 212, 217
Adriana A (aka DJ Adrian), 9–10, 15, 56–57, 75–76, 80, 84–85, 137, 144, 171–172, 192–193, 195, 203–204
Aesthetic judgment, 211
Aesthetic principles of mashups, 53–80
Aesthetics, content moderation's impact on, 199–201
Aesthetic Theory (Adorno), 104
Aguilera, Christina, 4, 11, 12, 74–75, 147–148
AH, 94–95, 116, 118, 130–136
AHA, 94–95, 116, 118–130
Alan Copeland Singers, 49
Algorithmic content-identification technology. *See also* Content moderation; Takedowns
  automaticity of, 203
  increased use of, 182–184
  shortcomings of, 228–230
All Day (Girl Talk), 146
Allen, Graham, 96

"Alone Again" (Biz Markie), 167, 177
"Alone Again (Naturally)" (O'Sullivan), 167, 177
AmsterJam, 11
AnDyWuMusicland, 5, 71
Appropriation. *See also* Acknowledged appropriation
  arrangement of sources and, 34–36
  concept of, 29–31
  nature of, 31–33
  perspective and, 37–38
  variables relating to, 21
Apter, Michael, 101–102, 135
Araya, Tom, 112–113, 114, 116, 117
Aristotle, 107
As Heard on Radio Soulwax, Pt. 2 (Soulwax), 9
Assassination of Jesse James, 131
Associative sources, 35–36
Attardo, Salvatore, 107–108
Attribution, right of, 159–161. *See also* Crediting
Audio Mashup Construction Kit (Roseman), 69–70
Aufderheide, Patricia, 166–167, 172, 174, 187, 220
Authenticity, 213–214
Authorial agency, 98
Authorship, 222–223
Autotelic mind-set, 89, 216
Ayers, Michael D., 4, 50

". . . Baby One More Time" (Spears), 127
Bach, 48
Bad faith inquiry, 164
Bakhtin, Mikhail, 43, 95–96, 97, 100, 113, 114
Banging, 81
Barlow, John Perry, 174
Barthes, Roland, 97–98, 99, 104–105, 110, 224
"Basic" mashups, 5
"Bastard," 7
"Bastard pop," 7
Beatles, The, 17, 27, 49
Beattie, James, 107
Beauty, experience of, 94, 130–136
Beebe, Barton, 162, 163–166
Beethoven, 27, 48
Begault, Durand, 224
Bello, Bryan, 172
Benkler, Yochai, 220
Bennett, Andy, 30
Bently, Lionel, 222–223
Berg, 48
Berio, Luciano, 48
Berlioz, 48
Berry, John, 133
Best Bootlegs in the World Ever, The, 8–9
Beyoncé, 70
"Beyoncé—Sorry, Single Ladies (feat. Justin Bieber) [Remix]" (AnDyWuMUSICLAND), 71
Bicknell, Jeanette, 57
Bieber, Justin, 71, 78, 141
Billi, Mirella, 42
Binding, 81
Bisociation, 95, 104–106
Bisociative sources, 35–36, 46–50
Biz Markie, 167, 170, 177
Black, Matt, 148
Black Album, The (Jay-Z), 17
"Black Eyed Peas—My Humps (feat. Mozart), The" (Maranci), 75

Black Eyed Peas, 75
Black Lives Matter, 126, 127
Black Sabbath, 124
Blanch v. Koons, 164
Blending, 81
Blondie, 61–62, 79
Bloom, Harold, 33, 48
"Blue Monday" (New Order), 11
"Blurry" (Puddle of Mudd), 125–126
"Blurry in the USA" (DJ Cummerbund), 71, 125–130
Bogost, Ian, 86, 90, 92
Bomb Squad, 177
Boom Selection, 8
Boom Selection_Issue 01, aka *Never Mind the Bootlegs*, 8
Boon, Marcus, 30
Boone, Christine, 69
Bootie: Beyond Thunderdome, 85
Bootie: Gay Pride! 84
Bootie Goes Goth, 84
Bootie Loves Bowie—Mashup Tribute to David Bowie, 85
Bootie Loves Prince, 85
Bootie Loves Whitney: Mashup Tribute to Whitney Houston, 85
Bootie Mashes Michael Jackson, 85
Bootie Mashup, 171
Bootie website and clubs, 10, 20, 84–85, 195
"Bootlegs," 7
Bootsy Collins, 11
"Bootylicious" (Destiny's Child), 9
"Borrowing," 28, 29, 33
Borschke, Margie, 13
Bourdieu, Pierre, 211
Bourriaud, Nicolas, 215
Bowie, David, 11
Boyle, James, 220
Brackett, David, 120
Bradley, Catherine A., 47
Bridgeport Music, Inc. v. Dimension Films, 167, 223

Index

BringMeTheMashup, 80, 109, 145, 147, 149, 191, 192, 194
British Phonographic Industry, 172
Brown, Kenneth, 146, 159
"Bruno Mars vs. Caravan Palace(24K Digger)—Mashup" (Happy Cat Disco), 72, 131
Buchanan, Bill, 27
Buffalo Springfield, 123
Bürger, Peter, 104
Burkholder, Peter, 27, 28, 29
Burlesque, 40
Burns, Lori, 29, 115
Burrough, xtine, 30
Bush, George W., 123
Buyout fees, 140–141
"By the Time I Get to Arizona" (Evolution Control Committee), 49–50

Cage, John, 75
Caillois, Roger, 82, 88
Calderone, Tom, 11
Call-and-response technique, 70
"Call Me Maybe," 87
"Camelot Wheel," 63
Campbell v. Acuff-Rose Music, Inc., 163–164, 165, 166
Cantata Carmina Burana (Orff), 85
"Can't Get You Out of My Head" (Minogue), 11
Capitol Records, 17, 173
"Careless Rebel (George Michael + Billy Idol Mashup)" (Wax Audio), 55–56
"Careless Whisper" (Michael), 55–56
Carlin, Richard, 216
Castle Rock Entertainment, Inc. v. Carol Publishing Group, Inc., 163
"Catalyst, The" (Linkin Park), 85
"Catalyst Carmina Burana (Linkin Park vs. Carl Orff)" (DJs From Mars), 85
Cave, Nick, 131
Certeau Michel de, 90–91

CFLO, 53, 70, 76, 78, 145, 148, 194, 195, 196, 202–203, 207
Chambers, Robert, 81
"Chemical Warfare" (Slayer), 111–114, 116–117
Chic, 56
Childish Gambino, 125
"Children of the Grave" (Black Sabbath), 124
"Children of the Revolution" (T-Rex), 124
Children's Corner (Debussy), 47
Childress, C. Clayton, 121–122
Chuck D, 49
Cicero, 107
Cicierega, Neil, 109
"Closer" (Ne-Yo), 124
Code of Best Practice in Fair Use for Online Video, 167
Colatron, 14, 15, 58, 84, 134, 195
Collage/montage works, 34–36, 215
Collision Course (Jay-Z/Linkin Park), 11
Composite creativity, 216
Concept mashup, 83–84
Constraints, mastering and overcoming, 82–88
Consumption, participation and, 90–91
Content-identification technology, 182–184
Content ID system, 182–183, 186, 189
Content moderation. *See also* Algorithmic content-identification technology; Takedowns
  aesthetics and, 199–201
  copyright and, 1, 2
  copyright exceptions and, 184–187
  development of, 175–176
  distribution and, 196–198
  evolution of, 17–18
  frustrations caused by, 193–195
  licensing and, 188–190
  parody and, 25–26
  pros and cons of, 180–190
  workaround strategies for, 199–200

Cook, Nicholas, 105
Coombe, Rosemary J., 230
Copeland, Alan, 27, 49
Copyright. *See also* Fair use/fair use doctrine
   authorship and, 222–223
   content moderation measures and, 1, 2
   ethics and, 142–150
   exceptions to, 150–170, 184–187, 207, 220–221, 227–228, 229–230
   historical changes in enforcement of, 177–180
   jurisdiction and, 151–152
   lack of full understanding of, 142–143
   locating holders of, 138–139
   market control and, 219
   monetizing content and, 191–192
   myths about, 205
   notification requirements regarding, 18
   purposes of, 141, 226
   takedowns and, 16
   types of, 138
Corporations, positional power of, 25
Covach, John, 113
Craig, David, 184
Creation, definition of, 215
Creative Commons, 174, 219–220
Creativity, composite, 216
Credit, conscious effort to give, 4
Crediting, 54, 55–59, 73, 83, 147–150, 169
Cross-posting, 198
Cruger, Roberta, 7, 9, 74
Crumplbangers, 20, 76, 84
Csikszentmihalyi, Mihaly, 87–88, 91
Cultural appropriation, 31
Cultural hegemony, theory of, 215
Cultural participation, democratic, 216–218
Cunningham, Stuart, 184

"Cut-up" technique, 70
Cyrus, Miley, 79–80, 125–126, 127

Dada, 104
Dancers/dancing, 91–92
Danger Mouse (aka Brian Burton), 13, 17, 173, 219
Danielsen, Anne, 128
"Danube Incident, The" (Schifrin), 62
DAWs (digital audio workstations), 12
Debussy, Claude, 47–48
DeeM, 79
Deep End, 80, 88
Defamiliarization, 92, 132–133, 216
De La Soul, 64, 141, 178
Deleuze, Gilles, 99
De Man, Paul, 99
Demers, Joanna, 220
De minimis, 168, 205
Democratic cultural participation, 216–218
Dentith, Simon, 41, 43
Derrida, Jacques, 97, 99, 120, 122
Destiny's Child, 9
Dialogism, 95–96
Dicksoak, 80, 109, 131
DiCola, Peter, 138–139, 140, 142, 146, 148, 168, 175–176, 204–205
Digital Millennium Copyright Act (US; 1998), 17–18, 186
Digital Single Market (DSM) Directive, 189, 226–228
Di Maio, Sara, 108
Dimension Films, 168
Disney Mashed, 85
Disparate genres, blending of, 74–77
Distanciation, 30
Distribution
   alternative outlets for, 197–198
   content moderation's impact on, 196–198
"Disturbia" (Rihanna), 124

DJ Cummerbund, 63, 71, 76, 118, 125, 148–149, 202
DJ Earworm, 5, 69, 93, 109, 124–125, 131, 136, 143, 198, 199
DJ Faroff, 65, 76, 83, 137, 140, 143, 145–146, 175, 192, 196, 199, 201
DJ Hero, 12
DJ Paul V., 9, 57, 74, 84, 143–144
DJ Poupli, 87, 93, 123, 133–134, 141, 143, 149, 194
DJ Prince, 63, 141, 196
DJ Schmolli, 63–64, 67, 84, 123–124, 132–133, 144, 191, 194–195, 198, 201
DJs From Mars, 85
DJ Surda, 74, 90, 192, 197
DMCA (US Digital Millennium Copyright Act), 180–182
"Dogme 95 Manifesto" (Trier and Vinterberg), 86
Döhl, Frédéric, 152, 153–154
Double-codedness, 16, 95, 100, 105–106, 111, 132, 134
Double-voiced, 100
Doubling, 99–104
Downhill Battle, 17, 173, 219
Drake, 168
DSM Directive, 152
Duality, sensation of, 35
Dub music, 6, 27, 32, 37, 50
Duchamp, Marcel, 215
Duffy, Kevin Thomas, 167, 171, 177, 223
Dyer, Richard, 37, 39–40, 41, 42

E-Commerce Directive (ECD; EU; 2000), 17–18, 181, 182
EDM remixes, 36
Eechoud, Mireille van, 223
Eisenstein, Sergej, 35, 105, 128
Ellis, Warren, 131
Eminem, 75

"Eminem—Lose Yourself But It's 4'33" by John Cage" (Maranci), 75
Empire of the Sun, 124
Endorsements, 148–149
Entertainment Weekly, 8, 9, 10
Eriksen, Asbjørn, 113
Escapism, 88, 92
Esotericism, avoidance of, 56
"E.T." (Perry), 75
Ethical guidelines of mashups, 23–24
Ethics of sampling in mashups, 142–150
EU law, 152–161
"Evaluatively open," 39–40, 41
"Evaluatively predetermined," 39–40
Evolution Control Committee, 49–50
Expectancy violations, 134–135, 157

Facebook, 14, 20, 178, 192, 193
Fair use/fair use doctrine, 142–143, 150, 161–168, 174, 185–187, 188, 219. *See also* Copyright
False attribution, right against, 159–161
Familiarity with sources, importance of, 56–58
Federation against Copyright Theft, 172
"Feel Good Inc." (Gorillaz feat. De La Soul), 64–65
"Feel Good Inc.—Gorillaz feat. De La Soul vs. Flo Rida feat. T-Pain (mashup)" (oneboredjeu), 64–65, 131
Feist Publications, Inc. v. Rural Telephone Service Co., 163
"Fighter" (Aguilera), 12
File sharing, illegal, 171, 172–173, 178
"Firework" (Perry), 57
Flair, Ric, 125
Fleetwood *Mashed*, 84
Fleischer Studio, 72
Flo Rida, 64–65
Flow, theory of, 87
Fluxus, 104

"Flying Saucer, The" (Buchanan and Goodman), 27
Folk culture/music, 216–217
Followers, loss of, 194–195
Foo Fighters, 148–149
Forensic musicologists, 224
Formula criticism/formulaic critique, 212–213
"For What It's Worth (Stop, Hey, What's That Sound)" (Buffalo Springfield), 123
"For What It's Worth Impeach the President (Buffalo Springfield, Honey Drippers)" (DJ Prince), 123
Foucault, Michel, 99
"4'33"" (Cage), 75
Free culture movement, 219–220
Freedom of expression, 2, 16, 156, 158, 160, 169, 190, 220, 228–230
"Free Fallin'" (Petty), 70
Freelance Hellraiser, 4–5, 9, 11, 12, 74–75, 147–148
Free use, 174, 219
Friedman, Thomas, 217
Frith, Simon, 91–92, 212
Funkadelic, 167–168

Gallagher, Owen, 6, 30, 79, 123, 173, 190
Garbage, 11
Gates, Henry Louis, Jr., 99, 101–102, 103
Genderplay, 116
General theory of verbal humor (GTVH), 107–108
Genette, Gérard, 40, 41, 42, 43, 136
"Genie in a Bottle" (Aguilera), 4, 74–75
Genre, subversion of, 118–122
Genre clash, 74–77
Genres, music, 114–115, 117–118
Gestalt psychology, 94
"Get Off Your Ass and Jam" (Funkadelic), 167–168

Gillespie, Tarleton, 176, 207
"Gimme More" (Spears), 124
Girl Talk, 5, 13, 146
Givan, Benjamin, 48
"God Bless America" (Smith), 125
"God Save the King [or Queen]," 48
"God Save the Queen" (Sex Pistols), 5, 74–75
Go Home Productions, 4–5, 74–75, 84
"Golliwog's Cakewalk" (Debussy), 47–48
Good Copy Bad Copy, 13
"Good King Wenceslas," 49
Goodman, Dickie 27
"Good Times" (Chic), 56
Goodwin, Andrew, 213
Google, 179, 189
Gorillaz, 64–65
Gould, Glenn, 48
Governing law, 151
Gramsci, Antonio, 215
Grande, Ariana, 200
Grand Upright Music, Ltd. v. Warner Bros. Records Inc., 167, 170, 177, 223
Grey Album, The (Danger Mouse), 17, 173, 219
"Greyhound," 87
Grey Tuesday, 17, 173
Grohl, Dave, 149
Grossberg, Lawrence, 213
Guardian, 11
Guitar Hero, 12, 91, 214
Gunderson, Philip A., 173
Gunkel, David, 6
GYBO (GetYourBootlegOn), 7–8, 9, 10, 13, 14–15, 60, 68, 84

HAHA, 94–95, 106–118
Halloween Bootie, 84
Hanneman, Jeff, 112
Happy Cat Disco, 59, 64, 66–67, 72, 131, 141, 143, 198
"Hard to Explain" (Strokes), 4, 74–75
Harkins, Paul, 49, 173

"Harmonic mixing," 63, 73
Harmony, 60–65
Harper & Row v. Nation Enterprises, 165
Harris, Calvin, 124
Harry, Debbie, 62
Hart, Lorenz, 49
Hauer, Josef Matthias, 86
Hawkins, Stan, 115, 116
Hearthis, 193, 195
"Heart of Glass" (Blondie), 61–62, 63
Hebdige, Dick, 15, 120, 121, 171, 214
Heise, Heather D., 224
Hempelmann, Christian F., 108
Hendrix, Jimi, 125
Herb Alpert's Tijuana Brass, 49–50
Hestholm, Marion, 48, 104–105
Hindemith, 48
Hip-hop music
  lawsuits, 141, 167–168
  sampling 3, 27, 29, 32–34, 36–37, 47, 50, 56–57, 64, 146
  sampling and copyright, 140, 176–178
"Hold It," 72
Holfelder, Chase, 125, 127
Homage, 39–46
Home Taping Is Killing Music campaign, 172
Homme, Josh, 133
Homo Ludens (Huizinga), 82
Honey Drippers, The, 123
Householder, Fred W., 41
Howard-Spink, Sam, 173
Hughes, Lucien, 72
Huhn, Mary, 11
Hui, Alan, 141, 152, 153–154, 188, 189
Huizinga, Johan, 82, 87, 88–89, 90, 91, 92
Humanities in the European Research Area (HERA), 223
Humor, 44–45, 76–77, 94, 106–111, 115–116, 117–118, 157–158, 224–225

Huron, David, 134–135
Hutcheon, Linda, 40, 41, 42–43, 44, 99, 100–101
"Hymnen" (Stockhausen), 48, 49

Iddol, Simon, 11, 66, 84, 147
Idol, Billy, 55–56
"If I Were a Boy" (Beyoncé), 70
"Impeach the President" (The Honey Drippers), 123
InanimateMashup, 75
Incongruity/incongruity theory, 44, 47–48, 107–109, 110, 111–118, 136, 224
InfoSoc Directive, 150, 152–155
Ingarden, Roman, 99
Instagram, 192
Integrity right, 159–161
Intellectual enlightenment, 94
Intellectual Property Office of Singapore, 172
International Federation of the Phonographic Industry, 172
Intertextuality, 23, 29, 31, 95–99, 215
Intrinsic motivation, 89–90, 216–217
"Iron Chic—Rime of the Ancient Mariner" (Iron Maiden), 56
Ironic critical distance, 37–38, 41–45, 46, 111
Ironic distancing, 54, 74–78, 83, 224
Iron Maiden, 56
Isosine, 70–71, 77, 135, 191–192, 196, 199, 200, 202, 203
iTunes, 8, 171, 206
Ives, Charles, 28

Jacobson, Maya, 80, 90, 123, 199
Jacques, Sabine, 41, 156, 158–161, 165, 169, 205, 221
Jameson, Fredric, 42
Jaszi, Peter, 166–167, 174, 220, 222
Jay-Z, 11, 17, 70, 125, 127
Jazz, 101

Jenkins, Henry, 90, 129, 216–217
"Jesus Walks" (West), 70
Johan Deckmyn and Vrijheidsfonds VZW v. Helena Vanersteen and Others, 155, 164
Jones, Ellis, 12, 13, 173
Jurisdiction, 151–152

Kamps, Garrett, 210, 212
Kap Slap, 56, 83–84, 87, 91, 192, 194, 195, 197, 216
Katrina and the Waves, 111–114, 116–117
Keen, Andrew, 217, 221
Key, 60–65, 73
Kierkegaard, Søren, 99, 107
King, Kerry, 112
Koch, Ludovica, 42
Koestler, Arthur, 23, 35, 94, 105–106, 118, 130
Koons, Jeff, 164
Kraftwerk, 154
Kristeva, Julia, 95, 96–97, 98–99, 114, 224
Kuhn, Virginia, 122–123

Labor, value of, 211–215
Labor theory of property, 211–212
Lacasse, Serge, 29, 30
Lai, Amy, 159, 161
LaPolt, Dina, 168
LazyTown, 75
Lee, Monica, 121–122
Legal reasoning and artistic practice, 25
Lelièvre, F. J., 41, 43
Leskanich, Katrina, 112–114, 116–117
Lessig, Lawrence, 6, 13, 174, 209, 218, 219–220
Leval, Pierre N., 162–163
Lévi-Strauss, Claude, 99
Liability issues, 180–181
Linking options, 198
Linkin Park, 11, 85

Lipogram, 86
"Little Girl Blue" (Simone), 49
Locke, John, 211–212
Lombardo, Dave, 112
"Lose Yourself" (Eminem), 75
"Love Lockdown" (West), 62
"Love Shine a Light" (Katrina and the Waves), 112
"Low" (Flo Rida feat. T-Pain), 64–65
"Lucifer" (Jay-Z), 70
Lyrics, 68–73

Machine-learning technology, 25–26, 228–229
Madeira, Angelica, 210
Mad Max beyond Thunderdome, 85
Madonna, 5, 74–75, 168
"Magic circle," 87
Mahler, Gustav, 48
"Make-believe" synergy, 102
Maranci, William, 75
Market substitution, 166
Martelly, Elizabeth de, 47–48
"MASHED: Mashup Music, Copyright, and Platform Regulation," 19
"Mashional Anthem—50 Songs of America" (DJ Earworm), 125
"Mashup 2016 'We Were Young' [Best 90 Songs of 2016]" (AnDyWuMusicland), 5
Mashup concerts, 11
Mashuptown.com, 14
Matching, 54, 60–73, 83
McCartney, Paul, 11, 12
McClintock, Bill, 111–114, 116–117, 129
McGranahan, Liam, 9, 19, 69, 70, 210
McLeod, Kembrew, 117, 119, 138–139, 140, 142, 146, 147–148, 168, 175–176, 204–205
McSlzy (aka Mc Sleazy), 7–8, 12, 14, 68, 80, 84
Medleys, 4, 28, 34, 37

Megamixes, 5, 68–69, 77, 155–156
Memes, 20, 37, 129, 161
Menninghaus, Winfried, 135
"Metall für Metall" (Kraftwerk), 154
Methodology, 19–20
Meyer, Leonard, 134–135
Michael, George, 55–56
"Miley/O'Connor Mashup—Nothing Compares to a Wrecking Ball" (ragaman7 aka Gallagher), 79
Miller, Kiri, 91, 214
Milosevic, Tijana, 172
"Minimixes," 5
Minogue, Kylie, 11
"Mission: Impossible" theme, 27, 49
Mitchell, David, 146, 159
Mixed in Key, 63
Mixmag, 210
Monetizing content, 183, 184, 188–190, 191–192, 226–228. *See also* Profit
Montage works, 34–36, 46–50, 104–106, 127–128, 215
Moore, Allan F., 213
Moral rights, 159–161
Morcheeba, 131
Morrisette, Alanis, 75
Morsi, Mohamed, 124
Morson, Gary Saul, 100
Motets, 47
Motion Picture Association, 172
Motown, 31, 112, 139
Mouth Moods (Cicierega), 109
Mouth Silence (Cicierega), 109
Mouth Sounds (Cicierega), 109
Mozart, 75
MsMiep, 65, 72–73, 79, 84, 85–86, 109, 131, 136, 145, 147
MTV Mash, 11
Mukařovský, Jan, 129–130
Multifunctional appropriation, 46
Munch, Edvard, 97
Muse, 124
My Chemical Romance, 57

"My Humps" (Black Eyed Peas), 75
Myspace, 178, 179
Mysterious D, 9–10

Napster, 172, 178
National anthems, 48–49, 125, 127
Navas, Eduardo, 30
Needle, Simon, 69
Neutrality, presumed, 24–25
New Corporation, 179
New Order, 11
New York Post, 11
New York Times, 8, 9, 10
Neyman, Danny, 5, 65, 72, 132, 200, 203
Ne-Yo, 124
Ngai, Sianne, 211, 212, 217
"99 Problems" (Jay-Z), 127
Nixon, Richard, 123
NodaMixMusic, 76, 79, 84, 134, 195, 214
"No More Gas" (DJ Earworm), 124
"No One Knows" (Queens of the Stone Age), 133
"No One Knows When the Sky Falls (QOTSA vs Adele)" (DJ Poupli), 133–134
"Norwegian Wood" (The Beatles), 27, 49
Nostalgia, 40, 72
"Nothing Compares 2 U" (O'Connor), 79–80
Notice and takedown system, 176, 181–182
Novović, Miloš, 152
"Nur Mir" (Setlur), 154
N.W.A., 167–168

O'Connor, Sinéad, 79–80
Of Authorship and Originality (project), 223
Oneboredjeu, 64–65, 131
"100 Miles and Runnin" (N.W.A.), 167–168

Online service providers (OSPs), 181, 227
On the Orator (Cicero), 107
"Ooh, I Love It (Love Break)" (Salsoul Orchestra), 168
Orff, Carl, 85
Oring, Elliott, 108, 109
O'Sullivan, Gilbert, 167, 177
Oswald, John, 27–28
Osymyso, 5
Oulipo, 86

Palimpsestic nature of music, 29
Palindrome, 86
Paratelic mind-set, 89, 216
Parody
　aesthetic principles and, 54–55
　content moderation issues and, 25–26
　copyright exceptions for, 16
　definitions of, 2, 163–164, 224–225
　as doubled-coded, 100
　essential characteristics of, 155
　as noninfringing on copyright, 1
　typology of appropriation and, 39–46
　work of, 81
Parody exceptions, law on, 155–161. *See also* Copyright
Participatory culture, 17, 90, 179
"Party in the U.S.A." (Cyrus), 125–126
Pastiche, 39–46
Peirce, Charles S., 128
Pelham GmbH and Others v. Ralf Hütter and Florian Schneider-Esleben, 153–155, 161, 223
Peltier, Christopher A., 224
Permission
　fees for, 140–141
　obstacles to obtaining, 58–59, 138–142
　survey on, 137, 141
Perry, Katy, 57, 75

Petty, Tom, 70
Phillips, Dom, 11
PhilRetroSpector, 56, 63–64, 79, 84, 109, 131, 134
Piracy Kills Music, 172
Pitchfork, 8, 9, 10, 72
Plagiarism, 39–46, 148, 171
Play
　mashups and, 53, 81–92
　as motivation, 4, 22
　as voluntary, 88
Playframe, 87, 92
Playing Along (Miller), 91
Plunderphonics (Oswald), 28
Poetic reference, concept of, 129–130
Political commentary, 122–125
PomDeter, 76
Poolboy, 60, 109, 131, 148, 174, 194, 202, 206, 214
Portishead, 61–62, 79
"Portishead vs Blondie vs Kanye West—Sour Glass (mashup)" (Reborn Identity), 61–62
Possessive individualism, 222
Postmodernism, 42
Post-production, 215
Pregnant moments, 105
"Prelude" (Wagner), 47
"Pretty Vacant" (Sex Pistols), 5, 74–75
Private forums, 196–197
Profit. *See also* Monetizing content
　copyright and, 159
　ethics and, 144–147
Promotional value, 145–146, 169
Property, labor theory of, 211–212
Protestant work ethic, 211
Public Enemy, 49–50, 177
Puddle of Mudd, 125–126
Pudovkin, Vsevolod, 35

Queen—Mash Aid, 85
Queens of the Stone Age, 133
Quotation exceptions, 152–155

Raheem D, 53–54, 58–59, 70, 77–78, 84, 134, 200, 202
Raskin, Victor, 107, 108
Ravel, 48
"Ray of Gob (Madonna vs Sex Pistols mashup)" (Go Home Productions), 4–5, 74–75, 84
"Ray of Light" (Madonna), 5, 74–75
Readerly text, 97, 110
"Rebel Yell" (Idol), 55–56
Reborn Identity, 61–62, 79
Reddit, 232
Red Hot Chili Peppers, 11
Relief theory, 106–107
Remix, definition of, 6
"Remix, The" (radio show), 7
Repetition with ironic critical distance, 37–38, 39, 41–45
Repurposing, 54, 78–81, 83, 132
"Respect Copyright" campaigns, 172
"Revolution" (DJ Schmolli), 124
"Revolution 9" (The Beatles), 27
Reynolds, Simon, 210
Rhetoric (Aristotle), 107
Rhythm, 60–65
Ricoeur, Paul, 30
Ridicule, 40–41
Rights enforcement organizations (REOs), 179, 182
Rihanna, 124
"Rime of the Good Times," 56
RiP!: A Remix Manifesto, 13
Rock Band, 91, 214
Rock ideology, 25, 214
Rodgers, Richard, 49
Rosati, Eleonora, 157
Rose, Margaret, 40–41, 42, 43, 44
Roseman, Jordan (aka DJ Earworm), 69–70

"Safe harbor" provision, 181–182
Sag, Matthew, 162
Salsoul Orchestra, 168

Sample-based appropriation, 32–33, 46–47, 223–224
Sample databases, 58
Samuelson, Pamela, 162
Sanjek, David, 170
"Satch Boogie" (Satriani), 112
Satire, 39–46
Satriani, Joe, 112
Saussure, Ferdinand de, 95, 96
Savage, Randy, 125
Schaeffer, Pierre, 27
Schifrin, Lalo, 62
Schoenberg, Arnold, 48, 86
Schopenhauer, Arthur, 107
Schumann, 27
Schuster, Mike, 146, 159
Script-based semantic theory of humor (SSTH), 107–108
Semiology/semiotics, 95, 128
Serazio, Michael, 15, 210
Setlur, Sabrina, 154
"72," 85
Sex Pistols, 5, 74–75
SF Weekly, 210
Sheldon, Daniel, 8
"Shelter Search" (DJ Schmolli), 123–124
Shifman, Limor, 129
Shifrin, Lalo, 49
Shiga, John, 15, 60, 171, 210
Shklovsky, Viktor, 132–133
Sibelius, 27
Signifyin(g), 101–102, 103
Silver, Daniel, 121–122
Silver, Jon, 184
Simone, Nina, 49
Simpsons, The, 72
Simpsonwave, 72
Sincerity, notion of, 213
Sinfonia, 48
"Single Ladies (Put a Ring on It)" (Beyoncé), 71
Sinnreich, Aram, 19, 205

Skull and crossbones logo, 171
"Skyfall" (Adele), 133
Slayer, 111–114, 116–117
"Slayer and Katrina & The Waves—'Chemical Warfare (Don't It Feel Good?)'" (McClintock), 111–114, 115–117
"Smells Like Booty" (Freelance Hellraiser), 9
"Smells Like Teen Spirit" (Nirvana), 9
Smith, Kate, 125
Snoop Dogg, 11
Sony Corp. of America v. Universal City Studios, Inc., 166
Sony Music, 166, 181
"Sorry" (Bieber), 71
Soulwax (aka 2ManyDJs), 9, 11–12
Sound, 65–68
SoundCloud, 14, 20, 179, 192, 193, 196–197, 206
"Sour Times" (Portishead), 61–62
Spears, Britney, 124, 125, 127
Speech genres, 96, 113–114
Spiegel Online GmbH v. Volker Beck, 153
Splice, 58
"Star-Spangled Banner," 48
Staydown options, 189
Stems, 58–59, 83
Stockhausen, Karlheinz, 48, 49
Story, Justice, 162–163
Strauss, 48
Stravinsky, Igor, 48, 86
"Stroke of Genius, A" (Freelance Hellraiser), 4–5, 9, 74–75
Strokes, The, 4, 74–75, 147–148
Structure, 68–73
Subcultures, trajectory of, 15
Suits, Bernard, 82, 88
Superiority theory of humor, 106
Surrealism, 104
Swift, Taylor, 200
Synergy, 101–103, 106, 134–136

Tactics, 91
Takedowns. *See also* Content moderation
  copyright/copyright exceptions and, 16–19, 184–187
  disputing, 186–187, 201–203
  producers' experience with, 190–208
  survey on, 175
Taylor, Charles, 50, 119–120
Tempo, 60–65, 73
Test mixes, 198
The_Dr, 8
Theme-based challenges, 84–87
Theory of the Avant-Garde, The (Bürger), 104
"This Is America" (Childish Gambino), 125
Timberlake, Justin, 78
To Kill a Dead Man, 62
Tom Boates Everybody, 61, 198, 205
Tong, Pete, 210
ToToM, 86
T-Pain, 64–65
Transcontextualization, 78, 100
Transformativeness, 33, 80, 162–164, 166, 169, 203, 224
"Transmitting Live from Mars" (De La Soul), 141
Travesty, 40, 41
T-Rex, 124
Tristan und Isolde (Wagner), 47
Trugoy, 178
Trump, Donald, 125, 127
"Turkish Rondo" (Mozart), 75
Turtles, 141
Tushnet, Rebecca, 164, 190, 217
Twelve-tone composition, 86
Twin Freaks, 12
Twitter, 20, 179, 193
2Pac, 84, 134
Tynyanov, Yury, 100

Index

"United State of Pop 2014 [Do What You Wanna Do]" (DJ Earworm), 5
"United States of Pop" (DJ Earworm), 5
Universal Music Group, 181, 200
"Uprising" (Muse), 124
Urban, Jennifer M., 184, 187, 206
Urish, Ben, 115
US Copyright Act, 142–143, 150, 161–168, 185
US Digital Millennium Copyright Act (DMCA), 180–182

Vaidhyanathan, Siva, 174, 178, 205, 219, 229
Vaporware, 72
Veatch, Thomas C., 108
Vergo, Peter, 105
Very Bootie Christmas, A, 84
Viacom, 181–182, 184
Viacom International Inc. v. YouTube, Inc., 181–182
Video, 68–73
Vimeo, 178, 192
Vinterberg, Thomas, 86
VMG Salsoul, LLC v. Ciccone, 168
"Vogue" (Madonna), 168
Von Trier, Lars, 86
"Vows of Chastity" (Trier and Vinterberg), 86

Wadsworth, Benjamin K., 69
Wagner, Richard, 47–48
"Walking on Sunshine" (Katrina and the Waves), 111–114, 116–117
Walser, Robert, 114
Warner Music Group, 181, 200
"We Are Extraterrestrial—Robbie Rotten vs Katy Perry (Mashup)" (InanimateMashup), 75
"We Are Number One," 75
"We Are the People" (Empire of the Sun), 124

Web 2.0, 12–13, 178–179, 181, 217
Webern, 48
"Weeknd vs. 2Pac & Eazy-E ft. Lucien Hughes & Memeguy1997 (I Feel The 90's Ḉoming), Ŧhe" (Happy Cat Disco), 72
"We Found Love" (Rihanna feat. Calvin Harris), 124
West, Kanye, 62, 70, 79
Whipped Cream and Other Delights (Herb Alpert's Tijuana Brass), 49
"Whipped Cream Mixes, The" (Evolution Control Committee), 49
White Album, The (The Beatles), 17
Williams, Justin, 29, 57
Winkie, Luke, 120, 122
WIPO Internet Treaties, 180
Woodmansee, Martha, 222
Woods, Alyssa, 115
Work of Authorship, The, (Eechoud) 223
"Wrecking Ball" (Cyrus), 79–80
"Wrecking People (Village People vs Miley Cyrus" (DeeM), 79
Writerly text, 97–98, 110
Wu, Tim, 185, 188

XFM London, 7

"Y.M.C.A." (Village People), 79
"You Showed Me" (Turtles), 141
YouTube, 14–16, 20, 179, 181–183, 186, 192–194, 200, 206
Yunek, Jeffrey S., 69

Zijderveld, Anton, 118–119

Parody in the Age of Remix